# THE GOVERNANCE OF JESUIT COLLEGES
# IN THE UNITED STATES, 1920–1970

# The Governance of Jesuit Colleges in the United States, 1920-1970

Paul A. FitzGerald, S.J.

With a foreword by
Theodore M. Hesburgh, C.S.C.

UNIVERSITY OF NOTRE DAME PRESS
NOTRE DAME, INDIANA 46556

Copyright © 1984 by
University of Notre Dame Press
Notre Dame, Indiana 46556
All Rights Reserved

Library of Congress Cataloging in Publication Data

FitzGerald, Paul A.
   The governance of Jesuit colleges in the United
States, 1920-1970.

   Bibliography: p.
   Includes index.
   1. Jesuits—Education—United States—History.
2. Catholic universities and colleges—United States—
History.    I. Title.
LC493.F56   1984     377'.82'73       83-25927
ISBN 0-268-01010-2

Manufactured in the United States of America

# Contents

Foreword, *Theodore M. Hesburgh, C.S.C.*      ix

Preface      xiii

1. The Inter-Province Committee, 1921–1931      1

2. The Commission on Higher Studies, 1931–1934      21

3. The General Appoints a "Commissarius," 1934–1937      36

4. The Executive Committee, 1937–1946      54

5. Postwar Expansion, 1946–1950 (Commissions and Institutes)      74

6. Accent on Quality, 1950–1955      92

7. The Emerging Role of Jesuit Presidents, 1940–1960      110

8. Coordination and Cooperation, 1955–1965      131

9. Three Areas of Concern, 1960–1965      149

10. The Revised Constitution, 1959–1964      169

11. The New Order, 1964–1968      188

12. The Presidents Assume Full Responsibility, 1968–1970      209

Epilogue      221

Appendixes      223

Abbreviations      234

Notes                                                    235

Bibliography                                          299

Index                                                    303

# Foreword
*Theodore M. Hesburgh, C.S.C.*

As ONE ENGAGED in the work of higher education for a lifetime, I can testify that profound changes have come about in the past half century. That is even more true of Catholic colleges and universities than of other American institutions of higher learning. When I look back now at the Catholic colleges and seminaries I knew in the late 1930s, they appear so strange and different that I am almost tempted to believe that they existed on another planet.

But while those of us involved know that things have changed enormously, we don't have any connected account of just *how* all these changes came about. The historical literature on Catholic higher education in this country is sparse at best, but for the most recent period it simply isn't there at all. That is the context within which we have to set Father FitzGerald's book; its pioneering quality makes his contribution all the more important. He tells a story that is fascinating in its own right, but he has at the same time opened a whole new territory for historical investigation.

The Jesuit Educational Association, which Father FitzGerald uses as the prism of his study, was brought into existence in the 1930s to deal with the problems besetting Jesuit institutions of higher education, especially in the realm of graduate work. The story of the JEA is thus the story of Jesuit efforts to come to grips with the major challenges that have confronted their schools over the past fifty years. Its history is, of course, most directly informative about Jesuit developments. But it also casts a most revealing light over the whole area of American Catholic higher education, because the same forces that affected the Jesuits also affected other Catholic institutions.

Father FitzGerald is a scholar, a professional historian. As such, he doesn't try to pretty up the record or gloss over shortcomings that his research has brought to light. He deals frankly with these matters in discussing the weaknesses the Jesuits were trying to correct and in reporting tensions that arose among them from differences in personal temperament or conflicts of institutional interest. But his love for the Society of Jesus and his commitment to its educational tradition, as well as his affection and respect for the men whose story he is telling, shine forth on every page. By telling their story so well, Father FitzGerald has erected the most enduring kind of memorial to their struggles. For he gives us a lively sense of the genuine perplexities they faced and the difficulties that complicated their efforts to overcome them. And that kind of understanding is enough to awaken our sympathy and admiration.

Three themes in Father FitzGerald's account strike me as particularly interesting and significant. The first is the central role of graduate work in bringing about a major change in the focus and orientation of leading Jesuit institutions in the period extending from the 1920s through the 1960s. Almost equally notable was the broad scale on which the Jesuits attacked this problem — an inter-province committee in the 1920s, a special commission in 1931-1932, the appointment of a personal representative of the Jesuit General soon after, and in 1934 the creation of the JEA. This is all new material and it is very valuable, not least in suggesting the importance of graduate work as an agent of change across the board in American Catholic higher education.

The second theme concerns the rector/president problem, and I suspect that it, too, is related to the expanding role of graduate work and the changes it wrought in Jesuit institutions. Traditionally, the chief executive officer of a Jesuit college or university was known as the *rector*. Although he was the top academic administrator, the office was primarily a religious one. It was part of the chain of command of the Society of Jesus, and its powers derived from that realm of authority rather than from any source in the sphere of knowledge or learning. As Jesuit schools transformed themselves into modern universities, with heavy emphasis on research and scholarship in many fields of specialization, increasing strains grew up between the religious-superior functions of the rectorial office, and the academic-administrator requirements of the presidential role. Father FitzGerald shows that the Jesuits grappled with this problem for a long time and tried out a variety of solutions to it. Here again his account has a bearing on the history of many other Catholic institutions besides those run by the Jesuits.

In the 1960s, the rector/president tension was in practice resolved in favor of the presidential office. This outcome leads us into the third theme, namely, the gradual attainment by presidents of Jesuit universities of autonomy with respect to external supervision on the part of the JEA — or on the part of any other agency in the traditional religious-order chain of command. What this development suggests is that the Jesuit presidents convinced their confreres in religious life that the successful operation of a modern university cannot be contained within the traditional religious-order framework of priorities, administrative procedures, and structures of authority. This shift in thinking was interwoven with other major changes of the 1960s, such as the establishment of independent boards of trustees for Catholic universities. These developments are both very important and very complicated, and Father FitzGerald makes a great contribution in giving us some details as to how they took place in Jesuit institutions.

Besides being grateful for the light it sheds on these critical matters, I personally treasure this book because it is peopled with old friends of mine. I knew and admired Father Edward Rooney, the long-time president of the JEA, whose innumerable services to the cause of Catholic higher education are explored in these pages. The same is true of many other Jesuit educators who figure in this account — men like my presidential comrades-in-arms, Paul Reinert of Saint Louis University, Mike Walsh of Boston College, Laurence McGinley, now president-emeritus of Fordham, and Robert Henle of Georgetown. It gave me great pleasure to meet them here again, and to be impressed once more by their intelligence and vision, their seriousness of purpose, and their high-minded commitment to the cause of truth.

Father FitzGerald, too, has rendered yeoman service in the past, both in his earlier work as an assistant to Father Rooney in the JEA and as graduate dean at Boston College. But I would have to say that in his present role as University Archivist at Boston College, he has crowned his achievements with this fine study of university work by American Jesuits over the past half century. In congratulating him upon it, I pay honor to the dedicated Jesuit educators whose story he has told so well.

# Preface

SOME YEARS AGO, a thoughtful observer of the national scene pointed out that "American Catholic universities and colleges represent a direct large-scale venture into higher education such as the Catholic church has never attempted in the past or elsewhere in the present."[1] As an integral part of that movement, the Jesuit apostolate of education in the United States represents an achievement without precedent or parallel in the history of the Society of Jesus. The results of this concerted effort by American Jesuits have amply justified the huge investment in men and money, and largely fulfilled the expectations of those who worked so hard to overcome the handicaps of a modest beginning. Today, Jesuit colleges and universities compete on an equal footing with the finest schools in the country.

Although segments of this story have appeared in other pages, the complete account, from the early attempts to modernize Jesuit institutions to the present structure of the fully integrated American university, has never before been documented. Since I was involved for a number of years in the activities of the Jesuit Educational Association (JEA), first as an administrator at Boston College and later as an officer in the national office of the Association, I became convinced that there was a need to bring to a larger public the details of this extraordinary chapter in the history of the Jesuits in America.

Fortunately for the researcher, the entire JEA collection, which includes official documents, correspondence, personal papers, and printed materials, is now in the University Archives at Boston College. The main collection has been augmented and supplemented by additional documents from cooperating institutional and provincial archives. Particularly important, for example, is the Daniel M. O'Connell File from the Roman Archives of the Society of Jesus, which I used as a basis for chapter 3. As a consequence, the narrative is based almost exclusively on primary sources, which include the private papers of Edward B. Rooney. Secondary sources were used solely to weave the Jesuit account into the larger picture of American higher education.

No author works in isolation. He is always dependent on friends and colleagues for advice and encouragement, and I am particularly indebted to three members of the academic community at Boston College: Joseph D. Gauthier, S.J., of the Department of Modern Languages; Edward J. Power, Professor of Education; and Charles F. Donovan, S.J., former Academic Vice President and presently University Historian. I am also under obligation to two other competent observers of the American educational scene: Philip Gleason, Professor of History at the University of Notre Dame, and John W. Donohue, S.J., Associate Editor of *America* magazine. These five discerning critics, who read the typescript in whole or in part, offered valuable suggestions to improve the text. They also brought to my attention what could have been, if not detected, embarrassing mistakes.

J. Donald Monan, S.J., President of Boston College, not only encouraged me to persevere in this project but was helpful in ways that merit the gratitude of the author. I am, of course, also indebted to Theodore M. Hesburgh, C.S.C., President of the University of Notre Dame, who generously agreed to write a Foreword to this book. Actively involved for thirty years in all aspects of higher education, on the national and international scene, he is in a unique position to comment on the intellectual apostolate in the United States. In addition, I would like to thank James Langford, Director, and Ann Rice, Executive Editor, of the University of Notre Dame Press, for their friendly advice and professional competence.

James E. Powers, S.J., New England Province Archivist, and Georges Bottereau, S.J., of the Roman Archives, were especially helpful in making available copies of essential documents. Edna Reed typed the manuscript, patiently enduring last-minute corrections and emendations.

Needless to say, I take full responsibility for factual data and for the interpretation of the documents.

Paul A. FitzGerald, S.J.
Boston College

# 1. The Inter-Province Committee, 1921–1931

In 1918, as the German High Command signed the articles of surrender at the end of World War I, President Woodrow Wilson confidently announced that the world had been made safe for democracy, but he proved to be a poor prophet when the United States Senate, in a historic vote, rejected the Covenant of the League of Nations and the Treaty of Versailles. Moreover, a presidential appeal to the people, in a "solemn referendum," was turned down by the electorate which, in a Republican victory, sent Warren G. Harding to the White House. It was the beginning of a new era.

The summer of 1920 set events in motion that colored the American political and social landscape for the decade known as the Roaring Twenties. The Eighteenth Amendment, which legislated the consumption of alcohol, and the Nineteenth Amendment, which allowed women to express their opinions at the polls, had repercussions beyond the decade. The arrest and indictment of Nicola Sacco and Bartolomeo Vanzetti, denounced as dangerous anarchists for the payroll murder in Braintree, Massachusetts, confirmed even skeptics of the reality of a "red scare." More frivolous and transient were the trappings of the Jazz Age, the Gatsbys of the Lost Generation, the novelty of the "flapper," and the vulgarities of Wall Street speculators. As F. Scott Fitzgerald wrote, in those days "it was always three o'clock in the morning."

Yet the serious business of life, much less flamboyant than the shallow and the superficial, has always engaged the attention of responsible people. At this very time, in fact, certain members of the Jesuit order, faithful to the traditions of the Society of Jesus, were to illustrate this truth in the quest for excellence in their chosen apostolate of education.

1

While the accumulated tensions of World War I were alleviated in the seductive attractions of New York City, a relatively minor event took place in the famous borough called the Bronx which, in retrospect, proved to be the germinal cell of an important movement in the history of Jesuit education in the United States. On a sunny June day in 1920, taking advantage of their attendance at the annual convention of the National Catholic Educational Association in New York City, a group of concerned Jesuits held an informal meeting on the Rose Hill Campus of Fordham University. For the most part, these men were products of nineteenth-century Jesuit schools which still bore the imprint, in method and curriculum, of their European origins. After the restoration of the Society of Jesus in 1814, Jan Roothaan, the energetic Jesuit General, of stolid Dutch ancestry, made a brave but futile attempt to impose a revised *Ratio Studiorum*, which incorporated the Jesuit plan of studies, on the Society's schools in America.[1]

The failure to achieve uniformity was largely due to geography. Jesuit schools in the East, influenced by Georgetown College, the *alma mater* of Catholic colleges in the United States, and by established institutions such as Harvard, Yale, and Columbia, were close to the classical tradition. Elsewhere, Belgian and Swiss Jesuits cultivated the educational apostolate along the Mississippi River and north to the Great Lakes; Italian Jesuits brought their particular genius to the Rocky Mountain region and the West Coast; and French civilization permeated the Jesuit effort in Louisiana and north to Kentucky.

By the end of the nineteenth century it was clear that even a modified version of the *Ratio* had to be reconciled with the type of educational institution that was developing in America. The Jesuit General himself, Francis Xavier Wernz, "authorized this flexible approach when he admitted that the pre-suppression program in Jesuit schools was a thing of the past."[2] Newly established standardizing agencies, together with pressure from competing colleges, forced Jesuit institutions to modernize the curriculum, enlarge the library, and strengthen laboratory facilities. Although some Jesuits looked back nostalgically to the glories of the past, others, convinced of the advantages of the American democratic tradition, looked to the future. J. Havens Richards, the president of Georgetown University, was of that number. "We must be on the alert," he wrote, "to adjust our colleges to the altered circumstances of the times. We must be prepared to modify our schedules."[3]

The total number of students in Jesuit schools at that time was not particularly impressive, but enrollments were increasing. In 1900, in the two American provinces (Maryland–New York and Missouri) and several mission areas, 7,200 students were enrolled in the collegiate programs — that is, in a seven-year program that began with grammar courses and ended with philosophy and a B.A. degree.[4] (In the first decade of the twentieth century, all Jesuit schools conformed to the American pattern, with four years of high school and four years of college.) Twenty-one years later, reflecting the post–World War I increment, 25,477 students were enrolled in collegiate programs and 12,723 were registered in university courses and professional programs, making a grand total of 38,200.[5] The apostolate of education was obviously growing, and decisions had to be made. Yet, in a system that had conformed for almost four centuries to a European model, based on the celebrated *Ratio Studiorum*, it was more difficult for Jesuit institutions in America to adjust and adapt than for others of more recent origin. But this was the challenge.

The initiative for the Fordham meeting came from Father Edward P. Tivnan (1882–1937), one of those Jesuits whose talents, disposition, and character combined to make the perfectly balanced man. A versatile student, a diligent worker, and an able executive, he could do many things well. Born in Salem, Massachusetts, he left Boston College to enter the Society of Jesus at Frederick, Maryland, in 1899. Following a brilliant course in the Society, which included a five-year regency as a teacher of chemistry at Boston College and Fordham, he pursued his theological studies at Valkenburg, Holland, and was ordained at Milltown Park, Dublin, in 1914. Assigned to teach chemistry at Fordham University in 1916, he was appointed its president three years later. Leaving Fordham in 1924, Father Tivnan served successively as rector of Weston College, procurator of the recently established New England Province, and superior of Bellarmine Retreat House in Cohasset. In his later years, he became a popular preacher, a skillful retreat master, and a sought-after counselor.[6]

The small circle of Jesuits to whom Father Tivnan had extended his invitation had serious doubts about the caliber of Jesuit education at high school, college, and university levels in the United States.[7] In comparison to other recognized schools, Jesuit institutions, as these men realized, were inadequately staffed, underfinanced, and unevenly administered. The disbanding of military units after the Great War had suddenly increased enrollments beyond the operating capacity of collegiate facilities at some institutions and had forced reluctant Jesuit administrators to broaden and modernize the ancient curriculum. At the same time, the regional accrediting associations, in areas where they were beginning to exercise effective supervision, began to question the quality of Jesuit education at the collegiate level. There was a distinct possibility that the apostolate of Jesuit education, which had been the envy of the academic world in the seventeenth and eighteenth centuries, might be ignominiously eliminated in the United States or, at the very least, condemned to perennial mediocrity.

As a result of their deliberations that June afternoon, the fathers "had expressed a wish that the Very Reverend Father Provincials [*sic*] should call together during the year representatives of our Provinces in America to discuss various plans whereby we might eventually help one another and become more closely united in the Society's great work, education of youth."[8] Shortly thereafter, the fathers provincial, persuaded of the necessity of a regional exchange of ideas by qualified representatives of each province, approved the petition for a committee that would be truly national. This was a crucial decision that marked provincials who made it as men of courage and vision.[9]

Reflecting the urgency of the situation and having won the support of the provincials, eleven Jesuits, representing five provinces and eleven institutions, met on March 27, 1921, at Campion College, Prairie du Chien, Wisconsin, to form the first Inter-Province Committee on Studies. These prominent rectors and deans, men of ability and experience, elected Father Albert C. Fox, rector of Campion and the host, chairman of the committee.[10] The administrators at that historic meeting (which was a benchmark in the history of Jesuit education in the United States) quickly identified the basic deficiencies of the past and bravely charted a new course for the future. Sad experience had taught them that a system of education that was fragmented by regional divisions, and plagued by serious inconsistencies, must be replaced by continuity, union, and cooperation. These characteristics, they emphasized, would lead to a renaissance of Jesuit education.

The Jesuits who met at Campion College made two seminal recommendations that were to bear abundant fruit in the years ahead. Stressing immediate implementation, their first piece of advice to the fathers provincial was "that each Province should have a permanent committee on studies which shall meet at fixed intervals."[11] To ensure cohesion within the province and to maintain contact beyond the province, "a secretary should be appointed whose sole duty it is to communicate with the secretaries of other Province committees," which "will tend to unite our colleges in the great work of education."[12] This resolution was the modern origin of the office of Province Prefect of Studies, which, at the province level, played such a prominent role in the reorganization of the colleges and high schools and in the designation of Jesuits for graduate degrees.[13]

The second recommendation was even more important. Convinced of the necessity of national cohesion and cooperation, the committee at Prairie du Chien "recommended most strongly that from the American Provinces there be constituted a Committee on Studies."[14] The personnel of such a committee, moreover, "must be made permanent" in order to promote the mutual understanding of common problems, eliminate the unnecessary repetition of discussions, and ultimately save valuable time. By this means, "confidence and trust will be engendered, without which indispensable factors the meetings would result, as has so often happened in the past, in nothing constructive."[15] It seemed self-evident that "permanent members of a committee will certainly take greater interest in our educational problems and will aid in removing the deplorable apathy [which is] so widespread."[16] The members of the committee had decided that, in placing before the provincials the true state of affairs, the time had come for frankness, and they did not apologize for their candor.

The American provincials, as stipulated by a Roman ordinance, held their annual meeting one month later, at Xavier High School in New York.[17] They "expressed themselves as thoroughly pleased with the Report and congratulated the Committee on the thoroughness of its work."[18] On the edge of a new movement, the provincials quickly forwarded the report, which contained additional recommendations, to the General of the Society.[19] To American Jesuits of that era, Wlodimir Ledochowski was a name that evoked vivid though ambivalent images. An Ignatian hero to some, he represented to others the Curial mentality that insisted on clerical law and order.

His family background undoubtedly influenced his character. He was born in Loosdorf, Lower Austria, in 1866, the son of Count Antoine Kalka-Ledochowski, whose family had migrated from Poland after the partition of 1795, and Josephine Salis-Zizers of Swiss aristocracy. His uncle, Miecislaus, who may have influenced his choice of religious life, was cardinal-prefect of the Sacred Congregation of the Propagation of the Faith. Ordained a priest at the age of twenty-eight, and appointed vice provincial of Galicia on the day of his solemn profession, he was elected twenty-sixth General of the Society of Jesus (February 11, 1915) by the Twenty-sixth General Congregation. Mildly autocratic by nature and habit, but a superb administrator, he ruled the Society for twenty-seven years, until his death on December 14, 1942.[20]

Although the General was familiar with the policies and practices of European governments, he was less at ease with the American political system and only superficially acquainted with the development of the Catholic Church in the United States. The implications of Pope

Leo XIII's apostolic letter on Americanism, *Testem benevolentiae*, may have served to make him even more cautious.[21] In any case, Father Ledochowski's letters to the American Assistancy in the 1920s and '30s were, initially at least, a valiant effort to shape the emerging apostolate of higher education in the mold that had been cast by Father General Jan Roothan, after the restoration of the Society, with the publication of the revised *Ratio Studiorum* (July 25, 1832). Ledochowski clearly recognized the necessity for certain differences in the American and European approaches, but he always feared that the American tendency to improvise and innovate, even to accommodate, would in the end dilute the Ignatian goals of Jesuit education.

On this occasion, however, Ledochowski seemed impressed. Province and house consultors from the American Assistancy had for some time been commenting upon the deficiencies of Jesuit high schools and colleges in the United States. In an unusually prompt response to the provincials, written in the precise Latin phrases for which the Roman Curia is justly famous, the General approved both recommendations. The fathers provincials, he wrote, each in his own province, should appoint committees to supervise studies within the provinces and these committees should coalesce in one common committee.[22] Those appointed to this common, or inter-province, committee, the General reminded the provincials, must be "men who are familiar with the policies of other institutions but who, nevertheless, esteem the Jesuit method."[23] It was clearly stated, however, continuing the tradition of Roman caution, that the committee had neither legislative nor deliberative authority. Indeed, the provincials were forbidden "to sanction any innovation in the collegiate plan of studies without the approval of the Superior General."[24]

Although the letter was typically cautious, and paternally restrictive, the General and his Assistants realized that a national, or inter-province, committee "was not only useful but even necessary" in addressing the problems that confronted the apostolate of education in the United States.[25] The Inter-Province Committee, which met annually from 1921 to 1931, although little known by later generations, and poorly recognized by contemporaries, was in fact the basic vehicle by which a provincially fragmented effort slowly expanded into a body that had a national dimension. The fathers who insisted upon it, the provincials who supported it, and the General who approved the committee were charting a new course. It had its limitations, as the record shows, but without this initial effort a national movement would have ended in failure.

The committee, with Roman sanction, met for the second time, at the invitation of Father Provincial Joseph H. Rockwell, at St. Joseph's College in Philadelphia, June 30 to August 2, 1922.[26] Father Rockwell, a native of Boston and neighbor to Beacon Hill brahmins, was, according to contemporaries, tinged with the mannerisms associated with New England Puritanism. Active in convert work in Boston, this thoroughly disciplined Jesuit later served as socius to Father Provincial Joseph Hanselman, rector of Saint Francis Xavier College in New York and Brooklyn College. Appointed provincial of Maryland–New York in 1918, he continued in that office until 1922.[27]

The members of the committee, having been successful beyond their expectations in the first meeting, now made mention for the first time of a proposal that would be repeated, revised, and refined for the next twelve years. While acknowledging the importance of maintaining ties to the National Catholic Educational Association, the Inter-Province Committee thought it opportune "that an association of Jesuit institutions of the United States be formed and given publicity for the purpose of unifying standards and gaining general recognition."[28] Directing nearly 75 percent of Catholic higher education in America, according to their calculations, "we need to stand together as leaders in education," wrote the committee, "and we shall be welcome in the field by standardizing agencies who have great respect for the standards, ideals and methods of the Jesuits."[29] In this instance, the fathers seemed to confuse "more" with "better" (a persistent mistake in Jesuit higher education in the years to come) and, as the future would reveal, they were more optimistic than the facts warranted. The standardizing agencies were, on occasions, less than respectful of Jesuit pretensions. The basic idea, however, was good, since the goal of the proposed association was "to help and encourage each college and high school to secure recognition from the regional association" and to conform to the minimum requirements generally prescribed."[30] To be effective, the proposal rested on the premise that "every Jesuit college and high school should . . . be a member of this association."[31] Such an organization, in the opinion of these veteran Jesuits, "would be the one safeguard and chief solution of our difficulties in any educational crisis that may arise."[32]

Actually, there was ample reason for uneasiness since, in all this planning, lurked an unknown equation. Although the members of the committee annually made a brave attempt to accentuate the positive, with an appeal to the ancient glories and rich heritage of Jesuit education, they were extremely worried about the potential power and imminent intrusion of the so-called accrediting agencies. These agencies, whether regional or national, are an American invention which grew out of the rapid proliferation of colleges, with distinct cultural, denominational, geographical, and ethnic differences. In essence, accreditation was an attempt to ensure quality without unnecessary uniformity. In a real sense, the catalyst came from the University of Berlin when, in 1905, the Faculty of Philosophy refused to recognize an American bachelor's degree unless it were taken at a member institution of the Association of American Universities. With some reluctance, this association, on the eve of the First World War, agreed to assume the responsibility of a standardizing agency.[33] Subsequently, it was against the standards of this association, whose approval was eagerly sought and gratefully received, that Jesuit colleges and universities had to measure their academic quality.

At about the same time, especially in the Midwest and North Central areas of the country, the regional associations were beginning to exercise a more active role in evaluating programs in institutions of higher learning. In the East, particularly the Northeast, the long traditions of independent, nonpublic education, fortified by the prestige of the powerful Ivy League, combined to blunt the control that the regional association might otherwise exercise. As a matter of fact, the colleges and universities in New England were able to retain "a cherished sense of individuality, accompanied by an unmistakable unwillingness to be subjected to the critical scrutiny of outsiders."[34] The Jesuit colleges in this geographical area benefited from this protection and initially were immune from outside interference. But this security would not last forever, and Jesuit institutions, like others, would have to stand on their own merits. If they stood together, so the Inter-Province Committee reasoned in accordance with biblical advice, there would be less chance that they would fall separately.[35]

The movement toward accreditation was very much on their minds when the members of the Inter-Province Committee met at Loyola University in New Orleans in April 1923.[36] Albert Fox was again elected chairman of the committee, and he was a good choice. Having received his A.B. degree from Saint Xavier College, Cincinnati, in 1898, he entered the Society of Jesus shortly thereafter and, in the course of a distinguished career, became one of the best-known Jesuits in the United States. On the occasion of an honorary degree from Columbia University on June 5, 1928, President Nicholas Murray Butler paid a remarkable tribute to Father Fox. "As a member of the Society of Jesus," read the citation, "pursuing an earnest and devoted career of scholarship, religious teaching and educational administration; exercising large influence in the movement to raise the standards and improve the methods of college and university work throughout the United

States, easily taking rank with the foremost educational leaders of the land, I gladly admit you to the degree of Doctor of Laws."[37] Returning to his *alma mater* as dean in 1913, he found, pigeon-holed in an old desk in his office, an invitation to Saint Xavier College to become a charter member of the North Central Association of Colleges and Secondary Schools. This incident, apparently, was the beginning of his highly successful efforts to work with and to win the favor of that association. Having finished a six-year term as rector of Campion College, Prairie du Chien, Wisconsin, Father Fox was at this time president of Marquette University.

After repeating their plea for a national organization of Jesuit colleges and high schools, the committee members, assembled at Loyola University, addressed the serious question of accreditation. The fathers admitted that "while they [accrediting agencies] may at present have no jurisdiction over our schools, their many exactions, if not lived up to, can hurt our work and impede our students and graduates from gaining proper recognition when they are obliged to pursue professional or technical courses elsewhere."[38] Having acknowledged the problem, their solution — proof once again of Jesuit ingenuity — was undeniably simple and unique. "If we organize ourselves into a standardizing agency that will be recognized," they reasoned, "our position is secure."[39] To achieve this recognition, the movement, initiated by and dependent upon the proposed National Jesuit Organization, would ultimately convince "secular educators and State Departments of Education . . . that *Jesuit college* is synonymous with *standard college* and thus compel them unfailingly, without doubt or question, to accord our colleges the complete and proper appraisal that is justly their due."[40] In assessing this proposal, which postulated an intramural accrediting agency, one can only admire the bold confidence with which the Inter-Province Committee attacked this national issue. There is no record that anything ever came of this desperate effort, the implications of which would have been clearly and immediately perceived by the agencies in question. Its importance, however, lies in the fact that there was among Jesuit administrators a mounting concern for quality and the standards against which it must be measured.[41]

Meanwhile the provincials, meeting in St. Louis, approved the 1923 report of the Inter-Province Committee, with an important exception. It was argued that a National Association of Jesuit Colleges and Secondary Schools might "create antagonism and be regarded by other Catholic educators as a manifestation of Jesuit exclusiveness."[42] A year later, the proposal of the committee was again "seriously discussed" by the provincials. They remained convinced, however, that "the advisability of giving publicity to the existence of the Association of Jesuit Colleges and High Schools of the United States" would not be in the best interest of the Society.[43] In the end, the provincials, concluding that there was neither sufficient time nor information for an immediate decision, agreed that the question should be submitted to province consultors.[44] As a partial solution, the provincials proposed that the Inter-Province Committee on Studies organize subcommittees, representing each province, and that the prefect general be *ex-officio* chairman in his province. Furthermore, in a continuing effort to avoid friction, they directed the national (Inter-Province) committee to hold its annual meeting at the same time and place as the National Catholic Educational Association to discuss matters of mutual interest. The provincials appeared to be moving toward a national Jesuit association, but at a prudent pace.[45]

But there was a more pressing problem. Standards, the basic prerequisite for accreditation, became the watchword of the day for the Inter-Province Committee. In drawing a blueprint for the proposed National Association of Jesuit schools, the committee enumerated "the unified standards to be exacted of each institution entitled to membership."[46] On a preferred list, which included administration, curriculum, publications, and endowment, faculty and library were accorded priority.[47] Libraries had been the glory of the Society of Jesus before its suppression in 1773, and, generally speaking, a serious attempt was made, to the extent that finances allowed, to maintain this tradition at the undergraduate level. It was at the graduate level that reservations were subsequently voiced by the Association of American Universities. In further refining the order of preference, faculty was granted the primacy on the universally accepted premise that the reputation of a college or university matched the distinction of its professors.

There was general agreement at this time, among the regional associations, that a postsecondary institution in America should have a faculty in proportion to the number of students and that heads of departments should possess the doctorate or its equivalent.[48] In those early years, the number of Jesuits with earned doctorates from approved, or prestigious, American universities was very small. Those with theological degrees from Europe were teaching in scholasticates which depended on ecclesiastical approval. Therefore, in order to strengthen the position of Jesuit colleges against the impending day of reckoning, the committee urged "that every effort be made to give as many men as possible the opportunity of preparing for the Ph.D. degree."[49] The committee was on high ground when it reminded the provincials that "no professor is today in our country considered 'praestans'

. . . unless he has the Ph.D. degree."[50] However, to achieve this ideal, the high-minded committee members were not above proposing an original solution that, if successful, would give the appearance of cutting academic corners. Exaggerating the elasticity of equivalency beyond its intended meaning, "as a substitute in some respects for the actual degree," it was suggested that Father Tivnan, who as president of Fordham could more easily approach the educational officials of New York State, should systematically classify and describe, in modern educational terms, the studies pursued by Jesuits during the four years of theology.[51] The plan was to present this curriculum, with graduate overtones, to the regional accrediting agencies "with the request that evaluation be given to these studies for the Ph.D. degree."[52]

Since it would be impossible to justify such a request today, even though the courses in theology and scripture are more research oriented, it is difficult to understand the naiveté of those cosmopolitan and enlightened Jesuits who had convinced themselves, "that the studies of our four year theological course . . . will receive a favorable verdict for the Ph.D. degree from the standardizing agencies of the United States."[53] There is no evidence that anything ever came of this artless scheme.[54] Nevertheless, though somewhat innocent of academic realities, these fathers understood that advanced degrees were essential for this recognition and prestige; that, without them, the Jesuit college would always be second class. Unfortunately, their advice was not heeded until the middle and late '30s, when the lack of doctorates became a source of acute embarrassment to Jesuit administrators.

In its crusade for academic excellence, the concern of the Inter-Province Committee for qualified teachers went beyond the Jesuit community. At its fourth annual meeting, which was held at Marquette University in June 1924, one of the sessions concentrated exclusively upon the increased demand for lay professors to augment and support the Jesuit staff. To meet this emergency, the committee called for "an immediate and adequate organization of graduate schools in our universities where these lay teachers may be prepared not only for our Jesuit colleges but . . . for other Catholic institutions as well."[55] The advantage to this crash program, the argument went, would be in the fact that, in addition to academic competency, Jesuit deans would "have a knowledge of the [lay professor's] personality and character."[56] Although the motive was above reproach and the justification admir- able, a graduate school that was organized in haste for a practical purpose would not impress the world of scholars. The committee itself evidently had second thoughts on the rationale for advanced studies. Two years later, with an eye to research and publication, the committee insisted that "no university is considered complete without a graduate school, which should be organized and conducted according to approved standards."[57] The committee then described the components of a good graduate school, the type of courses to be offered, and the degree requirements. The design, on paper at least, would have had the approval of the deans of established graduate programs.[58]

It is not superfluous to add that, in the preparation of teachers, the Jesuit high schools had their own problems. Due to the pressure of concrete cases in particular provinces, the committee had early recognized "the pressing necessity of regular courses in *Education* for our teachers as a prerequisite to State recognition and certification."[59] With the passage of time, the need became "more pressing than ever" and the committee warned that something definite must be done "as the very existence of our schools is imperilled."[60] The steady pressure for special courses in pedagogy came from members of the committee who represented the interests of the Midwest and Northwest, where a specific number of semester hours was required for teacher certification. Forwarding the report of the Milwaukee meeting to the fathers provincial, the secretary of the Inter-Province Committee, in a covering letter, made the following prediction: "At this year's meeting, the topic which excited greatest concern on the part of all was that pertaining to courses in Education for Ours. . . . We are absolutely sure that practically none of the present studies pursued in the Society will receive recognition in Pedagogy. As Your Reverence will remember, each year as far as was allowed us we have urged the necessity of something adequate being done."[61] For Jesuits, the juniorate and summer schools seemed to offer the best opportunities for these courses, while the "philosophers" were urged to utilize their short vacations. It was a makeshift arrangement at best, and nothing was done in an organized way until Jesuits themselves began to take advanced degrees in education.[62]

In his letter to Father Provincial Piet, Father Nevils, referring to the next provincials' meeting, expressed the hope of the committee that Father Francis M. Connell "may be allowed to explain the details of the report to the Very Reverend Fathers Provincial."[63] The committee could not have sent a more competent or eloquent emissary to plead its cause. Father Connell (1866–1935) joined the Inter-Province Committee in 1922, attended almost all of the subsequent meetings, and was frequently elected chairman. His appointment, in 1922, as the first prefect general of studies of the Maryland–New York Province was the natural consequence of a career devoted almost exclusively, but generously and brilliantly, to the education of Jesuits. For many years a revered member of the faculty at St. Andrew-on-Hudson, he was remembered by his contemporaries and students as a model teacher, an exacting mentor, and a genuine classical scholar. Immaculately groomed, meticulously prepared, he brought "dignity, seriousness and earnestness" to the teacher's platform. Humor was not his long suit, however, and one of his students, Father Leonard Feeney, a literary light in his own right, later recalled that Father Connell "never told a joke or a funny story in class." His principal publication, *The Study of Poetry*, an original analysis of literary esthetics, contained his famous definition of poetry, which is widely used today. During his years as province prefect of studies, Father General and the American provincials leaned heavily upon his learning and prudence.[64]

In his appearance, by invitation, before a special meeting of the provincials at Kohlman Hall in New York, August 1924, Father Connell gave an impressive exposition of the "present position" of Jesuit education. By way of preamble, he laid to rest the nascent impression that the Inter-Province Committee conspired to interfere with the legitimate autonomy of each province. The sole purpose of the committee was to set up common ideals, standards, and goals for all Jesuit colleges.[65] His explanation of the problems to be faced and the remedies proposed persuaded the provincials to become more sympathetic toward and actively implicated in the work of the committee. Under Father Connell's gentle persuasion, the provincials then rapidly approved the recommendations of the 1924 report. One suggestion was of special interest because of the subtlety with which it pursued its objective. The committee urged publication of an Inter-Province *College Directory* which, Father Connell admitted, was partially designed "for the purpose of forcing the unaccredited institutions to get to work to improve their standing."[66] Again, under prodding of the committee, the provincials were focusing their attention on the academic training of young Jesuits in preparation for their future apostolate of education. They favored early selection of promising scholastics, a particular discipline for specialization, and the counsel of older Jesuits in organizing a plan of studies leading to A.M. and Ph.D. credits.[67]

The persistent efforts of the Inter-Province Committee were beginning to exercise a positive impact on the Jesuit educational scene, and the fathers provincial, overcoming their initial reserve, openly encouraged the collaboration of this high-level assistance. Yet the feeling remained that, for long-range benefits, a better structure was necessary to protect the prerogatives of province and college officials. At the fifth annual meeing of the committee, at Canisius College, the first item on the agenda, taken up at the suggestion of the provincials, was "a statement outlining the purposes and procedure of the Committee."[68] The resulting format, though unspectacular in its originality, further refined a practical instrument by which the committee could have access in an orderly manner to the provincials' meeting. Article II of the statement, while careful to acknowledge the advisory capacity of the committee, in conformity to Father Ledochowski's instructions, stipulated, nevertheless, that the committee should annually draw up resolutions and submit them to the provincials, who, in turn, would transmit those that were approved to the province prefects of studies for implementation.[69] The same article specified that, as the committee looked to the future, at the end of each five-year period a quinquennial digest should collate the recommendations which had been duly approved, together with amendments that may have been added. These resolutions would then be printed, distributed, and recognized as authoritative.[70]

The format proved to be more complicated than had been anticipated. The proposed procedure also illustrated the basic weakness of the Inter-Province Committee which ultimately depended upon a consensus of several provincials for a final decision. The first quinquennial digest (1921–1925) was submitted as an attachment to the committee's report for 1926.[71] The recommendations contained in the digest were consolidated under three titles, all of which had prior but conditional approval of the provincials.[72] However, the provincials, at their June 1926 annual meeting, moderating their earlier zeal for harmonious collaboration, decided that the digest should be sent out "to the colleges now, not as approved but, with a view to its approval after it had been returned with recommendations from the rectors and deans."[73] It was then to be submitted in final form the following year, with comments appended. In obedience to the wishes of the provincials, the digest was duly circulated, comments were recorded, a slight revision was made, and it was again submitted to the provincials. But, alas, the provincials still hesitated to give the digest their unconditional approval.[74]

There were two reasons why they withheld their blessing. At Santa Clara, when Father Charles Carroll, province prefect of studies in California and secretary of the Inter-Province Committee, presented the 1926 report to the provincials, Father Provincial Edward Cummings, of New Orleans, urged that each report be submitted at least a month in advance of the provincials' meeting. This would give the provincials time "to consult men competent to talk on matters educational in their respective provinces."[75] The response of the provincials, meeting at Saint Louis University, was even more to the point. They complained "that a member of the Inter-Province Committee should have been present to explain the two reports; that is, the Quinquennial Digest 1921–1926, and the report of the 1927 meeting."[76] Secondly, the provincials had probably been receiving unsolicited advice from several sources. Although not explicitly stated in their response to the committee, an interlinear reading suggests that the provincials had been cautioned to avoid an outright approval of the digest. In a forthright petition, "the schools of the Maryland–New York Province with practical unanimity requested that the Digest be not put into the formality of print until a more complete description of Jesuit ideals in collegiate education can be drawn up."[77] The principals and deans felt strongly "that a printed document of this kind might be misinterpreted as representing the fullest conception of what a Jesuit college is expected to achieve."[78] The provincials acceded to this request and authorized the circulation of the digest in mimeograph form. Disappointed at this decision, the members of the committee, convinced that a printed document would be more effective, continued to urge its official publication as soon as possible.[79]

Even dearer to the hearts of the hard-working committee members was the formation of a national Jesuit association of schools, which they had originally urged in 1922. But disappointment and frustration continued to defeat their best efforts. It is surprising — to an extent mysterious — that the digest, which purports to recapitulate the resolutions of the past six years, omits any reference to the recommendation for a national Jesuit association, which had been considered a cornerstone in the new educational edifice. The decision taken by the provincials in 1924, to avoid a collision with the NCEA, was still in force.[80] There was, however, a compromise. The title page of the 1927 version of the digest bears the inscription "Association of Jesuit Universities, Colleges and High Schools," and in allowing this title, the provincials, in order to anticipate unwarranted conclusions, explicitly noted that the committee proposed this designation "to give permanency of form to what the committee is now accomplishing, not to destroy the autonomy of the Provinces."[81] The "association" would continue to derive its authority from and function through the Inter-Province Committee.[82]

Mildly chastened by recent responses of the fathers provincial, the Inter-Province Committee, at the invitation of Father Provincial James Kilroy, met at Weston College in January 1928.[83] Father Kilroy (1876–1969) had entered the Frederick novitiate in 1896. After theology, he was prefect of studies of Georgetown (College and Preparatory School combined), then became the first principal of Regis High School, New York, which had opened its doors in 1914. He succeeded Father J. Havens Richards as rector of the 84th Street community in 1919 and was appointed provincial of the newly established New England Province in November 1926. Partly due to his longevity and partly to his successive rectorships, Father Kilroy became a legend in New England. This tall, spare Jesuit, whose stern visage disguised a warm heart, was noted for oral permissions since he preferred to avoid the written word.[84] The meeting at Weston was the largest to date, with three representatives from each of the five American provinces.[85] Fathers Connell and Carroll, elected in 1925 for a three-year term, acted as chairman and secretary respectively. Father Carroll, who had attended every meeting except the one in 1923, was subsequently elected chairman for the next three-year term. He deserved the honor, and his background amply prepared him for this office.

Charles F. Carroll (1877–1934), born in San Francisco, entered the Society of Jesus from Saint Ignatius College at the age of fifteen. After his course of philosophy at Spokane and regency at Saint Ignatius, San Francisco, he studied theology at Oña, Spain, and was ordained at Burgos in 1907 by Gregorio Maria Cardinal Aquirre. As a result of his years in Spain and Italy, he developed an excellent gift in languages and spoke Spanish "with a fluency rare in a foreigner." His entire priestly life, with the exception of parish assistance and retreats to religious communities, was literally spent in the apostolate of education. He was successively appointed rector of Seattle College, dean of Gonzaga College, and dean of the Law School and Evening College at Saint Ignatius. In 1924 he was appointed province prefect of studies for California, and at the time of his death, which came suddenly, was chairman of the College Section of the National Catholic Education Association. Commanding and dignified in bearing, Father Carroll had a remarkable talent for administration. He is a good example of those Jesuits in the 1920s and '30s who, though lacking the advantages of advanced training in an academic specialty, labored courageously and intelligently to improve the standing of Jesuit education.[86]

In deference to an elaborate agenda, three subcommittees were appointed to consider three general topics. These were vitally important questions, involving the role of student counsellor, with the first Jesuit definition of that office; the whole range of religious instruction, which included the reorganization of the sodality; and the place of honors courses in Jesuit colleges. As chairman of the subcommittee considering gifted students, Father Connell reminded those present that Saint Ignatius regarded the educational apostolate as the best means for training leaders and that the *Ratio* itself was a method to that end. "We have produced comparatively few real leaders," the committee noted, and "our *best* students complain that they did not know how to work alone until they entered a professional school."[87] As a solution to this complaint the committee recommended, as essential elements of an "Honors Course System," selection of students, arrangement of their work, and proper supervision with special examinations.[88]

Beyond questions of the academic curriculum, the committee again urged that Jesuit delegates from each college and high school, or their local proxies, should attend the annual convention of the National Catholic Educational Association. Moreover, "on the evening preceding the opening session of the College Section, the Jesuit delegates should meet at the place and hour fixed by the Prefect General of the Province where the convention is being held."[89] Presumably, this was an attempt to form an unofficial lobby of Jesuit educators who might exchange views, plan convention strategy, and represent the interests of Jesuit education at every level. In a final, desperate appeal to the fathers provincial, the committee members insisted that their work would be much more effective if the quinquennial digest and annual reports could be sent, at least in their essentials, to all the schools. The hard-working committee lamented that "quite a number [of Jesuits] are still unfamiliar with the purpose and work of the committee" and predicted that "cooperation could be at once secured and strengthened through a better understanding of our common problems and the means proposed to solve them.[90]

Their plea fell on deaf ears. It is clear, in fact, that — for reasons which will emerge as the story continues — the committee was beginning to lose the support of the provincials and was not making a good case for its own existence. The provincials, meeting in New Orleans in April, concluded that it "was not feasible at this time" to publish the digest or the *Reports*.[91] Rather, as a less controversial alternative, it was decided to publish what amounted to a watered down version of the digest, with additional modifications, and to provide every teacher with a copy.[92] From the viewpoint of the committee, this could only be interpreted as dissatisfaction with, or lack of confidence in, their efforts over the past eight years. It is a tribute to the spiritual resilience and apostolic zeal of the committee members that they continued to devote their time and talent to a worthy cause with diminishing cooperation from above.[93]

In the last three years of its existence, the committee omitted its previous emphasis on curriculum, library, and faculty in order to focus its attention on the external constituencies of a college or university which would help to extend its influence beyond the campus walls. The provincials themselves, with prodding from Father General, had begun to suggest projects to the consideration of the committee, which had become resigned to a reduced level of national importance.[94] Gathering at the University of Detroit for their ninth annual meeting, and augmented by representatives of the recently erected Chicago Province, members of the Inter-Province Committee proposed a concrete plan for fostering a Catholic atmosphere in Jesuit professional schools;[95] urged the immediate formation of Jesuit alumni associations; documented, from the experience of prestigious institutions, the benefits of soliciting the advice of qualified laymen in the management of financial investments; and recommended concrete means for increasing the visibility of the Jesuit educational apostolate before the academic world and the general public.[96]

Members of the committee, appealing to the successful practices of nationally ranked universities, strongly recommended that Jesuit institutions cultivate their alumni, profit by their advice, and use their services in staffing a professional placement bureau.[97] The committee recognized, as many superiors did not, that, without professional advice to guide Jesuit boards of trustees in making mundane decisions, colleges of the Society would be overshadowed by their more aggressive, and modern, competitors. To refute the impression that "the Society is a rich corporation interested in education as a hobby," administrators should persistently explain to a sometimes prejudiced public "that the educational work in which we are engaged is a public service . . . deserving not only of a tolerant interest but also of active cooperation and support."[98] As an antidote to allegations of complacency, Jesuit publications ought to appear in the scientific and literary journals; attendance at and participation in national conventions should be the rule; and — very important — each institution would do well to organize a press bureau under "faculty control."[99]

Father Louis J. Gallagher, socius and province prefect of studies in New England, was delegated to interpret the 1929 *Report* for the provincials who were meeting at Boston College. It was hardly an attractive assignment, but his colorful career had not been characterized by timidity. Born in Boston in 1885, Father Gallagher entered the Society in 1905, was ordained in 1920, and after completing theology at Woodstock, was appointed prefect of studies at Xavier High School, New York. Shortly thereafter, he joined Father Edmund A. Walsh, director of the Papal Relief Mission in Russia, and assisted in the distribution of food and medicine to the starving children of that famine-stricken country.[100] In 1923, after a third request by Pope Pius XI and diplomatic pressure by Fathers Gallagher and Walsh, the Bolshevik government released the relics of Saint Andrew Bobola, a Polish Jesuit martyred in 1657, whose body had been removed from White Russia to Moscow.[101] In a cloak-and-dagger operation, reminiscent of Agent 007, "Dr." Gallagher smuggled the relics across several borders and on to Rome.[102] After tertianship at Paray-le-Monial, France, he was appointed prefect of studies at Georgetown University, where he remained until he was transferred to his native New England in 1927.[103] He subsequently served as president of Boston College.

The response to Father Gallagher's advocacy was less than a ringing endorsement of the prescient proposals of the hard-working committee. As the provincials had, in the past, occasionally faulted the committee on not allowing adequate time for decisions, the General now complained "that he had not received sufficient information" on subjects concerning which he was expected to make a judgment.[104] Taking their cue from Ledochowski, who cautioned against making a national alumni association "an exclusively Jesuit affair," the provincials, adopting the large view, preferred "to build up the Catholic Alumni Federation, not to make it Jesuit controlled but at the same time to prevent it from becoming anti-Jesuit."[105] Although the provincials agreed that an "all-time" spiritual director should be appointed to professional schools and "recognized the advantages . . . of a qualified head of Department of Religion," they did not seriously consider the committee's proposals. It would appear that, even for that period, the provincials were unduly intimidated by Father Ledochowski. On the option of sending Jesuits to The Catholic University of America for higher studies, "the Provincials agreed that no action should be taken on the matter unless full information on the subject was previously forwarded to Very Reverend Father General."[106] In fact, caution exceeded normal bounds when, as Father Gallagher later explained, the fathers provincial decreed that "the reports of the Inter-Province Committee on Studies were not to be circulated as minutes of the committee's meetings even after the reports had been approved by the Provincials."[107] For reasons that are difficult to assess, the life of the Inter-Province Committee was in danger and its future in doubt.

Despite the provincials' cool reaction to practical proposals for the organization of an active alumni association, the committee returned to this topic with additional arguments.[108] Moving from secular to spiritual and religious reasons, the committee reminded the provincials, in what should have been a persuasive point, "that to train a student for four years and then altogether to sever connection with his intellectual and, for us, his religious pursuits is a great waste in efficiency." Indeed, alumni from Jesuit professional schools could be enlisted "for public, civic and social service" and for "that Catholic action which the Holy Father has so much at heart."[109] There is no evidence that the provincials were moved to reconsider their commitment to a national

Catholic alumni association. However, in a related area, with the ambiguous approval of Father General, "the Fathers Provincial approved of the plan of Advisory Boards, judging them to be of real assistance to our Colleges."[110] Actually, the provincials were merely confirming a practice which had been introduced at Georgetown in 1914 and was subsequently established at four other Jesuit universities.[111]

The committee, in its waning months, and with diminishing influence, was the recipient of one last instruction. In the provincials' directives to the committee in 1929, "it was suggested that a draft of a schedule of studies of all Juniorates should be drawn up by the Inter-Province Committee on Studies and submitted to the Fathers Provincial."[112] The draft would then be forwarded to Father General for his approval. Convinced, no doubt, that they had exhausted their contribution to the renovation of Jesuit education at the secondary and collegiate levels, the committee concentrated its remaining energies on preparation of an innovative report on juniorate studies. In fact, it went beyond the parameters of the original instruction and designed a comprehensive plan for "the usual course of training in the Society."[113] Demonstrating its habitual instinct for essentials, the committee proposed a comprehensive schedule of studies that would safeguard the traditional requisites for both the sacred ministry and secular teaching, the twin elements of a Jesuit's vocation. In particular, the expertly organized plan ingeniously provided for required courses in education, laid a solid foundation for future doctoral work, and anticipated regional specifications for accreditation.[114]

The provincials, "praising the assiduous and devoted labor of the Inter-Province Committee," accepted the report "as a valuable directive outline" and agreed that it should be recommended for consideration to the faculties of the juniorates and scholasticates.[115] This was the last report submitted by the Inter-Province Committee to the fathers provincial of the American Assistancy.[116] By the time the provincials had gathered in Toronto — May 1931 — Ledochowski had already communicated his decision to appoint a Special Commission on Higher Studies which would replace the Inter-Province Committee. The continuity, tenuous at best, would be provided, in Father General's expectations, by the active and unselfish cooperation of the committee in supporting the initial steps of the new commission.[117] The work of the members of the Inter-Province Committee, during the eleven years of its existence, was best appreciated, and duly acknowledged — as the record will show — by those who would now carry forward the high aspirations of the Jesuit apostolate of education in America.

# 2. The Commission on Higher Studies, 1931–1934

ONE DAY IN FEBRUARY 1927 (the exact date is not certain), Father Ledochowski left the Jesuit Curia to keep an appointment with the cardinal-secretary of the Holy Office. Rafael Cardinal Merry del Val, gifted son of a Spanish marquis and an English mother, had been the controversial secretary of state during the pontificate of Pope Saint Pius X. Shortly after Pius' death in 1914, he was appointed secretary of the Holy Office, one year before Father Ledochowski's election to the generalate. The cardinal, who had requested the General's presence, came immediately to the point and said that several charges had been brought against Jesuit universities in the United States. Almost as an *obiter dictum*, he quickly added that, according to his sources, which he did not reveal, in addition to The Catholic University of America there was only one other truly Catholic university in the United States, namely, the University of Notre Dame.[1]

With that startling introduction, and to the General's continuing amazement, the cardinal then enumerated the charges, which he summarized under four headings: Jesuit universities in the United States can in no sense of the word be called *Catholic* universities; in Jesuit universities, professors were, for the most part, Protestants, Jews, even atheists; rectors had little or no authority in the universities in choosing professors or determining policy; Jesuits exercised practically no influence on the spiritual and religious welfare of the students.[2] After reciting this litany of accusations, His Eminence admitted that he was astonished at their seriousness. Though taken completely by surprise, the General came to the defense of the Society and explained that some of the charges were false while others were exaggerated.[3]

After describing this tense interview in his letter to the American provincials, the General added that while the charges "may be false or exaggerated," he could not ignore the fact of the admonition and must do something about it.[4] As a first step, Ledochowski wanted hard information. "I am submitting to Your Reverence, therefore, a Questionnaire which I ask you to have answered with the greatest care and precision possible."[5] The General emphasized the importance of cooperation on the part of the provincials, and through them the rectors, prefects, and deans, in compiling "exact and definite information" as soon as possible in order that he might exonerate the reputation of the Society.[6] His instructions were very specific: the questionnaire should be completed in English; it was to be answered for colleges as well as for universities; and the whole process was to be considered confidential.

The questions were designed to elicit facts and figures which the General could utilize in refuting the cardinal's charges. Although some respondents felt that the questions were too narrowly drawn, and the language unnecessarily blunt, the responses, as later established, were honest and reasonably accurate. Father Francis Connell, taking advantage of his prerogative as an elder statesman, cautioned the General against making too much of the whole business. In particular, he advised him not to refer to Jews in a pejorative way nor attempt to restrict the attendance of female religious in Jesuit institutions, which, if insisted upon, would penalize Religious and weaken Church apostolates. Nor, wrote Father Connell, should non-Catholic students be compelled to take religious courses and attend Catholic services. In fact, it would be counterproductive to multiply regulations beyond the strictly necessary.[7] In receiving this sensible advice, the General was selective; he accepted some ideas and ignored others.

One year and three months later, "after many unavoidable delays," Father Ledochowski "was able to take up the subject of last year's Questionnaire."[8] Always the diplomat, the General noted that "if in some cases the statistics were inaccurate and the data vague and incomplete, I may say that for the most part the replies were thoroughly satisfactory, and showed a care and diligence proportionate to the importance of the matter in hand." A close reading of this ten-page letter, addressed to the American Assistancy, reveals unmistakably that it was considered a very important document, both from the viewpoint of the Roman Curia and from the reaction of the American provincials.[9] For this reason it merits close analysis, since it helps to understand the General's philosophy and theology of education.[10] Sensing, perhaps, that the dramatic growth of the American provinces and their schools was placing the direction of the apostolate of education beyond his customary control, his letter was an overt attempt to contain those institutions, and their administrators, within the nineteenth-century European tradition of the Society. Written with the best of intentions, the epistle reflects a conservative mentality which, unfamiliar with the educational concomitants of a pluralistic society, assumed the automatic acceptance and enforcement of obsolete regulations that had been effective in another time and place. The list of prescriptions is long and the language was intended to preclude interpretation.

Invoking a hierarchy of values, the General's strongest strictures were directed against four "abuses" which corresponded roughly to the cardinal's complaints. Since the presence of non-Catholic students "is not in itself desirable, and can at most be tolerated," consistent efforts should be made to decrease their number.[11] The question of non-Catholic professors was a more important problem; that of non-Catholic deans was beyond discussion. Ledochowski conceded that 7 percent of non-Catholic professors in college departments was tolerable but far from ideal; the more than 50 percent in the professional and technical schools, however, was entirely unsatisfactory. In regard to non-Catholic deans, the General was neither counselling nor cajoling. He "positively ordained that in the future no one who is not a Catholic must under any circumstances be given the office of dean."[12] Furthermore, where prudently possible, non-Catholics who occupied that office should be replaced.

Despite the prudent advice proffered by Francis Connell, His Paternity remained inflexible on the admission of women students to Jesuit institutions. "Since the whole idea of co-education is disapproved by the Church," the General insisted that "in the high schools and colleges, Jesuit administrators must continue to close the doors against female students," no matter what pressure might be brought upon them.[13] He saw more justification for admitting women at the university level, but he could not approve the practice as a policy. His position on the attendance of women religious at Jesuit institutions was, even for those with an open mind, difficult to understand and practically impossible to implement. Though the General conceded that permission had previously been granted by Rome for religious women in summer courses for degree programs, he reminded superiors that the situation was "merely tolerated for the time being, and the Rectors should withdraw from it as soon as other provision can be made."[14] It would be difficult to imagine what other provision could be made, and he did not suggest any.

It would not be accurate to imply that the letter was entirely negative. Father Ledochowski was, in general, satisfied with the provisions made "for the religious instruction of Catholics in our college departments."[15] In fact, he slyly observed, "if everything outlined were really carried out, this part of our work would seem to be almost perfect."[16] On this point, at least, he was able to submit a consoling response to Cardinal Merry del Val. Although the General, in his concluding paragraph, made a brief reference to Jesuit institutions "as educational centers," the letter neglects almost entirely the academic aspects of the colleges and universities in order to focus exclusively on the religious responsibilities of the Society in its educational apostolate. This approach is understandable since the cardinal himself had singled out this issue for censure and the questionnaire was designed to yield this kind of information. Nevertheless, the letter did little to advance the proposition that a university is in substance an academic and intellectual enterprise, involved in the pursuit of knowledge and the search for truth.

For this reason, if the letter had been fully implemented, the consequences would have seriously impeded the growth of Jesuit colleges and universities in the United States. Jesuit universities were officially Church related, and identified as such, and the spiritual formation of the students, if not co-equal, had not been — as implied by the cardinal — callously subordinated to the academic programs. Yet the controversy concerning Divine Revelation in relation to the pursuit of truth in a Church-related university, radicated in the well-known Shavian comment, "a Catholic university is a contradiction in terms," continued to plague the intellectual aspiration of denominational institutions. In any event, the fathers provincial, rectors, and deans, guided by the advice of province prefects of studies, quietly implemented those instructions which were clearly beneficial and wisely disregarded those injunctions which, anachronistic and unrealistic, were beyond the possibility of fulfillment.[17] There is no evidence that there was extended discussion of the letter in the provincials' annual meetings. However, the chairman, Father Edward Phillips, of the province of Maryland–New York, reminded his fellow provincials that they were to inform His Paternity how the letter of June 7, 1928, "had been put into execution and what difficulties had been encountered in doing so."[18] With this gentle exhortation, the chairman had fulfilled his obligations.

The patience, or passive resistance, of the American administrators was rewarded. As a result of consultations with delegates to the Congregation of Procurators in 1930, visits from American bishops in Rome, and advice from distinguished laymen, Father Ledochowski came to realize that there was more to the apostolate of higher education than its religious dimension.[19] After reflecting for two years on the proper role of Jesuit colleges and universities in America, which he considered "precious jewels of the Society," he concluded "that our Society in the United States could and should take a more influential share in determining the intellectual policy of the country."[20] To the General's credit, this was the first intimation from Rome that the Society of Jesus in the United States should envision and prepare for an intellectual apostolate. Several years before Robert Hutchins, the youthful president of the University of Chicago, charged Catholic institutions with imitating the worst features of secular education while ignoring the best, Father Ledochowski had said it better. "As things are now," he wrote, "we have too often become followers rather than leaders, and have allowed some of the best features of our educational system to vanish wholly or in part from our curriculum, adopting instead the tentative methods and changing standards of the day."[21] Moreover, the solutions to serious problems, according to His Paternity, "have been haphazard and makeshift," without getting to the root of the difficulty or establishing a common purpose.[22]

The General, in order to construct a successful program, proposed a formula for improvement which involved four steps on the road to revival. In the first place, there was an absolute need for "united purpose and concerted action," which could only be accomplished through national cooperation.[23] Secondly, it would be very helpful, in establishing the comparative standing of Jesuit colleges and universities, to study the policies and practices of those institutions, public and independent, which had attained acknowledged preeminence in academic circles. Furthermore, admitting the ascendancy of standardizing agencies, Jesuit educators in America should carefully calculate their future impact and prepare to satisfy their demands. Finally, and as a corollary to the perils of accreditation, each province should make provisions, without detriment to priestly formation, for the advance training of Jesuits who, with doctoral degrees and pedagogical practice, would add distinction to the graduate schools.[24] The implementation of this ambitious program, the General was convinced, "can only be done by a special commission formed for this purpose, and consisting of a representative Father from each Province of the Assistancy."[25] He then requested each provincial to submit the names of one or two fathers "whom he judges to be most fit and competent to participate in this study": men "who not only know education in general, and Jesuit education in particular," but who are thoroughly familiar with educational conditions in the United States.[26] As a final step, the General would appoint the commission, from the names suggested, and a presiding officer who would direct the work and report directly to him.

The following March, in an unusually warm and cordial letter, Father Ledochowski appointed six fathers who thereafter constituted the famous Commission on Higher Studies. Its members were Charles F. Carroll, general prefect of studies of the Province of California and regent of the School of Law of the University of San Francisco; Charles J. Deane, dean of the college and the university, Fordham University; Albert C. Fox, dean of the college and dean of administration, John Carroll University; John W. Hynes, president of Loyola University, New Orleans; Edward P. Tivnan, procurator of the Province of New England, Boston College; and James B. Macelwane, dean of the graduate school, Saint Louis University.

Writing in Latin, His Paternity urged the fathers provincial, in cooperation with the commission, to allow the commissioners to choose the time and place of their meetings, to prepare materials, to propose conclusions and resolutions. The provincials were reminded, however, that the minutes of the commission's meetings were to be sent directly to His Paternity and that nothing was to be publicly approved or sanctioned unless first approved by him. The General had one last piece of advice: the commission, overcoming the American inclination to do everything, should emphasize deeper commitment to established educational priorities. The educational world, he wrote, would not fault the Society for lack of "variety and multiplicity," but for lack of "authority and solidity." He proposed the ancient glory of the Society, in its preeminent schools, as an example of dedication.[27] Impressed by his brilliant academic career and demonstrated organizational abilities, Ledochowski, in a separate letter, appointed Father Macelwane chairman of the commission.[28]

James Bernard Macelwane (1883–1956) was a man of many talents, an internationally recognized scientist, and an inspiration to fellow Jesuits. Born near Port Clinton, Ohio, he entered the Society of Jesus in 1903 and was ordained to the priesthood in 1918. Although his early preference was in the field of classical studies, he later manifested a marked talent for science, subsequently earning a Ph.D. in physics, seismology, and mathematics at the University of California at Berkeley, where he also taught for two years. But his extraordinary career was associated with Saint Louis University, where, beginning in 1925, he was appointed director of the newly established Department of Geophysics; later, he served as dean of the Graduate School. In 1944 Father Macelwane founded, and was the first dean of, the Institute of Technology. Due to the prestige he enjoyed at the national level, he was appointed to the boards of several government agencies and also to important committees of educational associations. Author of several books and over one hundred technical papers, he was the recipient of a number of honorary degrees, president of the American Geophysical Union, and a member of the National Academy of Sciences. In poor health for over a year, he died in February 1956.[29]

Since his career in educational administration had been relatively brief, the commission member from the Deep South was, even to his admirers, something of a surprise. Plainspoken, energetic, and intelligent, John W. Hynes is even today recognized as a giant in the history of the New Orleans Province. Born in El Paso, Texas, in 1886, he entered the Society of Jesus in 1901, just short of his fifteenth birthday, and served the province in a variety of apostolates. After receiving his doctorate from the Gregorian University, he taught theology at Mundelein Seminary near Chicago. His second career was associated with Loyola University, New Orleans, where he was director of athletics, later dean of the College of Arts and Sciences, and finally president (1931–1936). During Father Hynes's presidency — as was the case with other institutions at that time — Loyola faced the harsh reality of the Depression years, but his talents and energy were equal to the emergency. It was during these years that he was a member of the special commission. In later years, in a third career, he became widely known and beloved as director of the Manresa Retreat League. He died in 1952, at age sixty-four, a year after the celebration of his golden jubilee as a Jesuit.[30]

The representative from the Maryland–New York Province was a rugged individual and, to his credit, Charles Deane was also a self-made man. His strong character, native talent, and worldly wisdom moved him from relative obscurity to positions of prominence. Born on April 2, 1881, in the small Connecticut town of Cheshire, he worked for several years after his graduation from the public high school, first for the New Haven Street Railway Company, then for the Thompson Shop (interior decorating). Following his student years at Fordham University, he entered the Society of Jesus in 1904, made the usual course of Jesuit studies, returned to Fordham as a priest in 1921, and for the rest of his long life was associated with that university. From 1921 to 1925, Father Deane taught history and, as faculty moderator of athletics, watched the athletic program at Fordham gain national recognition. Appointed dean of Fordham College in 1925, and shortly thereafter regent of the School of Pharmacy, he assumed, in 1938, the posts of vice president and secretary general of the university. Due to his long tenure at Rose Hill, it was said that Father Deane knew, and was recognized by, more alumni than any other faculty member. Except for a four-year period as superior of the Jesuit community at Fordham, he continued as vice president and secretary until his death, at age eighty-five, in 1966.[31]

With two exceptions, the members of the special commission were not Jesuits of remarkable distinction. All of them, however, were men of judgment and balance, whose corporate experience, as the General recognized, extended to the inner workings of Jesuit colleges and universities and their relationship to external agencies. Strengthened by the inclusion of four veterans of the Inter-Province Committee, which forged a link of continuity with the efforts of the past, all were totally committed to revitalization of the Jesuit apostolate of higher education in the United States. Determined to be charitably aggressive and completely honest, they addressed their responsibilities with enthusiasm, optimism, and, most important, the active support of the General.

The commission held its first meeting, at Philadelphia, in June 1931. Thereafter, the commission met at intervals of two or three months in five additional locations which ensured that the commission members made an on-site visit to each of the six provinces.[32] The minutes of each meeting were forwarded to Father General, who, furnished with every detail of the proceedings, acknowledged the reports with encouragement and advice. Working with deliberate speed and efficiency, the members submitted to the General the results of their labors (in August 1932) in a 234-page document entitled REPORT OF THE COMMISSION ON HIGHER STUDIES OF THE AMERICAN ASSISTANCY, 1931–1932.[33] As stated in the covering letter to His Paternity, the commissioners "made a sincere and earnest effort to give as exact a picture as possible of the general educational field and the position occupied by our Jesuit institutions."[34] In submitting its report, the commission paid a "sincere and deserved tribute to its Chairman, Reverend James B. Macelwane, S.J., to whose zeal and ceaseless labor, whatever success achieved may be largely attributed."[35]

At the first meeting, in formulating a plan of procedure, a decision was made to send out a series of questionnaires to faculty and administrators in the colleges and universities.[36] The questionnaires were divided into three categories, and a four-page form was addressed to deans and a two-page form was sent to registrars. The consolidated report from each institution yielded a fairly complete profile of the college or university. More complicated than the other two, a four-page form, to be considered confidential, was mailed to Jesuit faculty. Constituting a detailed academic biography from juniorate to theology, it followed the Jesuit through graduate studies (if any) and on to research and publication. With questions on teaching and nonteaching activities, the respondent was asked to indicate the difficulties, if any, under which he had worked and to suggest changes that would have improved his academic career. The data from those questionnaires were used by the commission to form its recommendations for a revision of the Jesuit course of studies. Rewarded by a conscientious response, which painted a candid picture of the difficulties faced by the institutions, "the members of the Commission were able to proceed with their work in a much surer and more satisfactory manner."[37] In both the process and the report, the commission followed the order suggested by the General himself in his letter of December 8, 1930, and responded to the four points he had raised.[38] While it would be profitable, indeed, to focus attention on all four sections of the report, each of which contains a wealth of information, it is more to the point of this study to examine in detail the first section — that is, the organizational structure proposed by the commission for obtaining unity, harmony, and cooperation within the apostolate of education in the American Assistancy.

The idea of a mechanism that would nurture a "united purpose and concerted action" in reviving the apostolate of higher education within the American Assistancy did not originate in the Commission on Higher Studies. The Inter-Province Committee, as explained above, had earlier recommended a national association of Jesuit institutions for the purpose of unifying standards and gaining academic recognition; the same idea had been carried forward by regional committees and had found expression in at least one provincial's letter to Father General. On March 15, 1929, Father John M. Salter, provincial of the New Orleans Province, had written to Father Provincial Edward Phillips, who was preparing for the April meeting of provincials at Boston College: "In accordance with your Reverence's wish to receive in advance matter which should be brought up in the coming Provincials' Meeting, I herewith submit an excerpt from a letter of Very Rev. Fr. General's concerning a proposal of mine that a Jesuit Educational Association be formed in the States of such a character and with such high requirements as to be recognized by the various standardizing agencies, and that thus our freedom in following out our educational policy [is] to be safeguarded."[39] Moreover, according to the General himself, an "eminent American bishop" had made the same suggestion.[40] Actually, the provincials, in an unofficial version of the quinquennial digest, had already given nominal approval to such an organization.[41] However, it was left to the commission to design an association of Jesuit schools that would ensure the union and cooperation that were so earnestly sought and desperately needed to project a new Jesuit image in American academic circles.

The commissioners had embarked on their assignment with the active assistance of the provincials, and in an appearance before them at their annual meeting in Toronto, Father Macelwane, taking advantage of the General's suggestion for a personal encounter, stressed the magnitude of the undertaking "and earnestly urged the Provincials to help him to secure all possible information that could serve the cause."[42] On their part, after promising prompt cooperation, the provincials, recognizing the necessity of making allowances "to the regrettable exactions" of the standardizing agencies, urged Father Macelwane zealously to maintain the spirit of the traditional studies of the Society.[43] Taking this admonition seriously, and prudently allowing for regional and cultural differences, the commissioners appealed to part IV of the Constitutions of the Society, the *Ratio Studiorum*, and the entire philosophy of Jesuit education, as the sources of unity in the Jesuit apostolate.[44] Yet, as St. Ignatius had envisioned, the Constitutions, and the *Ratio*, had to be interpreted for time and place. Granted that the Society was legally free in the United States to give expression to a narrowly conceived method of education, "can we expect continued recognition . . . if we set up a plan of our own?" the commission asked.[45] It answered that the Society would only gain "the confidence of our colleagues in the college and university world . . . if the training and achievement of our teachers, the equipment and use of our libraries and laboratories, and the requirements for our degrees are above the minimum standard."[46]

To overcome the inertia that continued to frustrate the best efforts of a few, the commission was convinced that the American provinces must "cooperate closely with one another in a spirit of sympathetic mutual understanding . . . even to the extent of considerable self-sacrifice when necessary for the common good of the entire Assistancy."[47] In an age of organization, the Society could not afford to claim exemption from the normal rules that govern efficiency and cooperation. As the most effective means to this end, the commission proposed a concrete solution which, when finally and fully implemented, had a profound influence on the apostolate of education in the United States and subsequently affected the decisions of other provinces in the Society.

The commission "earnestly recommended and strongly urged" a truly functioning inter-province organization which should be known as The Association of Jesuit Universities, Colleges and Secondary Schools of the United States.[48] The design for this instrument was clear and concrete. The Association would function through a National Executive Committee composed of as many members as provinces, "each province being represented by one member chosen from its own Standing Committee on Studies."[49] In a notable revision of the procedure of the Inter-Province Committee, the National Executive Committee (which would meet once a year, or oftener) would report directly to Father General and to the fathers provincial.[50] For supervision, direction, and leadership, a full-time executive secretary, nominated by the Executive Committee, approved by the provincials, and appointed by the General, would preside over the association. He would, of course, be provided with a suitable office and, administering this central bureau with an adequate staff, maintain contacts with superiors, academic offices of the Society, and external agencies.[51] Specifically, the executive secretary would preside at meetings of the Executive Committee, give full time to the study of current educational questions and the collection of accurate data concerning them, attend educational meetings, maintain friendly relations with other associations, and act as advisor to provincials, presidents, and deans.[52]

In the judgment of the commissioners, the executive secretary would be the key to success. It was the opinion of the commission, fully conscious of mistakes of the past, that the reason for the ineffectiveness of the Inter-Province Committee "was the absence of concerted action under central direction." In other words, the committee "should have reported directly to Father General."[53] To remedy that defect, it was the unanimous conviction of the members of the commission that, for prompt execution of their recommendations, the first executive secretary should be selected by the General himself, and, in a bold proposal, the father who was selected "should be given the powers and responsibilities of a 'Commissarius' over all educational matters in the Assistancy for as long a period as seems advisable to His Paternity."[54] To be precise, he would supersede provincials in decisions affecting education.

According to the commission, there were cogent reasons to justify an extraordinary procedure. In the first place, it was necessary to draft an educational expert in order to assist the provincials who, because of their ordinary preoccupations, were not always familiar with the complicated aspects of higher education, which had become more and more technical. Moreover, the vast territory embraced by the provinces of the American Assistancy precluded united action without a central authority to direct it. Finally, in facing the academic world, including educational associations and accrediting agencies, the Society of Jesus in America stood in need "of an authoritative, well informed spokesman, recognized as such, for our Jesuit institutions at this critical time of reorganization."[55] For all of these reasons, argued the commission, a special American commissarius, appointed by the General with "super-Provincial authority," was necessary to meet the exigencies of the moment.[56]

The *Report* of the Commission on Higher Studies was completed in July 1932 and, by direction of the General, was submitted to the American provinces for criticism.[57] As far as the picture can be pieced together, comments on the *Report* were candid and generally constructive; a few responses, however, were negative. Due, perhaps, to the adverse criticism, the General postponed action on implementation of the *Report*. As could be expected, most of the comments, and much of the criticism, focused on parts II, III, and IV, which, as indicated on an earlier page, were not entirely germane to this study.[58] For example, one critic, in a ten-page letter to his provincial, while conceding room for improvement did not agree "that our men in High School, College and Graduate work are as a whole far inferior in training and teaching capacity to the corresponding men in other Catholic, and especially in non-Catholic schools." The writer concluded that "this point of view colors the whole *Report* and in my judgment is unfair and not warranted in fact."[59] Writing from an Eastern theologate, a faculty member found it difficult to reconcile certain proposals of the commission with the requirements of papal documents in training Jesuit scholastics for the "de universa" examination in philosophy and the licentiate examination in theology. Furthermore — moving to another concern — the same commentator was "against the notion of a Commissarius." In his opinion, it would be difficult to find such a man, and secondly, the system would not work smoothly because the office would intrude "too much into the field of the authority of the Provincial."[60]

Historically, ecclesiastics and academicians are reluctant to question the methods of the past or to risk innovative projects in the future. Yet the *Report of the Commission*, in anticipation of its implementation, had begun to generate a momentum in the intellectual apostolate that would one day affect the careers of younger Jesuits in the United States. Three months before the 1932 report was officially submitted, His Paternity expressed surprise that, in the catalogs of the American provinces, very few fathers were identified by the title "writer."[61] He then suggested, in order to encourage the publication of articles, that this title be used more often. Moreover, in preparing for the future, more young Jesuits, of ability and promise, should be assigned to special studies for advanced degrees, even at great sacrifice to the province. As an added appeal to the provincials, the General invoked his conversations with Pope Pius XI, who exhorted the Society to excel not only "in virtue but in science and letters." Indeed, the proposed ideal was to emulate, even surpass, the scholarship of secular institutes.[62] As he had recommended on other occasions, the General clearly preferred fewer colleges and universities so that the accent would be on substantial courses, qualified professors, and professional administrators, "without which little by little, our American institutions will find themselves rejected and deserted."[63]

As criticism of the commission's work (even before it was completed) began to reach Rome, Father Macelwane felt obliged to defend the recommendations that were being formulated. Since someone had evidently written to His Paternity, "causing the General to think a few strange thoughts about us and our work," the chairman considered it only fair that the commissioners be allowed to defend their position before the Roman Curia.[64] Father Tivnan, although he dreaded the prospect of the trip "more than I can say," was the first to present their case to the General.[65] He was followed by Father Hynes and, as the last man in this procession, Father Macelwane himself.

Father Tivnan, who became progressively more pessimistic (and was fond of putting everything on paper), found the General ambiguous in his reaction to the report. At their last three-hour session, "[the General] seemed pleased with the [report], appreciated the work done by us, but thought we were extreme in some of our views and demands."[66] The General singled out Father Hynes as unduly innovative in his suggestions for change. In Hynes's defense, Tivnan pointed out to the General that it was an excess of zeal, since "Fr. H. was interested, heart and soul, in the Society's welfare."[67] With a final bit of advice, culled from his own experience, Tivnan urged that Macelwane, in his discussions with Ledochowski, "let him have the truth"; otherwise, "the standpatters [who] seem to wield the most influence" would gain the day.[68] Father Macelwane, who had guided the commission through some heavy seas, was not the man to need encouragement of that kind from a colleague. Honesty and courage had always marked his dealings with superiors.

As further evidence of his customary prudence, Father Ledochowski supplemented the commissioners' interpretation with selected interviews of informed Jesuits. One of those to whom His Paternity turned for advice was the distinguished educator from Saint Louis University, Alphonse M. Schwitalla. Even though, as is now clear, there were gray areas in the educational picture, there was always a small group of American Jesuits who continued to give integrity and credibility to the Society's historical reputation, and Father Schwitalla was such a person. Born in Beuthan, Upper Silesia, Germany, in 1882, he came to St. Louis with his parents when he was three years old. He entered the Society of Jesus in 1900, was ordained in 1915, and was awarded a Ph.D. in zoology from Johns Hopkins University in 1921. Appointed dean of the Saint Louis University School of Medicine in 1927, he held that post until his retirement, due to ill health, in 1948. Although a non-medical doctor, he was high in the councils of the American Medical Association, co-author of a famous minority report on the costs of medical care, member of a committee to evaluate the nation's medical schools, and the recipient of many academic honors.[69]

In his discussion with the General, Father Schwitalla spoke in support of cooperation with standardizing agencies and the rigor that should replace complacency in the administration of Jesuit graduate schools and in the granting of academic degrees. He explained to His Paternity the academic consequences of having a nonaccredited school in America; the necessity of restoring the confidence of non-Catholic educators in Jesuit institutions, which could be accomplished only through intense emphasis on research and publication; and the rigorous norms that should be applied before additional graduate programs were permitted in Jesuit institutions. He also exhorted the General to insist upon the selection of outstanding young Jesuit scholastics for advanced degrees and pleaded that they be given the opportunity to pursue their studies unencumbered by other commitments.[70]

Moreover, in his conversation at the Roman Curia, Schwitalla emphasized the necessity of grasping the earliest opportunity to secure public recognition for Jesuit institutions in their efforts to serve the Church in the United States. This suggestion was undoubtedly prompted by a move on the part of Catholic University to preempt the academic market in graduate education and so to garner the lion's share of publicity and acclaim before the eyes of the academic world. In an interesting exchange of correspondence with Wilfred Parsons, S.J., Robert Johnston, S.J. (President of Saint Louis University), and Schwitalla, Monsignor Maurice Sheehy, acting president of The Catholic University of America, complained that Francis M. Crowley, dean of the School of Education at Saint Louis, had indulged in unfounded and unfair innuendos against the position of Catholic University in his *America* articles.[71] Sheehy reminded the three prominent Jesuits that Catholic University had the approval of the Pope and, he added for good measure, the approval of the Association of American Universities. He did not foresee the possibility of any other Catholic university qualifying for *membership* in the association for the next twenty years. To add insult to injury, he suggested, as a solution to these problems, that degrees could be granted through the Catholic University charter to other Catholic graduate schools. Predictably, this was an unacceptable solution to Jesuit administrators, but it was an added reason for a national response to the challenge presented by Catholic University.[72]

As chairman of the Committee on Graduate Studies of the NCEA,

Schwitalla was in a good position to evaluate the evidence that was beginning to generate apprehension in Jesuit circles. In January 1933 an article appeared in the *Catholic University Bulletin* which stressed three points: (1) the necessity of graduate education, (2) Catholic University as the only school fully equipped for this service, because of (3) its "membership" in the Association of American Universities and the rescript of Pope Leo XIII.[73] Although Monsignor Sheehy subsequently modified his position and advocated five Catholic graduate schools, the Jesuits were not entirely mollified. Meeting in June 1933, Jesuit representatives, including Fathers Schwitalla and Wilfred Parsons, editor of *America*, passed a resolution at a convention of the NCEA: "It is the sense of this meeting that the relationships between the Catholic University and our Universities, especially concerning graduate work, should be recalled to the Fathers Provincial of the American Assistancy since the situation is one which warrants serious consideration and action."[74] It is possible, of course, that Catholic University itself felt threatened, since, in the statistics developed by Father Schwitalla for the years 1931–1932 and 1932–1933, of the thirty-three Catholic institutions that offered graduate degrees, the thirteen controlled by Jesuits, in relative terms, awarded the largest number of degrees, both master's and doctor's; enrolled the most students; and employed the most instructors.[75] In any event, it was unfortunate that this running controversy within the Catholic academic community took place at a time when professional harmony would have better served the Church.

Although the assertion would not be easy to document, it seems quite possible that the 1932 *Report of the Commission on Higher Education*, and his subsequent conversations with prominent members of the Society, hastened the General's decision to address a major document to the whole Society. His Paternity's "Letter Concerning the Choice of Ministries and Works," addressed to provincials throughout the world, contained many of the suggestions he had previously brought to the attention of the American Assistancy.[76] In particular, he repeated and emphasized the absolute importance of the intellectual apostolate and, indeed, gave it high priority in the order of choice. There was now no doubt about his conviction or commitment. Within one year, an announcement in American academic circles would act as a catalyst in moving the General to implement the recommendations of his special commission.

# 3. The General Appoints a "Commissarius," 1934–1937

THE AMERICAN COUNCIL on Education in the 1930s was becoming very influential in shaping the course of American higher education. Founded in 1918, the council was, from the beginning, an umbrella organization which, in addition to individual colleges and universities, sheltered local, regional, and national educational associations under its broad cover.[1] Its influence and authority, especially in its early years, filtered through these educational associations and could be decisive in affecting the destinies of particular institutions. Though not technically an accrediting agency, the educational *imprimatur* of the council was avidly sought by institutions that were moving from mediocrity to a higher ranking on the educational ladder. By the same token, its disapproval, intended or implied, could be a serious disadvantage for those intent on gaining entrance to the inner sanctum of academic respectability.

On October 7, 1932, the Executive Committee of the ACE appointed a Committee on Graduate Instruction, under the chairmanship of Raymond M. Hughes, president of Iowa State College, to identify those American institutions which, in the opinion of the specialists who collaborated with the committee, were qualified to prepare candidates for the doctor's degree. In the first nationwide survey ever made, seventy-seven graduate schools, known to offer programs for the doctorate, were unofficially ranked in an informed consensus by the members of the committee. Two years later, in its house journal, the council published the results of its survey in an explosive article which excited the interest of the academic community in the United States.[2]

To the twenty-eight members of the Association of American Universities, which comprised the previous official list, the committee added thirty-five institutions that it considered had adequate staff and facilities in one or more fields to prepare students at the highest level. Besides rating these institutions as "qualified," the report listed some as "distinguished" in one or more of the departments under consideration.[3] The committee conceded that "the report is neither complete nor free from mistakes. It is, however," it claimed, "a reliable guide as to the judgment of a large group of our leading scholars relative to American graduate work."[4]

Sensing the serious implications of the committee's report, the *New York Times* printed a long article with a comprehensive enumeration of the departments surveyed, and identified the sixty-three institutions and their departments on the approved list and those designated "distinguished."[5] A subheading read: "14 Graduate Institutions Fail of Endorsement as Qualified to Prepare for Doctorate." Two Catholic universities were on the approved list: The Catholic University of America, in five departments, and the University of Notre Dame, in chemistry. No Jesuit institution was found worthy to be numbered among this distinguished company. The omission was tantamount to an embarrassing accusation, and it was subsequently alleged that at least one hundred copies of the article were sent to the General's Curia in Rome.[6]

Whatever his reasons for hesitating to act upon the recommendations of the Commission on Higher Studies, Father Ledochowski realized that he could no longer afford to vacillate. The public indictment of Jesuit graduate education by a peer group could not go unanswered; and in the end, he acted quickly and decisively. In August 1934, less than three months after the article appeared in the *Educational Record*, His Paternity sent three documents to the American Assistancy which, for efficacy and long-term influence, are—in retrospect—three of the most important documents ever addressed to the American provinces.

In a letter to the fathers and scholastics of the American Assistancy, the General announced that he was sending, under the same cover, an "Instruction on Studies and Teaching."[7] Briefly reviewing the record of the past, including the work of the Commission on Higher Studies, His Paternity explained that the *Instruction* was, in effect, "an effort to give a new direction and a fresh impulse to the labors of Ours [and] a systematized attempt to secure for our educational activities their due recognition and rightful standing among other groups of a similar rank and grade."[8] He was particularly anxious, since they form the *spes gregis*, that the scholastics be convinced "that a great deal is expected of them"; that they "eagerly embrace the studies assigned to them, and do their best to make them a success."[9] In a spirit of exhortation, he noted that "teachers must have degrees, they must write books and ar-

ticles of scientific value [and] keep in contact with learned organizations."[10] Binding everything together was the watchword "cooperation": "cooperation of the Provinces among themselves, cooperation of
the several Colleges of each Province, cooperation lastly of all the members of the Province, old and young, Superiors and subjects, each un-
selfishly looking to the general good."[11] In conclusion, and as a source
of inspiration, His Paternity noted that the *Instruction* was promulgated "on the four hundredth anniversary of the day when our holy
Father Saint Ignatius and his six companions consecrated themselves by
vow to the service of God and of the Church."[12]

The General was more technical, explicit, and legal in his official
letter to the American provincials.[13] In a reference, perhaps, to the
report of the American Council on Education, he repeated that union
and mutual cooperation were absolutely necessary "if we wish to hold
our own in the modern education world, and to meet the new conditions that are challenging us on every side." He became, in fact, explicit. "The position of your Graduate Schools, which have hitherto
received so little public recognition, must be courageously examined into. This is a matter of supreme moment to be handled with unselfish
cooperation on the part of all the Provinces, and with the single purpose
of bringing the schools to the level of the best in the country."[14] Convinced that union and cooperation could not exist without a central
organization, he created the Association of Jesuit Universities, Colleges
and High Schools of the United States, in which all such institutions,
without exception, would enjoy *ipso facto* membership.[15]

In the organization of the association, transposing (almost verbatim) the recommendations of the commission, the General provided
for a national secretary of education and, as his personal selection, appointed Father Daniel M. O'Connell, of the Chicago Province, to that
office. Moreover, "for a limited time," His Paternity gave Father
O'Connell the title and prerogative of a "commissarius," by which he
was "invested with all the authority needed to carry into effect the
prescriptions and recommendations contained in the *Instruction*."[16] But
foreseeing the possibility of fraternal friction, the General attempted a
jurisdictional balancing act. Although the provincials were dependent
on the commissarius in matters educational, the commissarius, in turn,
would ordinarily communicate his decisions through the provincials. As
events would prove, this shared arrangement was not entirely successful. In any case, there would be room for amendments, as the *Instruction*, which was from the beginning mandatory, would be tested
for three years. "It will then become permanent with whatever additions and modifications experience shall dictate."[17]

The third document was the *Instruction* itself.[18] Written in Latin and organized under three main headings and thirty-five articles, it treated, first, of education at the Assistancy and province level; second, of the administration of universities, colleges, and high schools; and third, of the preparation of Jesuit teachers. Articles 2–4, under title I, provided for the formation of a Jesuit Educational Association, an Executive Committee, and a national secretary, with enumeration of his principal functions. The language was borrowed, even to punctuation, from the recommendations of the Commission on Higher Studies. Under other circumstances, the General could have been indicted for plagiarism.

Anticipating the necessity of a long-term intellectual infusion to fortify the academic life of the association, title III of the *Instruction* drew a comprehensive blueprint of a Jesuit's intellectual growth, from the simple classes of the novitiate to the donning of the doctor's hood. In fact, article 34 implies that pursuit of the doctorate should be the ambition of those Jesuits, priests and scholastics, who have the aptitude and desire for that distinction. For former members of the Inter-Province Committee and the special Commission on Higher Studies — vindicating, as it did, their hopes and labors — the *Instruction* was a dream come true.

Father O'Connell opened his office in Chicago on September 8, 1934. By the common consent of those who applauded his tireless efforts as national secretary of education and commissarius, as well as those who found themselves in disagreement with his *modus procedendi*, "Father Commissarius," as he was frequently called, never received the recognition he deserved. More than any other Jesuit — in the author's opinion — he was responsible for improving the standards of Jesuit colleges and universities, for inculcating much-needed professionalism in the offices of administrators, and for persuading superiors to send talented men to advanced studies. In three short years he gave Jesuit education a new direction, a new spirit, a new name, and the legacy inherited by Jesuit educators of today is in large measure a testimony to the unselfish dedication of this man.[19]

Daniel M. O'Connell was born in Louisville, Kentucky, on August 27, 1885. After completing both his high school and college training at St. Mary's, Kansas, he entered the Society of Jesus at Florissant, Missouri, in 1903. He was ordained to the priesthood in 1918, and after tertianship in Parma, Ohio, he was assigned to Xavier University, Cincinnati, where he spent nine years: three as an instructor in philosophy and six as dean of the college. Appreciating the importance of advanced degrees, Father O'Connell began graduate studies in English literature at Fordham University, where he was awarded the doctorate in 1930. At the same time, he gained national recognition as a Newman scholar, and desiring to introduce John Henry Cardinal Newman to Catholic college students, he edited the cardinal's most famous works: *The Present Position of Catholics in England, The Idea of a University,* and *Apologia pro Vita Sua.* Appointed prefect of studies for the Chicago Province in 1930, he was Father Ledochowski's choice for national secretary of education in 1934.

For reasons that will become clearer as our narrative continues, Father O'Connell's term of office was abruptly terminated in 1937, and it is a measure of his strong character and spiritual strength that, as many Jesuits recorded, even to his closet friends "not a word was mentioned revealing anything of his disappointment at the early termination of the national work."[20] After his three-year term, Father O'Connell was, successively, minister of Campion House, New York City; librarian at the University of Detroit; and spiritual father to that Jesuit community. Ill health forced his retirement to West Baden College, where he died on July 29, 1958.

In his letters to the American Assistancy, Father General had identified three problems which demanded immediate attention: efficient and competitive development of graduate schools; preparation of Jesuit teachers by means of advanced studies, leading to the master's and doctor's degrees; and establishment of a sound and professional relationship with accrediting agencies. As he addressed these problems with determination, intelligence, and vision, it is astonishing, in retrospect, to read the record of Father O'Connell's activities. As a first step, he undertook a visitation of every Jesuit university, college, high school, and seminary in the United States. His inspection of each institution (admittedly hasty on some occasions) followed a uniform pattern which conformed to the instructions of the General, honored the authority of provincials, and protected the prerogatives of a commissarius. Father O'Connell's directions and recommendations were normally communicated to local superiors and subjects through the regional provincial, who, in his turn, forwarded copies to Father General and to Father O'Connell. It was routine practice for the commissarius to send copies of his reports and correspondence to Rome.[21]

Reflecting his sense of urgency, Father O'Connell visited Boston College, the College of the Holy Cross, and Boston College High School in the fall of 1934.[22] In submitting his recommendations to the provincial of the New England Province, the commissarius reminded him that "Father General gave me the not pleasant task of making suggestions and giving directions. In doing so, I pray that I am not critical or worse still, unappreciative of the splendid educational work being done by the New England Province."[23] With this preventive warning, and admitting "the splendid history of Boston College," he gave concrete directions for improvement of that institution.

In the first place, expressing complete agreement with the results of an inspection by the Association of American Universities (AAU), Father O'Connell directed that "the Ph.D. degree, as given in the past at Boston College, should be entirely discontinued until the (AAU) approves the inauguration of particular Ph.D. degrees at Boston College."[24] Moreover, he continued, a Jesuit Ph.D., trained in an American university recognized by the AAU, must be appointed dean of the Graduate School, with authority to organize it according to accepted standards. Master's degrees, though permitted, were to be confined to departments whose heads held a Ph.D. and were also full-time professors. In addition to the Graduate School, Father O'Connell was very specific in his instructions for administration of the undergraduate college, its library, curriculum, admission of students, examinations, and — very important — the recommendation of students for graduate and professional schools.[25]

From Boston, the commissarius motored to Worcester for his visit to Holy Cross College, which, he noted, "well deserves its high reputation among S.J. Colleges in the United States."[26] Among its credits, Holy Cross, with AAU recognition, restricted its graduate courses to a master's degree in chemistry; and although its library was admirable, attention to certain details would make it even better. He suggested making Greek an elective, "since having so many disinterested students does not conduce to scholarship"; and students should be allowed to develop more initiative with library assignments. Moreover, the enrollment should be controlled so as to avoid having three students "in the same small room," which precluded serious study. Finally, "a faculty building, science hall and more gymnasium room [were] desirable."[27]

In his memoir to the provincial, James T. McCormick, O'Connell added two final directives in order to ensure permanency and continuity to his more detailed instructions for the New England Province. First, he urged that "Father General's plan for developing Jesuit Ph.D.'s should be immediately inaugurated, even though expensive in men and money, by placing scholastics at recognized Jesuit universities for their M.A. and assigning priests to the best universities for their Ph.D."[28] Secondly, he appointed a blue ribbon committee to supervise implementation of the demands of the AAU and to monitor the curricula changes he had suggested at the two colleges and the novitiate at

Shadowbrook.[29] His "notes" (as he called them) to the provincial contained several additional points which served to buttress his principal directives. (To avoid repetition as our analysis continues, it might be helpful to remember that the program devised for the visitation of the New England Province was followed in other provinces.)

As time went on, it became clear that Father O'Connell had an obsession which was not shared by everyone involved in Jesuit education. He was utterly convinced that the blessing of the AAU was a magic formula that would open the doors of the American intellectual "establishment" to Jesuit expectations of ultimate equality. His preoccupation, moreover, was not without foundation. The constitution of the AAU, adopted on February 28, 1900, is brief and to the point. Article II clearly states that the association "is founded for the purpose of considering matters of common interest relating to graduate study."[30] Member institutions took this mandate seriously, and the association, as already noted, became — almost by default — the *de facto* accrediting agency for graduate schools and departments.[31] In fact, at the thirty-sixth annual conference in 1934, the association drew up an "Accepted List" which, predictably, included the best schools in the country.[32] It is understandable, in this context, that O'Connell, under serious pressure to improve the standing of Jesuit higher education, would regard approval by the AAU as his norm for excellence. Throughout his visitations, consequently, endorsement of Jesuit universities by the AAU was considered the key to success and the acme of academic achievement.

A decision by the AAU precipitated a *contretemps* between the commissarius and Aloysius Hogan, the distinguished president of Fordham University, during and after the former's visitation of that institution. Father Hogan, a cultured, intelligent, and charming Jesuit, had completed his graduate work in classical studies at Cambridge University, England. Returning to his province, he served for two years as dean of studies at Saint Andrew-on-Hudson and was then appointed president of Fordham University in 1930, at the relatively youthful age of thirty-nine. As the controversy continued, it was mildly surprising that the commissarius, holding a Fordham doctorate, should press for innovations and standards while the cosmopolitan scholar-president argued for the academic *status quo* at Rose Hill.

Two inspectors from the AAU made a formal visit to Fordham in the fall of 1935 and, after careful evaluation of the documentation supplied by the president, made their recommendation to the chairman of the Committee on the Clarification of Universities and Colleges of the AAU. The chairman, dean of the Graduate School at Indiana University, then informed Father Hogan that the committee had "voted at its recent meeting to omit Fordham University from its list of accredited institutions."[33] This action, the dean explained, was based primarily upon the "unsatisfactory showing of Fordham graduates in other professional and graduate schools," and the inadequacy of the libraries both in the Bronx and Manhattan.[34] Reference books, he added, "were locked in cases in inaccessible rooms" and the availability of other library facilities in the city "does not compensate for the deficiencies."[35]

Disturbed by this report, O'Connell lost no time complaining to the American Assistant in Rome that Fordham's censure by the AAU was a "national disgrace."[36] In a second letter to Father Maher, the commissarius contrasted the intransigence of Father Hogan, who made it clear that he would carry out instructions "only within the letter of the law," with the diplomacy of Father Gallagher at Boston College, which remained on the approved list of the AAU.[37] "The pity is," he lamented, "that Fordham could be our outstanding Graduate School."[38]

Despite this adversary relationship, O'Connell was forthright and specific in his recommendation to Joseph A. Murphy, provincial of the Maryland–New York Province. Fordham should seek "complex organization" status, which had improved the standing of Saint Louis University and Marquette with the AAU. To this end, Fordham, "which has the greatest opportunity of any Jesuit Graduate School in the United States," should build up a separate graduate library, transfer the Graduate School to the main campus, engage full-time professors, secure full-time students through partial or complete scholarships, and separate the Graduate and Teachers' colleges. Pressing forward, he submitted directions for the Law School, the School of Social Work, and, to the surprise of many, wondered "if Fordham should not abandon its Pharmacy School. Among the advantages would be much needed room for the Catholic undergraduates."[39] He also recommended for doctorate studies several Jesuits (e.g., he urged the provincial to send Demetrius Zema to Columbia for a Ph.D. in history) who subsequently brought distinction to the Society.[40]

For the undergraduate College of Arts and Sciences, he suggested an honors course, reduction in class hours, majors in addition to philosophy and science, greater use of the library by students, and better departmental organization.[41] Many of the changes prescribed by O'Connell did not go unchallenged. Francis Donnelly, province prefect of studies, was not happy with an honors program, which he characterized as hostile to the *Ratio Studiorum*, and Father Hogan objected strenuously to the proposed undergraduate program.

In a seven-page memorandum, entitled "Objections to the Proposed A.B. Schedule," President Hogan appealed to the *Instruction*, to Father General's letters, to the Commission on Higher Studies, and even to accrediting agencies to demonstrate that the proposed changes were not in the best interest of Fordham.[42] Actually, the new directives were mandated at a previous meeting of Maryland–New York deans (June 1935) in which Father O'Connell outlined the proposed A.B. course, which was prescribed for the opening of class in September 1935.[43] According to President Hogan, the objections of the deans were noted at that meeting, but "apparently no consideration has been given the opinions regarding the schedules of those who have been intimately engaged in this work in this section of the country." As a parting shot, he referred to a recent letter from Father General, dated June 29, 1935, in which His Paternity assured Father Hogan that "he was very anxious that the ancient and approved traditions of the Society be preserved intact."[44]

Father O'Connell's experience at Fordham must have confirmed his growing suspicion that the life of a commissarius could never be described as a pleasant interlude. Happily, as he traveled to the southern jurisdiction of the Maryland–New York Province, his reception at Georgetown University was characteristic of traditional Southern hospitality. Tracing its academic ancestry to Archbishop John Carroll and honored as the "alma mater of all Catholic colleges in the U.S.," Georgetown was presided over by Arthur O'Leary, who had only recently inherited his presidential mantle from the handsome and urbane W. Colman Nevils. Father O'Leary, well over six feet tall, dignified, and imposing, had no special background that would entitle him to a presidency. Yet, according to O'Connell, he had the instincts and "the proper qualifications" for that position. On his part, O'Connell never seemed to grasp or appreciate the historical pattern of Georgetown's growth — nor, apparently, was he familiar with the academic feud that had developed between Georgetown University and The Catholic University of America.[45] Moreover, his growing insistence on quality over quantity, without any awareness of financial realities, appeared to local administrators to inhibit the growth of Jesuit institutions.

True to form, he immediately noted that the Georgetown University Graduate School (as had been the case at Boston and Fordham) "will likely have an inspection of the A.A.U. this year."[46] As though that were not warning enough, he added that "Georgetown is also under the critical eye of the Catholic University."[47] He then posed a rhetorical question which, if known by the rank and file, would not have made him popular on the Georgetown campus. "As the Catholic University

has a graduate school at Washington," he asked, "is there need of a
Graduate School at Georgetown, except for the M.A. in Philosophy at
Woodstock, and possibly in the Law School?"[48] Since, as the commissarius admitted, "most of ours here think we should continue with
some Graduate work, very limited and high class," he permitted the
continuation of certain programs within severe limitations.[49] His directives were precise, and to avoid misunderstanding were to be clearly
stated in the graduate bulletin. In astronomy, seismology, economics,
and philosophy, no new Ph.D. candidates were to be accepted. In
chemistry, the Ph.D. could be offered, but only under the personal
research direction of Dr. Michael X. Sullivan, whose competence was
everywhere acknowledged. As for the remaining departments, "no
other Master's or Doctor's courses may be offered without the written
permission of Father Provincial and Father General's representative of
education."[50] Finally, the graduate programs should show exclusively
Graduate credits and the Ph.D. thesis must be published.

The commissarius seemed impressed, or at least satisfied, with the
management of undergraduate programs at Georgetown College. In
view of the fact that Georgetown had received undergraduate recognition from the AAU, he was expansive in concluding that "our eldest college is keeping up the standards and traditions, which have been the
pride of the Society in this country for so many years."[51] But this did
not mean he was completely satisfied; he had several suggestions for
strengthening degree majors, improving the library, and organizing departments; but he reserved his strongest criticism for the lack of continuity in administration. "Georgetown's saddest experience," he observed,
"has been some ten or so deans in as many years."[52] On the other hand,
he congratulated the professional schools whose success was in large
measure due to the caliber of their deans or regents. Edmund A. Walsh,
an internationally recognized diplomat and the reigning authority on
the Russian Revolution, was founder and proprietary dean of the School
of Foreign Service. A compatriot from New England, Francis E. Lucey,
was at this time province prefect of studies and regent of the Law
School. The commissarius noted that "Father Lucey has educational
ideals" which "the next Rectors at Georgetown and Fordham should
push."[53] This advice was uncharacteristically vague and probably reflected fatigue at the end of an academically demanding visitation.
It was also the termination of his visit to the Maryland–New York
Province.[54]

Leaving the banks of the Potomac, the commissarius continued his
survey on the shores of the Mississippi. Saint Louis University, whose

roots go back to 1818, recalls the almost legendary Louis W. B. Dubourg, the Sulpician bishop of the vast territory which stretched from New Orleans to Missouri; Charles VanQuickenborne, who led the seven Flemings to Florissant; Peter J. Verhaegen, who combined religious observance with executive talent; and Bishop Joseph Rosati, who lent his energy and authority to the Jesuit enterprise.[55] Saint Louis University was the pride of the Missouri Province and, in a wider context, was treated with academic respect by the educational *cognoscenti* of the American Assistancy. This esteem was implicit in the decision of provincials to assign Jesuit scholastics to that institution for the master's degree. In Fathers William J. McGucken, Thurber M. Smith, Schwitalla, and Macelwane, Saint Louis could lean upon resourceful, responsible, and experienced educators who commanded the confidence of their peers at the national level. Due to the work of these men (and others), the university was recognized by the AAU, and its constituent schools, professional and undergraduate (with the exception of the School of Finance and Commerce), had been accorded accreditation by appropriate agencies.

Impressed by its reputation and accomplishments, Father O'Connell hoped to make this institution the centerpiece of Jesuit higher education in the Midwest. His proposal, to Father Provincial Samuel Horine and to Father Maher, the American Assistant in Rome, was — in essence — to retard or delay the development of other institutions in favor of concentration at Saint Louis.[56] According to this grand design, he was inclined to think "that Marquette in the plan of the whole Province should be content with its present recognition."[57] He admitted that this "was throwing strength to St. Louis but again it is a question of a plan for the next twenty or thirty years from the viewpoint of the whole Province."[58] But that was not all: the foundation at Denver must also sacrifice itself for the common good.

Since Regis College, according to the commissarius, had no academic future, was a heavy drain on manpower, and could pay no province tax, he urged the provincial, in the face of these perennial problems, "to formulate a plan for closing Regis College and High School."[59] Needless to say, the president of that institution did not greet this astonishing advice with enthusiasm. (As history records, the point was not well taken.)[60] As for the two remaining institutions in the Missouri Province, it was suggested that Creighton University strive for AAU undergraduate recognition, while Rockhurst, which "seems to have a future as a small college," should get a financial infusion from the province and immediately seek accreditation from the North Central Association.[61]

With such a solid foundation, O'Connell felt that Saint Louis should strive for membership — far more prestigious than mere recognition — in the AAU. He conceded that this "will probably take from ten to fifteen years," but, when accomplished, it would be proof that Saint Louis could claim equality with the best schools in the land.[62] However, he subscribed to the thesis that in universities, as in every other human endeavor, there is always room for improvement.

There was also a hierarchy of values. Although he worked hard to improve the academic quality of Jesuit colleges and universities, he was, if anything, even more insistent that they be thoroughly Catholic. On occasions, truth to tell, he was almost *too* eager to preserve the prerogatives of Church affiliation. In the present case, fearful that Saint Louis University, in pursuing its intellectual goals, might lose its Jesuit character, he tested the policies of the university against the stipulations of the *Instruction*.[63] It was a matter of co-equal objectives, which involved both will and intellect.

In any event, returning to the academic program, he imposed certain directives which, he thought, would facilitate the much-sought-after, but elusive, membership in the prestigious AAU. The most visible problem at Saint Louis was the persistent emphasis on the professional schools, to the detriment of the undergraduate College of Arts and Sciences.[64] For added prestige, he urged more Jesuits, at whatever level, to apply for membership in associations of their discipline and to gain visibility through attendance at meetings. A corollary was the necessity of research and the publication of articles in learned journals. The weakest link in the academic structure of Saint Louis, according to the commissarius, was the library. "I can say without fear of giving offense," he wrote, "that the material quarters make one feel one's heart contract. I trust a new one will take precedence in any building program."[65] Yet, taking everything together, he was very optimistic about the academic future of Saint Louis.

Although Father O'Connell was positive in his praise of Saint Louis University, lavish in his approval of the Jesuit scholasticate, and ranked the Florissant juniorate "as probably the best in the Assistancy," his visitation was not without intramural conflicts. Never the complete diplomat, his candid assessment of personalities, especially those who employed a strategy of passive resistance, only served to augment the ranks of his detractors. Writing to Father Assistant Maher, he referred to Father Horine as a "defeatist," accused him of a "*laissez faire* attitude," and questioned his cooperation. Robert Johnston, president of Saint Louis University, was "a charming gentleman but no educator or executive."[66]

One is tempted to mitigate the harshness of these judgments in the light of O'Connell's total dedication to the apostolate of Jesuit education, his sense of urgency, and his accountability to Father General as commissarius. No one would deny his ability or commitment, but certain Jesuit superiors, in the American Assistancy and in Rome, began to question his discretion.

Two of his more conspicuous confrontations involved the provinces of New Orleans and Oregon. During his visitation of the New Orleans Province, he directed the provincial, Joseph Walsh, to transfer Andrew Smith, dean of Spring Hill College and province prefect of studies, to Loyola University, New Orleans, as professor of English and chairman of the department. Father Smith, a gregarious personality and beloved by all who knew him, had recently completed a doctorate in English at the University of Chicago, and O'Connell's point was that only Smith could give proper academic leadership to Loyola. The provincial and his consultors disagreed, and in two courteous letters Father Walsh asked the commissarius to be released from his directive. Since O'Connell was adamant, the provincial, as a last resort, appealed to the General. Among other reasons for avoiding the move, Father Walsh, whose dealings with the commissarius were "disappointingly brief," thought that Father Smith would be "seriously damaged by contact with the irregulars of Loyola."[67] This brought the president of the university into the picture. John Hynes, as the provincial had informed the General, supported O'Connell's point of view, and for good reason. In December 1934, an unfriendly Southern Association, after a survey of the campus, placed Loyola on probation for one year, with the threat that it would be expelled from the association unless criticisms were answered and resolved. Criticisms were answered, and Loyola was admitted to full membership in December 1935.[68]

In a previous disagreement with the Oregon provincial, Walter F. Fitzgerald, future bishop in Alaska, O'Connell seemed to take an unreasonable position in the face of solid arguments from the provincial. The commissarius had directed Father Fitzgerald to arrange a summer quarter at Seattle College. Because of the shortage of manpower, the provincial and his consultors were opposed to this plan, but O'Connell insisted. Obviously upset, the provincial replied: "From [your] statement I understand that you order the Provincial by authority of Father General to establish a Summer School at Seattle immediately."[69] The commissarius, in his turn, regretted "that in this matter you have from the beginning shown less than cooperation. I had not expected that."[70] When the provincial read that letter to his consultors, "they were shocked by its tone and by the charges of lack of cooperation with you on my part."[71] Father Fitzgerald then ordered the summer session to be held as directed.

On these occasions, as on others, the problem was partially a conflict of authority, as well as personality. More than that, however, these exchanges represented the difference between the immediate and well-defined objectives of the commissarius and the perceived needs of the whole province by the regional superior.

In discharging the General's mandate, O'Connell visited every university, college, and high school in the assistancy.[72] It would be instructive — if only to satisfy the record — to document his visitations to the remaining institutions; such a procedure, however, would involve the reader in details that would ultimately create confusion rather than enlightenment. Those institutions that we have selected for review sufficiently illustrate the problems that were addressed, the areas of concern, and the administrative style and *modus procedendi* of the commissarius.[73] Beyond the visitation of institutions, Father O'Connell made additional contributions which, as time goes on, stand as a more permanent memorial of his zeal and vision. The picture would be incomplete if mention of these were excluded from the catalog of his activities.

Title III of the *Instruction* provided a framework for the "Preparation of Teachers," scholastics and priests, from the baccalaureate degree through the master's and on to the doctorate. The process begins in the juniorate, normally a two-year period, devoted to study of the humanities, which precedes the more arduous course in scholastic philosophy. Father O'Connell immediately recognized that the major obstacle to pursuit of higher degrees in the Society was the absence of collegiate credit, from accredited institutions, for courses completed in Jesuit houses of formation. The inherited system was an unfair handicap. As his biographer observes, he "saw clearly that our houses of study were more than seminaries . . . and accordingly he integrated the Juniorates, Philosophates and Theologates with our universities so that the former could share a university status and acquire a university atmosphere."[74] This concern reflected his sensitivity to the intellectual respectability of Jesuits who carried the reputation of the Society into the halls of the learned laity.

For these reasons, he was the first to devise an official integration of the juniorate courses at Shadowbrook and the philosophy courses at Weston College with Boston College. The juniorate at Saint Andrew-on-Hudson was attached to Fordham. (Florissant and the scholasticate in St. Louis were already academically tied to Saint Louis University.) The plan was put into practice in every province where Jesuit scholastics had been cheated of academic credit for courses they had completed. The juniorate at Saint Isaac Jogues Novitiate, Wernersville, illustrates the commissarius' concern for detail and the importance he attached to this phase of his work. In complete agreement with the administrators at Wernersville, Father O'Connell approved the academic integration of these courses with Georgetown University. Georgetown, he noted, had a federal charter, and was recognized by the AAU; and to simplify course identification, all credits would come from that institution.[75] To ensure shared responsibility, as he had done in New England, he appointed Francis Connell as representative of the provincial; Hugo McCarron, prefect of studies at Wernersville, as representative of Joseph Didusch, rector; and John Grattan, dean of the college, as representative of Georgetown, to draw up details of the integration.[76] What seemed commonplace in later years was novel then. To Father O'Connell, more than to any other man, should go the credit for insisting upon this total integration and coordination of a Jesuit's effort to plan an organized academic career envisioned by the *Instruction.*

In his visitation of complex institutions (undergraduate, graduate, and professional schools) Father O'Connell's primary, immediate attention was focused on the graduate school. It was almost a fixation. Not only was this responsibility made a priority in his instructions from Father General, but the commissarius realized — as few others did — that a truly representative graduate school was the key to academic prestige for a particular institution.

The history of American graduate schools, it has been said, is the history of the Ph.D. degree. Imported from Germany, and incorporated into the American higher education system, the Ph.D. became the hallmark of the trained scholar, scientist, and researcher. As evidenced by the unhappy results of the AAU survey, this would now be the test of Jesuit achievement, and as *ex-officio* chairman he proposed that the Executive Committee of the Jesuit Educational Association establish a Committee on Graduate Studies.[77] This committee, which was chaired by Father Macelwane, elaborated a series of norms to guide Jesuit graduate schools in undertaking master's and doctor's programs. At a meeting in Louisville in 1937, the committee, with the approval of Father O'Connell, completed and published its statement, officially entitled *Norms Proposed by the Committee on Graduate Studies of the Jesuit Educational Association for Its Guidance in Appraising Graduate Work.*[78]

Samuel Knox Wilson, whose name is legendary in the Chicago Province, was a member of the Committee on Graduate Studies and his contribution, regionally and nationally, to Jesuit higher education should be acknowledged. Father Wilson, born in 1882, was ordained in 1917, and after his tertianship was assigned to Saint Ignatius High School in Chicago. His talents were quickly recognized, and in 1922 he began a graduate program in history at Cambridge University, England, where he earned his degree in 1924. After several years of writing and teaching, he was appointed dean of the Graduate School at Loyola University and served as its president (1934–1942). During his presidency, Loyola University received AAU recognition.

On the subject of Jesuit education, O'Connell and Wilson were in close agreement, and Wilson supported the commissarius in his recommendation to close Saint John's in Toledo. In fact, O'Connell, writing to the American Assistant, made a bold proposal: "Father Wilson (with Father Clifford out?) is our outstanding educator—*facile princeps*. Though he would be a great loss to Loyola, the Province needs him more and immediately. Is there any hope?"[79] On the other hand, Wilson disagreed with O'Connell and Macelwane on the type of governmental machinery by which the JEA would operate. He contended that the association "remains a paper organization, and the only element of life in the whole affair is the annual meeting of the General Prefects of Study."[80] He conceded that "[his] plan of making the Jesuit Educational Association function through a group at the top consisting of the various Provincials of the American provinces is somewhat hazardous."[81] However, the intrinsic merit of his proposal depended on the fact that "in the last analysis the normal government of the Society in this country must be carried on through Provincials."[82]

To return to the norms. An authority on the history of Catholic higher education in the United States has written that "these norms recognized every issue facing Catholic colleges in their efforts to realize excellence in undergraduate and graduate programs. Also, they were the first general statements on the subject of graduate school standards for Catholic colleges in this country."[83] In a later work, the same author has an excellent description and analysis of these "norms," showing the relevance of the five key points—faculty quality, academic organization, adequate libraries, research facilities, and degree requirements—to the Jesuit institutions of that day.[84] What Professor Power fails to point out, however, is that these "norms" were the natural extension of Father O'Connell's experience as commissarius and were the ultimate expression of his philosophical commitment to excellence in Jesuit higher education.

The operative word is always "Jesuit." The standards that the commissarius had imposed on each graduate school had coalesced into a coherent set of regulations that applied to all. This is clear from a practical application of the cooperation that should characterize a community of Jesuit universities. In fulfilling the requirements for graduate degrees, "we must . . . visualise our degrees, not as given by this or that institution, but as conferred by a *Jesuit university* so that, rightly or wrongly, praise or blame will attach to the Jesuits. Therefore, the requirements laid down everywhere should be a little above the average of what is generally considered good practice."[85] Through imposition of these "guidelines," which were conscientiously applied, Jesuit graduate schools began to move from a stationary position of survival to true academic competition and equality. In its first attempt at regulation for improvement, the Jesuit Educational Association had acted with authority, courage, and influence.

At the 1937 meeting of the Executive Committee in Louisville, Father O'Connell is quoted as having said "that in his mind the heart of the *Instruction* is special studies."[86] Whether that judgment is objectively true or not, there is solid evidence for his insistence — even though provincials were short of funds in those years — that talented priests and scholastics be set aside, so to speak, to study the disciplines which they were destined to teach. Although some older Jesuits, as is clear from the record, had already completed their doctorates at distinguished universities, they were too few in number to support the academic reputation of twenty-five colleges and universities. Many, indeed, had been "sacrificed" to administration. Statistics show a dramatic increment, in the late '30s, in the number of those sent to special studies. Whether there was a direct, causal connection between this increase and Father O'Connell's personal crusade would be difficult to establish. Undoubtedly, provincials, province prefects of studies, presidents, deans, and personal ambition played their part. It is undeniably clear, however, that, as part of his report to each provincial, on the basis of information supplied to him, he submitted the names of priests and scholastics who, in his judgment, should be assigned to special studies, either for the Ph.D. or, in the case of most scholastics, for the master's degree.[88]

The necessity of special studies was the final detail in the picture painted by the *Instruction*. Not only were doctoral studies logically tied to adequate preparation for teaching, but advanced degrees were absolutely necessary for implementing the graduate "norms," which, in turn, would guarantee recognition by the AAU and accreditation by the standardizing agencies. Each of these elements responded to the charge imposed by Father General on the American commissarius. In the end, it would be the total effort of Jesuit personnel, trained in research and productive in publication, that would open the doors of the American academic club to the aspirations of Jesuit scholars and their universities. No other route would lead to the desired goal.

In a three-year period, Father O'Connell gave a powerful stimulus to Jesuit education in the United States. The foundation, it is true, had been laid by his predecessors in the Society; he, however, accelerated construction of the superstructure and helped to form the shape of the edifice. In challenging the *status quo*, he persuaded Jesuit colleges and universities to abandon sectarian isolation on the periphery of the academic world and forced them to assume a responsible role on the American scene. His profound knowledge of the history of American higher education, his instinct for excellence, and his total commitment to the apostolate gave credibility to his crusade. His years as commissarius were not without disappointments; yet, in his retirement, as he watched the growing prestige of the Jesuit Educational Association, it must have been consoling to remember that he had served as the principal architect.

# 4. The Executive Committee, 1937–1946

THE FRENETIC PACE that distinguished Daniel O'Connell's first two years as national secretary of education was gradually moderated by the intrusion of other events. Some were closely connected with application of the *Instruction*; others were only marginally linked to the apostolate of higher education. In the fall of 1936 the General appointed John Bolland, provincial of the English Province and later English Assistant, Visitor to the New Orleans Province.[1] To avoid a conflict of authority, and in the interest of diplomacy, His Paternity suspended the office of commissarius. Although deprived of his badge of authority, O'Connell remained, nevertheless, national secretary. The following year, in preparing for a general congregation of the Society of Jesus, the American provincials concentrated on the organization of provincial congregations in order to choose delegates for the main event.[2] Happily emancipated from the pressures exerted by a zealous commissarius, they endeavored to divert the attention of the General to less controversial business. Ledochowski, however, though sympathetic to the prerogatives of provincials, had no intention of abandoning his program for achieving excellence in Jesuit higher education in the United States.

For his part, having completed a survey of individual institutions, O'Connell turned his attention to the first three articles of the *Instruction*, which were basic to the whole structure. *Union*, the efficacious coalition of American Jesuits, so ardently advocated by the Inter-Province Committee and the special commission, and given primacy of place in article 1, would be achieved through the cooperation of the provinces and individuals in the provinces. More specifically, as prescribed in article 2, this *cooperation* would become a reality by means of an active and effective "Association of Universities, Colleges

54

and High Schools." The association itself, under mandate of article 3, would be directed by an Inter-Province Executive Committee whose membership included (and was restricted to) the province prefects of studies, with the national secretary as chairman *ex officio*.[3]

The function of this committee, which in time became the nerve center of the whole operation, was twofold. It was originally constituted to take under advisement new trends, movements, and initiatives in education and to present its views on them to the provincials and the General. Secondly, it was the responsibility of the committee, and its members, to assist provincials in the execution of those policies which, after approval within the provincials' meetings, had been duly authorized. In the end, it was the Executive Committee, taking the larger view and representing a national constituency, that welded disparate, geographically separated Jesuit entities into a formidable organization with a common goal.

The General, as the original architect, was more aware than the provincials of the potential for progress in an energetic, properly motivated, and skillfully managed Executive Committee. The provincials, who had their doubts, as a result of their deliberations at Los Angeles in 1936 submitted several questions to His Paternity which involved an authentic interpretation of the *Instruction*.[4] In his reply, after reminding the provincials that the office of commissarius had been suspended, Ledochowski added: "I am very anxious that the Inter-Province Executive Committee, described in Article 3 of the *Instruction*, be immediately activated and convened. . . . I am persuaded that many of the difficulties which now plague you can be solved if this Committee . . . plays an active role."[5]

Still dubious, the provincials approached the idea of a national executive with caution. With the experience of a commissarius happily behind them, they were understandably suspicious of a national committee whose chairman operated under another title but with almost the same authority. The similarity brought to mind the French adage, *Plus ça change, plus c'est la même chose*. They were most curious about the jurisdictional origin of future educational regulations, the appointment of administrators, and, in summary, the weight that would be attached to the committee's recommendations.[6] In answering these *quaesita*, the General made an honest effort to alleviate apprehensions and to correct misunderstandings. Selecting article 3 as the focus of discontent, Ledochowski ruled that if a point in dispute extended to the entire assistancy, the provincials should solicit the opinion of the Executive Committee. If, however, only one province was affected, the case should be resolved within that jurisdiction. When *everyone* was in doubt, the General would be happy to arbitrate.[7] Presumably, this latter solution was intended to bring a measure of reassurance and consolation to the worried provincials.

Technically, the Executive Committee met for the first time, in joint session with a Committee on Graduate Studies, at the Stevens Hotel in Chicago on April 25, 1935. It was a historical event, as any "first" is bound to be. Father O'Connell invited Father Macelwane, chairman of the Graduate Committee, to present his report on "Standards Proposed for Judging Graduate Schools" (which was approved the following year).[8] It is understandable that, at its first meeting, the Executive Committee was uncertain of its role and timid in addressing national issues affecting Jesuit education. However, in its continuing effort to reach a working relationship with the provincials, it would gradually gain confidence with the passage of time.

Again accommodating itself to the schedule of the NCEA, the first adequately organized and truly national meeting of the Jesuit Educational Association (though that name was not yet official) took place in New York City in April 1936. On the evening of April 15, at Fordham University, where delegates were guests of President Hogan, there was an extended discussion of the relationship of the Jesuit association to the NCEA. Father O'Connell argued that the Jesuit meeting "should always be held in advance of the National Convention in order to achieve unity of viewpoint and action in voting on the different questions proposed at the sessions of the National [Catholic] Educational Association."[9] Stressing the importance of cooperation with external organizations, the chairman announced that, during the past year, the JEA had been admitted to membership in the American Council on Education. He felt that this was official recognition of a Jesuit presence that was moving in the right direction. In a further plea for Jesuit visibility, O'Connell recommended that individual Jesuits attend the meetings of learned societies and participate in their programs, and that those who were fully qualified accept invitations to deliver papers. In his view, this was the formula for admission to professional circles.[10]

On the following day, the Executive Committee met in a joint session with the Graduate Committee and graduate deans. The Executive Committee seemed reluctant to take charge and again voted to continue its meetings with other groups. The "Graduate Norms" were approved, and a committee was appointed to draw up a list of periodicals for the libraries of institutions that offered graduate courses. In point of fact, under O'Connell, who was not at his best in this role, the Executive Committee had become identified with graduate schools instead of the broader constituency it was designed to represent. It was neither a popular nor a prudent precedent.

At the Brown Hotel in Louisville on April 2, 1937, Father O'Connell, though he did not know it at the time, chaired his last two meetings as national secretary. The first meeting was a joint session of the Executive and Graduate committees.[11] The distinguished members of these groups considered substantive questions which were beginning to emerge: the progress of Ph.D. candidates in each province; application of the "Graduate Norms"; development of an efficient central office for the national secretary; national and international recognition of Jesuit universities. Samuel Wilson, always perceptive and loyally uninhibited, observed that, for national recognition, it would be necessary to mold the JEA into a more distinctive and effective organization than was then discernible. In supporting Father Wilson's remarks, Edward C. Phillips, highly regarded for his educational acumen when he was provincial of Maryland–New York, urged that Jesuits be more aggressive in letting their academic light "shine before men."[12] Taking everything together, it was a productive session, and the attendants were more optimistic that the new mechanism might work.

In the evening, Father O'Connell convened a second meeting which — with the exception of Father Macelwane, an invited guest — was restricted to prefects for higher education.[13] In the words of the secretary, "the entire meeting was given over to a frank and lengthy discussion of the *Instruction*."[14] With Father O'Connell's blessing, Allan Farrell, province prefect, Chicago, insisted upon a unified approach to issues within the committee, if the committee had expectations of success in pressing effective recommendations. William McGucken, going to the heart of the matter, linked the *Instruction* to the meaningful organization of a Jesuit Educational Association, to a justifiable collaboration with learned societies, and to recognition by regional and national accrediting associations. There was particular emphasis by the committee on compliance with the *Instruction* in the assignment of scholastics and priests to recognized universities for the master's and doctor's degrees. All of these ideas were then cast in the form of resolutions which were incorporated into the report prepared for Father General.[15] The committee was beginning to operate at the level of expectation.

Since his reticence was always respected, it would be idle to speculate whether, in later years, Father O'Connell recalled his sojourn at the Brown Hotel with pain or pleasure. In either case, the curtain was coming down on his role as a national figure in Jesuit education.

In October the General, endorsing the recommendation of the American provincials, appointed the prefect of studies for Maryland–New York to succeed Daniel O'Connell.[16] If success can be measured by longevity in office, it was an inspired choice.

Edward Bernard Rooney (1900–1976), Buffalo born and bred, entered the Society of Jesus (followed later by his brothers Albert and Joseph) on September 4, 1918, at Saint Andrew-on-Hudson. After a three-year teaching period at Regis High School, New York City, he began his theological studies at Louvain, Belgium. His professor of canon law at the Jesuit theologate was John Baptist Janssens, twenty-seventh General of the Society of Jesus. (The young theologian could not have foreseen that his subsequent career would bring him often to the General's *ante camera*, which, due to their continuing friendship, would be the more easily accessible to him.) Ordained to the priesthood in 1931 at Milltown Park, Dublin, and a tertian at Poughkeepsie in 1932, in 1933 he was assigned to Saint Joseph's College, Philadelphia, where he taught moral philosophy. In 1935 he was appointed prefect of studies for high schools in the Maryland–New York Province, and two years later succeeded Father O'Connell. Fluent in French and Spanish, widely traveled, and internationally known, he guided the Jesuit Educational Association for twenty-nine years. He was an acknowledged leader in educational circles, a fearless defender of Catholic education, and an outstanding spokesman for Jesuit education. (Famous for his liking for the convenience of commercial aircraft, he was frequently the object of good-natured ribbing for his intimate knowledge of international airports.) After his retirement in 1966, he acted as a consultant for Catholic educational interests in Latin America and represented the Inter-American Education Association at the United Nations. He died at Long Beach, New York, on July 30, 1976.[17]

Father Rooney, who had a definite vision of the function of the Executive Committee and realized the enormous potential of the Jesuit Educational Association, over the years molded these two entities in that vision. Presiding at his first meeting of the committee in December 1937, he moved quickly to establish his identity as national secretary.[18] At the suggestion of John Hynes, who had replaced the affable Andrew Smith, the committee accepted a list of topics for discussion, arranged in order of perceived priority, and an old problem immediately came to the surface. There was general agreement — from a distillation of various sources — that an unfortunate rift was developing between the American hierarchy and the Society of Jesus that had its origin in the apostolate of higher education, but it was difficult to place the blame. On one hand, there were responsible Jesuits who admitted that the Society may have exaggerated its canonical independence, which appeared to place the interests of the Jesuits above the Church. On the other hand, the hierarchy—so the argument went—was guilty of parochialism, resented the popularity of the Society, and was unwilling to cooperate with a superdiocesan organization. It was also alleged that while bishops were apathetic toward Jesuit colleges and universities, they were, by contrast, strongly supportive of Newman Centers at secular universities, which tended to reduce enrollment at Jesuit institutions in urban centers.[19] Finally, it was rumored that a few bishops abetted the campaign undertaken by an official at Catholic University to discredit Jesuit schools.[20] Though enlarged beyond its intrinsic importance, this unfortunate *contretemps* ultimately drew the General into the controversy.

The tempest originated in the so-called "affiliation program" that had been established at Catholic University, and for a proper understanding of the sequence of events it is necessary to appreciate the implications of that system. According to the original statutes of Catholic University, "the University is empowered to affiliate other Institutions for the purpose of conferring academic degrees."[21] The statutes were supported by the apostolic letter of Pope Leo XIII, *Magni nobis gaudii* (March 7, 1889), which read in part: "We exhort you all that you should take care to affiliate with your University your seminaries, colleges and other Catholic institutions . . . in such manner, however, as not to destroy their autonomy."[22] Armed with this papal endorsement, Father Thomas E. Shields in 1912 organized the first phase of an "affiliation program" which involved the mechanics of accreditation. This program was revised, in 1939, under Professor Roy J. Deferrari, who explained that this new phase in affiliation operated on the principle of cooperation and service for academic improvement. There was no mention of accreditation.

It was Professor Deferrari, whose long tenure at Catholic University made him a national figure (at least in Catholic circles), who became the great crusader for the promised benefits of affiliation. A product of Dartmouth College and Princeton University, where he received the Ph.D. in classical languages, Deferrari was promoted to professorial rank at Catholic University in 1923. Director of the summer session in 1929, he served as dean of the Graduate School from 1930 to 1938; he was then appointed secretary general of the university, and continued in that post until 1967.

Dr. Deferrari was undoubtedly sincere in offering the prestige and services of Catholic University for the improvement of academic standing in Catholic colleges.[23] However, the trouble started when, in citing the papal mandate, Catholic University flaunted its membership in the Association of American Universities. This resulted in implicit and, on occasions, explicit censure of Jesuit graduate schools, which did not belong to that inner circle.[24] The implications of the position of Catholic University were, in fact, alarming and had to be addressed.

After the Executive Committee meeting in December 1937, Father Rooney communicated to the provincials the committee's assessment of the strained relationship between the hierarchy and the Society, arising from the alleged position of Catholic University. The provincials, in turn, transmitted this information to the General, who was placed in a very difficult position. In his response, Ledochowski, who had "received the complaints with sadness," reminded the provincials of the Society's traditional relationship to the hierarchy.[25] Since Catholic University enjoyed the prerogatives of a papal university, it had a preeminence that the Society should recognize. For this reason, His Paternity directed that Jesuits continue to enroll at that institution for advanced degrees; moreover, the Society should be prepared to assign professors there if Catholic University requested them. In conclusion — and reverting to a more familiar role — he reminded provincials that the Society should not be intimidated in the management of its schools according to approved traditions.[26]

But the General did not let it go at that. In a second letter, he informed the provincials that he was sending Father Assistant Maher to the United States, "not as a Visitor, although he would have the faculties of a Visitor, but rather that he might, in my name, discuss certain grave matters with the Provincials which touch on the relationship of our colleges with the local ordinaries."[27]

When the Executive Committee met in November 1938, Father Maher was present as an invited guest. In the ensuing discussion, it was apparent that Jesuits were irked by Catholic University's pretension, based exclusively on the fact that it enjoyed membership in the AAU and thus was the only Catholic university fully qualified to award graduate degrees. However, in a series of interviews, reported by members of the Executive Committee, a number of ranking administrators within the AAU denied that it was in any way an accrediting body. The point at issue revolved around the alleged cases, vaguely documented, of discrimination against teacher applicants who had not taken their graduate degrees at a member institution of the AAU. This was the substantive accusation by the Executive Committee against the position taken by Catholic University. The academic credibility of Jesuit graduate schools was at stake.[28]

Invited by Father Rooney to express his opinion, Father Maher repeated the points made by the General. He emphasized that His Paternity wanted "ours" to support Catholic University and not to criticize it. In addition, he quoted Francis S. McMenamy, a revered member and former provincial of the Missouri Province, to the effect that the Society should express willingness to acknowledge the primacy of Catholic University while preserving the autonomy of Jesuit institutions.[29] On the recommendation of a subcommittee, which had been appointed to deal with this question, Father Maher agreed to join Rooney and Joseph W. Parsons (at that time associated with Georgetown University Graduate School) in a high-level meeting with Monsignor Joseph Corrigan, rector of Catholic University, to discover the policy behind "affiliation," to present Jesuit objections to that policy, and to discuss the future of Catholic higher education in the United States.[30]

The subcommittee also recommended that the national secretary, in his report to the provincials, urge the necessity of selecting and developing a Jesuit university for membership in the AAU. *One* university on that magic list, the committee argued, would be sufficient to guarantee the degrees of all Jesuit universities. This, of course, was wishful thinking, as the AAU had no intention of abetting such a plan. Nor were the provincials prepared to make a decision that would have provoked dangerous rivalry within the Jesuit Educational Association.[31]

As a substitute for the proposed meeting (which was aborted by Father Maher), Rooney, in rather strong terms, sketched the complaints of the JEA in a letter to the rector of Catholic University. Summarizing its alleged position, Rooney pointed out that Catholic University went beyond the required standards of accrediting agencies and, in so doing, ran the risk of destroying Catholic graduate education in the United States.[32] In implementing such a policy, "representatives of the Catholic University of America are casting aspersions on other Catholic educational institutions and are giving an impression of division in the ranks of Catholic higher education when all signs point to the need of unity and cooperation, and a united front among leaders of Catholic education."[33]

In his courteous reply, Bishop Corrigan explained in detail the policy of affiliation as he understood it. Addressing the specific point at issue, Corrigan stated that "graduate degrees from departments of those institutions which are not members of the AAU are to be considered satisfactory when the departments concerned are held in high repute in their respective fields of learning."[34] His Excellency singled out as departments of high repute "certain departments in the University of St. Louis and Fordham and the University of Notre Dame."[35] As for other charges made by Father Rooney, the bishop would appreciate more information which, in this context, meant evidence. In the meantime, as proof of his concern in finding a solution to the controversy, the bishop arranged a meeting between Rooney and Deferrari.[36]

Within the deliberations of the Executive Committee, as far as the record is concerned, this seems to have been the end of the controversy. In his report to the Executive Committee, at a meeting in September 1940, the national secretary confirmed the fact that a house of studies for Jesuits, which had been under consideration for some time, had been established at The Catholic University; Wilfred Parsons had been appointed superior and a few students were already in residence.[37] This happy arrangement was interpreted, apparently by both sides, as the basis of an armistice in what was fundamentally an intramural competition for ascendancy in American Catholic higher education.

In retrospect, one wonders if the Jesuits had not overreacted to a poorly enunciated policy by Catholic University that, in practice, was unsuccessful and posed no real threat to Jesuit institutions.[38] On the other hand, it showed that the Executive Committee of the JEA, with little support from the upper echelons of authority, was willing to accept the challenge. As a final legacy, the controversy gave Father Rooney, as defender of the Jesuit ramparts, instant visibility in both camps.

Of course, other issues were concomitantly claiming the attention of the Executive Committee. Rooney, on assuming his national office, saw the immediate necessity of a constitution to govern the association, and tentative steps were taken in that direction. At their December 1937 meeting, committee members voted unanimously in favor of calling the association the "Jesuit Educational Association," regulated the biannual meetings of the association, sanctioned the title "National Executive Secretary," and designed the official stationery letterhead. The committee also recommended that each province prefect be known as "Regional Director of Education," and it divided the association into five divisions. Finally, the committee agreed upon a common procedure for visitation of schools and colleges.[39]

While these discussions were valuable in refining ideas, there was need of a formal, written document, and the legal basis for a constitution was rooted in article 2 of the *Instruction*, which proposed a "vigorous and effective association" of Jesuit institutions at every level. With a covering letter to the provincials, Rooney enclosed the draft of a constitution and described the process by which it had been constructed.[40] According to his account, after discussing the matter in the meetings of 1937 and 1938, he had appointed a special committee to draft a document.[41] The proposed constitution had been "submitted to all the members of the Executive Committee at least three times and their suggestions have, as far as possible, been incorporated into the document."[42] After he received the opinions of the provincials, Rooney wrote, "I intend to submit the constitution to Very Reverend Father General."[43]

The final draft was hammered out in an important meeting of the Executive Committee in November 1938. Matthew Fitzsimons, province prefect from Maryland–New York and for many years an influential member of the committee, summarized the opinions of the provincials on the draft that had been sent to them. Three provincials approved, without reserve, while the others approved the draft "in the main, and commended the work as a forward-looking step."[44] One provincial, with an instinct for practical results, expressed the hope "that the J.E.A. would be an *effective working* organization and not merely a paper organization, and would do things that need to be done, and not merely philosophize about them."[45] Another provincial suggested strongly that the regional groups (or divisions) be eliminated in favor of a national body with province entities. The Executive Committee resisted this recommendation and voted unanimously to retain the regional groups, and in a more precise revision expressed a formal opinion that these groups should meet annually.

A final objection to the draft, from a provincial who thought the Executive Committee was overly exclusive, proposed that "a few college presidents" should be added to the committee — "that is, at least one college or university president from each province."[46] The reasons for this proposal were not calculated to impress the committee. The well-meaning provincial thought it would be helpful to have well-known names on the committee; moreover, "Presidents have a wider knowledge of what goes on in a university."[47] Predictably, the committee voted down this suggestion, which, the members felt, would enlarge the committee beyond workable size. If necessary, they reasoned, the presidents were available for consultation.

Responding to a request from the fathers provincial, Father General approved the constitution in a letter sent from Rome on the Feast of Saint Ignatius. The General made it clear that while the committee was under pressure to formulate a document "which would be easily understood by externs unfamiliar with our organization and system of government," the changes he had introduced into the original text "have been prompted by the conviction that in this Constitution the hierarchy of authority in the Society should be explicitly stated."[48] He further ordained that "whenever this Constitution is printed for the use of ours a copy of this my letter shall accompany the publication."[49] In a strange maneuver, after the General's letter had been received, the committee petitioned Ledochowski for permission to make additional modifications in the text. As a result, Father Maher declared "that the Constitution in this its latest form is now approved and is to be duly promulgated in the Assistancy."[50] As was the case with the *Instruction*, the constitution was to be tested for a period of three years, after which it would become permanent "with whatever additions or modifications experience shall dictate."[51]

The "Constitution of the Jesuit Educational Association," its proper title, was officially promulgated through publication in the *Jesuit Educational Quarterly*.[52] The document has ten articles, with many subparagraphs, all of which — as stated in article III — were designed "to promote and make more efficient all Jesuit educational activities in the United States." Other articles, which will be treated as our narrative continues, delineated the divisions, officers, and government of the association, the commissions, schedule of meetings at each level, voting procedure, and the mechanism for amendments.

National authority in the government of the association rested with the Board of Governors, which consisted of the provincials superior of Jesuit provinces of the United States. The other national officers were the executive director and members of the Executive Committee. The national body included all Jesuit educational institutions in the United States, geographically divided into three groups (East, Midwest, West Coast), and their respective academic officers. Within this framework, "all recommendations of the Executive Director and of the Executive Committee, all resolutions passed at the national meetings of the Association, as well as all actions of the Executive Director that affect the educational policy or practice of the whole membership of the Association, shall be subject to the approval of the Board of Governors."[53]

The authority of the Board of Governors, which was insisted upon by the General, combined with the broad prerogatives of the executive director, made for a concentration of power that, from the beginning, some Jesuits resented.[54] It may have been necessary in the early stage of development in order to establish the national character of the organization; in the end, however, the presidents challenged a system which placed ultimate decisions in the hands of those who were not responsible for their implementation. Yet few would deny that the constitution gave stability, legality, and force to a national effort. It was also an important source of union and cooperation, the necessary ingredients of progress.

Another source of union was mandated by the constitution. Article IX stipulated that "there shall be an official bulletin of the Association to be known as *Jesuit Educational Quarterly.*" (Actually, this confirmed what was already in existence.) It is generally acknowledged that interest and allegiance within an organization are notably enhanced through publication of a journal whose pages are open to contributions of the members, and the Executive Committee was quick to appreciate the importance of such a project. In April 1938, with very little discussion and no opposition, the committee voted to establish a house organ to be known as the *Jesuit Educational Quarterly.*[55] It was envisioned as a sounding board to delineate the character and purpose of the JEA, to enlighten a national Jesuit leadership on trends in education, and to publish notes and notices of national importance.[56]

While its content and expression may be uneven, as is the case with every serial, the *Quarterly* contains some of the best articles ever written on the inner workings of Jesuit education.[57] It was called, by Rooney himself, "a powerful influence in achieving union and cooperation among the Jesuit provinces," and is found today in the reference section of many libraries.[58]

It was appropriate that the office of editor-in-chief be reserved, *ex officio*, to the executive director, but the Executive Committee had the good judgment to appoint Allan P. Farrell the first managing editor. Under his direction, the *Quarterly* got off to an excellent start. An acknowledged leader in the early councils of the committee, he had written a classic work, *The Jesuit Code of Liberal Education*, which is probably the finest treatment available in English on the development and scope of the *Ratio Studiorum*. His life, in fact, was dedicated to the advancement of Jesuit studies at every level.

Born in 1896, Allan Farrell entered the Society of Jesus in 1916, finished his philosophy course at Saint Louis University, his teaching experience at Marquette, and his theological studies at Naples, Italy. In 1930, immediately after his seminary training, he pursued graduate studies in the humanities at National University, Dublin, where he was awarded the doctorate. Following tertianship in Cleveland, Father Farrell spent the next ten years as province prefect of studies in Chicago while, at the same time, serving successively as dean of West Baden College and the Milford novitiate. Assistant to Rooney and managing editor of the *Jesuit Educational Quarterly* for two years, he was assigned to America House in 1944 as a writer. The years from 1947 to his death in 1976 were spent, for the most part, at the University of Detroit as professor of education and dean of the Graduate School. Avuncular in appearance and disposition, Father Farrell was loved by all who knew him. Seated in a comfortable chair, puffing his favorite pipe, he would sagely comment on the vagaries of life in general and the uncertainties of Jesuit life in particular. He was, in short, one of those thoughtful and prudent Jesuits who is not easily replaced.

Protected by an approved constitution, the Executive Committee renewed its efforts to revise the *Instruction*. This document, which, it will be recalled, was promulgated in 1934, had been in operation for five years. The proposed changes had been discussed in Rome and submitted to the provincials for their approval.[59] If the committee could have foreseen the delays that were to be encountered before its approval was obtained, it might have lost some of its enthusiasm.

In his 1939 annual report to the provincials, the executive director pointed to a misunderstanding in the minds of many concerning the prescriptive force of the *Instruction*.[60] According to Rooney, some Jesuits assumed that, since the office of commissarius had been suspended (or suppressed), the *Instruction* had lost its validity. There was need, therefore, to clarify a gray area. The committee then recommended that the occasion for clarification would also be an appropriate time for a new edition, but changes in a document that had originated in Rome would require Roman approval, and this procedure uncovered a problem.

In October 1939 Father Assistant Maher, an invited guest, explained to the Executive Committee that reprinting the *Instruction* must await a report from the Commission for the Revision of the *Ratio Studiorum*, which, unfortunately, had been delayed.[61] As the *Ratio* was the more comprehensive document, as the basic plan for the whole Society, the General wanted assurance that the recently recommended revisions of the *Instruction* were in harmony with it. His Paternity, according to the Assistant, "planned to have the report of the *Ratio* Commission ready for distribution before the beginning of the school year, 1940–1941."[62] Looking at the situation from its point of view, the Executive Committee was unhappy at this decision and "urged again the importance of publishing a revision of the *Instruction* at the earliest possible moment."[63] The executive director and members of the committee, as the provincials realized, had good reason for urging revision and early publication of the *Instruction*. Their privileges, prerogatives, and responsibilities were directly derived from the *Instruction* and only indirectly tied to the *Ratio*.

In point of fact, the changes that were proposed, and those that were ultimately approved, were neither many nor radical. While it is not necessary to compare the revisions against the original text, it may be helpful to indicate three areas in which additions and deletions strengthened the text in the light of five years of experience.[64] In addition to duties already enumerated, article 4 provided for appearance of the executive director before the provincials' meetings in order to plead his cause; he is also charged with execution of the constitution and is made *ex officio* editor of official JEA publications.[65] Article 5 added two consultors to each province prefect of studies, both at the secondary and collegiate level. Father Rooney, in fact, had sometimes openly, sometimes subtly, promoted the important role of the prefects general. On one occasion, in reporting to the provincials, he had bravely observed: "I am sure that in the minds of the Provincials, he [the Province Prefect] must be more than simply a reporter."[66]

Article 22 was brand new. Drawing on an ancient tradition, this article recognized the crucial importance of the library at every academic level and mandated the acquisition of books and periodicals. Moreover, it prescribed that a suitable sum of money be set aside for the library, which money, it stated, could not be used for any other purpose. This article also authorized a librarian who should receive the "technical training necessary for such an important office." Title III, in the new version, is even more explicit in prescribing the course of studies, at both the undergraduate and graduate levels, for Jesuit scholastics and the order in which the curriculum in philosophy is to be arranged. Articles 31 to 34 describe the academic life of scholastics and priests who are destined for and assigned to special studies for the master's and doctor's degrees. It was the implementation of title III that measured the success of the *Instruction* in giving new life to the Jesuit apostolate of education in America. The ideal product would be the Jesuit Ph.D., trained in research and eager to publish.

A detailed account of the persistent efforts of the Executive Committee to secure official promulgation of the revised *Instruction* would only subject the reader to a dreary tale of postponements. There were a few substantive disagreements on the wording of the text;[67] the basic problem, however, appears to have been the reluctance of a succession of superiors in Rome, in those difficult years, to take ultimate responsibility for the revised *Instruction*. With the death of Father Ledochowski on December 14, 1942, Maurice Schurmans lost his authority as vicar general, since he did not have the right of succession. In a letter

dated November 13, 1942, Ledochowski, knowing he did not have long
to live, had appointed Alexis Magni, the Italian Assistant, vicar general
upon the General's death.[68] But Father Magni himself died on April 12,
1944, which left the office vacant. As prescribed by the Jesuit *Institute*,
the regional assistants and senior professed fathers in Rome, meeting in
a special congregation, elected Norbert de Boynes, French Assistant,
vicar general. The oldest among the assistants, and former Visitor to the
American provinces, he presided over the Society until the election of
the new General in 1946.[69]

Father de Boynes, therefore, inherited the intramural debate over
promulgation of the *Instruction*. It was not difficult to discover the
problem. The commission, which had been appointed in 1938 by the
twenty-eighth General Congregation to bring the *Ratio* up to date, had
not yet submitted its draft. Its task, in fact, was not easy. The commissioners had to incorporate two new decrees, which affected Jesuit
scholasticates, and at the same time reconcile the *Ratio* with the papal
document, *Deus Scientiarum Dominus*.[70] To make matters worse,
Rooney, in an exchange of views, insisted that the wording proposed by
the Executive Committee (in certain articles) was clearer than that proposed by the vicar general and more in accord with American practice.[71] Moreover, the Executive Committee worked very hard to bring
the Jesuit scholasticates in the United States under the purview of the
committee.

While the *Ratio Studiorum* clearly places the administration of
philosophy and theology in the hands of deans and faculties duly constituted for this purpose, article 5 (no. 2) of the *Instruction* just as
clearly states that it is the office of the prefect general to assist the provincial "in everything that pertains to the studies of Jesuits or externs."
In addition, the committee argued, since there was direct concern in the
philosophates with civil degrees, many of the courses were offered to
that end, and indeed the recognition often came from a college or university. These considerations alone — not to mention the advantages of
an external opinion — should have been sufficient to warrant the
privilege of visitation by the general prefect of studies.[72]

Wearied by the endless importunities of the Executive Committee,
Vicar General de Boynes, in a letter dated February 8, 1946, granted
permission for the *Instruction* to be "reprinted *ad interim*."[73] The vicar
general purposely avoided an official promulgation, which was clearly
understood by Rooney, who asked — perhaps to emphasize his disappointment — if the document should be printed or merely mimeographed and
distributed.[74] Writing three weeks later, in connection with the annual
meeting of the JEA, de Boynes said: "I think it better to leave it to the

new Father General to give them [the constitution and *Instruction*] definitive approbation." That turned out to be an academic question, since the provincials, meeting as the Board of Governors, cancelled publication of both the constitution and the *Instruction* until they had received satisfaction on the wording of article 31.[75] There the matter rested until the action of the next General.

Besides wrestling with the intricacies of the *Ratio* and the *Instruction*, the Executive Committee had to face other problems. Certain questions were proposed *to* the committee, other initiatives were taken *by* the committee. Most of these questions concerned the emerging role of Jesuit colleges and universities and their apostolic influence in the larger picture of the Church's mission.

Rome, especially in the Ledochowski era, had never admitted the principle of co-education, and was unhappy over the practical necessity of accepting women at Jesuit institutions. Nevertheless, an inordinate amount of time was spent by the committee in justifying a practice that was already a *fait accompli*. To prevent more stringent legislation, a closely reasoned document "concerning the admission of women to our colleges and universities" was sent to American delegates to the 1938 General Congregation. This was followed in 1939 by a *Tentative Draft of Norms*, particular and general, which described the dilemma facing nuns and Catholic laywomen in pursuing undergraduate, graduate, and professional training. These documents are models of clarity and sanity, but the whole exercise had an air of unreality, almost hypocrisy. The pretense was abandoned after the death of Father Ledochowski, and women applied for admission, and were accepted, in greater numbers and at every level.[76]

In these years, it should be remembered, the JEA was operating under particularly difficult conditions. The United States was fighting a global war. While internal affairs continued to occupy the Executive Committee, the patriotic cooperation of Jesuit institutions in the war effort and the exigencies of postwar planning gradually came to dominate the discussions of committee members, presidents, deans, and principals.[77] On January 3, 1942, at a meeting of administrators of Jesuit colleges and universities, Rooney read the contents of a New Year's letter sent to President Franklin D. Roosevelt from the American Assistant, Zacheus Maher. He "offered to the President all the facilities of the Jesuit institutions in the United States and pledged Jesuit cooperation to the fullest extent for the successful prosecution of the war."[78]

The Executive Committee projected a sober analysis of the possible effects of this emergency. "Jesuit education in the United States," the committee wrote, "faces the gravest crisis in its history. We are involved in a total war. Many Jesuits do not seem to realize this fact, nor the fact that for our schools the questions will be one of survival, of *esse* rather than of *bene esse*. At the least our institutions face the necessity of accepting curricula prescribed by the government and of making radical changes in existing curricula — or of being eliminated from the educational scene."[79]

With that assessment, the committee then made a number of suggestions for the better use of manpower. The executive director received explicit advice from his colleagues. Under a heading "Executive Director's Function in the War Emergency," which appears in the Executive Committee minutes, Rooney would be the principal source of up-to-date information for the JEA and the contact with government agencies and educational associations. The committee felt it was particularly important that he "obtain early information on emergency measures"; send out special bulletins "to keep Jesuit schools informed of significant plans, trends, developments"; urge the colleges to make a survey of facilities "with a view to sharing in the war effort," as recommended in the ACE bulletin, *Higher Education and National Defense*; and make sure that all Jesuit institutions were on the mailing lists for all releases issued by the government and other sources.[80] The members of the Executive Committee agreed to attend all regional institutes or conferences dealing with the war effort. They also made early visitations of the colleges, universities, and high schools in their provinces to see how they might be helpful to administrators.[81] Obviously, day-to-day decisions on the involvement of the colleges were made by the respective administrators, who were responsible for the contribution of their institutions.[82]

As a reward for its cooperation, the JEA earned an unexpected bonus. The spontaneous response of the Jesuit organization to the national emergency gave JEA almost instant equality with other educational agencies and abbreviated what would normally have been a protracted period of probation. Rooney, who appears to have exercised leadership in Catholic circles and influence in others, had a close working relationship with Guy Snavely, the knowledgeable executive director of the Association of American Colleges.[83] He was also in a position to speak candidly to Dr. George Zook, president of the American Council on Education and the leading authority on the history of accreditation. Although the relations of JEA with ACE had been cordial, Rooney let it be known that, in proportion to Catholic members in the council, the number of Catholic representatives among elected officers and committee appointees was disappointing.[84] Dr. Zook was sympathetic to the complaint, and in the years that followed, Catholics played a larger role in the inner councils of that organization.

In one of his designs, however, Rooney was frustrated. In his 1942 report to the provincials, he indicated that efforts were being made (by friends in Washington) to secure for him an appointment to the War-time Manpower Commission, which operated in conjunction with the U.S. Office of Education. Although the Honorable Paul V. McNutt, chairman of the commission (to whom Rooney had offered the facilities of Jesuit institutions), seemed to favor the appointment, it was not forthcoming. Nor was Rooney appointed to the Advisory Committee, which, if it had occurred, would have made the intercessions less embarrassing. To mask his disappointment, he later informed the provincials that he had "dropped the matter entirely as I saw that the U.S. Office of Education was exerting very little influence on the war-time programs for education—especially on the Army and Navy Specialized Training Programs."[85]

The Executive Committee had not only to meet the challenge of current events, but of necessity had to plan prudently for the future. Hugh Duce, province prefect of studies in California and an emerging personality in the councils of the Executive Committee, urged publication of a "Jesuit manifesto for Post-war Jesuit Education."[86] At the same time, Raphael Hamilton, of Marquette University, directed the committee's attention to an ACE release on "problems and plans for post-war college education."[87] These initiatives led to appointment of a committee—proposed by Julian Maline of the Chicago Province and seconded by Edward Bunn, president of Loyola College, Baltimore—to prepare a "Statement on Postwar Jesuit Education."[88] An advisory committee was also appointed, to act as a resource body for the first committee. On the motion of Arthur Sheehan, province prefect for New England, it was agreed that the executive director should request the administrators of Jesuit institutions to keep the central office informed of future plans, and especially plans to accommodate the influx of returning veterans.[89]

During the war, as the record abundantly shows, administrators at each institution were working overtime to attract military units to the campuses or, where this was not successful, to keep the colleges financially solvent with limited enrollments. Yet the national office was probably as helpful as could be expected in the circumstances, and in any event the Jesuit Education Association, as an organization, enhanced its national standing and acquired professional credibility.

One of those who had worked hardest to enlarge the image of the JEA was a casualty of wartime exertion. William McGucken, in the opinion of his contemporaries, was the most vocal, most experienced, and most courageous member of the Executive Committee in proposing recommendations that would advance the purpose and reputation of the association. Unfortunately, his health, precarious for years, did not match his zeal. It has been said that a man's death epitomizes his life, and this was stunningly true of Father McGucken, who collapsed and died on the evening of November 4, 1943, at Loyola University, Chicago, as he and his fellow members of the Executive Committee were preparing for the next day's meeting. His death, immediately marked as an irreparable loss, touched his companions deeply. It was unanimously acknowledged "that his generosity was truly phenomenal, and that his wide interests, his incisive and brilliant mind, his unfailing good humor and selflessness gave a unique quality to all their discussions, to every task undertaken, to every decision arrived at."[90]

William J. McGucken, born in Milwaukee (1883) and educated at Marquette University, joined the Jesuit order at Florissant in 1910. After completing his theology in Europe and a doctorate at the University of Chicago, he was assigned to Saint Louis University. He was an outstanding teacher and administrator, but his career was more closely identified with his years as province prefect of studies in Missouri, his contribution to the nascent Jesuit Educational Association, and his inspirational work with Jesuit scholastics. His contemporaries marveled at the extent of his charity, whereby "he could suffer fools gladly." A familiar figure at conventions, "he was recognized by secular educators and secular organizations, national and regional, as perhaps the ablest spokesman for the Catholic viewpoint." Two of his widely read publications are *The Jesuits and Education* and *The Catholic Way in Education*.[91]

Paradoxically, when the war ended in Allied victory in 1945, the JEA was a stronger organization than when hostilities began. Circumstances had combined to produce this result. The executive director and the Executive Committee, operating at a national level and confronting common problems, had established their credibility with constituent members. The executive director, in particular, had moved with surprising assurance in the upper echelons of national planning and made contacts which were to prove helpful in later years. In the colleges and universities, more than in the high schools, the presidents, in assuming authority for critical decisions, became more independent of the close supervision of provincials.

In one particularly important area, involving financial management, these institutions were forced to adopt more professional procedures in auditing and budgeting institutional resources. Federal agencies, in calculating the remuneration of Jesuit teachers, were intrigued with the notion of "contributed services" and generally mystified by the formula for Jesuit salaries in relation to the vow of poverty. As a result, most of the trustees at Jesuit institutions revised the regulations for payment of Jesuit salaries and for their application to the Jesuit community and the university.[92]

Although it was not their custom to indulge in exuberant encomiums, the provincials appeared to recognize the work of the committee. In 1944 the Board of Governors instructed the executive director "to communicate to the members of the Executive Committee of the JEA its sincere appreciation of the excellent service that the Committee has performed in studying the problems of our schools and in assisting schools to meet the problems. . . . While circumstances at times prevent the acceptance of some suggestions offered by the Executive Committee, the Board of Governors has the fullest confidence in the work and judgment of the Committee."[93] Jesuits are *not* emotional people.

# 5. Postwar Expansion, 1946–1950 (Commissions and Institutes)

WITH THE CESSATION of hostilities and the resumption of international travel, Vicar General de Boynes summoned to Rome the eligible electors from around the world for the election of a Superior General. The Twenty-ninth General Congregation elected the fifty-seven-year-old provincial of Northern Belgium the twenty-seventh General of the Society of Jesus.[1] He ruled the order for eighteen years.

John Baptist Janssens, of Flemish origin, was born in Malines, Belgium, December 22, 1889; entered the Jesuit novitiate at Tronchiennes in September 1907; and was ordained a priest on September 7, 1919. While a scholastic, he obtained a degree in civil law at Catholic University of Louvain, where he came to the attention of Arthur Vermeersch, the noted Jesuit moral theologian. After tertianship, and continuing his specialization, Janssens completed his doctorate in canon law at the Gregorian University, pursued advanced studies in the Jus Ecclesiarum Orientalium, and began his teaching career at Louvain in 1923. His intellectual gifts, linguistic ability (he was fluent in six languages), mature judgment, and religious stability combined to mark him for positions of authority in the Society. In quick succession, he was appointed rector of the scholasticate at Louvain, delegate to the Congregation of Procurators (in 1933), instructor of tertians, an elector at the Twenty-eighth General Congregation, and provincial superior during the difficult years of the war. His election to the generalate, on September 15, 1946, was not a surprise to those who had followed his career.

Father Janssens, so confident and competent as a Jesuit administrator, was unhappy and uncertain in his role as a distinguished ecclesiastical personality. From the earliest days of his administration, his contacts with the press were painful to him, and he never accepted the importunate demands of "public relations." This was due partly to temperament and partly to a frail constitution, which forced him to conserve his energy for primary responsibilities. Throughout his life he was troubled with asthma, a tendency to vertigo, which precluded travel, and poor eyesight, which worsened with age. However, he presided over an expanding Society, which was growing in numbers and works, and his letters are evidence of his concern for preservation of the Ignatian spirit.[2]

A new American Assistant was also elected at the Twenty-ninth General Congregation. Vincent A. McCormick, a member of the New York Province, had already had a distinguished career and was familiar with the intricacies of Roman relationships. Born in 1886, he entered the Society in 1903 and was ordained at Woodstock College in 1916, where he later served as rector from 1927 to 1933. In 1933 he was appointed *rector magnificus* of Gregorian University and in 1941 moved to the General's Curia, where he remained during the war years. Known for his urbanity, intelligence, and discretion, he was a confidant of bishops and cardinals. Because of his precise diction (which disguised his Brooklyn origins), proper manner, and distinguished appearance, he was, on occasion, referred to as "the Oxford movement." He served as Assistant until 1960, when, in failing health, he returned to New York and pastoral work. He died at Saint Andrew-on-Hudson in 1963.[3]

In his early years as General, Janssens was particularly anxious to define the major ministries proper to Jesuits. The thesis is not irrefutable, but it would appear, from the tenor of his letters, that he assigned a certain primacy to the apostolate of education, and within that ministry, he emphasized the importance to the Church of higher education. In any case, it is clear that he was intrigued with the unlimited potential afforded American Jesuits in the orderly expansion of their educational apostolate.

Eight months after his election, as a signal of his preoccupation, the General sent a letter to all provincial superiors setting down "certain norms to be followed in the pursuit of higher studies."[4] While this letter was directed to members of the Society who were destined to teach the sacred sciences in Jesuit houses of study, it was an important segment of a total program. Two weeks later, on the occasion of the canonization of Saints John de Britto and Bernardine Realino, the General addressed to the whole Society his justly famous letter *Jesuit Ministries.*[5] This thirty-seven-page document, though composed with little regard for color or style, merits extended analysis. A distillation of Janssens' deep convictions, and formed in the context of his intellectual experience, it is the expression of long and mature reflection on areas in which the Society could make its maximum contribution to the Church and its Sovereign Pontiff.

Part III of the letter is devoted to the ministry, or apostolate, of education.[6] This section is again divided into two academic levels, *"labor scientificus,"* which supposes graduate, specialized, and original research; and secondly, the "normal" contribution expected of college and university faculties. Janssens insisted that, whether there is question of sacred or profane disciplines, "scientific work, properly so called," is absolutely necessary to the intellectual life of the Church. There is a natural process of assimilation, whether the source is pure or polluted, whereby seminal ideas, sown by creative intellects, are filtered through the writings of learned men; these concepts are then the property of cultured people and, finally, become the patrimony of everyone. The General, in a marginal comment, agreed with Pope Pius XI, who had observed that priests should be as cultured and cultivated as other cultured men,[7] but Janssens went beyond that standard in his analysis of Jesuit preparation. "Is it not similarly necessary," he asked, "that at least some clerics and religious, according to the ancient tradition of the Church, should be equally strong in learning?"[8] Referring again to papal incentives, he quoted several sentences from the address of Pope Pius XII to the electors of the Twenty-ninth General Congregation: "It is your duty . . . to be not only religious men," the Pope said, "but also men of great learning. And if they [Jesuits] ought especially to cultivate the faith, they ought . . . to pursue the advancement of sciences as much as they can and in whatever way they can, being convinced that along this path, rugged though it be, they can make a great contribution to the greater glory of God and upbuilding of his Church."[9]

Emphasizing the necessity of dedication (without disguising the cost), Janssens conceded that scientific study, on the frontiers of knowledge, demands rigid discipline and unremitting labor, with little in the way of visible consolation. In a brief summary of his thesis he wrote: "I am persuaded that we [Jesuits] would make our greatest contribution to the Church if we returned to the practice of a large number of Jesuits of the Old Society who cultivated studies, especially at the higher levels, more assiduously than we do."[10] In brief, motivated by love of learning and the Church, research and publication should be the laudable ambition of gifted Jesuits.

The General then turned to the "instruction of youth in Colleges and Universities," which he considered a separate ministry. Having recalled that the Society, from its earliest history, manifested a distinct preference for this apostolate, he refuted those fathers and scholastics who argued that, in changing times, the Society should relinquish it in favor of a more direct apostolate to the people.[11] Janssens saw Jesuit colleges and universities as bulwarks of Catholic faith and morals, but, as a man trained in the university, he also emphasized the academic rewards of this apostolate. With reference to their intellectual formation, "those [students] who are educated in our schools should in no way yield the palm to those in other institutions; in fact, they should rather surpass them."[12] Moreover, it is not sufficient to form public-spirited men of good morals; "it is absolutely necessary that they so excel in knowledge, ability and talent that their works will be acknowledged by all, even by those of other faiths, to be outstanding. As a result, our graduates will be prepared to serve when called upon to assume the onus of public office."[13] The conclusion was inescapable. "You will see how important it is that Jesuits, chosen for special studies, should become experts in the disciplines they will be assigned to teach."[14] The "generalist," he noted, surely has his place in the Society, but the "specialist" is now a necessity.

In summary, the letter *On Ministries* was a classic statement of the Society's commitment to the academic apostolate. In years to come, since Rome had determined the priority, it would serve as authentic justification of the huge investment in men and money that the American provincials were called upon to provide.

In response to this cogent appeal, JEA made a valiant effort, in its postwar expansion, to implement the expectations of the General. It was, in fact, a case of fraternal reciprocation, as His Paternity had early shown a personal interest in that organization. On the eve of the first annual meeting of the JEA after his election, he sent a warm letter of support to the Jesuits gathered in Boston. "The field of education," he wrote, "offers an apostolate to the Society in the United States without parallel."[15]

The advantages of official support from Rome were not lost on Rooney. In his report to a plenary session of the JEA in 1948, Rooney alluded to the 400th anniversary of the founding of the first Jesuit college at Messina, Sicily, in 1548. Then, reviewing other historical highlights — which included a generous reference to the Inter-Province Committee of the '20s — he said: "To my mind no event of this past year is of greater importance to Jesuit education in the United States than this letter of Very Reverend Father General."[16] In the years that followed, it enjoyed, in some quarters, the authority of an inspired text.

The General, however, did not stop with a theoretical (albeit inspirational) statement. Always conscious of the latent possibilities in the

United States—and abetted, perhaps, by the personal intercession of the executive director—he finally approved the revised text of the *Instructio*. In a letter that recalled the initiatives of Father Ledochowski and the probationary period of the original document (which had reached the unforeseen length of fourteen years), Janssens commended it to the prayerful consideration of fathers and scholastics.[17] "I say prayerfully because its immediate aim gives it a place among the *spiritual documents* sent to the Assistancy."[18] Moreover, it was a "spiritual" document because "according to the mind of our holy founder the work of the Society in this field is primarily a spiritual work."[19]

But this did not emancipate Jesuits from the obligation to excel in the classrooms and lecture halls of the academy. On the contrary, Janssens urged the provincials to increase the number of fathers and scholastics in higher studies so that "with their staffs eventually strengthened by these specially trained scholars, your Colleges and Universities should take a more prominent place in that group of centers of learning and culture that by their erudite publications extend their influence far beyond their own walls."[20]

The Executive Committee, in order to emphasize the interdependence of both documents, decided to publish the *Instruction* and the constitution of the JEA within a single cover.[21] The General was aware of the connection. "The chief instrument," he wrote, "forged by the *Instructio* itself for the consistent carrying out of its prescriptions is the Jesuit Educational Association . . . [which] represents a union of efforts in the educational field on the part of all our Provinces in the United States."[22] The work of the Society would be futile, he predicted, "unless men of special talents, especially prepared, and defended against the fateful burden of administrative office, are free, encouraged and urged to devote their time and energy to research and scholarly productivity."[23] Taking everything together, the General had made his position clear as an enthusiastic patron—even partisan—of the American effort.

The executive director and his associates, who deeply appreciated this testimonial from headquarters, accepted the challenge implicit in the General's directives, and slowly but surely, the association came to grips with the emerging problems. Preoccupied, as were all American institutions, with the educational complexities arising from conversion of a universal wartime draft to the more normal pattern of peace, the JEA felt the strains of rapid adjustment.[24] First of all, there was the unusual increase in student enrollments at all levels. When the war ended, during the academic year 1944–45, there was a total enrollment of 28,108 full-and part-time students in the twenty-five Jesuit colleges and universities in the United States. Four years later, the total had grown to 98,452.[25] Jesuit administrators in high schools, colleges, and universities faced the enormous task of increasing faculty, facilities, and classroom space to accommodate the flood of applicants in that short, four-year period. President Harry Truman captured the essence of the problem when, in the letter to members of the President's Commission on Higher Education, he wrote: "As veterans return to college by the hundreds of thousands, the institutions of higher education face a period of trial which is taxing their resources and resourcefulness to the utmost."

Although not fully prepared for the long lines of returning veterans, the JEA was not taken entirely by surprise. As the war ended, the Executive Committee realized that it would be neither practical nor appropriate for the committee to infringe on the prerogatives of local administrators who had to make day-to-day policy decisions. These judgments were the responsibility of the presidents, advisors, and trustees of the various institutions.[26] However, the committee was entitled to suggest norms for guidance.

In the months immediately following the war, the executive director brought to the attention of Jesuit administrators the various directives and announcements issued by government agencies in Washington. These included the availability of government-surplus property, the intricacies of tax exemption, the process for veterans' applications and the GI Bill, as well as the provisions of the Fulbright Program and the newly introduced (and controversial) bill on federal aid to education and its application to Church-related institutions.[27]

In 1944, at a meeting in Boston, the Committee on Postwar Jesuit Education was reorganized into a subcommittee of the Executive Committee.[28] Its purpose "was to draw up a statement or manifesto which would redefine in a vital way and perhaps in modern terminology the main objectives of Jesuit education and the principal means of attaining them, with the idea that such a manifesto would furnish a background for all postwar planning in our individual colleges and universities."[29] To reassure critics in the colleges, who were suspicious of the committee's intentions, Rooney explained to the Board of Governors that the name was not descriptive. "The function of the committee is not the drawing up of plans on curricula to meet specific postwar needs."[30] With that understanding, a statement was composed, then sent to a select group of thirty-five Jesuits, who returned their comments to Wilfred Mallon, prefect of studies of the Missouri province. In attempting to respond to their constructive comments, the project became more ambitious, the procedure more complicated, and the text more ornate than had been anticipated. The project, in short, got beyond the control of the subcommittee.

It was decided that the new draft, which would contain theological, philosophical, historical, and educational elements, would be prepared by one man and then submitted to a distinguished panel of three scholars, who would edit it for final form.[31] (Julian Maline bravely volunteered to fashion the first draft.) In the end, the mandate proved to be beyond the capacity of the subcommittee, which began to doubt the feasibility of a single statement that would serve to describe ambitious plans for the future of Jesuit higher education in the United States. As a last — and novel — resort, it was suggested to the provincials that the task be transferred to a promising young Jesuit who might make this assignment the subject of a doctoral dissertation.[32] The provincials favored this idea — assuming, no doubt, that nothing would come of it. Poorly conceived and weakly supported, the project faded from view in the press of other unfinished business.

Necessity ordains that when one plan fails another must be adopted. In the present instance, failure forced the Executive Committee to concentrate its energies on a better program, which, in the end, gave departments, faculties, and schools a healthy push along the road to modernization and professional competence. This was the committee's decision to reactivate, develop, and motivate the commissions provided for in article VII of the constitution, which had become stagnant during the war.[33] The article created five permanent commissions whose members were nominated by the Executive Committee and appointed by the Board of Governors.[34] The broad function of these commissions was "to study specific problems in their respective areas," then "present the results of their findings to the Executive Director of the Association."[35] As they became more active, the commissions added a large pool of experts to the academic resources of the JEA and, indeed, formed an unofficial extension of the Executive Committee within the college and university departments. While other phases of postwar expansion within the JEA deserve to be documented, the work of the commissions and the sequence of academic institutes were the most important in accelerating the remarkable and sustained growth of the association. In the opinion of many, the commissions added a final dimension to the executive organization of the JEA. At the same time, the national institutes fostered interprovince cohesion, Jesuit and lay faculty involve-

ment in a common cause, and, finally, brought about a more professional approach to the apostolate of modern higher education.

The work of the commissions, as implied, had been sacrificed to
the exigencies of wartime improvisations. After the war, however, they
were the first units of the JEA to receive attention from the executive
director, who was anxious to propose specific studies to their consideration. But there were problems. In 1945 Hugh Duce, the hard-working
and durable province prefect from California, and one of the most
cooperative members of the Executive Committee, submitted a report
originally drafted by William G. Gianara, president of Santa Clara and
chairman of the Commission on Liberal Arts Colleges.[36] The initial difficulty highlighted a problem that was, and to a lesser extent still is,
endemic to Jesuit higher education. Father Duce regretted the instabil-
ity of the commission since two of the members, Joseph R. N. Maxwell
and Percy A. Roy, had been removed from college administration,
which made them ineligible for this appointment.[37]

The concerns and composition of the commissions indicate the
areas of interest and priority in the association. Originally, the Liberal
Arts Commission—perhaps the most important, though not the most
successful of the five—had been charged to investigate the A.B. curriculum in Jesuit colleges as a prelude to a postwar update of course offerings. This recommendation was later rescinded in favor of the more
ambitious postwar project, which never materialized. In its place, in an
effort to narrow the focus, the commission was instructed to examine
the effectiveness of teaching philosophy, which, as understood from the
inception of the *Ratio*, is the capstone of a Jesuit education. The
elaborately conceived investigation would review course offerings,
teacher preparation, texts, and objectives in the arts and sciences colleges, as well as requirements in the professional schools.[38] In response
to Rooney's report, the Board of Governors gave its unqualified support
to this project and asked to be kept fully informed of its progress.[39]

The Commission on Graduate Schools, due in part to the calibre
of its members, was the most persistent, effective, and successful commission in the 1940s and '50s.[40] In a sense, the problems were more
manageable and the solutions less elusive than in the undergraduate
areas. As an initial assignment, the commission was asked to analyze the
implications for Jesuit institutions of the recent report of the AAU on
the accreditation of graduate programs.[41] This was a new development,
since, in past years, the AAU had concentrated on the accreditation of
undergraduate colleges. The Graduate Commission, however, with
foresight, was anxious to anticipate, and comply with, the standards

that might be imposed by the AAU on graduate programs and, thus, avoid the unhappy experience of the colleges.

In that connection, the position of the JEA vis-à-vis the AAU was, unfortunately, static.[42] After citing the relevant statistics in his report to the provincials, Father Rooney had to admit that "this record is not very impressive."[43] It was an old story. Apparently a certain apathy, combined with timidity, made Jesuit institutions reluctant to approach this prestigious association; but the association itself was encouraging. Dr. Frank H. Bowles, secretary of the AAU Committee on Classification, told Rooney "he would be happy to see more of our [Jesuit] institutions apply for approval."[44] The Board of Governors, justifiably disturbed at this poor record, showed more than ordinary interest in the statistics submitted by the executive director and instructed the province prefects to discuss with individual provincials an effective program that would lead to approval of more institutions. More specifically, the provincials wanted to know which institutions were in a position to seek approval and what improvement would be necessary in individual cases before the AAU could be approached.[45]

This was not a congenial assignment for the Commission on Graduate Schools, which, in a true sense, was now obligated to monitor in-house programs. In the flush of postwar expansion, a number of Jesuit institutions were contemplating the introduction of graduate programs at the master's level, and Xavier University, Cincinnati, was a case in point. In December 1945, Julian Maline submitted a report on "The Projected Graduate Work to Be Offered at Xavier University Beginning in June 1946."[46] Although Xavier did not anticipate a problem with the North Central Accrediting Association, Maline did not hide the hazards that would attend approval by the AAU. In his report, he quoted a standard educational monograph which carried the following warning: "Certainly a college not accredited by the Association of American Universities should delay the offering of a graduate program until such accreditation has been attained."[47] It is sufficient to note that Xavier was not on the approved list at that time. (If Father Daniel O'Connell was aware of this discussion, the French expression, *déjà vu*, might have come to his mind.)

In the postwar period, the AAU had become preoccupied with the increase of students at the graduate level and less concerned with undergraduate education.[48] The association felt that the quality of graduate degrees would be diluted because of the dearth of qualified faculty members — or, conversely, by the rapid increase of professors who would be neither properly trained nor sufficiently concerned with standards. In a paper delivered at the Forty-eighth Annual Conference of the AAU, Dean N. Paul Hudson of Ohio State University posed this question: "Are we turning out high grade gas station attendants or are we contributing extra-well-trained individuals who will have a proper perspective in regard to their social obligations?"[49] This was a fair question, which could also apply to the standards and objectives of Jesuit graduate schools.

The Commission on Professional Schools was a special case and had a distinction of its own. In a surprise move, it was recommended that this commission be appointed from members of the Executive Committee and that "subcommissions for each of the professional fields be chosen from among the Jesuit Deans or Regents of the professional schools."[50] Other explanations are possible, but it would appear that this unusual procedure, which required members of the Executive Committee to review their own decisions, was the result of a dearth of Jesuit administrators and faculty members in the schools of medicine, law, dentistry, business administration, and social work. There is no denying that in these years the Jesuit Educational Association was a descriptive title. At the suggestion of the provincials, who endorsed this procedure, Fathers Rooney, Maline, and Mallon, three trusted stalwarts, were named to the commission.

As it turned out, this arrangement was mutually advantageous to the commissioners and the professionals. Each group educated the other. To begin with, a meeting of the regents of Jesuit dental schools (at St. Louis in 1945) was a successful experiment in establishing contacts and cooperation between the schools.[51] The commissioners, Rooney, Mallon, and Maline, met with the deans and regents of the Jesuit law schools at Loyola University, Chicago, on December 28, 1947, on the occasion of the meeting of the Association of American Law Schools. Chiefly an organizational meeting, the group made plans for future sessions and appointed a committee to prepare an agenda. Topics suggested for consideration included the Catholicity of Jesuit law schools, the relative standing of these schools in the Association of American Law Schools (AALS), and the place of jurisprudence in Jesuit law schools.[52]

The medical schools posed special problems. The first meeting with medical regents was held at Lewis Towers, Loyola, Chicago, in February 1948. Since the American Medical Association was planning a visitation of medical schools that very year, Jesuit schools of medicine were advised by the Executive Committee to anticipate this official visit with an intramural audit of their own. "It was clear from this meeting," Rooney reported, "as well as from other contacts with our administrators and with officials of the AMA, that the paramount problem of our medical schools is their financial status, present and future."[53]

The *Minutes* of the meeting at Lewis Towers paint a gloomy picture. Since the Council on Medical Education had indicated that a minimum of $400,000 annually was needed for acceptable education, the Jesuit regents "[agreed] that our ability to carry on with a good level of education is in serious doubt."[54] It was then recommended "that the three Provincials be acquainted with these major considerations and the urgency of the situation placed before them."[55] Apart from other considerations, the Commission on Professional Schools and the Jesuit regents had a direct line to the Board of Governors which would have been unavailable to the medical deans.[56] The Executive Committee wanted to go further, and submitted a proposal to canvass American bishops in support of Catholic medical education. The committee noted that "an inspection of the enrollment in our medical schools shows that they go far beyond caring for the immediate needs of their own localities." Since there were only five Catholic medical schools in the United States, "one might reasonably expect that some support for these schools might come from localities other than those in which the schools are situated." It was Rooney's opinion, therefore, that if the schools were to meet proper standards, the problem should be brought to the attention of the American hierarchy, since, in the last analysis, "the Bishops are ultimately responsible for providing Catholic education."[57] If the provincials approved, the committee offered to prepare "a very significant report" for presentation to the bishops. The Board of Governors took this suggestion under advisement, but made no further move.

In time, these professional groups adopted their own procedures, elected officers, and formed conferences. Although standards are primarily the responsibility of each institution, the meetings of academic officers from professional schools, by addressing common problems within an association with a common set of objectives, the Jesuit medical, dental, and law schools moved gradually from a level of adequacy to parity with peer schools.

The commissions were established to monitor the academic health of institutions at various levels, to identify problems, and, as far as possible, to propose solutions.[58] The work was done in committee or in consultation with qualified colleagues in the same academic area, and the reports that followed had limited circulation. The institutes sponsored by the Jesuit Educational Association, however, gathered together in one place, for an extended period, representative Jesuits and lay colleagues, drawn from the American assistancy, for in-depth examination of a segment (department, faculty, school) of the educational process. It would be difficult to exaggerate the importance of the institutes (or "Workshops") which, over the years, scrutinized every major aspect of Jesuit education at the undergraduate level.

The first JEA Institute was held at Regis College, Denver, for high school principals.[59] Under the direction of Fathers Wilfred Mallon and Julian Maline, the participants read papers and discussed topics connected with admission policies, courses of studies, secondary school standards, examinations, faculty supervision and stimulation.[60] The provincials, highly pleased with the results, congratulated the participants, the director, and the Executive Committee.[61]

Impressed with the success of the "high school experience" in Denver, the Board of Governors began to appreciate the potential advantages in a national institute. Accordingly, when Rooney reported to the Executive Committee that "certain Fathers Provincial have mentioned the value of an institute for college deans similar to the Institute for High School Principals," there was enthusiasm on all sides.[62] The committee, eager to prove itself at the collegiate level, immediately agreed to prepare for such an institute, which would necessarily be more elaborate than the first one. During the inclusive dates of August 1 to 15, 1948, the participants would again take advantage of the salubrious climate and comfortable campus at Regis College. It was understood that the provincial of each province would designate those who were eligible to attend — deans, assistant deans, and doctoral candidates who were prospective college administrators. The declared purpose of the institute was to emphasize the distinctive elements of Jesuit education, the academic administration of admissions (a conceded weakness), improvement of instruction, faculty recruitment and supervision, degree requirements, examination grading, and library and curriculum specifics.[63] The agenda was nothing if not comprehensive. Once again, because of his experience and generosity, Father Mallon was appointed director. Father Maline was an unselfish (and unsung) assistant.

These two Jesuits, conspicuous for their contribution to the work of the Executive Committee, were the trusted lieutenants of the executive director. Always generous, they offered their services whenever there was a need for drafting reports, conducting surveys, or preparing policy papers; in addition, they gladly acted as committee secretaries (the ultimate affliction of those who attend meetings). They also offered sound advice on academic trends and educational innovations. Men of experience — today they might be called "executive managers" in a corporate hierarchy — their lives reflected daily dedication to assigned tasks, whether agreeable or disagreeable.

Julian Maline, who entered the Society of Jesus in 1913 and was ordained to the priesthood in Italy in 1927, began his Jesuit life in the Missouri Province, passed to the Chicago Province in 1928, and to the Detroit province in 1955. With a rich background as a graduate student, teacher, and dean, he was appointed province prefect of studies in Chicago in 1933, first for high schools and then (in 1940) for all institutions. To that experience, Father Maline added unflagging zeal for the apostolate of Jesuit education. Always smiling and genial, a legend in his own time in the Midwest, he is, at this writing, still active in his chosen apostolate at Saint John's in Toledo.

Maline's companion in arms, Wilfred M. Mallon, was a compulsive worker in the Ignatian mold. His passion for perfection in the tasks assigned to him, resulting in periods of exhaustion, caused anxiety to his friends and counsels of moderation from his fellow members of the Executive Committee. Born in 1899, he entered the Society in 1921 and was ordained in 1934. Associated for many years with Saint Louis University as dean and professor of education, he was appointed province prefect of studies for Missouri in 1944 and served in that capacity until 1953. Now a member of the Wisconsin Province, Father Mallon continues his parochial apostolate at New Hope, Minnesota.

The format of subsequent institutes followed (in general) the pattern of the first in preparation, direction, participation, and implementation. For this reason, and to avoid needless repetition in future references, it will be instructive to examine the process used at this time. Planning for the "Deans' Institute" was thorough and professional. The director immediately noted that, since the institute "is not a convention but a teaching instrument," the choice of those who would write papers or lead discussions would be made on the basis of competence, not on geographical representation.[64] After the parameters of the institute had been agreed upon, it was decided which topics would lead to further discussion, which would not. Deans were requested to submit topics within the general framework; they were also asked if they were prepared to present a paper. A library, with the latest titles in relevant fields, was assembled for the use of participants.[65]

In drawing up plans, an important decision was made to let in academic fresh air from the outside world. This was not to be just another Jesuit conclave, a closed circle, Jesuits talking to one another without benefit of a "second opinion." It was agreed that outside experts could make a healthy contribution to both the atmosphere and the substance of the institute by bringing the latest trends in collegiate policy and procedure to the consideration of a national group of concerned Jesuits. Although not all were able to attend, invitations were sent to Dr. Milton Eisenhower, president of Kansas State University; Dr. Earl McGrath, dean of the College of Arts and Sciences at the University of Iowa and an authority on "general education"; and Professor Floyd Reeves of Chicago. At ease in his specialty, McGrath clarified for his attentive audience "The Objectives and Procedures in General Education." Dr. Russell Cooper, of the University of Minnesota, who gave an entire day to the institute, read an excellent paper on the "Marks of a Superior College."[66] Professor Gilbert Wrenn, of Minnesota, regretted that his schedule would not permit attendance, but submitted a paper on "Procedures for Evaluating the Organization of Personnel."[67] To minimize the dangers inherent in an intramural convention, there was provision for honest comparison, in the areas selected for treatment, between Jesuit institutions and three other types: urban universities, state universities, and private (independent) colleges.

The director was determined to fasten the discussions to concrete facts. To avoid philosophical excursions on the ideals of Jesuit higher education (for which Jesuits are justly famous), a questionnaire was sent to administrators of colleges of arts and sciences and autonomous schools of business administration. This instrument was designed to document, in ten areas of concern, the actual practices in Jesuit institutions. The facts reported in the questionnaire, which had elicited a highly satisfactory response, were painstakingly collated and sent to each participant for study in preparation for the institute.[68] Those who attended the institute, therefore, arrived at Regis College fully informed of current practices pertaining to admissions, curriculum, instruction, standards, faculty, and student personnel offices in Jesuit institutions across the country. In addition, this item contained suggestions for seeking approval by the AAU, for application for accreditation, and for Phi Beta Kappa recognition.[69] It included, besides, an excellent bibliography on higher education — for those who had time and energy to mine this lode of information furnished by national authorities. By every index, Father Mallon made it clear that those assigned to participate in the institute could expect ten days of hard work.

The norm for attendance, perhaps the least enlightened stipulation, requires a comment. While the decision to invite distinguished educators from other institutions was a good one, it would have been an even more progressive sign to include competent lay faculty members from Jesuit colleges for a more equitable and ecumenical representation. The Executive Committee had recommended, and the provincials approved, that membership be limited to Jesuit administrators of liberal arts colleges, schools of business administration, and schools of adult and evening divisions.[70] This was unfortunate, since the deans of schools of business administration (with few exceptions) were lay colleagues.[71] Moreover, it was statistically documented that in the basic arts courses (with the sole exception of philosophy), lay faculty taught more class hours than Jesuits. Thus it would have been advantageous if selected lay professors had joined their Jesuit partners in assessing institutional objectives in a fraternal setting.[72]

By normal measurements, the institute was successful in terms of its objectives, but its focus became rather narrow, despite the profusion of papers. The director recognized that "the entire Institute . . . could well be devoted to the clarification of objectives of Jesuit colleges and to the religious and philosophical areas of the curriculum and of college life."[73] It was also clear to him that "an assembly restricted to administrators would not include many of the American Jesuits who could make the best contribution to discussions of objectives and of the curricula in religion and philosophy.[74] However, Father Mallon was convinced that, as a first step, the academic effectiveness of the college could be strengthened only through improvement of administrative policies in strategic areas. Consequently, "to express the purpose of the Institute in the briefest form, it was increased academic quality of the Jesuit college through administrative functioning."[75] In other words, the director envisioned a logical progression in which a skillful dean would mobilize, supervise, and inspire a quality faculty, which, in its turn, would implement a revitalized curriculum.

For the seventy-eight participants, the benefits were tangible and enduring. The recently appointed deans "found in the Institute a school of comprehensive and realistic instruction in all phases of their office."[76] Those who had many years of experience "felt the broadening influence derived from an exchange of experimental knowledge."[77] According to many participants, "perhaps the most important result, though the least tangible, is the elevation of morale of Jesuit administrators."[78]

Those Jesuits who attended the institute, and are now retired, still consider it a benchmark in Jesuit higher education and a concrete illustration of the "united purpose and concerted action" that was the rallying cry of Father Ledochowski. The resolutions, drawn up at the end of the institute, paid ample tribute to the exceptional cooperation of the provincials, rectors, presidents, and administrators in this assistancy-wide effort.[79]

In view of its success, corroborated by the enthusiasm of the participants, the Board of Governors approved "the plan to hold similar institutes every five years."[80] The provincials were also anxious, as a return on their investment, that the *Proceedings* (edited by Father Mallon) "should be used constantly by presidents and deans as the basis for thorough institutional self-studies of their institutions."[81] Finally, in a gesture of appreciation, they sent a message of satisfaction and congratulations to the Executive Committee, with particular gratitude to Fathers Mallon and Maline, principal architects of the institute.[82]

In addition to commissions and institutes, the third major source of union and cooperation within the association was the annual meeting. Mandated by the constitution, article VII stipulated that "the Association shall convene once a year in a general session of both departments during the week that the National Catholic Educational Association holds its annual convention."[83] Truly national in comprehension and membership, the meeting brought together presidents, deans, high school principals, and resource experts from every university, college, and high school in the United States, and frequently from foreign countries where schools were staffed by American Jesuits. The program, comprising a main theme, with individual topics and in-depth papers complementing the theme, was designed at the previous spring meeting of the Executive Committee, which allowed almost a year for preparation.

In what became a ritual, all delegates (from both departments) assembled for the first general session on Easter Sunday evening; the sessions continued through Monday; and the meeting climaxed with a dinner meeting that evening.[84] No one would argue that the format was perfect, but the delegates who heard the reports of the commissions, absorbed the papers, and participated in the discussions agreed that the exercise was worthwhile.[85] The social encounters and informal gatherings were almost as important as the formal meetings. It is helpful for a dean to know that his problems are not unique; and in a corridor or room, administrators from Holy Cross, Rockhurst, and Gonzaga could find solace and advice in an exchange of views and experiences that would be beneficial when they returned to their campuses.

Truth to tell, one feature of the program was neither anticipated nor remembered with universal enthusiasm — and Jesuits who attended these meetings will recall the executive director's annual report to the association. Always delivered at the dinner meeting, when the delegates were restive, the well-intentioned report, in length, scope, and complexity, would have intimidated the General Assembly of the United Nations. Whether diplomatic or undiplomatic, representations were unsuccessful in syncopating the text. Despite this, the annual program was an ecumenical expression of the common objectives and purpose of institutions geographically separated, each with its individual, academic personality and character. There was the inescapable impression that the delegates belonged to a large, active, and effective organization, and they returned to their daily decisions with new ideas and new resolve.[86]

The Executive Committee was less successful in addressing other questions that either originated within the committee or were proposed to it from without. As a rule, the committee was on firm ground in its effort to shape policies and procedures that were susceptible of national application; it was less persuasive in particular applications. The National Office met opposition, or at least passive resistance, when it attempted — even with the blessing of the provincials — to influence the curriculum, invade the departments, oppose new degree programs, or challenge the prerogatives of an individual president. While the committee could be helpful in developing background materials or providing a historical perspective on a particular issue — as, for example, in the rector–president controversy, the projected promulgation of a general set of statutes, the bylaws for a national Jesuit alumni association — these proposals were always distilled, amended, and adjusted through boards of trustees and their advisors.[87]

From time to time the committee endorsed laudable plans and projects that proved too ambitious for the human resources that were available. William J. Codd, province prefect of the Oregon Province, had begun to codify regulations for seeking accreditation and for establishing honor societies,[88] but, as had happened in the past, the work had to be shelved when he was assigned to new duties. The Executive Committee then decided, as a substitute for Codd's work and in the interest of assistancy uniformity, to prepare a manual or handbook for the inspection of Jesuit institutions by the province prefect.[89] This concept was later enlarged to embrace a "codification of Province and Assistancy Regulations" on studies. At this point, and with second thoughts, the prefects complained that the records were so incomplete as to make virtually impossible the completion of a meaningful text.[90] With admirable courage, but some confusion, it was then decided to edit college and high school manuals with the list of regulations between the same covers. In this way, many projects were on the committee's agenda year after year, with varying degrees of progress or success. Many of these loose ends can be traced to the divided interests and duties of the prefects themselves, who, through no fault of their own, were unable to concentrate their time and energy on the demands of the moment.[91]

Despite these disappointments in the completion of overambitious projects, there was ample cause for satisfaction in what had been accomplished. In the immediate postwar years, JEA became the active partner of other associations and agencies in coping with the rush of students to campuses across the country. In his annual reports to the Board of Governors, Rooney always listed the addresses he gave, the meetings he attended, and the associations with which JEA was interacting.[92] By any standard, it was an impressive show. Other Jesuits were also active, but the executive director, by taste and temperament, enjoyed national and international exposure: conferences in Rome with the General, UNESCO meetings in Paris and Versailles, South American visitations to Bogatá or Quito.[93]

As he continued in office, with a clear perception of its possibilities, he guided the Executive Committee, established a businesslike relationship with provincials (who accepted his advice on most occasions), and became the educational consultant of the General. But he was never on easy terms with the presidents of Jesuit colleges and universities, who remained suspicious of his friendships at the Roman Curia.

# 6. Accent on Quality, 1950–1955

On Tuesday, September 16, 1947, Father Rooney had his first conference with Father General Janssens, since the latter's election, at his office in the Curia on Borgo Santo Spirito.[1] It was a friendly reunion between two Jesuits who had similar, though not identical, views on the apostolate of Jesuit higher education. Of that lengthy conference (almost two hours), Rooney wrote: "I outlined briefly the work of the Jesuit Educational Association in the United States: the meetings we hold, the activities of the Executive Committee, Reports to the Board of Governors etc., etc., and the fine results we have from all this in the growing unity and cooperation among our institutions."[2] Two topics, one of which was becoming a mild obsession of the executive director and the other a legitimate preoccupation of the General, received special attention. The first dealt with the office of the province prefect of studies and the second emphasized the essential role of special studies in establishing the academic reputation of the Society in America.

The executive director had every reason in the world to strengthen the hands of province prefects who formed the Executive Committee of the JEA. It was the heart of the operation, and at this audience Rooney "spoke at some length of my views on the importance of the office of the General Prefect of Studies and what great assistance the General Prefect can be to a Provincial, if the office is well organized and if proper use is made of it."[3]

Throughout his tenure as executive director, Rooney composed variations on the same theme, urging the General and provincials to appoint capable prefects who would be free from other responsibilities. His insistence on full-time prefects was a key point, and in taking this position he had history on his side, for there had been an early experiment with the office of province prefect. William F. Clark (1856–1947), whose Jesuit career spanned seventy-one years, was the earliest incumbent. He had served as moderator general of studies of the Maryland–New York Province in 1905 and 1906, after which the office lapsed. Technically, the office was inaugurated, though not immediately implemented, by the prescriptions in the *Memorial* left by Father Norbert de Boynes at the close of his official visitation of the American provinces in 1922.[4] In his *Memorial* the Visitor wrote that, in an effort to improve the schools, "it would help very much to appoint a General Prefect according to the regulations given to the Provincials."[5] These regulations, or "ordinations," were contained in a special document, entitled *Directiones*, which was addressed personally to the provincial. This document clearly stated that "for promoting studies in colleges and other schools, a Prefect General of Studies should be assigned, free from all other duties, whose office would be determined by the Provincial with advice from his consultors and other knowledgeable men."[6]

In official conferences and written reports, Rooney appealed to this document in support of his thesis. He argued, *a fortiori*, that the growth and size and complexity of Jesuit institutions "made it impossible for any provincial to exercise personally that supervision necessary if there is to be any unity or even a semblance of uniformity among the schools of a single province."[7] The provincial simply had to delegate supervisory authority, "and the natural person to whom to delegate it is the province prefect of studies."[8] In a sense, that point was not in dispute. The debate revolved, rather, around how much authority was to be delegated, how it was to be exercised, and how it was to be reconciled with the advisory function of the socius to the provincial. A secondary, but important, consideration addressed the question of full-time versus part-time prefects.[9] These questions were finally resolved, but the process took time, patience, and diplomacy. The resolution of the problem illustrates the tense relationship that sometimes existed between the Executive Committee and the Board of Governors.

After 1934, the province prefects appealed to article V of the *Instructio* for whatever authority they might possess. Yet that article merely says that the prefects are to assist the provincials in whatever pertains to education in the province. The extent of authority, therefore, was uneven and depended upon the paternal largesse of a particular provincial. The Executive Committee correctly felt that clear lines of responsibility should be established that would be adhered to equally by all provincials. Responding to this request, "the Board of Governors [instructed] the Executive Committee of the JEA to begin work on drawing up a clear statement of duties and function of General Prefects of Studies."[10] There was, however, a *caveat*. "In drawing up such a statement attention should be paid to the regular functions of the Socius to the Provincial."[11] In a final charge, since the province prefect was often the director of special studies, the provincials asked the Executive Committee "to prepare a statement of the functions of the Director of Special Studies."[12] This was at least a recognition of the problem, for which the committee was grateful, but it would take an unbelievable five year period to approve such a statement. In the provincials' meetings, the wheels turned slowly.

The chairman of the subcommittee, charged to prepare a draft, was Arthur Sheehan of New England. After a Roman biennium, he taught theology at Weston College for a number of years and in 1940 was appointed province prefect of studies. A man of decision, quick of step and mind, he did not suffer delays gladly.[13] Each province prefect was asked to complete a questionnaire which factually detailed his duties and discretionary powers. He was also asked for suggestions. A year later, at Jesuit High School in New Orleans, the chairman submitted to the Board of Governors a draft statement on the "Duties and Functions of Province Prefects."[14] In a historical *praenotanda*, which was a monument to research, the committee faced the question: whether the functions of a province prefect "are purely advisory or whether they are to be considered as being, to some extent administrative also."[15] Comparing the evolution of the province prefect to the dean in relation to the president of a college, the *praenotanda* came down on the side of administrative authority. The statement itself, entitled *Duties and Functions of Province Prefects*, contains six articles, with several paragraphs under each heading.[16] It is an excellent document, which, if accepted as written, would have given the province prefect the necessary discretion to move among the academic officials of the colleges and universities with authority and prestige.

Unfortunately, the Board of Governors felt that the draft, as presented, competed with the powers of the provincial or, at the least, did not make sufficient provision for delegation in certain circumstances. In their response, the provincials, "realizing the importance of such a statement," informed the executive director that the draft "deserves more thorough study than can be given to it at the present time."[17] Suddenly taking the initiative, to the chagrin and disappointment of the Executive Committee, the provincials appointed a subcommittee of their own to edit the draft that had been submitted to them.[18] The provincials, as they had promised, held perfunctory consultations with their respective prefects, but the final document was entirely the product of the Board of Governors. This process, which dampened the enthusiasm of the prefects, took three years to complete. To repeated inquiries from Rooney, the provincials replied with assurances of steady progress in composing a formula, that would be acceptable to all parties. Finally the statement, dated April 23, 1953, was officially approved by the Board of Governors, with the stipulation that it be published in the *JEQ* with offprints sent to rectors, presidents, deans, and principals.[19]

In a letter addressed to the fathers and scholastics of the American Assistancy, John J. McMahon, chairman of the board, promulgated the statement, entitled *The Duties and Functions of the Province Prefect of Studies*.[20] The so-called legal aspects of the document were derived from the *Instructio* and the JEA Constitution, which could not be changed. Where the provincials exercised originality, the provisions make it quite clear that the function of the province prefect is advisory and not administrative. Although the members of the Executive Committee could accept the constant refrain, "with the approval of the Provincial," they were dismayed to learn that "[the Prefect] shall endeavor to conduct his office in a manner analogous to that prescribed in the *Rules for the Socius to the Provincial* and the *Rules for the Consultors of the Province*."[21] Rooney, who did not mask his immediate disapproval of the statement, was quick to recognize the reason for the provincials' analogy.

Shortly after the statement was promulgated, he scheduled his annual conference with the General. With the courtesy customary on those occasions, he told the General that the statement "as it stands is good" but that he and the province prefects found no great comfort in it. "We felt," Rooney told the General, "that it had been cut too much and I, myself, was afraid that it might possibly give an impression of playing down the functions of the Province Prefects of Studies or of 'cutting them down to size.' I said I had objected — and still do — to the quotations from the rules of the Socius and the Province Consultors in such a statement."[22]

He was more explicit in his complaint to Father Assistant McCormick. "There is an essential difference," he reminded the Assistant, "between the office of Socius and that of Province Prefects of Studies: The Socius as such, has no authority at all and must not even give the appearance of it; the Province Prefect has. His authority is delegated, but it is authority none the less."[23] The approved version had differed so much from the original draft submitted by the Executive Committee "that the Province Prefects of Studies had lost their enthusiasm."[24] However, Rooney assured McCormick, "the Prefects will be loyal to its prescriptions."[25]

Although it was technically a separate office, the provincials specified that "normally the province prefect of studies shall supervise and direct the province program of special studies for members of the Society."[26] In this capacity, the director should "study the future needs of the various universities, colleges, and high schools of the province as a basis for long-range planning of a program of studies leading to graduate degrees in those fields of education which are the distinctive and special work of Jesuit education."[27] It was Father General himself who brought up this question in his first conference with Rooney. Referring to his letter *On Ministries*, and conceding that "a fine, broad training" had been adequate in former times, he repeated that "we are living in an age of specialization and we must have highly trained men, specialists, to meet our needs and to meet the competition."[28] The executive director in total agreement, noted that the *Instructio* had been the basic incentive for the development of a program in special studies and that he, himself, made an annual report to the provincials on the status of Jesuits in special studies. In a moment of generosity, he could have added that the original impetus was inspired by Daniel O'Connell.[29]

Although the provincials were protected by a document, in practice they were rather liberal in interpreting their own restrictions. They were understandably reluctant to allow the province prefects to come between them and the officials of the colleges and universities. However, in their capacity as directors of special students and special studies, the province prefects enjoyed a good deal of autonomy and discretion, even authority — and it was in this area that they may have made their greatest contribution to the improved quality of Jesuit higher education.

The assignment of priests and scholastics to special studies in the postwar years was not new. That is clear from the outstanding examples already mentioned in this narrative. What was new, however, was the official emphasis on advanced degrees; the national awareness of the need; the long-range planning and careful preparation of scholastics for further studies, especially in the profane disciplines; the matching of disciplines with particular needs; the self-interest manifested by presidents and deans. It was, in summary, clearly understood by all concerned that earning advanced degrees was basic to a successful apostolate of higher education. The province prefects, as directors of special studies, can take much of the credit for the success achieved in their respective provinces. The provincials had to pay the bill, but the General reminded them that the price, if not exactly a bargain, was money well spent. In his second exhortation to the Congregation of Procurators on September 30, 1953, Father General said:

> Time and again I have pointed out the present day need that in addition to their traditional general formation given in the Society, which more than ever before must today be solid and sound, many of Ours should

receive training in those special branches of knowledge, now so multiplied by progress in research. Although many more men have been set
aside for such studies, yet in some places their numbers are still too small.
It is not a sacrifice to send Scholastics to Universities, even though there
arises a temporary curtailment of manpower for existing works. Who will
call "a sacrifice" the allocation of funds which will reap richer returns in
the future? Such investments are the marks of wisdom and foresight.[30]

It would be tedious, though impressive, to document the procedures of the directors of special studies in their efforts to identify, encourage, and prepare young Jesuits for a life of scholarship. The directors, some of whom lacked the very advantages they offered others,
visited the scholasticates, listened patiently to proposals, and offered
advice. Once the decision was made to plan a course of studies at a particular university, the priest or scholastic, as those who were selected
later agreed, received every consideration and total cooperation as a
full-time doctoral (or master's) candidate.[31]

As the program continued, the Board of Governors showed renewed interest. In fact, a certain inner-province rivalry appeared to
develop. In any case, in their 1952 response to the executive director's
annual report on special studies "the Provincials [agreed] that it would
be useful to have a more detailed report showing the record of the
respective provinces and, hence, request the General Prefects to prepare
such a report."[32] Additionally, the provincials asked for a "comprehensive report . . . covering the last ten years," which would indicate "the
comparative numbers of Jesuits attending Catholic and secular universities and the subjects studied."[33]

The Executive Committee moved quickly on this request, but
assembling the statistical data was more complicated than anticipated.
Although Rooney regularly submitted his annual report on studies, it
was confined to simple numbers. At this point, it was necessary to determine accurately who had begun graduate studies during these years,
who had continued, and who had finished, together with universities
attended and choice of field. When the report was finally submitted,
Father Rooney acknowledged the technical assistance of his office
associate.

William J. Mehok, now of the Wisconsin Province, became Father
Rooney's assistant and managing editor of *JEQ* in 1947. Able and
energetic, for eight years he provided the statistical data (with interpretation) for national enrollments, special studies, and Jesuit manpower. Suited both by temperament and physical stamina for this
science of numbers, which many would find boring or baffling, Mehok

was one of the first in the Society to recognize the implications of the applied science of statistics. His hard information grounded the Jesuit philosophy of excellence in the hard reality of concrete facts and figures. In later years he was associated with the Cambridge Center for Social Studies, where he published several comprehensive surveys on international and geographic trends in the Society.[34]

Fathers Mallon and Maline, in their customary role, were asked to incorporate the suggestions of the Executive Committee in the ten-year report. In its final form, the report covered the eleven-year period, 1943–44 to 1953–54, and was officially distributed to the Board of Governors on July 7, 1953.[35] In one sense, the figures were disappointing. A few months earlier, in making his annual report, Rooney noted that "we have gone from a total of 254 full time graduate students in 1949–50 to a low of 173 for 1952–53."[36] He offered an interesting theory for this decline, which, in light of future growth, may have been correct. His explanation was predicated on the unexpected decrease in the increment of priests in the American Assistancy in the late 1940s and early 1950s.[37] Scholastics, who finished their course in philosophy in those years, reflected the diminishing vocational picture during the war period. Those who were available for special studies, therefore, were in shorter supply. There may have been something to this theory, since there was a change for the better after 1954.[38] Clearly, the emphasis on special studies was not keeping pace with enrollments in the schools, and every official in the JEA recognized that more must be done. That was the hopeful part about it. There could be no satisfactory quality in Jesuit higher education without the advanced degrees that would prepare men for research and publication, the real test of academic achievement.[39]

It is not necessarily cynical to note that advanced degrees do not, of themselves, guarantee quality; and since the special studies program involved large sums of money, both the Board of Governors and the Executive Committee were anxious to know if the return was commensurate with the investment. The committee sensed that, to realize expectations, it might be helpful to publicize the successful efforts of industrious Jesuits.

At a meeting in Kansas City, when Rooney expressed misgivings "whether or not we are making the right kind of studies for the improvement of our schools,"[40] the committee came to the fairly obvious conclusion that there were two ways in which to measure the academic impact of special studies. The first norm, anticipating the days of "publish or perish," measured the list of publications of Jesuits who had profited by the advantages of graduate studies; the second, in a more sensitive area, attempted to identify established Jesuit scholars. The province prefects were asking basic questions. "How can we make more effective studies of the quality and efficiency of our schools?" "What practical steps can be taken to improve our schools?"

It became clear in these discussions "that the topics are of the utmost importance and need much more discussion before our conclusions can crystallize."[41] Responding to these queries within the Executive Committee, the Board of Governors asked the committee to make an annual report on the scholarly publications of Jesuits in the United States and further, that it be presented each year in *JEQ*. This procedure would give the results the widest possible publicity among Jesuits; it would also, as a human reward, focus attention on the accomplishments of the authors. In referring to scholarly activities of Jesuits, Rooney, who first made this suggestion, wrote: "It has occurred to me that it might be well to compile and publish in each province Newsletter an annual report of this type. A most interesting feature of the annual meeting of the Conference of Jesuit Historians is the report made by each one present [and published in the minutes of the meeting] of his scholarly writings and publications during the previous year. I suspect that this report serves as a stimulus to all our historians to keep writing and publishing."[42] The provincials also suggested — an index of their seriousness — that in the short notices under "News from the Field" a list of publications in progress be added.

The subcommittee that was appointed to this thankless task had the not unexpected problem of defining the elusive word "scholarly." It finally agreed upon a twofold purpose in compiling such lists: "an indicative measure of the fruits of graduate studies and a stimulation for further production."[43] With this clarification, appropriate forms for this purpose were distributed by province directors of studies to the proper agents (rectors and deans) for completion by Jesuits who had authored books or articles since 1953. The first list, which was accompanied by a brief history of the project and a definition of "scholarly," was published in 1955.

The criteria for identifying and including these publications were reasonable and traditional. "Actual appearance in print" was the prime requisite. In addition, a work must be the result of "original and independent research, whether pure or applied." Finally, the judges looked for a product of "high quality which is generally recognized as a scholarly contribution."[44] The listing, which became an annual feature of the *Quarterly*, was one gauge of the scholarly activities of Jesuits in the American Assistancy. For those who perused the lists, the authors and their works would furnish concrete evidence of the depth and extent of Jesuit research. Basically, this exercise provided a statement on, or index to, the quality of schools these authors staffed. On the generally conceded assumption that publication is an index to quality, this internal, academic audit showed that Jesuit professors must continue to haunt the laboratory and the library.

In identifying scholarly publications, Father Mallon proposed a parallel list of Jesuit scholars. Since an institution depends on the reputation of its faculty, it was another attempt to measure the quality of excellence that characterized Jesuit institutions; it was also a stratagem to inspire scholastics to emulate their distinguished mentors in the Society. It was Mallon's plan to prepare, by province, a list of "living Jesuit scholars." The provincials, sensing the possibility of injured academic egos, sanctioned these lists, but they were to be shared exclusively with other province prefects and provincials. "Since star differs from star in magnitude," the Board of Governors wanted to avoid unseemly regional competition and institutional rivalry. For that reason, perhaps, "the Board of Governors [did] not approve the proposal to prepare a national list of Jesuit scholars" that would be publicly available.[45]

Reporting for the subcommittee, composed of Midwest prefects, Father Maline explained that his committee discussed a method of selection that included purpose, criteria, and form design. In defining the purpose of the project, the committee envisioned a reference list of scholars in the American Assistancy that would be available to provincials for special assignments, for representation at high-level academic meetings, and for consultation and advice.[46] As a secondary benefit, the list would serve as a partial basis for evaluating undergraduate and graduate programs and for identifying institutions which consistently produced outstanding graduates — those that instilled a driving inclination for research and those that did not.[47] The criteria for induction into this "Jesuit Hall of Fame" were similar to those demanded by the Catholic Commission on Intellectual and Cultural Affairs.[48] Taking the doctorate for granted, as the badge of success in a program of special studies, the ground rules called for noteworthy publications, originality, ongoing research, recognition by peers, significant awards, and active membership in the learned societies.[49]

While the total was small in comparison to the number of Jesuit faculty members across the country, the Society could boast of a number of genuine scholars who were acknowledged by colleagues in the same disciplines. As one would suspect, they were generally in the large institutions with graduate programs at the doctor's level. Walter J. Ong, now an established scholar, was then gaining recognition in the field of comparative literature. William L. Lucey of Holy Cross, John F. Bannon of Saint Louis, Ernest J. Burrus of New Orleans, and Peter Masten Dunne of the West Coast were appearing in the historical journals and publishing monographs in their special areas of interest. Herbert Musurillo, whose career was cut short by an unfortunate accident, and William M. A. Grimaldi, both of Bellarmine College, opened fresh approaches to reading and appreciating the classical languages. A young group of philosophers, the fruit of special studies, was dazzling students on several campuses: Norris Clarke and Quentin Lauer at Fordham, George Klubertanz and Robert Henle at Saint Louis, and Robert Harvanek at West Baden; and William C. Bier of Fordham, and James F. Moynihan of Boston College were charting new courses in psychology. John C. Murray, John C. Ford, and Walter J. Burghardt were associated with *Theological Studies,* which was — and is — a learned journal of the highest caliber. Charles A. Berger, at Fordham, was training younger Jesuits who later became preeminent in biology. Francis J. Heyden in astronomy and Daniel Linehan in seismology brought distinction to the Society in those sciences.[50]

As no list is ever exhaustive, the names of equally brilliant men have been omitted, but those who were selected for citation are good examples of Jesuits — especially young Jesuits — who had taken advantage of special studies to work at the outer edge of knowledge, to introduce their students to the mysteries of research, and to burnish the name of the teaching Church. They fulfilled the expectations of Father General, envisioned in his letter *On Jesuit Ministries,* and, more particularly, his understanding of *labor scientificus* in the apostolate of higher education.

It is generally agreed that "more" is not always "better," and in its drive for excellence the Jesuit Educational Association was forced to search for a solution to this conundrum. The temporary emergency caused by the sudden influx of students under the GI Bill in the immediate postwar years was met at all institutions with hastily devised programs.[51] However, an increase in the birth rate, with scientific predictions of a steady increase in enrollments for years to come, called for a policy decision on expansion of Jesuit institutions of higher learning in the foreseeable future. It was not an easy decision. Some Jesuits protested that expansion meant dilution of Jesuit education; others argued that expansion was necessary, inevitable, and beneficial. Yet, as rectors and deans realized, the question could not be considered in isolation. Expansion was not related only to quality, it was closely connected with financial resources, manpower, and the recruitment of lay faculty.

The General's position, which gave the impression of inconsistency and ambivalence, served to encourage decisions at the local level.

As far back as 1949, Rooney had reminded the provincials that new departments, new schools, and new degrees required the General's approval.[52] Except for the controversy over the Latin requirement for the A.B. degree in Jesuit colleges, the provincials refused to become alarmed,[53] and under the new statutes for province prefects, the Executive Committee was not in a position to interfere. It was up to the executive director to make the case. In his conference with the Father General in 1954, Rooney carefully explained the growth, present and projected, in student enrollments in the United States in postsecondary education. He told the General "that a number of our Provincials and Rectors are concerned and perplexed."[54] Although constantly reminded that the Father General was opposed to expansion, they heard of permissions granted to open new schools.[55]

In his initial response to Rooney's fairly frank assessment, the General, manifesting surprising unfamiliarity with the system, felt there was an automatic selection process because "[Jesuits] have one kind of an education."[56] Rooney quickly corrected the General's misapprehension and explained that, in addition to the literary and humanistic, there were professional schools and departments at the undergraduate and graduate levels in the university complex. Then he offered his advice: "In general our principle should be that we shall be willing to take those students who can profit by the education we wish to give them," provided the faculty, Jesuit and lay, and the necessary physical facilities were available.[57] The General seemed to agree with this principle, and "stated quite clearly that we cannot say we will not expand."[58] But, he quickly added, we cannot so expand "that we cease to give a Catholic and Jesuit education."[59] Father Rooney seemed satisfied for the moment and noted that "the General felt that he could go along with what I had suggested."[60] At the end of the next conversation, he asked Rooney to put his thoughts in writing and send the draft to him.

When Rooney returned to his New York office, he addressed a ten-page memorandum to the General on "Expansion of Jesuit Education in the United States."[61] An excellent statement, it included a technical but clear explanation of the roles of public and independent education in the United States, the proportion of Catholic institutions, and a summary of college-age population trends (1940–1970), with statistics and predictions from the latest government publications. With that introduction, Rooney then outlined the two positions that could be taken: "We can decide to hold the line where we are now; or, we can be ready to expand but only after having determined what relative strength we must preserve in any degree of expansion."[62] The first position, he argued, would be untenable in view of the history of the United States, the Church in America, and the traditions of the Society. Therefore he opted for the second position and submitted a draft, "General Policies and Procedures," which he felt "would assist superiors and other administrators . . . to face the problems of expansion and to give an answer to those who have a right to know what our policy on expansion will be."[63] The memorandum was designed for the undergraduate colleges.

The "Policy" was simple and straightforward. Borrowing words from Father Janssens, it said that Jesuit institutions should accept as many students as "furnish solid grounds for the hope that they will go through with their studies . . . with real success" and for whom physical facilities and teaching staffs would be expanded insofar as their costs were compatible with financial resources.[64] The "Procedures" were more elaborate and quite explicit. Rooney's position was that expansion, which he openly supported, should not change the character of Jesuit schools, and the Procedures' twelve points were constructed on this premise. Plans, it was assumed, would be submitted to the approval of superiors, and administrators should remember, first of all, that Jesuit institutions have traditionally been a rich source of priestly and religious vocations to the Society and the Church. At the same time, expansion should not encourage competition with the hierarchy's plans. Important in Rooney's draft was development of a process to identify students who would profit from a Jesuit education. Similarly, in the recruitment of lay faculty, which he recognized as a necessary component, a program on instruction must be provided to introduce lay colleagues to the spirit, history, aims, and methods of the Jesuit system. Finally, recalling the function of the JEA, plans for expansion should be long-range in scope and assistancy-wide, "so that our total American Jesuit personnel, facilities and resources will be used most advantageously."[65]

In contrast to the attention to detail exercised at the General's Curia and in provincials' offices, the history of this document is rather bizarre. In his 1955 conference with the General, Rooney, "looking for a statement"—in reality or reaction—obliquely alluded to the draft he had sent to Rome. The General seemed surprised at Rooney's allusions, "since," as Rooney noted, "[the General] had evidently sent something through on it."[66] Suspecting that something had gone awry, Rooney searched the files of Thomas Henneberry, New York provincial, for the missing document. He found nothing. Ironically, in his *Report* to the Board of Governors in 1956, Rooney wrote that "Father General has been studying this matter [of expansion] very carefully; it is possible that he may issue some directives soon."[67] The provincials were mysteriously noncommital.

To make a long story short, at the meeting of the Board of Governors in 1958, Father Leo Burns, provincial of the Wisconsin Province, and Rooney made a methodical search of the provincial's file in Milwaukee. In Rooney's words, "there we ran across Father General's letter of July 29, 1955, actually expressing satisfaction with the Policies and Procedures approved by the Provincials concerning expansion. This was the very answer I had been requesting of Father General concerning a policy on expansion."[68] The Board of Governors had sent Rooney's draft to the General, with a covering letter dated June 30, 1955, and in return had received a statement of approval. Rooney, rightfully upset at this lack of communication on an important matter, which had bypassed him, made his complaint openly to the General. Father Janssens, mildly contrite, "said he saw no reason why copies of letters sent to all Provincials and which concern education or topics brought up in my report to the Board of Governors, should not be sent to me. [The General] made a special note of this and I feel certain that in the future, copies of such letters or documents will be sent directly to me."[69]

That very year, 1958, twenty-eight presidents of Jesuit institutions, forming a new conference within the JEA, met for the first time at Georgetown University. Among other important questions, they discussed the implications of expansion.[70] Edward J. O'Donnell, the capable and popular president of Marquette University, in an introductory paper facetiously proposed that presidents disqualify themselves from comments on expansion. At the heart of Parkinson's Law, he noted, are administrators who "want to multiply subordinates (not rivals) and make work for each other."[71] More seriously, he urged that, in any version of expansion, Jesuit institutions jealously aim for "that type of excellence which the needs of the Church require, and which the Society earnestly recommends — excellence which is quite within our reach."[72] However, in the discussion that followed, the presidents, descending from this lofty plane, focused on financial resources, campus facilities, and manpower. In a sense, the recruitment and formation of lay faculty was the crucial question. By and large, the presidents accepted the "Policies and Procedures" and continued to look to the General for further guidance.

After the meeting, inaugurating an annual feature, the presidents, with Rooney as a spokesman, held a press conference. The publicity was good, but one point in particular initiated a public controversy, which in a few journals turned into an attack on the Jesuit Educational

Association. In a press release, Rooney said that if federal aid to education were deemed necessary, "then that aid should be made available on an across-the-board basis, for all students and for all institutions." In an angry editorial, "Jesuits Seek Public Aid for Private Schools," the *Christian Century* wrote a sharp reply. "Congressmen would find it easier to bear the cross of greatness if they could see more examples of cross-bearing in the religious communities of our country. . . . This effort to strike for public aid for sectarian schools while the iron is hot may be followed by widespread agitation to that end. But fortunately the authoritative voice of the Roman Catholic hierarchy is not yet the Jesuit Educational Association but the National Catholic Welfare Conference."[73]

Despite the apparent satisfaction of the presidents with the "Policies and Procedures," the Executive Committee, as reported by the chairman, wanted a further clarification of the regulations on expansion. Rooney would have been better advised to drop the issue. It was an odd request in that there did not seem to be any good reason for it, and the provincials dealt with it in summary fashion. Inasmuch as the General had expressed his approval of the "Policies," Rooney's own handiwork, the Board of Governors insisted that "they are, therefore, to be taken as the approved policy for the American Assistancy on the subject of expansion."[74] There was to be no further debate.

Though tenuous at best, there was a possibility that the committee's request stemmed from a discussion in Rome which impinged on the question of expansion. It began in 1956 when Janssens had sent a memorandum to the American Assistant, Vincent McCormick, in which he expressed his concern that Jesuit institutions in the United States seemed to be placing "Over-Emphasis on the Immediately Useful."[75] The charge had a familiar ring. McCormick, of course, forwarded the memorandum to the Board of Governors, which shared its content with Rooney. Forewarned of this latest development, he prepared for his next conference with the General, which took place at Villa Cavaletti, the summer residence of the Curia fathers.

Janssens, as he had said in writing to McCormick, was disturbed by the curriculum in the professional schools which emphasized the "useful and the practical."[76] Rooney explained the difference between the graduate programs in law, medicine, social work, and business administration, which were mandatory for a particular degree, and the undergraduate curricula in engineering, nursing, and business administration, which allowed flexibility, at least in the first two years. In designing those undergraduate programs, Rooney said, the provincials, the Executive Committee, and he himself were deeply concerned "with the dangers of neglecting the more lasting values of the humanities, science, philosophy, history and religion; and that all of us were trying to watch these things constantly."[77] But he had to admit, in his summary of the conference, that the General "would like to see further evidence of our constant insistence on long range values in our education."[78] This must have been on the General's mind, for he confided to Rooney that "yielding to the immediately useful" was not peculiar to the United States. "It is true today also all through Europe."[79] It was, unfortunately, a losing battle, as Jesuit institutions were moving with the American tide, and Latin was one of the early casualties.

It was always understood that, in an expanded educational program, the JEA would avoid any overt challenge to the NCEA, especially in the graduate schools. In fact, it was explicitly stated that "plans for expansion should be made to coordinate with, rather than be in competition with plans of the hierarchy for expansion."[80] The implications of this policy went beyond the simple consideration of enrollments. From the beginning, the JEA had been sensitive to the importance of a good relationship with the American hierarchy, and with diocesan officials at the local level. On more than one occasion, as the provincials were well aware, and as Rooney had reported to the General, the canonical privileges and exemptions granted by the Holy See to the Society of Jesus were a source of irritation to or in conflict with the bishops in whose jurisdiction Jesuit colleges and high schools were located. Although the General, as a former canonist, always insisted upon the legality of the exemptions, he and the provincials were anxious, in the interest of religious harmony, to honor the bishops' legitimate authority. The complexities of diocesan relationships were on the agenda of every Executive Committee meeting. For this reason, it might be instructive to trace (however briefly) the efforts within the JEA to reach an accommodation with the hierarchy — an accommodation that would safeguard Jesuit exemptions and, at the same time, preserve the Ordinary's prerogatives.

Although there had been previous incidents of jurisdictional conflict, resolution of the problem became more urgent in 1947. At that time, the American bishops began to emphasize a Catholic Action program which involved students in Catholic institutions. In some areas, diocesan officials insisted that Jesuit schools, especially at the secondary level, participate in the program.[81] The situation was brought to the attention of the provincials, who discussed the problem at their meeting in Spokane. Shortly thereafter, Leo J. Robinson, the popular provincial of Oregon and chairman of the board, communicated the provincials' decision to the executive director. It had been determined, he wrote, "that a committee be appointed to study the relationships between the diocesan authorities and our institutions, the findings to be presented to Father General in Rome, if His Paternity grants permission for us to do so."[82] The committee was composed of Rooney, as chairman, "for matters concerning education"; Joseph MacFarlane, a member of the New England Province, assigned to Jesuit Mission, "for matters pertaining to Jesuit Missions"; and Daniel Lord, the nationally known, admired, and loved editor of *Queen's Work*, "for matters pertaining to the Sodality."[83]

Charged with a task that was altogether to his liking, Rooney lost no time in getting down to business. To get at the facts, he immediately sent out a questionnaire which asked for 126 "checked" responses. This was not an entirely successful exercise since several respondents, reluctant to respond in numerical terms, suggested that it was a risky way to accumulate complicated information. Since Rooney was told that "what is desired from Rome is a general statement, not a specific answer to difficulties," he sought counsel and advice from the experts. As cases of conflict were submitted, and responses requested, Rooney consulted canonists John Crowley and James Risk of Weston College, Timothy Bouscaren of West Baden, and Joseph Gallen of Woodstock.[84] In time, two committees were formed: a Committee of Five that met regularly with Rooney, and another that served in advisory capacity.[85] Finally, with all the necessary information at hand, including the report of the experts, the provincials asked Rooney and Sheehan, the province prefect of New England, to draft a statement on diocesan relationships.

In reviewing this situation, three points should be kept in mind. In the first place, most of the problems were at the secondary level.[86] Secondly, the conflicts in jurisdiction were the exception, not the rule.[87] Thirdly, there was, for the most part, an honest effort on both sides to resolve these conflicts. In drawing up policy suggestions, the five-man committee recommended that "every effort should be made to avoid anything like forcing an issue." Moreover, "if the regulation should be educationally sound and in accord with our own principles and policies, it might be well to accept it, in such manner that the *right of exemption* would not be at issue."[88]

At a meeting in Boston, Rooney and Sheehan submitted their draft ("Diocesan Relationships") and their case, in the form of a memorandum, to the Eastern provincials on October 3, 1952. It was a comprehensive statement which, in the Foreword, recognized "that in the operation of our schools, cases should occasionally arise which bring in question the jurisdiction either of the local Ordinary or of the religious superior."[89]

The technical explanation on exemption was taken *verbatim*, with attribution, from the report of the subcommittee of five.[90] (Actually, the Rooney-Sheehan document added a little flesh to the bare bones of the unimaginative canonists. Never intended to be a treatise on the subject, it was a very helpful statement for rectors, presidents, deans, and principals, who were duty bound to protect the exemption without, at the same time, assuming a belligerent or adversary position vis-à-vis the episcopate.) Jesuit schools were founded to assist bishops in the educational apostolate, not to oppose them. The statement was approved by the Board of Governors at its meeting in New Orleans on May 8, 1953.[91]

In addition to these activities and movements within the JEA in the early '50s, which attested to its growth and complexity, the ordinary work of the conferences, commissions, and institutes continued — indeed accelerated.[92] At the same time, the involvement of the JEA with federal agencies and national organizations gave the association visibility on the national scene. The voice of the president of the association was heard more and more often on the public issues of the day. The Korean GI Bill, Public Law 550, was vigorously opposed by the Association of American Colleges because, as the AAC saw it, the bill put pressure on veterans to attend public institutions, rather than private, in the interest of lower tuition. Rooney, whose intervention was sought by the AAC, prudently refused to take sides until enrollment figures clearly demonstrated the damage to independent colleges.[93]

Those were the days of Senator Joseph McCarthy's faculty witch hunts. According to the senator, Communists had infiltrated the lecture halls of the prestigious universities in the United States, and there was a movement in Washington to investigate the colleges and universities. It was the classical controversy of national defense versus academic freedom. In his message to Jesuit presidents and deans, Rooney wrote: "While I, myself, deprecate unlawful and unwarranted investigations of education institutions or of teachers, I fear that some educators in their denunciations of investigations have given bad example by their attitude toward governmental agencies and government officials and elected representatives."[94]

It was a balanced view, which did not match the clear-cut repudiation of government interference by President Nathan Pusey of Harvard, whose institution was under attack for having alleged Communist sympathizers on the faculty. But to be fair, Pusey was speaking for only one institution whereas Rooney was representing twenty-eight Jesuit colleges and universities with regional, cultural, and political differences. On another front, Rooney rallied support from the American Council on Education and the AAC to force the AAU (an old nemesis) to abandon its alleged obstructionist policy in restricting the newly formed International Association of Universities to a narrow group of prestigious institutions.[95]

All of these activities indicate that Rooney, as spokesman for the JEA, was willing to stand up and be counted on the educational issues of the day. In fact, he relished his role as leader of an organization which, despite its humble origins, was now courted as an ally or perceived as an effective opponent. However, with formation of the Jesuit Presidents' Conference, the picture began to change. Beginning in the middle '50s, newly appointed presidents who were academically trained, financially oriented, politically sophisticated, and sensitive to the importance of public relations were reluctant to operate under the old restraints. Rooney remained on the stage, but he was slowly moving from the center as the presidents began to speak for themselves. The change in the association was gradual but perceptible. The Executive Committee was more cautious, and in time even the Board of Governors had to take sides.

# 7. The Emerging Role of Jesuit Presidents, 1940-1960

Article 18 of the *Instruction*, as it was first promulgated by Father Ledochowski in 1934, provided for a chancellor or president of the university, in addition to the rector, if the complexity of the institution could profit by such an arrangement. In such a case, the president would be appointed by the General himself and, *sub alto Rectoris ductu*, would, *ex officio*, administer the educational affairs of the entire university. This brief article was the basis for the system of dual control which, after several experiments, became the normal procedure in the government of Jesuit colleges and universities in the United States. It was also the source of sharp debates which raised canonical and constitutional questions. In practice, especially in the beginning, it involved the delicate melding of highly motivated, but highly sensitive, personalities who were asked to inaugurate the new plan.

The "experiment," as it was originally called, began at Fordham University. On June 25, 1936, that institution welcomed its new rector and president, who, as former dean at Saint Peter's College, easily managed the transition from Jersey City to the Rose Hill Campus in the Bronx. Robert Ignatius Gannon (1893–1978) was broadly educated to move comfortably in the proper circles of society. A graduate of Georgetown College, and culturally broadened by a European tour, he entered the Jesuit order at Saint Andrew-on-Hudson on August 14, 1913. He completed his academic course in the Society with a graduate degree from Cambridge University. Short of stature but with an open, intelligent face, a first-rate mind, and a flair for words, he graced the head table at innumerable banquets. An after-dinner speaker *par excellence*, he entertained his audiences with wit and wisdom, and later gathered these "gems" into a small volume entitled *After Black Coffee.*

110

He was also the author of *The Poor Old Liberal Arts* (1961), which, semiautobiographical in content, makes a strong case for restoration of the traditional Jesuit curriculum. An able administrator, with impeccable credentials and a national reputation, he made Fordham University a vital presence in New York City.

In inserting article 18, which was personally composed by Ledochowski, the General was probably influenced by the Commission on Higher Studies. The commissioners, working in 1931, were convinced that the relatively brief tenure of a rector, who was also president, was an inherent weakness in the governance of Jesuit institutions. Moreover, "experience has shown that where individuals were eminently fitted either for the office of Rector of the community or for that of President of the institution, they were equally and unmistakably unfitted for the other, and especially for the office of President."[1] The commission concluded that "our American Jesuit universities . . . by their very nature, their size and complex organization would seem to demand a dual administrative organization."[2] It supported the validity of this innovative proposal by citing the Constitutions of the Society.[3]

The merits of the question continued to be discussed in the Roman Curia and within the JEA. In August 1940, as a consensus began to develop, *Norms* were conditionally approved by Ledochowski "which determined the relationship between the Rector and the President of Fordham University."[4] Citing article 18 as its legal source, the *Norms* attempted to accomplish the impossible: that is, to separate and, at the same time, reconcile the two offices. On the one hand, the president was solely responsible for the academic and financial administration of the university; on the other, he discharged that responsibility "under the higher command of the Rector," who, technically, was the source of the president's authority.[5] In brief, he was juridically an official of the rector, who, as established by the *Norms*, was *ex officio* chairman of the Board of Trustees. In cases of serious dissension or disagreement, either one could have recourse to the provincial. In this legal tangle, even with the best of intentions and good will, one could predict that clouds would eventually appear on the horizon.

To a large extent, success of the "experiment" depended on the two personalities who were asked to share this division of authority. The system of dual control went into effect when John Harding Fisher was appointed rector of Fordham University on August 5, 1940. (Born in 1875, he entered the Society of Jesus in 1896, and after twelve years as an associate editor of *America* had been entrusted with the training of young Jesuits.) A disciplined, cultured, and inspirational religious, he had been a successful master of novices at Shadowbrook, the New

England novitiate, and later at St. Isaac Jogues in Wernersville. A man of intelligence, judgment, and discretion, he seemed to be a good choice for the second member of the team. Although he was an authority on the Jesuit Institute, his contact with Jesuit universities had not been extensive.

It is painful to abrogate a 400-year-old tradition in which rector was synonymous with president. In the first four or five years of the experiment, Gannon, who had become a prominent educator with high public visibility, came to dominate the Fordham campus and its external constituencies. Fisher, the legal source of authority, was relegated to the wings and, for all practical purposes, reduced to the role of religious superior of the Jesuit community. After this arrangement had been in operation for four years, it was decided to reexamine and evaluate the experiment, but, unfortunately, circumstances combined to circumvent a thorough and satisfactory review. Father Ledochowski, who had approved the original norms, had died; the war was in progress; the American Assistant was in the United States; and Father Vincent McCormick, on the spot in Rome, was the vicar general's advisor. And the advisor was influential.

In 1943, in an effort to take the initiative, Rooney submitted to the consideration of the provincials a document entitled *Tentative Form of Statutes for Institutions of Complex Organization with Dual Control of Rector and President.*[6] Joseph P. Sweeney, the self-assured provincial of Maryland–New York, asked Gannon, Fisher, and Joseph Murphy (the former provincial) for their comments. In writing to Rooney, Sweeney did not reveal his views at this time but, transmitting the problems that arose from personalities, agreed that "there are real difficulties, as you know."[7] "The main obstacle for many years to come will be the changing of a tradition which has made Rector automatically the President."[8]

On their part, the respondents were frank and honest in stating their views. Gannon, who at this point had been rector-president for four years and president for three, saw "inherent difficulties which are independent of the personalities involved."[9] The office of rector has special significance in the Society "and always tends by virtue of Jesuit Tradition to regain its full strength, *normae* or no *normae.*" As a result, Gannon continued, "the one who receives from him delegated authority, *stabili modo*, has to fight constantly to retain it, thus giving the impression of being an aggressor."[10] Moreover, the office of president was so clearly understood in the United States "that no one who is merely an *'instrumentum rectoris'* would dare to call himself a President."[11] Granted these premises, Gannon doubted that "Rectors can be found who are willing to retire from the limelight" or that "Jesuit Communities can be found which will be reconciled to a Rector shorn thus by his own delegation of powers."[12]

J. Harding Fisher, in a comment of seven pages, complained that while there was no doubt about the president's position, there was confusion as to the rector's authority. To begin with, the practice of the president at public functions "has been not to address the Rector if present."[13] In fact, according to Fisher, Gannon had informed the deans that "if the Rector were present on public occasions of an academic character, he was present as a 'guest.' "[14] He felt that this was a falsification of the true situation and suggested the title "Chancellor," or, if the title "President" were retained, that his *potestas*," granted by the General, should be clearly defined, since "the interpretation in actual practice at Fordham . . . is that his authority in educational matters is universal and absolute."[15] In other words, the original design had been inverted: the dependent president had become the independent president; the rector had, in fact, become dependent.

Joseph A. Murphy, taking a constitutional viewpoint, agreed with Fisher that, with or without premeditation, "all public announcements from the first day of the appointment of the present Rector, have emphasized that he is merely 'Local Superior of the Community.' "[16] Moreover, "all public procedures of the University have either entirely ignored [the rector's] presence or . . . given him in public a markedly secondary position."[17] Since, according to Murphy, the *Instructio* itself had never been authorized by a General Congregation, he felt that such authorization should be obtained from the next congregation before the dual system could be imposed. In a final comment, he failed to find the office of president within the framework of the constitutions.[18]

In possession of these comments from the principal actors and other advisors, the New York Provincial appealed to Rome for approval of an amended version of the original *Normae*. Norbert de Boynes, the vicar general, unwilling to go beyond the conditional and temporary approbation given by Ledochowski, wrote to the American Assistant, who was living at Saint Andrew-on-Hudson:

> Because it is not clear that this dual arrangement, as proposed for the American Provinces, is not contrary to the Constitutions of the Society; and because it has not proved very satisfactory where introduced; and because the Provinces, in which are situated our large universities, have shown in practice . . . that they do not favor it, I do not wish to appear to give permanency to it by approving any norms for such a dual arrangement that would be of "universal" validity for the Assistancy.[19]

As the American Assistant and Rooney strongly suspected, Vincent McCormick had a good deal to do with the position taken by the vicar general. Explaining his ideas to Father Maher, McCormick wrote that "it seems to me only fair to you to let you know my opinion . . . as it may be supposed to have had some influence on the content of the decision."[20] He argued that "the Rector-President plan cannot be introduced into our American universities with sincerity to the public and fairness to the men concerned without violating the Constitutions of the Society."[21] In brief, he concluded that no one should be given the title of president who is not rector—"or, to put it from the other angle, no one should be Rector who is not also President, as Americans understand the term."[22]

This provoked a hasty rejoinder from Maher, who was in favor of the dual system because, in his opinion, it was impossible to find one man who could competently discharge the duties of both offices. Not only did he dismiss the charge of insincerity but, he pointedly added, "I cannot for the life of me see how the Constitutions are trespassed upon."[23] Rooney's response, characteristically, was longer and stronger. Although he was later to change his mind, he was at this time "convinced that the Rector-President arrangement is the best method yet thought of for the administration of our larger institutions." Moreover, he wrote, "if it were against the Constitutions, I would urge that a petition be presented to a General Congregation for a change in the Constitutions."[24] Referring to McCormick's modest admission of having been a counsellor to the vicar general, Rooney wrote: "This is careful wording and does not indicate just how much influence your opinon had."[25]

Despite this high-powered correspondence and top-level consultation, the dual system was not working well at the three institutions where it had been installed. In addition to Fordham, the plan was now in operation at Loyola University, Chicago, where Joseph Egan, who would shortly be named provincial of that province, had been appointed rector, with James Hussey as president. At the University of San Francisco, Carroll O'Sullivan assumed the office of rector to complement William J. Dunne, the president. Since the vicar general had refused to give permanent sanction to the revised *Norms*, and in fact had questioned their constitutional legality, American Assistant Maher predicted that the question would be debated at the next General Congregation.[26] In view of that prediction, Rooney believed that "a thorough study should be made at once, giving the reasons for some form of dual control system, the advantages and disadvantages of the President-Rector arrangement, the experience in the schools where we have the system, alternative proposals etc. Perhaps such a study might best be prepared by a committee."[27] The Board of Governors approved the proposed study by the Executive Committee, directed that the work be begun at once, and specified that suggestions be submitted "on what the powers of the president are to be under the dual system."[28] The board also directed that the study be completed by July 1, 1946, which allowed only seven weeks.

Working under pressure, a subcommittee of the Executive Committee, which had been appointed at the April 1946 meeting of the province prefects, submitted a "Report on Dual Administrative Control of American Jesuit Universities."[29] After a comprehensive listing of the duties and functions of an American college president, culled from secular sources, the subcommittee examined several alternatives. In connection with a review of the system then in experimental use, the subcommittee submitted a series of questions to John J. Crowley, professor of canon law at Weston College, on its constitutional implications. On the basic question of entrusting the administration of a Jesuit college to an administrator (president) who was not a religious superior, Crowley had no problem. Fullness of authority resides in the General, who normally acts through a local superior. However, according to Crowley, his power to act through others is not excluded by the constitutions.

But this response did not solve the question of personalities and the division of authority. The subcommittee, therefore, went back to the drawing board for alternatives. First, a wider use of the privilege of retaining a rector beyond the canonical limitation would solve the problem of frequent changes in administration. It would not, however, enable the rector to meet his paternal obligations toward his community. The committee, as a second alternative, then proposed that "the office of rector and president be united in one man, but he would delegate to a subordinate religious superior the duties ordinarily incumbent on a rector as superior of a religious community."[30] In this arrangement, the rector would have final authority in both the academic and religious spheres; the religious superior would have delegated authority over the community. Since subjects could appeal from the superior to the rector, it was felt that this system would not ease the rector's burden, which was at the heart of the problem.

The third proposal offered an administrative plan whereby "one individual would be the *rector of the university* and another would be the *religious superior of the community.*"[31] The rector's canonical title would be "Rector," his civil title would be "President." This proposal, which was substantially the recommendation of the 1931 special commission, was at this time in operation at several American colleges and universities that were conducted by religious of other orders and congregations. Although it was not Vincent McCormick's first choice, it was a proposal he could support.[32]

In summary, the subcommittee wrote that "of the solutions proposed, that which centers the academic administration in a rector-president and the religious government in a separate religious superior, in our opinion, seems to be the most realistic and practical."[33]

In the meantime, the "experiment" continued at the three institutions according to the prescriptions of the amended *Normae*. Joseph Murphy, the former provincial, had replaced J. Harding Fisher as rector of Fordham University. Given Murphy's constitutional reservations and rigid personality, this choice of succession did not solve the problems at the Rose Hill Campus. While no conclusions had been reached at the University of San Francisco, where dual control seemed more successful than elsewhere, a certain amount of dissatisfaction had surfaced at Loyola in Chicago, where Robert J. Willmes was about to succeed Egan, the newly appointed provincial. The provincials were weary of continually assessing the virtues of a method of governance that was admittedly based on trial and error and, indeed, might be canonically irregular; and Father Janssens himself was not particularly helpful. The General confessed to Rooney in 1947 "that up to the present he had not had time to go into this matter thoroughly but that he intended to do so with Father Assistant (McCormick)."[34]

The president of the JEA may not have found that promise of collaboration entirely reassuring. In any event, it was time to make a specific proposal to the new General and to petition a definite answer. Consequently, the two provincials who were most affected, John McMahon of New York and Leo Sullivan of Chicago, requested the Executive Committee once again to examine and propose constitutionally viable ways of providing for a division of executive functions in complex Jesuit institutions in the United States. As the provincials noted, article 18 of the *Instruction* gave legality to their mandate.

A subcommittee of five, which included most of the old guard, was appointed to this task.[35] To avoid the mistakes of the past, and profit by the experience of those in possession of hard information, Hugh Duce, as the province prefect on the scene in California, was asked to interview O'Sullivan and Dunne at the University of San Francisco; Maline would review the situation with Egan and Hussey at Loyola; and Rooney bravely agreed to approach Murphy and Gannon at Fordham. Originally scheduled for mid-November 1948, the meeting had to be postponed to December due to the sudden (but temporary) illness of two of the members. Rooney, one of those on the sicklist, explained to Mallon, the other casualty, and also to Edward Bunn, who had pleaded for more time, why it was imperative to hold the meeting before the new year. According to Provincial McMahon, Rome was anxious to resolve the matter, and "the end of January or the beginning of February might be too late for our views to be of any influence in the ultimate decision."[36] Moreover, Rooney continued — this piece of information was "strictly confidential" — there would be a change at Fordham in the near future. Obviously, this could only refer to the appointment of a new president. The form of governance, however, was cause for speculation.

The subcommittee met at Saint Louis University from December 16 to 21, 1948, and, in spite of the short period, produced an impressive document.[37] It was a last-ditch effort to provide reasonable recommendations that had a good chance of success and were, at the same time, consistent with the traditions and constitutions of the Society. On the eve of the meeting, and before he left New York City, Rooney had an interesting conversation with the New York provincial, John McMahon, who said that "Father Vincent McCormick has changed his opinion. He is definitely now of [the] opinion that [the] Superior of [the] Community should be subordinate to the Rector."[38] Given McCormick's influence in Rome, it was immediately clear to the president of the JEA that such a recommendation, or variation of the same, would be favorably received. It would appear, however, that the committee members approached their assignment without precommitments or notable preferences. All agreed — and this was the point of reference — that a division of labor was absolutely necessary in the complex universities. They understood also that if the committee did not contribute to a solution, the solution would be imposed, as it were, by remote control.

Building on the work of the 1946 committee, the subcommittee of five listed four possible *formulae* for an administrative design involving dual control. The members quickly passed over the first option, currently in place, which provided for a rector and dependent president. The second option called for a rector-president with an independent religious superior.[39] In this administrative design, the rector-president administered, with primary and full authority, the entire educational enterprise. However, he was not a local superior but was, in fact and in law, a religious subject of the superior who had the canonical status of a local superior.[40] In this arrangement there could be no appeal from rector-president to superior, or vice versa; a subject could have recourse to the provincial to whom both officials reported. Jesuit canonists agreed that, technically, the General, with plenary power, could provide for such a division of authority. However, the novel concept of a rector who was not a local superior seemed so contrary to the traditions of the Society as to jeopardize this *modus agendi.* In addition, as the subcommittee members admitted, such a division would tend to destroy the essential unity of a Jesuit's apostolic life; he would be forced to think of his academic work in the university as distinct from his life as a religious.[41] He might even run the risk, and biblical prediction, of trying to serve two masters.

The third form of governance, proposed by the committee, provided for a rector-president plus a dependent religious superior—an option which, in the immediate future, became the most successful, had the most advantages and the fewest disadvantages. In this form, which presented no canonical problems, the president had complete authority to administer the university; he was also the canonical *Superior localis.* Under him, the dependent superior had delegated authority and responsibility "to provide for the spiritual and temporal care of the Community."[42] This form completely satisfied civil and canonical requirements; it was also in accord with the traditional pattern of paternal government in the Society. Not only was the channel of authority, from General to superior, clear, but this design preserved both the moral unity of the institution and the integrity of the religious apostolate of higher education.[43]

After a description of the four options, with a candid enumeration of the advantages and disadvantages of each, the committee drew up a detailed set of norms for each option and a set of statutes governing the responsibilities of officials in a complex institution.[44] This was a valuable contribution. The norms for the appointment and office of a dependent superior were especially detailed and, with few emendations, were accepted by the provincials. The statutes were incorporated from those already formulated by the Executive Committee in 1940 and 1942. Since the committee was working under pressure, it was decided, on the recommendation of Rooney, that these statutes, forming part V of the report, should regulate the offices of president and vice president, if that option were installed.[45] Completed in haste, under pressure imposed by the provincials, the minutes of the December meeting, signed by Julian Maline, secretary, were dated January 4, 1949, and sent on to the provincials.

In one sense, the proposals became academic. It would appear that Rome had made a decision even as the special subcommittee was making its recommendations to the provincials. On February 2, 1949, in confirmation of Rooney's prediction, Laurence McGinley was appointed rector-president of Fordham University, without benefit—as everyone was quick to note—of a religious superior of the Jesuit community. But he was not one to avoid his responsibilities. (Father McGinley, who entered the Society in 1922, had earned a doctorate in sacred theology at the Gregorian University and had served for a number of years as dean of studies at Woodstock College. Distinguished in appearance and accomplishments, he enlarged the academic scope of Fordham, was prominent in the educational councils of New York State, and urged the administrators of smaller Catholic colleges to play a more active role in American higher education.) In his case, it was clear that the General, accepting advice from several sources, had decided that the "experiment" had not worked at Fordham. But the question of dual control, in some form, was still debated at provincials' meetings and at the Roman Curia.

The next move came quickly. In the fall of 1952, Edward B. Bunn, the former dynamic president of Loyola College, Baltimore, and energetic province prefect, succeeded J. Hunter Guthrie as rector-president of Georgetown University. Shortly thereafter, Vincent L. Keelan, who had served as the first provincial of the recently established Maryland Province, was appointed superior of the Jesuit community. It was the first appearance of a dependent superior, which, from the start, was the most successful division of labor in this new form of governance. This system was next installed at Boston College, where Joseph R. N. Maxwell, appointed rector-president in 1951, welcomed Urban W. Manning as the dependent superior of the community in 1954. In that same year, John J. Kehoe was named superior of the Fordham community when that institution entered another cycle, more successful than in the past, in the dual system of control.

Rome had finally become convinced that, of the options offered, this structure of governance was most in accord with the traditions of the Society. Father Rooney, who had now revised his opinion in light of the evidence, may have had some role in forming the General's mind. Recording his conversation with Janssens on September 11, 1954, Rooney wrote:

> I told Father General that it was now my firm conviction that the Rector-President arrangement wherein the Rector is over the President is a failure; that it is not working and cannot work; and I asked him not to allow it to be introduced in any other institution. I said that at present I favored the Rector (President) and Local Dependent Superior arrangement, and that, as far as I know, it was working well at Fordham, Georgetown and Boston College.[46]

Whether Rooney's intervention was persuasive or not, the preferred form of governance for complex institutions duplicated the pattern of those three schools. In the following months, Paul C. Reinert, rector-president at Saint Louis University, welcomed William J. Fitzgerald as dependent superior of the Jesuit community. Shortly thereafter, Albert C. Zuercher, former provincial of the Missouri Province, was named superior of the community at Marquette, where Edward O'Donnell was the president. However, both the University of Detroit, where Celistine Steiner had begun his long tenure as president, and the University of San Francisco were apparently satisfied to retain the old plan.[47]

Administratively, the *governance* of Jesuit colleges and universities was closely connected with Jesuit *control* of those institutions. There was a real, though intriguing, distinction between the two concepts, and the resolution of this question was initially complicated by the increase of lay colleagues in administrative positions. The discussion turned particularly on the role of Jesuit regents in the professional schools, where lay deans had administrative authority. This question, which had long claimed the attention of the Executive Committee and the presidents, involved technical distinctions applied to the general area of governance, that is, government itself, institutional control, administration, and supervision. The problem was compounded in the case of delegated authority. In all cases it was made clear that the dean was the administrator of his school, with direct authority from the president; the Jesuit regent was the liaison who represented the total university in the deliberations of a particular school. In theory, the lines were clearly drawn; in practice there could be gray areas. A strong dean might ignore the regent; a strong regent could intimidate a dean. But basically the discussion turned on who was in effective control of a particular professional school — law, medicine, dentistry, social work, management. The solution had profound implications for the Jesuit apostolate of education.

In 1954 a subcommittee of the Executive Committee recommended that "the office of regent be gradually discontinued where it exists, and not be established in any new situations."[48] Actually, the move to eliminate regents did not have the unanimous support of the presidents since, at a few institutions, regents continued to fulfill a useful function.[49] While the provincials appreciated the advice of the Executive Committee, the board, with its usual prudence, felt that "owing to peculiar province problems, the ultimate decision on this matter will have to be worked out on a province basis."[50] Two years later, answering a second appeal, the provincials were more specific. They urged the Executive Committee "to continue to study the subject of the role of regents, with emphasis on the basic problems of what control we wish to exercise in our professional schools, what is effective control, and what is the best administrative arrangement to secure this control."[51]

As the Commission on Professional Schools, at the suggestion of the Executive Committee, was debating the merits of the case, Rooney made a bold, but sensible, recommendation to the Board of Governors. He urged that the question of regents be remanded to the presidents since the subject was of intimate and ultimate concern to them. "The making of this study," he explained, "would afford an excellent occasion to hold a meeting of the presidents of our colleges and universities."[52] With the approval of the board, the Conference of Presidents was thus officially established, with enormous consequences that were not then appreciated by the president of the JEA.[53]

The meeting of the Conference of Presidents at Georgetown in 1958 was another benchmark in the history of the JEA. Already alluded to in connection with expansion, the annual conference provided the presidents a forum for high-level discussions and a platform for national announcements. It was through their conference, later raised to a commission, that the presidents began to play a more active, energetic, and aggressive role in the JEA. In fact, it was through this conference that the JEA began to gain national exposure through the media — more, indeed, than the president of the JEA had counted on. It was at this first meeting, therefore, that the presidents, in order to establish their Jesuit roots and in conformity to the mandate of the provincials, grappled with the problems of institutional control, the juridical aspects of ownership, and the function of trustees and consultors.[54] (There were, of course, other items on the agenda: tuition rates, admission standards, federal aid, and scholarships. These topics, however, affected the internal policies of individual institutions, which are beyond the scope of this study.)

One of the important steps taken by this conference was the decision to establish a Jesuit research council or commission. This development illustrated, once again, the national potential — indeed dimension — of the JEA and the residual benefits of union and cooperation. This was not a hasty decision. The plan had been under discussion since 1957, when, in common with all institutions of higher learning in the United States, the accent was on scientific research (after Russia had put the world's first satellite in orbit). The idea of a research council had grown out of a meeting (in 1957) of the research committee of the Conference of Jesuit Schools of Engineering. The prime movers were C. G. Duncombe and Ralph Trese of the faculty of the School of Engineering at the University of Detroit,[55] and the background is of some interest.

In 1956, at a meeting at Iowa State University, Victor J. Blum, S.J., chairman of the Conference of Jesuit Schools of Engineering, had appointed a committee on cooperative research. That committee submitted a report to the Executive Committee, which, in turn, approved the recommendations and returned them to the conference for implementation. On April 26, 1957, at the University of Detroit, the conference made a formal motion to establish a Jesuit Research Council. Although Rooney had originally planned to contact the presidents, he suddenly decided, due to movements in the world of science, to present these recent developments immediately to the Board of Governors.[56]

Convinced of the importance of such a council or commission, the provincials approved the initial recommendations of Duncombe and Trese and instructed Rooney to explain to the presidents (by letter) the purpose of the proposed council.[57] It was also agreed that, with added information on policy, purpose, and procedure, the president of the JEA would present the total package to the Board of Governors at its annual meeting in May 1958. The presidents, with Sputnik as a catalyst, anticipated the action of the board, and at their meeting in January 1958 "approved the establishment of a national Jesuit Commission on Research."[58] It was later recommended, and the provincials approved, that the name be changed to Jesuit Research Council of the JEA; it was finally, and officially, known as the Jesuit Research Council of America (JRCA). The bylaws were also approved, and included as an appendix to Rooney's report to the board.[59]

Since the JRCA enhanced the national image of Jesuit higher education, at a time when science was in the ascendancy across the country and the federal Government was sponsoring basic research, it will be to the point to give a brief explanation of its function. According to the bylaws,

> The purpose of the Council shall be to extend the potential for, and further the prosecution of, basic and applied research in all member institutions, insofar as such research is compatible with the purpose of the member institutions.[60]

Articles IV through X provide for the officers and directors of the council, their method of election, term of office, and duties. The two important officers were the chairman of the Board of Directors and the executive director.

Ralph Trese, who could claim distinction as one of the founders, was the first executive director. Due to lack of space elsewhere, his office was located at the University of Detroit, which — inevitably — tended to identify the council with that institution. His duties, as described in the bylaws, were to maintain an inventory of faculty and equipment in the cooperating Jesuit institutions and to locate research projects, formulate proposals, and contact sponsors.[61] He was also required to submit a semiannual report to the president of the JEA.[62] By most accounts, Trese was efficient, competent, energetic, and enthusiastic. According to his reports, he was cordially received during campus visitations (otherwise, he operated through an institutional representative). However — it will come as no surprise to those familiar with the academic mind — the vote for Ralph Trese was not unanimous. Senior science professors, who had already opened lines of communication to government agencies or private foundations, preferred to pursue contracts through personal contacts, rather than through the council. On the other hand, the JRCA was very helpful to young researchers who had not yet mastered the intricacies and diplomacy of research proposals.

Trese was succeeded in 1962 by the more sophisticated James L. Robillard, a Marquette graduate, who had been associated with the Office of Development at the University of Chicago.[63] Upon the initiative of the presidents, and with added financial support, Robillard moved his operation to Washington, D.C., where national organizations and prestigious universities maintained their offices. To counter the Russian challenge, the federal government had appropriated large sums of money which were distributed through the appropriate agencies. Contracts, more often than not, went to those who were familiar with the Washington scene and on hand to bring their proposals to the proper person and desk.[64]

The presidents of the twenty-two cooperating institutions elected the nine-member Board of Directors. The directors, in turn, elected as their first chairman the dean of the Graduate School at Saint Louis University. Robert J. Henle, who entered the Society in 1927 and was ordained in 1940, was already prominent in JEA committees and commissions. A man of robust health and boundless energy, he had, even as a scholastic, given evidence of future leadership in academic administration. In addition to his work as dean, he was conspicuous at the annual JEA meeting and he guided the sessions of the important Institute on Philosophy and Theology. (He served later as president of Georgetown University.) Henle appreciated the possibilities latent in a national Jesuit research effort and, with the assistance of the members of the board, worked hard to make an initial impact in the world of science.[65] Though impatient by nature, he was a realist, and realized that the new venture would require time to mature.

The presidents, meanwhile, encouraged by the progress made at Georgetown, began to campaign more actively for a greater share in the policymaking councils of the JEA. Meeting at Rockhurst College in 1959, the presidents were more and more concerned with national issues and events that affected higher education.[66] They analyzed the problems and opportunities created by enactment of the National Defense Education Act of 1958; calculated the implications of predicted legislation on loan programs, taxexemption, the required oath of allegiance; and assessed the advantages of cooperative planning among Jesuit institutions, as well as recruitment and retention of faculty.[67]

At the conclusion of the meeting, the presidents released a statement to the press which was derived from the NDEA. They praised the educational aims of the act, which was designed to correct an imbalance among college students in the pursuit of scientific studies. The Jesuit presidents also "appreciate[d] the contemporary circumstances which in the practical order have orientated the Federal Government's educational activities primarily toward defense"[68] — but defense should also include "some perception of those values of mind and heart which by his very nature man is committed to defend."[69] Then, taking advantage of the opportunity for national publicity, they concluded:

> For over four centuries Jesuit schools have sought to inculcate in their students a pursuit of excellence in mental and moral development, both as the duty of the patriot and the obligation of the Christian. The presidents judge that in pursuing this traditional ideal the Jesuit colleges and universities of the United States, currently enrolling 114,000 students, will best serve the defense of the nation.[70]

At Rockhurst, the presidents suggested "that for the next meeting plans be made well in advance, and that a group of presidents be named as a Planning Committee."[71] It had already been decided to hold the 1960 meeting in Boston, in conjunction with the annual meeting of the Association of American Colleges, and Michael P. Walsh, of Boston College, had offered to host the meeting. Suspicious of a move toward more independence on the part of the presidents, Rooney, in his report to the provincials, recommended that if the meeting of presidents were to become an annual affair, "it might be well if the presidents were constituted a JEA Conference of Presidents of Jesuit Colleges and Universities, so as to bring these meetings strictly within the Jesuit Educational Association."[72] In an attempt to persuade the provincials to follow his lead, he added that he had sounded out a number of presidents on this point "and each one to whom I mentioned it was quite enthusiastic about the idea."[73] This was not an accurate representation. The presidents were not interested in a "conference" status that would, in the JEA hierarchy of authority, equate them with historians, seismologists, and librarians, even though they admired the work done by those people.[74]

The Presidential Planning Committee, appointed by Rooney, held its first meeting at Fairfield University, March 30, 1959. Michael P. Walsh, who had assumed the presidency of Boston College in 1958, was the chairman. Holding a Ph.D. in biology from Fordham, and an admirer of Robert I. Gannon, Walsh was eager to build on the foundation laid by his predecessor, Joseph R. N. Maxwell, and move his institution along the road to a modern university. Combining the inherited instincts of a politician with the training of an academician, he worked hard to improve the standards of Jesuit colleges, and his own institution in particular. In this endeavor, he was not one to suffer gladly the constitutional restraints of the JEA.

The other members of the committee, all of whom had established reputations, were equally unhappy with the role assigned to them in the constitutional structure. Laurence McGinley of Fordham, who had emerged as the spokesman for independent higher education in New York, was keenly aware of the influence that could be exerted by twenty-eight college presidents. In hindsight, and upon careful reading of the record, the president of Saint Louis University could be considered the ringleader of this clerical, low-key rebellion. Paul C. Reinert, with a solid doctorate in educational administration from the University of Chicago, was a genuine professional. A strong administrator, he had continued, and strengthened, the academic traditions at Saint Louis, where he was successful in developing a public relations program that enlisted the aid of the business community in that city. Saint Louis University, always an important segment of the JEA, was becoming the leader of Catholic higher education in the Midwest. Reinert, more than any other Jesuit president, was determined to win for the presidents the position to which they were entitled within the organization. In the long run, he was successful.

Charles S. Casassa, a shrewd, affable, and able president, was slowly but surely transforming Loyola University from the role of a community college to the position of an influential urban university in Los Angeles. With intelligence and charm, he had persuaded the affluent citizens of Southern California to support his plans for a bigger and better Loyola. Preferring diplomacy to confrontation, he exhibited "the fine Italian hand" within the Presidents' Conference. His colleague on the West Coast was A. A. Lemieux, a straightforward, no-nonsense administrator, who would never blink when it came time to vote. Ruggedly built, he gave the impression of a strong character, which stood him in good stead at Seattle University. He would support a legitimate challenge to the authority of the president of the JEA. The sixth member of the Planning Committee, ensuring geographical representation, was W. Patrick Donnelly, president of Loyola University in New Orleans. Like his predecessors, he had to guide his institution through the hazardous intricacies of Southern associations and politics. An authentic agent of New Orleans hospitality, he could also be tough in protecting the rights and privileges of a Catholic university in a sometimes hostile environment.

The Planning Committee met morning and afternoon at Fairfield on March 30, 1959. As a result of their discussions, the six presidents made two substantive recommendations to the provincials. First, "the Jesuit Presidents recommend to the Board of Governors for their consideration and approval the establishment of a Council of Presidents of Jesuit Colleges and Universities within the framework of the Jesuit Educational Association."[75] Membership in the council would consist of the twenty-eight presidents and the president of JEA. In addition—and this was important—"a Chairman would be elected by the Presidents for a two year term and an executive committee of four additional members on a rotating basis."[76] The prerogatives of the council were specific: it would conduct an annual meeting and plan the agenda for the meeting; appoint, when necessary, standing committees to work on common problems; and concern itself with areas similar to those which were discussed at the past two meetings of Jesuit presidents.[77]

The second resolution was closely tied to the first. The presidents, in their own words, "unanimously convinced that there is an imperative need of creating the proper national image of the unique strength and quality of the Jesuit Colleges and Universities . . . recommend that the first project of their newly-formed Council be the establishment of a program to improve the public understanding and acceptance of Jesuit Higher Education."[78] This preeminent objective would be achieved "by the appointment of a qualified Jesuit whose full or at least part-time duty would be that of working with the Presidents in creating and projecting this national image."[79]

The committee suggested some ways in which this project could be implemented: accurate formulation of the unique characteristics of Jesuit higher education; closer cooperation with experts in communications to gain national publicity for Jesuit achievements; more effective use of statistics that would justify the legitimacy of Jesuit claims to federal and foundation grants.[80] To dispel the impression that they envisioned an independent operation, the presidents understood, and agreed, that the Jesuit who was charged with this responsibility "would work in immediate relationship to the President of the Jesuit Educational Association, since this would be a part of the Association's total program."[81]

The presidents, in fact, recognized the advantages of working within the organization which, through union and cooperation, had done much to advance the cause of Jesuit higher education. Moreover, they realized their critical dependence on the Board of Governors for manpower — for young, qualified Jesuits to staff their institutions. They were fully aware of the disadvantages of isolation. Nevertheless, they clearly — and understandably — wanted a greater voice in the policy-making machinery since execution of that policy was largely their responsibility. They were particularly concerned that province prefects for secondary schools were so intimately involved in shaping the academic life of Jesuit universities.

In their regular meeting, March 1959, the Executive Committee recommended to the Board of Governors "that the group of presidents be recognized as a Conference of the J.E.A."[82] However, at a supplementary session of the Executive Committee, held after the presidents' meeting at Fairfield, the committee voted to approve the first proposal, that is, that a Council of Presidents be established. It recommended, however, that the proposal for a structured program of public relations be returned to the committee for further study. It was now up to the president of the JEA to present the proposals of the presidents and the recommendations of the Executive Committee to the Board of Governors.

A very intelligent man, with twenty-two years of experience as executive director, Rooney immediately recognized the implications of the presidents' proposal for a council. The twenty-eight chief executives, organized as a council, might be considered a board of directors. With their own executive committee and chairman, and in control of their own agenda, the council would almost duplicate the structure of the JEA. In any event, it was clear to Rooney that this power play, if successful, would remove an important group from his jurisdiction and, without an intermediate buffer, could exert powerful pressure on the provincials. Indeed, since the presidents, by their very position, had a built-in guarantee of exposure and publicity which the president of the JEA could not match, they would be in a position to exploit this advantage to their own purposes.

After digesting Rooney's "Report," the provincials were in something of a dilemma. On the one hand, the presidents constituted a strong lobby; on the other, Rooney had seniority. The solution was, as is so often the case, a compromise. The Board of Governors approved "the establishment of a Council or Conference of Presidents . . . within the framework of the JEA."[83] However, the board wished that "for the time being, the term, Conference of Presidents, be used rather than Council of Presidents."[84] The question of changing "conference" to "council" at a future date should be discussed by a subcommittee on the revision of the JEA Constitution.[85] Moving on to a decision on the program of public relations, the board directed that this proposal be remanded to the Executive Committee, which, after further study, should forward its recommendation to the provincials.[86]

Rooney, in fact, had gone out of his way to shape this response. He admitted to the Executive Committee that when he reported to the provincials on the presidents' proposal, "I added orally that the attitude of the members of the Executive Committee seemed to be that before a Jesuit is appointed to the office of the JEA as an Assistant for Public Relations, it is much more important that two specialists be appointed, one for higher education and one for secondary education, to assist in the work of the JEA Central Office."[87] Again—off the record, as it were—he added: "Without putting this [comment] in the response to my report, the Provincials told me that they were sympathetic to this idea, but wished the Executive Committee to present specific suggestions, names etc."[88]

The twenty-eight presidents had lost the first round to a worthy opponent, but it was too early to predict the final outcome. At their 1960 meeting at Boston College (now with "conference" status), the presidents renewed their efforts to obtain satisfaction. With the president of the JEA in attendance, "many [presidents] expressed dissatisfaction with the present status of the Conference in relation to the JEA and several criticized the present structure of the JEA."[89] First noting that three groups were responsible for Jesuit higher education in the United States—the Board of Governors, the presidents, and the Executive Committee—the presidents articulated their criticisms. They alleged that the presidents were not kept adequately informed of major decisions, that the Executive Committee was too isolated and uninformed on the presidents' real concerns, that the structure made it unnecessarily difficult to process recommendations within a reasonable time. They also recommended that the Executive Committee be expanded so as to give better representation to the colleges and universities.[90] Finally, in a two-part resolution, offered by Father McGinley, the presidents unanimously recommended:

> That in redrafting the Constitutions [sic] of the JEA provision be made for a more direct advisory role of the Conference of Jesuit Presidents on higher educational policy;
>
> That meanwhile the Executive Committee of the JEA formally notify the Conference of Jesuit Presidents in advance of their January meeting about any matters of major concern to the colleges and universities which will be presented to the Board of Governors at their May meeting so that the recommendations of the Conference of Jesuit Presidents may be fully presented to the Board of Governors; and that the current Chairman of the Conference of Jesuit Presidents be available to make this presentation or explain it if necessary.[91]

After gently reminding the presidents that much of the information they sought had routinely been sent to them, Rooney promised to bring their comments, criticisms, and resolution to the attention of the board. He was faithful to this pledge in his report of May 1960.

Once again, however, the presidents were disappointed at the "Response" of the provincials, which was tailored to the known preference of the president of the JEA. In a covering letter to the presidents, attached to the provincials' "Response," Rooney wrote that, in his oral report, he explained in detail to the Board of Governors the resolution passed by the Conference of Presidents. "I did my best to interpret the desires of the Presidents . . . and answered many questions put to me by the Provincials."[92] Moreover, so that no stone would be left unturned to represent the mind of the presidents, Father Casassa, in place of the unavailable Paul Reinert, was invited to present the presidents' case to the board. Therefore, "the *Response* of the Board of Governors was made only after a most thorough discussion of all sides of the question."[93]

Be that as it may, the presidents gained very little satisfaction in this second skirmish with the chairman of the Executive Committee, whose influence was still paramount in the councils of the JEA. In their official reply, the provincials first congratulated the presidents on their cooperation, as a conference, with the Executive Committee and "the enthusiasm with which the Conference" had treated a number of problems in Jesuit higher education. With that introduction, which may have caused the presidents to smile, the board came to the point. First, in the revision of the constitution, provision would be made "for the role of all Conferences within the framework of the JEA."[94] Second, college presidents and high school rectors would be included in the membership of commissions; indeed, there might even be a Commission of College and University Administrators. Third, the provincials explained that since four of the ten provinces had only one province prefect, it would be impractical to divide the work of the Executive Committee into secondary and postsecondary responsibility. Fourth, the board declined to increase the Executive Committee with the inclusion of two members from the Presidents' Conference. The solution for closer cooperation, the provincials suggested, would be for a president to represent his conference at meetings of the Executive Committee, either by request or invitation. By the same token, the province prefects might attend the presidents' meetings, an expedient which the presidents had previously opposed.[95]

The presidents could only be unhappy at this negative response to what they perceived as reasonable demands. But they were not discouraged; nor did they contemplate surrender. If the president of the JEA thought he had put the fire out, he was mistaken. The embers were still smoldering, and so was the resentment. In the meantime, they continued to concentrate their major efforts on the expansion and academic excellence of their respective institutions.

MEMBERS OF THE INTER-PROVINCE COMMITTEE, WESTON
COLLEGE, DECEMBER 1928. Front row, left to right: William
T. Tallon (Md.-N.Y.), Joseph Walsh (N.O.), John Creeden
(N.E.), Charles Carroll (Cal.), and Albert Fox (Mo.); second
row: Samuel Horine (Mo.), Edward Tivnan (N.E.), John
McCormick (Mo.),   Charles Deane (Md.-N.Y.), and
William Lonergan (Cal.); third row: unidentified, Francis
Connell (Md.-N.Y.), Louis Gallagher (N.E.), Joseph Kearns
(N.O.), and Cornelius Bulman (N.E.).

MEMBERS OF THE 1931 SPECIAL COMMISSION ON HIGHER STUDIES.
Left to right: Edward Tivnan (N.E.), Charles Carroll (Cal.),
Albert Fox (Chicago), Charles Deane (Md.-N.Y.), James
Macelwane, chairman (Mo.), and John Hynes (N.O.).

PEDRO ARRUPE, S.J.
General of the Society of
Jesus, 1965-1983

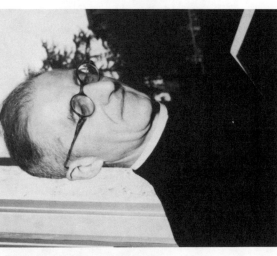

JOHN BAPTIST JANSSENS, S.J.
General of the Society of
Jesus, 1946-1964

WLODIMIR LEDOCHOWSKI, S.J.
General of the Society of
Jesus, 1915-1942

PAUL C. REINERT, S.J.
President of the Jesuit
Educational Association,
1966-1970

EDWARD B. ROONEY, S.J.
President of the Jesuit
Educational Association,
1937-1966

DANIEL M. O'CONNELL, S.J.
First National Secretary
of the Jesuit Educational
Association, 1934-1937

MEETING OF J.E.A. BOARD OF GOVERNORS, NEW YORK, MAY 7, 1952.
Seated, left to right: Joseph W. Egan (Chicago), John J. McMahon,
chairman (N.Y.), Harold O. Small (Ore.); standing, left to right: David
Nugent (Md.), William E. FitzGerald (N.E.), A. William Crandell
(N.O.), Daniel H. Conway (Mo.), and George Nunan (Upper Can.).
Joseph D. O'Brien (Cal.) was absent.


AMERICAN PROVINCIALS ATTENDING THE 28TH GENERAL CONGREGATION IN
GROUP PICTURE WITH FATHER GENERAL LEDOCHOWSKI. Seated, left to
right: Peter Brooks (Mo.), Zacheus Maher (Amer. Assistant), Father
General, James Dolan (N.E.), and William Magee (Chicago); standing,
left to right: Joseph Murphy (Md.-N.Y.), Thomas Shields (N.O.), Walter
Fitzgerald (Ore.), and Francis Seeliger (Cal.).

# 8. Coordination and Cooperation, 1955–1965

AT THE PRESIDENTS' CONFERENCE in 1959, Father Casassa, of Loyola University in Los Angeles, introduced a discussion on "the possibility of cooperative planning with regard to graduate programs."[1] The obvious reason for cooperation, as he succinctly put it, was to "bring about better quality in graduate programs and a consequent upgrading of Catholic intellectual activity."[2] The happy result, in Hamlet's immortal words, would be "a consummation devoutly to be wished." In adding this topic to its agenda, the conference was acknowledging the *raison d'être* of the Jesuit Educational Association. Union and cooperation were the twin pedestals on which the *novus ordo* of Jesuit higher education in the United States would be constructed. It was primarily a weakness at the graduate level which had persuaded Father Ledochowski to impose the *Instruction* on the American provinces. Cooperation, the heart of that document, had already been seized upon by combinations of other institutions in order to raise their standards and reduce their costs.[3] The same practice could, many Jesuits thought, lead to departmental preeminence in Jesuit institutions. In any case, it seemed self-evident that cooperation, by whatever name, must replace institutional competition if graduate programs were to command respect in the critical world of academe.

A campaign for ways and means to achieve excellence — although there is no magic to it — began in 1948 when the JEA Commission on Graduate Schools inaugurated its regular sessions. The commission, meeting at Marquette, recommended "that Jesuit graduate schools cooperate with other graduate schools in their areas."[4] This general statement, with which few could quarrel, was approved by the Executive Committee. Rooney, however, was more specific. He informed the committee that he intended to recommend to the Board of Governors "that our graduate schools attempt to consolidate their forces in certain departments in which each school might develop preeminence."⁵ True to his word, in his report to the board he repeated the remarks he had made to the delegates to the annual meeting of the JEA in San Francisco. His basic premise was that if uncoordinated expansion continued, it would be impossible for Jesuit graduate schools to build "top-flight departments in every field."⁶ If, however, the colleges and universities could develop strong programs at the undergraduate and master's levels, the graduates would then be directed — for the doctorate — to a particular institution for a particular program. As his examples, he chose Saint Louis for philosophy and Georgetown for political science or government.

Examples apart, Rooney told the provincials: "The point I am trying to make is that to attempt to build up sixteen Jesuit graduate schools with six or eight departments leading to the doctorate, to try to staff all of these schools with competent Jesuits and laymen, and to build up adequate libraries worthy of graduate work is taking on more than our share, and more than we can effectively carry out."⁷

This was, in general, a good description of the academic perils of duplication at the doctoral level, and over the years the problem was many times restated, often with added refinements. The Executive Committee resorted to various expedients to achieve compliance. As one means of securing, even forcing, the coordination of graduate programs, "the Executive Committee went on record to recommend that no permission for expansion in the doctoral field be requested from V. R. Father General until the Prefect of Studies of the province concerned has had the opportunity to discuss the request with the Executive Committee of the JEA."⁸ The warning was repeated the next year, with a reminder that the NCEA was considering the same question. The committee then enunciated its principle of coordination: *"Preeminence in a particular field by one institution in a definite region should be supported by all other Jesuit institutions in that region."*⁹

It is one thing, of course, to recognize a problem and quite another to solve it, and, it is painful to record that this lofty academic ideal, which depended upon so many variables, was never really implemented. Some of the problems were pedestrian. While they gladly admitted the benefits of cooperation in theory, the deans of Jesuit graduate schools, together with the commission, recognized the difficulties inherent in this grandiose plan. Geography, for example, was a factor. Jesuit universities were not clustered in localities; they were located regionally. Distances between Boston College, Fordham, and Georgetown, on the East Coast, would not be easily overcome by peripatetic (and frequently indigent) graduate students who did not normally enjoy the economic choices of established scholars. The problem would be even greater in the Midwest and Far West. Moreover, since members of the Society were largely involved in this grand design, provincials would have to cooperate in assigning Jesuits across province lines, if there were to be more than a token expression of support. At another level, presidents would be reluctant to lose a research professor to strengthen another institution. Exchanges and reciprocity would be difficult to arrange, especially in the sciences, where grants were made to a particular department and a particular researcher. An adjustment for lay professors and their families would be even more complicated.

The Executive Committee, despite the obstacles, persevered in its efforts to advance this worthy project. "While admitting the [Graduate] Commission's main point that complete integration and coordination of graduate offerings is, because of conflicting needs of local clientele, neither feasible nor desirable, the Committee felt that further study of the matter might result in the assignment of certain specialized areas, e.g., in the general field of history, to particular graduate schools, much as has been done in geophysics at Saint Louis University and in the Russian Institute at Fordham University."[10] The committee implied that emphasis on coordination would also tend to eliminate, at least partially, the danger of overexpansion.

Father General Janssens, through his ordinary sources of information, was very much aware of the problem. In 1948, in his letter to the American provincials on the eve of their annual meeting, he had made his position crystal clear. His sage advice — almost an admonition — deserves to be quoted at length since his analysis went to the heart of the matter.

> The multiplication of graduate schools in the universities and colleges of the Assistancy results in an uneconomical drain on very limited manpower, an inadequacy of scientific apparatus, e.g., libraries, and a possible consequent low level of scholarship. There may be external forces demanding graduate schools in most if not all the colleges; but is it demanded that graduate studies be offered by each in all departments? Cannot the Provinces pool, as it were, their resources and offer high-level excellently staffed and equipped graduate schools in philosophy in one university, in physical sciences in another, in political sciences in a third, in history and languages, etc. in still another? I can understand that it may be difficult and require much time to create this complete unifica-

tion of efforts in the same field; but should not a step be taken at once in that direction? Perhaps Provinces that are closer to each other historically, territorially, and culturally might form a group to initiate this unification. I would urge your Reverences to give serious consideration to this proposal and, after you have consulted with your officials in the educational works of the Assistancy and Provinces, to let me know your findings and resolutions.[11]

Providing further evidence of his personal interest in the matter, the General continued to press the provincials for some kind of action. He included the following paragraph in his letter to the chairman of the 1951 annual meeting:

In the response of the Board of Governors to the report of Father Rooney for 1950, I was pleased to note that the need of consolidating Graduate work in our Universities was stressed. Several years have passed since this was proposed to YRs [your Reverences]. Let it begin on a regional basis and in a restricted number of fields at first; but what is important is that it begin.[12]

One year later, he repeated the strictures of his previous letters. He reminded the provincials of "the proposal I made to pool and coordinate these resources—a proposal based not only on obvious reasons drawn from objective circumstances, but also on strong recommendations made to me from the Assistancy."[13] Janssens complained that, as far as he could tell, "no effective step has been taken to implement my recommendation."[14] In the meantime, he cautioned, "it seems more prudent to withhold approval of any new doctoral courses."[15] The General's letter had contained a hint of impatience at what he apparently considered the provincials' procrastination. In a hurry to correct that impression, John McMahon, a gentle man and observant religious, who was provincial of the New York Province, sharpened the focus of the agenda for the May meeting of the Board of Governors. It was decided that Rooney, who had led the fight for cooperation, should do yet another study "of Catholic Graduate Schools, in particular Jesuit Schools, to determine a policy of National or Regional Scope whereby graduate work, especially on the doctoral level, might be restricted, and arrangements be made for an interchange of professors."[16] The provincials also demanded an explanation of the "multiplication of Graduate Courses in the Colleges of the Assistancy."[17] The president of the JEA obviously had his work cut out for him. Actually, Rooney remanded this project to the JEA Commission on Graduate Schools, which, presumably, the provincials had expected.

In 1953 the commission, for the first time, made an attempt critically to address the questions raised by the General and provincials. On March 12, Rooney submitted to the Board of Governors a "Report of the Meetings of the Commission on Graduate Schools of the JEA held at Saint Louis University, December 6–7, 1952, and Loyola University, Chicago, February 7, 1953."[18] This report, edited by Stewart E. Dollard, dean of the Graduate School at Loyola, Chicago, and chairman of the commission, defined the members' understanding of "coordination" and "cooperation" in the context.

> By "coordination" we understand an ordering of our resources at the institutional, Provincial, inter-Provincial, or Assistancy levels which will best obtain the objectives of Graduate Jesuit education in the United States. By "cooperation" we mean helping to achieve an end agreed upon by doing the specific part assigned or by helping others to do their part. Coordination and cooperation understood in this sense will tend to integrate all Jesuit graduate work in the United States.[19]

Throughout the report, a valid distinction was made between the master's and doctor's levels with respect to resources, objectives, and the criteria for initiating or discontinuing such programs. The provincials approved the report, a copy of which was sent to the General, but requested additional information on part III, which was entitled "Doctorate Work for Preeminent Intellectual Leadership." This part of the report had never been completed.[20] Given the General's professed interest in this project, and the remarkable clarity of his letters on the subject, both the board and Rooney were surprised that he did not express any reaction to the report which appeared to answer some of his questions.[21] To assuage Rooney's disappointment, indeed puzzlement, Father McMahon promised to contact the General for his approval of the commission's work.[22]

The discussion on cooperation at the graduate level was not confined to the JEA; the NCEA was also interested in pooling resources for better results. At the fifty-first annual meeting of that organization, the Committee on Graduate Study reported that Dr. Urban Fleege, of the College and University Department, "suggested the possibility of cooperation among Catholic graduate schools for the investigation of certain important problems now facing Catholic education."[23] The following year, at Marquette University, the same committee "studied a proposal for research into the current status of graduate studies in American Catholic universities, but found it impractical at the present time."[24] Although nothing concrete was done, for the same reasons which plagued the JEA Commission, at least the NCEA, like the JEA, realized that something *should* be done. And here the matter rested until the question was dramatically revived by a national debate on the subject. It is a twice-told tale, but its relevance to the present discussion is beyond doubt.

The Catholic academic world in the United States was stunned by the seminal address delivered by Monsignor John Tracy Ellis at the annual meeting of the Catholic Commission on Intellectual and Cultural Affairs, held at Maryville College, St. Louis, on May 14, 1955. Monsignor Ellis, distinguished professor of Church history at Catholic University, took as his theme "American Catholics and the Intellectual Life."[25] His basic point was not new. The Reverend John J. Kane, of the University of Notre Dame, in a more modest comment had already brought this crucial question to the floor of the NCEA meetings. Noting that Catholic scholarship of the Middle Ages had yet to be matched in modern times, he added: "If the intellectual and social apostolate of the Church is ever to be realized in America, this condition must be changed, for scholarship is the heart of the intellectual apostolate and the basis for the social apostolate."[26] He reminded his audience that "eminence in scholarship means leadership in the world of thought which is or should be the very atmosphere of the campus."[27] But it was Ellis, whose academic credentials were solid gold, who marshaled the facts and drove the point home with dreadful accuracy. His presentation was so clear and cogent that he forced the Catholic academic community to confront his accusation.

His major premise was clearly (and bravely) stated: "Admittedly, the weakest aspect of the Church in this country lies in its failure to produce national leaders and to exercise commanding influence in intellectual circles."[28] What, he asked, "is the explanation of this striking discrepancy?" Among other considerations, Ellis elaborated on two reasons that were particularly relevant to the topic under discussion. Two major defects could be charged directly to the colleges and universities. First, "in their mad pursuit of every passing fancy that crossed the American educational scene," there had been a serious deficiency in the study of theology, philosophy, classics, subjects which should characterize Catholic universities.[29] Secondly, there had been what he called "a betrayal of one another" in the Catholic community. "By that I mean the development within the last two decades of numerous and competing graduate schools, none of which is adequately endowed, and few of which have the trained personnel, the equipment in libraries and laboratories, and the professional wage scales to warrant their ambitious undertakings."[30] As a result, he concluded, there is "a perpetuation of mediocrity and the draining away from each other of the strength that is necessary if really superior achievements are to be attained."[31]

The following year, Arthur A. North, dean of the Fordham Graduate School and a member of the JEA Commission on Graduate Schools, in an assigned paper responded to Ellis' indictment of the graduate schools.[32] While he was in general agreement with the charges that had been made, North's explanation was more sympathetic to the difficulties under which Catholics labored in the intellectual apostolate. With regard to duplication and competition, he had come to the meeting armed with statistics. In the United States, a large geographical area by any measurement, there were eighteen Catholic graduate schools, and only ten of them offered programs leading to the doctorate. Of those ten, only six offered doctoral programs in more than ten fields. Would this number justify Ellis's charge of "numerous and competing graduate schools?" Father North did not answer that question; he was more concerned with the implications of another aspect of Catholic graduate schools. The fact is, he claimed, that Catholic graduate schools [he was speaking of the mid-'50s] were relative newcomers to this level of academic achievement. While the undergraduate college was primarily concerned with the conservation and dissemination of knowledge, graduate schools, especially at the doctoral level, were interested in adding to that knowledge through the possession of evidence gathered through creative or original research.

In North's opinion, students in Catholic graduate schools had failed to understand their obligations as scholars; as first-generation scholars, they had not understood the importance of research in the discovery of truth. What accounts for this deficiency? North attempted an answer to *that* question. Catholic graduate schools, in company with Catholic elementary and secondary schools, were victims of a "crash" program to conserve and safeguard the faith. The graduate schools, in his opinion, did not mature gradually, nourished by the normal stimulants of academic inquiry, but imitated the external lineaments of the established schools without laying a solid foundation. The results were reflected in graduates who were not motivated by the personal satisfaction of discovery.[33]

In addition to North's analysis, there may have been a deeper, but less tangible, reason for the lack of Catholic intellectuals in the United States. As the advertisement for his book reads, Thomas F. O'Dea, a sociologist, "challenge[d] that attitude of his fellow Catholics toward the intellectual in today's society."[34] This, in fact, was the basic question: the *attitude* of Catholics toward the intellectual in America. He concluded that Catholics, even more than Protestants, distrust the man of science or letters who, through faith in the rewards of research, would appear to destroy their immigrants' value system. Working from a sociological viewpoint, O'Dea (a member of the Fordham faculty at that time) was "not concerned with establishing the existence of the problem — it is almost too self evident to need further documentation — but rather with the attempt to find some of its causes."[35] The dilemma he posed, therefore, was this: Will Catholics come to recognize and support the importance of the intellectual life, or will Catholics (and the Church) continue to stress immigrants' values of the past, which have inhibited scholarship and, therefore, intellectual leadership?[36]

This was the challenge. The members of the JEA Graduate Commission fully realized that Monsignor Ellis, when he lamented the multiplication of and competition among Catholic graduate schools, was indicting Jesuit institutions, among others, for choosing an alternative which he considered academically enervating. His language was diplomatic but the message was clear. It was against this background of renewed concern for intellectual respectability that the Jesuit Educational Association continued its search for a formula which, through cooperation and coordination, would produce academic leaders. As a first step, there was general agreement within the commission that the JEA must develop a preeminent graduate department in a substantive, traditionally Catholic discipline which would impress the academic world with the integrity of Jesuit scholarship and with indisputable evidence of intellectual growth.[37]

By a strange coincidence, at this very time, anticipating a decision by the commission, Raymond V. Schoder, a Jesuit classicist and classical archeologist of the Chicago Province, submitted to Rooney a proposal for a Jesuit Institute of the Humanities to be sponsored by the American Assistancy. The essence of the proposal, and its structure, are best described in Father Schoder's words:

> Essentially, the idea is to achieve the possible and much desired academic eminence which American Jesuits still lack, by concentrating in one place 15 or 20 of the top Jesuit scholars in the country in the various branches of the Humanities, so that at that place at least a top-level program can be offered to really interested and high-quality graduate students. . . . There are 15 or so Jesuits in the country whose academic quality is on a high level in the various branches of Humanities. Scattered among many schools, they lose impact. Concentrated at one school, the total force would be such as to command national attention. . . . The fields which I consider appropriate are: English, Classics, History, Philosophy, with

fewer men in such related subjects as Art, Music, European Literatures. The Institute staff would be kept to graduate teaching only, with time provided for their own research and writing.[38]

In thanking Schoder for his ideas on the institute, Rooney wrote that the "outline is just what I wanted and gives me the opportunity to discuss the matter with the Province Prefects at our next meeting."[39] At the suggestion of the Executive Committee, which anticipated several difficulties in implementing the plan, the proposal was sent to Paul A. FitzGerald, chairman of the Commission on Graduate Schools, for an evaluation of its merits and feasibility.[40] The commission, while admitting the merits of the proposal, judged that there were major obstacles on the road to implementation. In the first place, the institute included too many fields; for this reason, it would be difficult to administer and almost impossible to finance. As an added caution, it was noted that the Medieval Institute, begun at the University of Notre Dame in 1950, no longer functioned for the same reasons advanced by the commission.[41]

Although the commission did not approve Schoder's proposal, it considered other possibilities arising from that proposal. For some time, the commission had been considering ways and means to build, as a pilot project, a preeminent department at the doctoral level. In a series of meetings, from October 1957 to January 1958, the project was further defined. Finally, Arthur North, dean of the Fordham Graduate School, was asked if that institution would accept the responsibility of developing a preeminent Department of Classics.[42] North accepted the assignment, with the understanding that financial assistance and Jesuit manpower would be subject to discussion.

As evidence of serious intent, a distinguished committee of three Fordham classicists was appointed to prepare a report in response to the directives of the commission. No one could fault the qualifications of the committee. Rudolph Arbesmann, O.E.S.A., had been trained in Germany and understood the demands of scholarship. Edwin A. Quain, S.J., chairman of the committee, with a doctorate from Harvard, had observed at firsthand the real meaning of preeminence. James H. Reid, S.J., was a distinguished member of the Classics Department.

The Fordham Committee filed its report, dated March 15, 1958, with the Commission on Graduate Schools and the Executive Committee.[43] A comprehensive report, it acknowledged present strengths at Fordham and realistically documented future requirements. In the fields of study, which were carefully enumerated, "the primary emphasis of the training planned will be toward the development of fully-trained scholars in the fields of specialization, men who would be capable of consistently productive research." After listing the current faculty members and their fields, the report added the names of eight Jesuits—those in studies and those with established reputations—who would bring strength to the program. The cost to Fordham University would not be small, even with the donated services of Jesuits, and the library holdings would have to be expanded substantially in certain areas. Nor would the project take form overnight. In the opinion of the committee, "Fordham's department now possesses the nucleus of a preeminent department. It seems to us, that in ten years' time, the department could be actually 'preeminent' in the sense discussed by the Commission on Graduate Studies."[44] It was a sign of maturity that the committee was not seduced by the attractions of a "crash" program.

The provincials seemed genuinely interested, and instructed the Graduate Commission, together with the president of the JEA and Dean North, "to discuss the preliminaries of an agreement and the details of possible cooperation of other provinces in helping Fordham University's Department of Classics to achieve preeminence."[45] Six months later, since no official information had reached him, the chairman of the Graduate Commission reported that "the matter is languishing at Fordham."[46] This was not true, as recently available documents have clarified.

In a four-page memorandum to Edward F. Clark, academic vice president of Fordham, Father North had explained the General's several letters on the necessity of cooperation at the graduate level and reviewed the commission's search for the location of a preeminent Department of Classics.[47] Since Fordham was the "unanimous choice" for such a department, North summarized for Clark what Fordham's responsibilities would be, in terms of men and money, and the contribution that could be expected from other provinces. With that background, he asked if the authorities at Fordham "are willing to assume the leadership and the financial burdens involved, if the Board of Governors of the JEA, i.e., the Provincials of the Assistancy, approve of the Commission's proposal."[48] Under another cover, and in order to facilitate a decision, North forwarded to Clark copies of the report prepared by Fathers Arbesmann, Quain, and Reid.[49]

After a fairly long delay, the academic vice president sent to the president suggested responses to North's memorandum. In extenuation of the tardy reply, Clark felt that the president should preface his comments with the following paragraph:

> There has been considerable review and discussion of the proposal that Fordham University establish a preeminent Department of Classics. The

proposal is so important for Jesuit scholarship in this country and the long-range development of our own University that I wished to explore it thoroughly before answering.[50]

Then, borrowing Father Clark's language almost *verbatim*, Father McGinley framed a reply to the commission's proposal. He elaborated upon three main points. In his opinion, "it would seem to be educationally sounder to devise a national overall plan for establishing pre-eminent departments *before* requesting any individual university to commit itself to a specific area."[51] Moreover, "to any commitment by a University there should correspond a commitment that is clear, reasonable, [and] permanent to the effect that the Fathers Provincial of the Assistancy would support the pre-eminent department by supplying manpower."[52] Finally, reflecting current discussions in his own conference, he suggested that "Presidents of the Jesuit Universities should have a strong voice in the planning and establishment of such departments."[53]

These, then, were the prerequisites that would have to be met in exchange for Fordham's pledge to inaugurate a preeminent Department of Classics.

While the Fordham administration was studying the report prepared by Arbesmann, Quain, and Reid, the Commission on Graduate Schools was in the process of publishing a revision of its 1953 "Report." In the first "Report," which described the criteria for initiating or discontinuing graduate programs at the doctoral level, part III had never been completed. That section, "Doctoral Work for Preeminent Intellectual Leadership," had taken on a new meaning in the light of the discussion on Catholic intellectualism. The revised edition, with a new title, *Principles and Policies Governing Graduate Programs in Jesuit Institutions*, was approved by the Board of Governors on May 7, 1958.[54] This document, which was widely circulated, was the most detailed statement to date on graduate programs in the American Assistancy.

The commission considered the question of doctoral work from two standpoints: regional and institutional needs, together with area resources, and intellectual preeminence and influence. In clarifying the second point, the commission noted that "there are certain departments or fields of knowledge in which, for apostolic reasons, Catholic education would at least equal the best programs offered at non-Catholic institutions."[55] Once again, this was to be attained through cooperation in an exchange of faculty members, development of research teams, judicious selection of doctoral fields, and coordination of libraries' acquisition policies where feasible. That was an ideal. The commission also recognized the limitations in men and money, which would be difficult to overcome. Although not inconsistent with the ultimate objective, it was discouraging to note that the criteria that were imposed — financial support, library holdings, supporting departments, distinguished faculty, faculty exchange — would be the very factors that would defeat its efforts for preeminence.

The commission, in drawing a blueprint for "creative leadership in research and scholarship," was "thinking on a national rather than on a regional scale."[56] In this, the members were ahead of their time, because "the most important possible cooperation at this level would consist in the assignment of Jesuits on an Assistancy basis."[57] But this was a dream that would come true, and then only partially, fifteen years later. Although success is by no means accidental, many factors, some foreseen and some unforeseen, implement the emergence of a truly preeminent department.

> Departments of this excellence cannot be built simply by assignment nor [do] even the most careful planning and adequate financial resources guarantee the achievement of preeminent excellence. Many factors not fully under administrative control operate here. Management can be planned cooperatively; development often depends on genius or accident. For example the Department of Biochemistry of Saint Louis University has achieved an international reputation because of the unforeseen success of Doctor Doisy's research.[58]

Although a certain flexibility must be allowed, the commission recommended the following procedure. A discriminating list of fields, in which apostolic and academic influence would be paramount, should be drawn up; a study should be initiated to establish which of those fields was moving toward preeminence; a geographic survey should be made to determine, on the basis of population, resources, institutional competition, and student preparation, the best location for preeminent departments.[59] Finally, in part IV, fields of study were selected according to a prescribed set of criteria.

The criteria for selection, in the light of future developments in Catholic scholarship and research, now appear restrictive and parochial, perpetuating the image of the "immigrant Church." Preference, the commission wrote, should be given to those departments which are most important in the development of Catholic culture; to those areas in which a student could encounter danger if the subject were not taught under Catholic auspices; those areas which are most susceptible to Catholic leadership; fields most likely to promote Catholic educational prestige; fields calculated to offer the best preparation for the correction of social and intellectual problems in contemporary American society.[60] The commission was convinced that "if these principles, policies and criteria are invoked . . . graduate programs in Jesuit institutions will be maintained at a high academic level."[61]

This document, as approved in 1958, leaves much to be desired. It would not be written, or accepted, today. Yet, though the temptation is strong, it is an unpardonable error for the historian to read history backward. It was an honest attempt on the part of the JEA Commission to bring academic quality and intellectual integrity to graduate departments, especially at the doctoral level. The members of the commission, all of whom had earned the doctorate, knew the components of a good department.

Although preeminent departments did not materialize at that time, the commission kept alive the idea of intellectual leadership, influence, and achievement. To calculate the progress, one has only to compare *Principles and Policies* with the tentative steps taken by the Inter-Province Committee in the 1920s or with the justly famous report on graduate studies by Daniel O'Connell in the '30s. Those efforts were directed at adequacy or equality; the ultimate aim, of course, was distinction. In 1958, Jesuit graduate deans saw the possibility, even the necessity, of preeminence.

In the final analysis, material resources were not available; interinstitutional cooperation was in its infancy; and provincial superiors were not yet ready to tear down the fences that kept Jesuits within provincial boundaries. But the seed had been planted; the difficulties would be solved; and the garden would one day flourish.

To complement this discussion, it is of interest to trace the process employed by Marquette University to revive its doctoral programs. It is a good example of the serious intent with which Jesuit administrators pursued the goal of academic credibility. Due to the austerities imposed by World War II, which adversely affected all institutions, Marquette, on the advice of the North Central Association of Colleges and Secondary Schools, discontinued work at the doctoral level in 1943. The plan to restore the Ph.D. was first raised in 1955 in a long document that reviewed the history of the case in the six departments originally proposed. The financial cost was calculated, the faculty evaluated, and the facilities described.[62] For the required permissions, Marquette had to deal with two agencies: the North Central Association and the JEA. Compliance with Jesuit regulations proved more difficult than with those of the accrediting association.

Although John O. Riedl, dean of the Graduate School, was actively involved in the planning, the academic vice president was the prime mover in the restoration of doctoral programs. Though he anticipated problems, and was especially conscious of financial restrictions, Edward J. Drummond was determined to keep pressure on the president and provincial. Drummond entered the Society at Florissant in 1924, was ordained in 1937, and completed his tertianship in 1939. His graduate studies were undertaken at Saint Louis and at the University of Iowa, where he earned a doctorate in English literature. Successively professor of English and dean of the Graduate School, he was appointed academic vice president in 1955. An advocate of academic excellence, he had definite ideas and ambitious plans, for the leadership role of Marquette University in Milwaukee and Wisconsin.[63]

In October 1955, at the invitation of Father Drummond, a team of three highly qualified Jesuits visited the university to evaluate its programs.[64] Although Drummond had hoped for a definitive answer within the month, there was general agreement at Marquette that the shortage of Ph.D.s in the medical sciences posed a problem. Two years later, with renewed assurances by the administration, Father Eugene F. Gallagher recommended to the provincial that Marquette be granted permission "to reestablish the doctoral program in the fields of biology, philosophy and six basic medical sciences."[65] The recommendation, however, was not without qualification. Gallagher was unhappy that M.D.s outnumbered Ph.D.s in certain science departments, which gave the impression of "slanting research along professional lines rather than academic."[66]

Shortly after this exchange, good news came from the Commission on Colleges and Universities of the NCA. In a letter to President O'Donnell, the associate secretary wrote "that the Board was favorably impressed with both the thoroughness of your report and with the adequacy of the facilities and resources for the support of the proposed programs."[67] To make it official, "it [the board] voted to approve your plans for the introduction of Ph.D. work."[68] With that endorsement, Father O'Donnell informed the chairman of the University Board of Graduate Studies that its recommendation "for resumption of Marquette's doctoral programs has been approved."[69]

While the doctoral proposal was under consideration by the North Central Association, Marquette was also negotiating with Jesuit officials at several levels. Father Provincial Burns had already informed Drummond that he was "very sympathetic toward the plan of resuming the *doctoral program*" and that he would "drop a note to Father Rooney in Rome so that he may have whatever preliminary information may be necessary before his conference with Father General."[70] Rooney then, as an emissary of Father Burns, brought the matter to the General's attention. In his own words, "I explained very briefly the background of this request and I then told Father General that I am definitely in favor of Marquette going into doctoral work again, that it is necessary for the natural organic development of Marquette, that if Marquette does not expand in this direction the University of Wisconsin will surely open up in Milwaukee."[71] Furthermore, he told the General that he could have confidence in the judgment of Father O'Donnell, Father Drummond, and Dean Riedl. Rooney then asked if he might notify Father Burns, and the authorities at Marquette, "that the General recognizes the need of doctoral work at Marquette, that a specific request should be sent to him, and that specific fields should be asked for, and that the Marquette requests will receive very sympathetic hearing by Father General."[72] Janssens agreed that he could write in that vein.

Two years later, with a specific request from Father Provincial Burns, Rooney sent his formal approval of the program to the General. As he explained in his letter, he had received from the president of Marquette a document entitled "Request for Reestablishment of the Doctoral Program at Marquette University."[73] This document described in detail Marquette's resources and, according to Rooney, "substantiates its claim that it meets, more than adequately, the J.E.A. criteria for the inauguration of doctoral programs."[74] The administration specifically asked that Marquette be allowed to establish the doctoral program in philosophy and seven sciences. In Rooney's considered opinion, Marquette "is ready for the doctoral program in the fields for which it requests the permission; . . . there is need for such a program; and . . . it is able to bear the costs."[75]

But it was the anticipated cost of such a program that impelled certain members of the faculty to oppose it. In acknowledging Rooney's correspondence, Vincent McCormick acquainted the president of the JEA with an evaluation that was in contrast to his optimism. In January 1957 the General had received a letter from a Jesuit at Marquette, an excerpt from which the American Assistant communicated "confidentially" to Rooney for his reaction. The writer, "whose judgment," in McCormick's opinion, "commands respect," submitted a pessimistic analysis of financial realities.[76] The writer alleged that "all of the Jesuits admit that we do not have the financial resources to undertake such a burden." For this reason, the General should be "extremely slow in permitting a doctoral program at [Marquette] University."[77] Father Drummond admitted that his discussions with the business officers were not as extensive as they might have been, but he felt that the financial responsibilities had been assumed by the Budget Committee, the trustees, and the house consultors.[78]

Understandably, the president of the JEA was upset at this rebuttal of his testimony, which was based on the evidence furnished to him. Defending his original statement, he denied that "all" the Jesuits at Marquette were opposed to the program; secondly, he looked for "evidence" that the program was being forced on the faculty; and thirdly, he charged that the letter writer did not "understand the financial setup of Marquette School of Medicine."[79] In agreement with Drummond, Rooney added: "It seems to me that the ones who are able to judge best the financial ability of Marquette University to undertake a doctoral program would be the president, the treasurer, and the house consultors. If they agree to it, it seems to me that we are perfectly safe in going ahead."[80] With nothing in writing to the contrary, Marquette immediately made plans to accept students at the doctoral level.

It is unnecessary to review every program.[81] In his capacity as advisor to the General, Rooney went by the book in applying the criteria set by the JEA Commission on Graduate Schools. This procedure was, on occasions, a source of annoyance to the presidents, who resented the implied supervision, by the JEA, of graduate offerings. At Spring Hill College, for example, A. William Crandell, president, had developed plans to initiate a master's program in philosophy, and Rooney informed Crandell that when he was in receipt of further information, he would send his opinion to the General. Upon receiving the required letter from Spring Hill, and satisfied with its content, Rooney telephoned, and later confirmed in writing, his approval of the program to Father McCormick.[82]

In a similar situation, the president of the JEA initially refused to approve the application of Santa Clara University to begin a graduate program. "Maybe I was a bit hard on them," Rooney conceded, "but I felt that if they were given approval without actually meeting the criteria they may not be too diligent about meeting them."[83] In 1960, to everyone's satisfaction, Santa Clara inaugurated a master of arts degree in English, history, and education.[84]

Albert Lemieux, however, bravely decided to test Father Rooney's assumptions. In 1958 Seattle University established a graduate program without the blessing of the National Office of the JEA or Father General. The president of the JEA was surprised to learn from Herman Hauck, the province prefect in California, "that the authorities of Seattle did not think it necessary to submit the request to Rome."[85] Rooney insisted that such a petition must go to Rome because "Father General made it clear to me that in regard to the request to inaugurate graduate programs, he definitely wants the opinion of the Province Prefect and also of the President of the JEA."[86] In fact, "he [the General] said that I could tell this to the Provincials."[87]

This may have been a tactical error on Rooney's part. The provincials, it would appear, were beginning to question the wisdom of accepting uncontested oral messages from the General, communicated to them by the president of the JEA. In 1958 and 1959 the Executive Committee had devoted much of its time, with the aid of a subcommittee, to preparing a list of permissions that must be referred to the fathers provincial or to Father General. The provincials had actually approved a letter, directed to newly appointed superiors, which included a list of these permissions.[88] Approved with some caution, the letter would be "considered a suggested letter which will be sent by individual Provincials to new superiors of their province, with such modifications as they deem advisable."[89] In a later comment, with the Constitutions on their side, "it was the opinion of the Provincials that those things listed as being referable to Father General for which there can be found no documentation should be omitted from the list."[90]

With or without permission, the record clearly shows that, beginning in the 1950s, there was an earnest and constant effort on the part of Jesuit colleges and universities to improve their scholastic standing. At the department level—the basic academic unit—the larger universities recognized the necessity for, and took preliminary steps toward, preeminence in a chosen field. In a certain sense, it is irrelevant that the results did not entirely match their high expectations. The point is that those involved—provincials, presidents, deans, the president of the JEA and his Executive Committee—recognized the profound importance of academic excellence if Jesuit institutions were to exercise intellectual leadership in the United States.

Although an ideal is rarely, if ever, attained, the Jesuit effort was rewarded with a consoling measure of success. This was reflected in testimonials that were written in praise of Jesuit institutions by those who were in a position to judge their competitive standing and influence. Arthur S. Adams, the distinguished president of the American Council on Education, whose association had slighted Jesuit graduate schools in 1934, after applying the usual indices of appraisal, wrote: "As a result of all these considerations and in the light of the substantial contributions of the Jesuit institutions of higher learning to American education, Jesuit education in the United States enjoys full recognition for what it is and what it does in the entire American educational scene."[91]

The executive secretary of the National Commission on Accrediting, William K. Selden, after noting that "Jesuit education has been a constructive and positive force in American higher education," continued: "The faculty members and the administrative officers of these institutions are highly respected for their academic competence and educational foresight."[92]

The final testimonial to the academic progress and prestige of Jesuit colleges and universities came from a man whose opinion was greatly respected in the councils of higher education, Theodore A. Distler, who for many years was executive director of the Association of American Colleges. "In my position," he wrote, "I can testify that the Jesuit colleges and universities are among the leading institutions of higher education in the United States."

In our opinion the Jesuit schools represent a most important group in American education. They maintain a high standard curriculum. With the exception of a small group of older universities, popularly known as the Ivy League, there is no section of American higher education that enjoys a higher reputation for its concern with educational excellence or for the quality of its scholarship and teaching.[93]

# 9. Three Areas of Concern,
## 1960-1965

CONSCIOUS OF HIS RESPONSIBILITY, as ultimately accountable for the works of the Society of Jesus, Father General Janssens had no intention of purchasing academic preeminence at any price. As successor to St. Ignatius, he had inherited a glorious 400-year tradition in the apostolate of education, a tradition rooted in carefully guarded principles that were basic to the Jesuit system of pedagogy at the collegiate level. Although Edward Rooney was obviously a trusted and valuable advisor, the General decided that, due to the growing complexity of American Jesuit universities, it would be helpful to have a firsthand account, by independent investigators, of the Jesuit character of these institutions.

Accordingly, in November 1958 he appointed four prudent fathers as *Inspectores* with an official mandate to visit certain institutions. They were instructed "to report to him directly on how well these universities are achieving the aims of Jesuit education; what are the obstacles to the achievement of their aims; what means can be employed so as to be of greater use to the Church."[1] In order to create an atmosphere of impartiality, and to avoid the subtle influence of regional friendships, the inspectors were assigned to institutions beyond their own provinces.[2] Although the General's orders were confidential, Rooney had seen the letter of instruction, which, he confided to the Executive Committee, "yields a very clear idea of some of Father General's preoccupations concerning Jesuit education in the United States."[3]

The results of the inspectors' visitations began to filter back to Rooney in December 1959, and the first reaction was good. In a conversation with Vincent McCormick in Rome, he was told that Father General was pleased with the reports and relieved to note that "the

Catholicity of our institutions was upheld."⁴ The Assistant added, enigmatically, that it would be wise to remember "that they [the institutions] are being watched."⁵ In due time, the youthful (and recently appointed) provincial of the New York Province, John J. McGinty, received a consolidated list of topics which the General had distilled from the reports of the inspectors. He instructed McGinty, as chairman of the Board of Governors, to request the Executive Committee to study these topics and to submit a report on them at the next meeting of the members of the board, who in turn should present their own recommendations to Rome.⁶ This was not an easy assignment, as the list of topics was fairly long. At the same time, the General indicated that certain areas of concern had a high priority and that the provincials might concentrate their efforts on them. Of these, the three most important were the status of laymen in Jesuit institutions, the position of philosophy in the collegiate curriculum, and the objectives of Jesuit colleges and universities. The last topic was a perennial favorite at the Roman Curia.

From the beginning of his generalate, Janssens had a particular interest in the participation of laymen in the Jesuit educational enterprise. He had never indicated the slightest objection to lay colleagues, since, in certain countries of Europe, they comprised a large percentage of the teachers in secondary schools. Moreover, as provincial in Belgium he was familiar with their contribution to the local apostolate. His present concern, however, was their level of ascendancy on the administrative ladder, their involvement in the policymaking process of American colleges and universities, and their academic jurisidiction over Jesuit members of the faculty. What is today taken for granted, could have been looked upon as unusual twenty-five years ago. In any case, the General posed a number of questions. Should a layman, he asked, "be appointed as a vice president, a chancellor, or to any other such important office in our Colleges and Universities?"⁷ Should a layman be dean or assistant dean in the colleges of arts and sciences? To put it another way, "What should be the authority and composition of the committee, or committees, which formulate the major policies in our institutions?"⁸

The question of lay faculty was inextricably linked to the question of expansion, and the question first surfaced, in the Janssens years, in the General's *Letter on Ministries*, which seemed to favor a restrictive policy. He later explained to Rooney that he had in mind a number of schools in Europe "where the proportion of Jesuits to laymen was so small that they were Jesuit schools only in the sense that they had a rector or minister and a spiritual father who were Jesuits."⁹ In that long discussion with the General, Rooney supported the cause of laymen in

Jesuit institutions, a position he maintained with consistency during his tenure as president of the JEA. His notes indicate that his commitment was genuine.

> I also said [to the General] that it was my own opinion that even if by an almost absurd supposition we ever had so many Jesuits available that we could take care of all the administrative and teaching positions in our schools, . . . there will still be a place for a goodly percentage of Catholic laymen in a Catholic school . . . because the layman has something to contribute, by his very position as a layman, that no priest or religious could supply. Father General did not disagree with this viewpoint, although I cannot recall now what his comment on it was.[10]

Rooney had anticipated the General's query. A short time before the New York provincial requested a report on these selected questions, the JEA president had already sent to the General his considered opinion "on the appointment of laymen to the position of vice president or other administrative posts in American Jesuit colleges and universities."[11] In a long memorandum, originally encouraged by the American Assistant, Rooney painted an accurate picture of the unusual growth of colleges in the United States, with the consequent growth in teaching and administrative positions. After making the valid observation that "what is true of higher educational institutions is generally also true of Jesuit institutions," he reminded the General that "Jesuit manpower has not grown in the same proportion as the institutions."[12] His reminder, of course, was a subtle reference to uncontrolled expansion, against which he had often cautioned the General. In any case, this was the reason why the Society had "to depend more and more upon the assistance of laymen in our teaching and administrative staffs."[13]

Always the realist, Rooney, adjusting to a *fait accompli*, insisted that if laymen were employed, they must receive salaries commensurate with their positions and an equal opportunity to ascend the ladder of academic promotions and administrative responsibility. However, there were exceptions to the general rule. In his opinion, "the president of our institutions must be a Jesuit," as well as the academic vice president; laymen should be eligible for all vice presidencies that looked to the external management and development of the university.[14] Although laymen themselves had accepted this distinction, it was conceded by all that the intricacies of this question should be the subject of long-range planning.

The General's question, on the precise involvement of laymen in the Jesuit apostolate of education, was proper and legitimate. Their role as partners in an enterprise so closely identified with the Society of Jesus had to be evaluated. At this time, however, the question of lay participation in the JEA was, if not irrelevant, almost superfluous. The recruitment, appointment, and assimilation of lay faculty, their attendance at institutes and the annual meeting—these were questions that had been addressed several times at meetings of the Executive Committee and in Rooney's reports to the Board of Governors.[15] The attitude of the board was always positive. The board, it is true, vacillated before making an affirmative decision on the appointment of laymen to JEA commissions. The reason was that commission members were involved in the policymaking process within the association, and the provincials were waiting for the General's reaction to the reports of the *Inspectores*.[16] The letter from the General to Father McGinty made them even more cautious, and the office of vice president was now the real issue. Although he was not privy to the correspondence between Rome and New York, Rooney's instincts were correct.

In an earlier exchange with Harold O. Small, the New American Assistant in Rome, Rooney recalled that Vincent McCormick had raised his eyebrows "at mention of the fact that a layman had been appointed Vice President in some of our American Jesuit institutions."[17] Actually, Rooney had been asked about the propriety of this move by several conscientious presidents who were looking to Rome for guidance. Offering some advice of his own, he cautioned Small to be prudent: "I do not think it would be wise at all to come out with any prohibition against ever appointing a layman Vice President. . . . I think we must go carefully in this matter, since two or three of our places already do have laymen as Vice Presidents."[18]

Harold Small was introduced unexpectedly, and with little immediate preparation, to the concerns of the Roman Curia. It was not an ideal time to arrive at Borgo Santo Spirito. The General's poor health limited his customary energy and forced him to appoint a vicar general to lighten the burdens of office. He was also losing an experienced advisor. In a letter dated February 7, 1960, Vincent McCormick, citing reasons of health, asked to be relieved of office. As a result, Father Small, at that time rector and tertian instructor at Port Townsend, was appointed American Assistant *ad tempus*, that is, until confirmed by a General Congregation.[19] Though he was appointed without much warning, Father Small was quick to grasp the business of his large Assistancy and learned to reflect the mind of Father Janssens. As a former provincial of the Oregon Province, and member of the Board of Governors, he was broadly familiar with current issues of the JEA.

The new vicar general, from the day of his ordination, was marked for high office. After completing his term as provincial superior of the Province of Upper Canada, John L. Swain was entrusted, as tertian instructor, with the Ignatian formation of priests in Japan, where he met a Basque Jesuit, Pedro Arrupe, master of novices, with whom he would later be closely associated in Rome. Elected English Assistant at the Thirtieth General Congregation in 1957, he was later appointed vicar general and, due to the General's illness, he was confirmed in that office "to administer the ordinary business of the Society."[20] It was Father Swain who convened the Thirty-first General Congregation in 1965, at which he was elected a general assistant to Father General Arrupe and subsequently appointed his admonitor.[21] An excellent administrator, known for prudence and judgment, he became in time the right hand of Father Janssens and was his surrogate in matters of importance. His approach to the JEA was restrained, and in the controversies that developed within the organization, he appeared to sympathize with the position of the presidents.

The new American Assistant and the vicar general (to a lesser extent) acknowledged the necessity of augmenting collegiate faculties with lay professors. The need was obvious, and short of closing schools there was no alternative. Rome insisted, however, that lay professors understand the broad objectives of the Jesuit apostolate of education and, to the extent possible, contribute to them. Of particular concern was the contribution of non-Catholic professors, which had been an issue since the days of Father Ledochowski. Rooney, in a long memorandum to Father Small, constructed a remarkably cogent and valid defense of the practice of hiring non-Catholic teachers. In addition to the obvious arguments, he was not afraid to identify "a public relations problem arising from the fact that we are living in a pluralistic society."[22] The presence of a certain number of non-Catholics "who are sympathetic to the aims both general and specific of Catholic education helps much to create good will toward Catholic education."[23] To the president of the JEA, therefore, it "would be most inopportune" to issue regulations against the employment of non-Catholics, since there were too many critics "ready to say that Catholic institutions place limitations on academic freedom."[24]

Leaving philosophical questions to others, the presidents, and their deans, focused on the practical problems of recruitment and retention of lay faculty, both Catholic and non-Catholic. As men whose careers were identified with the Jesuit apostolate, they were also concerned, it is fair to say, with the *educational* attitudes of lay professors. Although each president was primarily interested in advancing the academic prestige of his own institution, all agreed upon a form of protocol that would secure their individual prerogatives and, at the same time, protect "the right of their faculty and administrative personnel to improve themselves personally and professionally."[25] This agreement, based on the practice endorsed by the American colleges, regulated the procedure to be followed between Jesuit institutions in negotiating the services of new faculty members. Given the normal academic rivalry between competing institutions, their formula for recruitment within the association was a unique example of fraternal cooperation for the good of all.[26]

In the face of hard statistics and common practice, Rome easily accepted the necessity and propriety of lay colleagues in positions of academic and administrative authority. Although the question was later revived in connection with the objectives of Jesuit universities, it was reconsidered only as part of the discussion on the philosophy and theology of Jesuit education. In the meantime, the Board of Governors had approved the appointment of laymen to JEA commissions, an important step forward, and invited their attendance at the annual meeting. Though the concession now appears ludicrous, the *Jesuit Educational Quarterly* was made available to lay faculty and placed on "open" shelves in libraries.[27] To all intents and purposes, lay colleagues were now full partners in the enterprise, members of the family, with all rights and privileges.

The second area for further study, as suggested by the reports of the *inspectores*, was the place of philosophy in American Jesuit colleges and universities. While other complaints might be overlooked, this was a basic issue in Jesuit education which Janssens was determined to pursue, as he made clear in his letter to the chairman of the next provincials' meeting. The General was diplomatic in his charge but specific in his instructions.

> The Inspectors whom I appointed to visit many of our universities in your Province accomplished their task with a care and thoroughness and charity that gave me much consolation and helpful information. All, if I recall correctly, found a weak spot where we ought to be especially strong, i.e., in the field of philosophy and theology. The weakness is not the same everywhere, but there it is. The *philosophia perennis* is being edged off the stage by a history of philosophers; honor courses are offered to young men who have not yet laid the foundation of our scholastic philosophy. It is not my purpose here to enumerate deficiencies; but I ask your Reverences to charge the Reverend President of the JEA, and his Executive Committee, to begin without delay a comprehensive study of the position of philosophy in the curricula of our colleges and universities and

to prepare a full report, with suggestions, to be transmitted to your Reverences and to me before the summer of 1961.[28]

In compliance with the General's request, the provincials commissioned the Executive Committee to carry out his orders. Father Provincial O'Sullivan, however, in his letter preparing for the spring meeting of the provincials, envisioned a more elaborate investigation. Addressing his regional confreres, he wrote: "It may be that we shall want to evolve a bit further the nature of this comprehensive study."[29] As events turned out, the Board of Governors endorsed an in-depth study which probably went beyond the General's intent.

Coincidentally, there was a convergence of interests from another group, which, anticipating the General's mandate, posed a different forum to accomplish the same result. At their meeting in Boston, the presidents were dissatisfied with the religious, moral, and spiritual formation of the students entrusted to their care.[30] Although the problem had long been recognized, it had formerly been discussed in small, homogeneous groups of concerned Jesuits, some of whom had claimed that the religious formation of the student should be co-equal with his academic training. Since these discussions usually proved to be inconclusive and ineffective, "the idea arose of preparing for a thorough examination of all these interrelated problems by a group representing every phase of pertinent activity."[31] All of this would be examined within the framework of philosophy and theology as academic disciplines. In short, it was a question of integration. "How can a unified combination of the academic disciplines of philosophy and theology be so integrated with the moral, spiritual and religious development of our college students that our graduates will lead lives approaching our ideal of the truly Catholic man of culture."[32]

Although there was a certain duplication, the Board of Governors, for the moment, treated each project separately, that is, the General's request and the presidents' proposal. The board was pleased to note that the president of the JEA had appointed a subcommittee to organize the study on the position of philosophy as requested by Father General.[33] In accepting the preliminary report, the provincials shrewdly observed that, in the revised report which they requested, the information should go beyond the statistical data printed in catalogs. The board was more interested in the hours of instruction in philosophy imparted by Jesuit and non-Jesuit teachers, as well as the content of the regular courses and, also, the honor courses. The second report of the subcommittee responded, more or less adequately, to the provincials' questions and was used by the presidents in preparing their own case.[34] Ultimately, the

General and the provincials recognized the redundancy of the report, and it was eliminated in favor of the presidents' plan.[35]

Impressed with the presidents' proposal, the Executive Committee recommended "that an institute on the moral, religious and spiritual education of Jesuit college and university students be held in the summer of 1962."[36] On their part, the provincials seized the opportunity to cooperate with the presidents to probe an area of Jesuit education that was of vital concern to the General and to satisfy their own qualms. With little discussion and no dissension, they approved "the proposal to hold an institute in the summer of 1962 on the Role of Philosophy and Theology in our Colleges and Universities."[37] They stipulated that the institute be (a) conducted as a workshop and (b) the membership be restricted to 60 delegates, distributed among eight groups. These included presidents, academic administrators, teachers of philosophy and theology, personnel directors, student counselors, spiritual directors, and province prefects.[38] Robert J. Henle was appointed director of the workshop and worked with a planning committee of six members.[39]

The Workshop on the Role of Philosophy and Theology, in the opinion of many, was one of the most ambitious, most rewarding, and most successful projects undertaken by the Jesuit Educational Association. It may, indeed, be the best example of that union and cooperation which was the hope of both Ledochowski and Janssens.[40] When he was informed of its scope and content, the General was enthusiastic about the workshop and looked forward to its positive results. Asked by Rooney if he intended to request a study of theology, as he had of philosophy, he answered "that if a study of the position of theology in our colleges is covered in the Workshop, it will not be necessary to call for another study."[41]

After two years of intense preparation, gathering of information, and circulation of discussion papers, the delegates arrived at the sun-drenched campus of Loyola University in Los Angeles. With Father Charles Casassa as a gracious host, the first session opened on August 6, 1962. Any attempt to summarize the proceedings of the workshop — the content of the papers, the enlightened discussions, the statement of positions — would be excessively long and, in the end, inadequate. The *Proceedings* fills five volumes, which even today would reward any brave soul who has the courage and persistence to read them.[42] For those who prefer a shorter version, there is an official resumé of the workshop by the director, who gives a splendid explanation of the intense preparation for the workshop and its unique aspects, as well as an authoritative commentary on the "positions" ratified by the participants.[43]

According to the director, two unusual features characterized the preparation for the workshop and contributed notably to its success. Taking advantage of the lead time of two years, the "Planning Committee laid out a series of surveys and studies to be made as the background for the work to be done at Los Angeles."[44] In Father Henle's opinion, "if the Workshop had no other fruitful result, it at least gave the Assistancy a set of excellent papers on some basic educational issues."[45] Two of the outstanding surveys, each of which answered the General's fears, presented a professional profile of theological and philosophical teaching, as it was in 1961, and set a historical point of reference for future surveys of the same sort. The second novelty, which for diversity and competence proved highly advantageous, was the great variety of participants. In fact, "the mixed composition was decided on in order to bring together in sustained face-to-face discussion representatives of all the different viewpoints pertinent to the discussion topics."[46] The result, of course, was a better understanding between campus categories that had formerly been, if not in competition, at least out of touch.

Out of the task forces, which again reflected a distillation of opinion from presidents to sodality directors, came the "position papers," the most important residue of the work of the participants, which "stand as a permanent valuable product of the Workshop."[47] Among the position papers, one of the most interesting, surely, is the "Profile of the Jesuit College Graduate," to which Father General referred in subsequent communications to American Jesuits. If fully realized in a large number of students, the living portrait of a Jesuit product would fulfill the dream of St. Ignatius in the apostolate of education. Other seminal papers, still applicable today, are "The Department of Theology and Its Discipline," "Approaches and Patterns for the Teaching of Philosophy in College," and "The Relationship of the Teaching of Philosophy and Theology to the Effectiveness of Religious Activities."[48]

In his report to the presidents, Father Henle said: "There are now in the various Provinces of the American Assistancy eighty Jesuits who were participants at the Workshop and are actively engaged in integrating the teaching of philosophy and theology with the moral, religious and spiritual life of the Jesuit student."[49] The presidents, completely vindicated in their original proposal, devoted a large percentage of their time urging implementation of the position statements. Although it was agreed that Father General not be asked to comment officially on the workshop, it was also agreed that if he did not openly question the papers, it could legitimately be concluded that he approved them.[50] The Board of Governors, "having heard from all sides the highest praise for the Workshop . . . recorded its sincere appreciation to all those who were responsible for [its] success," and in particular to the director and the members of the planning committee.[51]

It was, indeed, an Assistancy project which, better than any other effort, illustrated the potential rewards of union and cooperation among the American provinces.

There was a third source of anxiety to the Roman authorities as American Jesuit institutions grew in size and complexity. Apparently, a clear answer to this concern had also eluded the inspectors during their visitations to the colleges and universities. The issue must have surfaced in their reports, however, since Vincent McCormick was not the kind of person to invent problems which had not already appeared on his desk in epistolary form.[52] At any rate, Rooney reported a conversation with the American Assistant in Rome "in which [the assistant] stressed the need of a careful and deep study of the *objectives* of our universities."[53] The Executive Committee, fully occupied in preparation for the Loyola Workshop and in organizing the study on the position of philosophy, was reluctant to start another project. "However, since the study would ultimately be required . . . it was moved that this study on objectives be begun at once."[54] With that endorsement, the JEA president appointed a three-member Committee on Objectives of American Jesuit Universities.[55]

For the subject at hand, it was a blue ribbon committee. Robert F. Harvanek, the chairman, a recent arrival on the Executive Committee, was ideally suited to this assignment, and it was much to his liking. Harvanek, while a scholastic, had earned a Ph.D. in philosophy at Fordham University at a time when that department was notoriously demanding. After ordination, as a capable scholar with an analytical mind he gained recognition at West Baden College for his professional approach to his own discipline and to Jesuit education. He was appointed province prefect of studies for the Chicago Province in 1957.[56]

The second member of the committee, an enigmatic figure to some Jesuits but trusted by all, had been a prime mover in advancing the cause of special studies in the New England Province. After earning a brilliant doctorate in history and government at Harvard, James L. Burke had been an inspirational teacher at Boston College, director of the summer session, chairman of the Department of History and Government, and, briefly, dean of the Graduate School. He was appointed province prefect of studies for colleges and universities in 1951.

Herman Hauck, the third member, was the engaging, generous, enthusiastic, and energetic province prefect from California. Typical of the friendly, outgoing Jesuits of the Western provinces, he was a shrewd observer of men and manners. A former president of the University of Santa Clara, he understood the administrative mechanism of an institution of higher learning.

All three members had definite ideas on what a Jesuit college was supposed to accomplish. It would be difficult, however, to think of a subject on which more has been written and less known. Every college, at one time or another, has attempted to define its objectives, and collegiate catalogs abound with triumphal declarations which, alas, are often in sharp contrast with the reality. A satisfactory answer, it seems, is even more elusive when applied to Jesuit institutions. Beyond the accepted definition of a private, independent college, one must add the distinguishing marks of a church-related school; the distinction is then narrowed to Catholic and, finally, Jesuit. Moreover, although the question had been introduced in meetings without number, the literature up to this point had been unrewarding.[57] But the picture was changing. It will be clear, as our narrative continues, that the study suggested by Vincent McCormick, and undertaken by the subcommittee, sparked a spate of articles, and an excellent book, which advanced the argument through legitimate controversy.[58]

On the other hand, it was curious that, in 1960, the Executive Committee should be asked to address the subject of "objectives." Apparently, the General and his Assistants had not digested the excellent material recently made available to them. Although the focus had now been enlarged to illuminate the precise *raison d'être* of American Jesuit universities, much that had been done was basic, or at least background, to the new mandate. At the 1955 Deans' Institute, held at Santa Clara, seven first-class papers were delivered, with subsequent stimulating discussions, on the objectives of the collegiate enterprise. The papers, in logical sequence, were designed to trace the subject from a general statement, applicable to all colleges, to the specific characteristics of a Jesuit college.[59] Admittedly, it is not easy to distinguish between the objectives of a Catholic and a specifically Jesuit college.

A brief selection of basic concepts and key ideas will be helpful to clarify the progression of opinions from the general to the particular. In his closely reasoned paper, which is also a good example of his philosophy of education, Robert Henle, dean of the Saint Louis University Graduate School, examined the nature of the college within our society.

> Now the college is part of our system of higher education; that is, of the American university system. By a social and cultural commitment, the

university is, in our culture, the one institution that is formally dedicated to truth as such; that is, to intellectual knowledge, to its extension and development, to its preservation and communication. However necessary truth and knowledge may be in other parts of our culture, there is no other institution whose primary concern is the cultivation of truth and knowledge.[60]

Moreover, since the college "is established by a social commitment as an institution for the development of human beings, . . . it must be governed in all its activities by the truth about human nature, and this does not depend upon a social decision or consensus."[61] Henle concluded that the college is dedicated to truth, but truth that serves the development of human beings. "The objective, therefore, of the Catholic liberal arts college is to achieve the glory of God by (1) developing human beings as such to maturity in and through a dedication to truth and intellectual culture and (2) thereby serving society and the Church."[62]

Advancing the thesis, George E. Ganss, director of the Classics Department at Marquette, whose meticulous research in the rich resources of the Roman archives ideally qualified him for the task, contributed a paper on "Specifically Jesuit Objectives."[63] In addition to Jesuit sources, Ganss radicated his solution in canon 1372 of the *Codex Juris Canonici*, which prescribes the religious and moral education of the faithful, and in the well-known encyclical of Pope Pius XI, *Christian Education*. In that sense, as a complement to Henle's *philosophy*, he proposed a *theology* of education. Ganss addressed himself to two questions: In addition to the aims of all Catholic colleges, are there objectives specifically, even exclusively, Jesuit? Secondly, whether the answer to that question is affirmative or negative, what distinguishes Jesuit colleges from other colleges?[64]

Clearly in command of his sources, he derived fourteen principles, twelve of them from the Jesuit Constitutions and two from the practice of Ignatius, to demonstrate educational objectives which are characteristically Jesuit. He noted that, from 1550 onward, Jesuit administrators and teachers "have consciously striven to achieve the whole synthesis of educational objectives which Ignatius prescribed in Part Four of the Constitutions."[65] In summary, then, using the Constitutions of the Society, the *Instruction* of Ledochowski, and to a lesser extent the *Ratio Studiorum*, Ganss concluded that "the distinguishing mark of Jesuit education consists in our faithful adherence to the entire synthesis of the essential educational principles which Ignatius made obligatory upon officials and teachers alike in his schools."[66]

While not exactly begging the question, Ganss does not give an entirely satisfactory definition or explanation of "synthesis." Brian McGrath, then dean and academic vice president at Georgetown, questioned the validity of assigning specifically Jesuit objectives to a college. He may have come closer to the mark when he observed that "the Jesuit Liberal Arts College has a tradition, a method and a technique that gives the Jesuit teacher a different approach to the problem of education."[67] Other systems may borrow certain aspects of these components, "but no others have the combination of our tradition, our technique and our method."[68]

The papers and discussions at Santa Clara, though orientated toward the liberal arts college, identified the basic goals of the Jesuit apostolate of higher education. In this sense, the institute provided a solid foundation for the work of the subcommittee on the objectives of Jesuit universities. In fact, urged on by the energetic zeal of its chairman, the subcommittee moved quickly to put its thoughts on paper. Harvanek distributed a three-page progress report to fellow members of the Executive Committee at their September 1960 meeting.[69]

A close reading of the report reveals that the subcommittee had changed the focus from the "objectives" of Jesuit universities to "function." (Actually, "function" may have more accurately reflected Vincent McCormick's concern: "What are you trying to do with your university education in the United States?") As a prelude to his conclusion, Harvanek posited four components in a complex university: undergraduate schools, professional schools, and graduate schools of arts and sciences at the master's and doctor's levels. For this complex of schools and programs, adequate resources, which he listed as money, faculty, and students, are necessary. In his judgment, the Society in the United States did not have the resources to operate more than three such universities. According to his calculations—and his assumptions—Catholic universities in the United States should be limited to five: The Catholic University of America, the University of Notre Dame, and three Jesuit institutions.[70] Needless to say, this was a controversial opinion that, in the months ahead, would not go unchallenged.

Interestingly, to preempt the objection that, with only marginal means, the Society should not operate *any* universities, Harvanek insisted that there be three. In citing the reasons for this assertion, he moved his report a little closer to the concept of "objectives." According to his reading of the record, the history and tradition of the Society, the fourth part of the Constitutions of the Society, the decrees of the last (1957) general congregation, and the letters of Father General Janssens leave no doubt as to the obligation of Jesuits to engage in the apostolate of education at the highest levels. Moreover, the distinctive spirituality of humanism, characteristic of Jesuit intellectualism, combined with the Jesuit spirituality of action, confirm the apostolic imperative.[71]

The following March, the subcommittee filed a second progress report that was more controversial than the first one. Distinguishing between the "old image" of the Jesuit and the reality of the "new image," the subcommittee observed that the schools were not as "Jesuit" as they had been in the past. This change was not perceived by the committee members as an "unhappy or unwarranted development," but it should be honestly recognized. In that sense, the question is: "Are we building toward a lay university in which the Society provides the legal ownership, the president, a few top administrators, a few trustees and counsellors, but for the rest and for the most part the administration and the instruction is in the hands of the laymen?"[72] If that is the concrete situation, Father Harvanek asserted — and it was a position he would hold to the end — then it should have the official sanction of superiors.

Immediately aware of the explosive nature of this novel conclusion, the Executive Committee, looking for guidance before the matter got out of hand, moved to submit both progress reports to the Board of Governors. To test the water, the committee also recommended that Harvanek publish his draft as an article in the *JEQ*.[73] On their part, the provincials recognized a certain validity in the points that had been made and realized that they were being pushed toward a policy statement. For the moment, however, they wished the subcommittee to continue its work and to suggest some answers to the questions it had raised. The Board of Governors accepted the Executive Committee's recommendation and agreed that the province prefect from Chicago should publish his original draft in the *JEQ*, *as a personal article*.[74] "The discussion that such an article would occasion," the board felt, "might be of assistance to the subcommittee in formulating its draft statement."[75] (Unhappily, the board was not gifted with clairvoyance. If it had been able to anticipate the negative reaction of the Conference of Presidents, it probably would have buried Harvanek's paper in the file.) Surprised and shocked at the ideas propounded by the subcommittee, the presidents were quick to accept the challenge.

Father Harvanek's article, which appeared on schedule, deserves a brief analysis in virtue of the tart response from the Conference of Presidents and interventions from other sources.[76] After reviewing the history of the development of Catholic and Jesuit universities, the competition of state universities, the limited number of qualified Jesuits, and the lack of truly adequate resources, he articulated a basic question which had exercised not a few Jesuits who, up to this point, had kept their thoughts to themselves. The present situation "leads people to wonder whether we should not halt the drive behind the development of Jesuit universities, especially whether we not forgo developing our own professional and graduate education, but rather turn our attention to the educational apostolate within the secular universities."[77] To put it briefly, "What is the justification for the drive towards the development of Jesuit universities?"[78]

Following a broad survey of elements which might facilitate a resolution to this primordial debate, Harvanek proposed three possible responses. To avoid a long summary, it will be more succinct (and accurate) to quote his words:

> The first response is that which says that the decision and the commitment has already been made and that we are involved and cannot do otherwise than try to carry the venture forward as long and as well as possible. The second response develops a philosophy out of the exigencies of the situation and maintains that the developing modern Jesuit lay university is achieving a greater good than was achieved by the small liberal arts college with its theory of a select education of leaders, and a greater good than could be achieved by the small liberal arts college. . . . The third response would see the role of the Jesuit university as performing the work of the more intense Catholic higher education, recognizing that the less intensive, and the more laical education will be carried on in the secular universities, both state and private, as more and more Catholic students and professors enter into these institutions and are accepted there.[79]

The first to take up his pen and enter the lists in the pages of the *Quarterly* was C. Edward Gilpatric, then in his third year of theology at Alma College.[80] In a clever turn, he noted that there are two ways in which Harvanek's question could be phrased. (The tone of voice is important.) "Should there be Jesuit graduate schools?" is a straightforward interrogative. But, in a methodological sense, one might ask: "Why, indeed, should there be Jesuit graduate schools?"[81] Gilpatric understood Harvanek's responses not as choices in a philosophy of education, but as polarities or "pure types." They represent tendencies in a given direction. Moreover, the Society's commitment to university education, the first response, was the least satisfactory answer. However, if commitment includes obligation, the reason was compelling. In reference to the second response, which favors an expanded Jesuit university, instead of selection of elite students, Gilpatric was not impressed. He saw a basic flaw in abandoning the principle of the elite in favor of a large-scale operation.

> In such circumstances the quality of the education that our universities could offer necessarily declined. The word *necessarily* is used advisedly. The advocates of the expanding universities would maintain that large-scale operations and excellence are not in the very nature of things incompatible. No doubt some sort of case could be made for this position, although the experience of most human enterprises seems to argue that the opposite is more generally true. In any event the principle of maintaining excellence along with steady expansion is scarcely applicable in situations where the expansion far outstrips the available resources.[82]

In the end, Gilpatric chose the third response and came down in favor of the "intensely Jesuit University." The Jesuit and the Catholic scholar, he felt, "need the support . . . that is derived from a community with mutually shared ideals." Even more do they need access to a community of scholarship "which is beyond the competence of any single individual to master."[83] He admitted, however, that such a commitment would demand "a vastly greater degree of interprovince cooperation," which, he submitted, was not in evidence at that time. In summary, Gilpatric looked upon his contribution as "simply a strong vote for one of the several options open to us as we make our plans for the future."[84]

Allowed to comment in the same issue of the *Quarterly*, Father Harvanek was obviously pleased with Gilpatric's analysis, which added depth and, indeed, further refinement to his own preference. Gilpatric, he wrote, had "put his finger on the real difficulty in finding a solution: it is the absolute desire for institutional absolutism or complete autonomy of development."[85] The provincials could find no consolation in his indictment and the presidents even less, as Harvanek drove the shaft home. "We have not even had provincial planning, let alone regional or national planning."[86] Institutional autonomy, his *bête noir*, was the real point at issue. As long as that prevailed, he argued, "the first two responses will prevail and the third response will be only an ideal."[87]

This was not an academic debate, confined to the pages of the *JEQ*, that the presidents could safely ignore. The article, which encouraged partisans to take sides, stimulated discussions in Jesuit communities across the country. The presidents, their autonomy threatened, were compelled to respond and they chose Michael P. Walsh, president of Boston College, as their spokesman. Walsh did not disappoint them.

A resumé of the antecedents to Walsh's reply to Harvanek may be helpful in understanding the *dramatis personae* in this theatrical production. The chronology is also important. In February 1962 the subcommittee of five met at the provincial's residence in Oak Park, a suburb of Chicago, to consider comments and reactions to Father Harvanek's article. Two months later, the committee met again in Detroit to write a formal report for the Board of Governors.[88] This report, documented with Society legislation and quotations from letters of the Generals, supported, with some modifications, the so-called third response.[89] The Executive Committee submitted the report to the provincials at their 1963 meeting, and they, after expressing ritual appreciation to the committee of five, directed that it be referred to the presidents for their comments.[90] The presidents, without further urging, correctly interpreted this directive as an invitation to frame a frank rejoinder to Harvanek's article.

It was, then, with the provincials' blessing that Michael Walsh delivered his polished paper, "The Real Meaning of Jesuit Manpower Availability," at the conference of Jesuit presidents which met at Georgetown University in January 1964.[91] From the rhetorician's viewpoint, it was a masterpiece; measured by subsequent decisions, it was also effective. "The frank and fundamental analysis of the future of Jesuit higher education in the United States," Walsh began, "deserves a candid response."[92] He changed the *status questionis* slightly when he framed his topic sentence: "We are, it seems, asked whether we American Jesuits should be in the business of higher education at all except to run single-purpose, four year undergraduate colleges of liberal arts."[93]

In reply to this question, Walsh made three points. First, citing Earl McGrath and Alvin Eurich, of the Ford Foundation, he appeared to agree with their predictions that the A.B. degree, as we know it, would disappear before the end of the century.[94] (There is as yet, of course, no sign that this will occur.) Secondly, he urged that Jesuit universities be allowed to develop along American lines (a development in which size often means influence). He considered ten to twelve "solid Catholic universities" in the United States to be a reasonable goal, since "it would be a very grave matter, and hardly one that Jesuits would settle alone, to decide that henceforth there should be only four or five Catholic universities in America."[95] The Church itself, he wrote, should be involved in such a fundamental decision.

Father Walsh's third point was, perhaps, the most controversial. He seriously questioned the validity of the thesis that the *number* of available Jesuits should control the expansion of a Jesuit university — or, to put it another way, that the influence of the university was in direct proportion to the number of Jesuits on the faculty. In his judgment, which in time became the prevailing opinion, the critical requisite was the caliber, training, and strategic location of Jesuits in the university community. His philosophy of Jesuit education is quite clear.

> I personally believe that with a few outstanding Jesuit administrators, one very competent, scholarly Jesuit in each department of Arts and Sciences, one in each professional school, and with more, though equally well-trained, Jesuits in Philosophy and Theology, we could have a stronger *Jesuit* university, one that fulfills our objectives of quality education, with academic excellence and adequate moral, spiritual and religious formation of our students to a greater extent than we do at present.[96]

In his closing paragraphs, repeating the slogan of the JEA, he made an appeal for national planning and for the rigorous training of young Jesuits. In what appeared to be a parting word of advice to the provincials, he cautioned that "we pause long and prayerfully before we decide that running universities is not an appropriate enterprise for American Jesuits.[97]

Meeting at Santa Clara in August 1964, the JEA Commission on Colleges and Universities reproduced Walsh's article as a background paper for its discussions.[98] At this meeting, still pressing the attack, the commission prepared a draft "Statement on the Development of Jesuit Higher Education" which incorporated many of Walsh's ideas.[99] In conformity with the revised constitution of the JEA, the presidents submitted this draft directly to the Board of Governors "for direction and possible approval."[100] Eventually a copy of the draft statement was sent to Father Rooney, with a notation that Raymond J. Swords, president of Holy Cross College and secretary of the commission, would review the statement with the Board of Governors.

The question of "objectives" was again given priority at the meeting of the commission at Saint Louis University in January 1965.[101] The presidents found it difficult to reach any decision on the number, size, or complexity of "University Centers," which in translation meant graduate schools. As James Shanahan, provincial of the newly established Buffalo Province, who was in attendance at the meeting, remarked: "The crux of the problem is the inter-province cooperation on manpower."[102]

This was, indeed, central to the problem, but it was connected to another question which no one wanted to argue publicly. A development, which could have been predicted, was the muted disagreement between the presidents of universities and those of the four-year liberal arts colleges.[103] At Saint Louis, the presidents took an even stronger stand on those points in their statement to which the president of the JEA and his assistant for higher education had taken exception. The quarrel, again, focused on the freedom and self-determination which the presidents were demanding.

An anonymous respondent, who had been asked to comment on the Santa Clara Statement, characterized it as "a declaration of independence from Provincials and Province Prefects."[104] Another respondent, whose comment also had been solicited, replied: "It is evident that the Presidents do not wish any national body, e.g., the Board of Governors, to legislate on Jesuit higher education, or Provincials on the province level to be too concerned about what they are doing."[105] This was probably reading more into the statement than the presidents had intended, but it correctly identified the reaction which they had precipitated.

The controversy on objectives also introduced the first overt challenge to Rooney's position as president of the JEA. Although there was no such provision in the revised constitution, the presidents, at Georgetown and at Saint Louis, discussed and proposed the appointment of an executive director of the Commission on Colleges and Universities.[106] Such an office, if approved, would operate independently of the National Office of the JEA, report directly to the provincials, and duplicate many duties hitherto assigned by the constitution to the JEA president.[107] In a long lament to the vicar general, Rooney urged "that no such appointment be made without first giving the President of the JEA an opportunity to comment on the proposal."[108]

Rooney could find little consolation in Father Swain's response to his litany of complaints. After assuring the JEA president that the provincials had been reminded of their obligation to adhere to the revised constitution, he found it regrettable that, at the presidents' meeting at Saint Louis, Rooney had not "exercised his right to express to those present the ideas communicated to me."[109] Moreover, to set the record straight, wrote the vicar general, there was no document at the Roman Curia to support Rooney's statement that Rome had suggested the study on objectives in the first place.[110]

Astonished at this comment, which subtly impugned the origins of the whole controversy and, by implication, made him responsible for his own problems, Rooney appealed for justification to the memorandum of his conference with Vincent McCormick in 1959. It was not a formal order, he agreed, but he assumed that, as on former occasions, the Assistant's request "was Father General's wish."[111]

In a final observation, the vicar general informed Rooney that if the provincials wished to discuss the presidents' proposal for an executive secretary, they were free to do so. If, however, they wished to establish a new office that was not provided for in the revised constitution, the matter would have to be referred to the new General.[112] The tone of this letter, composed in cool, correct, and detached Latin, made it clear that Swain had offered his last animadversion on this subject. He would defer further decisions, if they were necessary, to the next General, whose election was imminent.

The great debate on the goals and aims of a Jesuit university had lost its excitement. Further discussion at this time would have been redundant. Sensing the futility of attempting to achieve a consensus, the Executive Committee voted to dissolve the subcommittee on objectives.[113] The province prefects were then asked to poll their respective provincials to determine their interest in continuing the work begun by the committee of five.[114] The responses revealed that the provincials themselves had ambivalent feelings and were not committed to a definite plan.[115] Even those who appeared to favor a standing committee on objectives did so without enthusiasm. In the face of that luke-warm support, the Executive Committee sensibly decided that it would take no further action. The Board of Governors, which had already recorded its appreciation for the work of the subcommittee and Father Harvanek, was now occupied with arbitrating the dispute that had erupted between Father Rooney and the Commission on Colleges and Universities.

The presidents, by presenting a solid front, had defeated the opposition. Although no one can say what would have happened if the Board of Governors, and Rome, had elected to follow Father Harvanek's lead, the presidents' program for unhampered, but orderly, expansion was probably the correct one. The dramatic growth of American higher education in the 1960s and 1970s, with accelerated enrollments, increased federal assistance, and private foundation support, vindicated the presidents' position. Far from falling behind, the prestige of Jesuit universities, enhanced by the infusion of qualified, often outstanding, lay colleagues, continued to grow; and the influence of these institutions matched the esteem in which they were held in academic circles in the United States. But to ensure permanency for their victory, the presidents were obliged to shape the 1948 JEA constitution in a new mold. Revision of the constitution was the key to their ultimate success.

# 10. The Revised Constitution, 1959–1964

AT THEIR MEETING in January 1960, several presidents complained that they had only recently learned that a revision of the JEA constitution was under consideration.[1] Actually, this was no secret, and, as Father Rooney was quick to point out, their ignorance of the matter was entirely their own fault. The JEA president, as was his custom, had sent each college and university president a copy of the pertinent items from his annual reports to the provincials. Although they were busy men, it was their responsibility to read the mail that arrived at their desks. In any case, what began as a modest effort to update the constitution ended with a decision for radical surgery, which drastically changed the course of events for Rooney and the JEA. It was the aggressive intervention of the presidents that made the difference.

The occasion that provoked a revision was not spectacular. In April 1958, William Schmidt, provincial in Chicago, sent on to Father Rooney a copy of a letter, dated April 14, 1958, which he had received from Frederick L. Moriarity of Weston College, secretary of the theologate deans, who at their recent meeting had voted "to apply for affiliation with the Jesuit Educational Association."[2] A problem, however, arose from the fact that article VII, 4, of the constitution limited seminary commissions to Jesuit philosophates and juniorates, since these were academically affiliated with Jesuit institutions. A "Commission on Theologates" would be the nomenclature most acceptable to the deans, but they were willing to consider alternative solutions. For his part, Rooney, who had not had an opportunity to discuss the proposal with the Executive Committee, gladly brought this request to the attention of the Board of Governors.[3] The provincials quickly approved the three commissions recommended by the JEA president, that

169

is, for theologates, philosophates, and juniorates. The board added: "It [the board] leaves to the President and the Executive Committee to work out any further details of nomenclature and necessary amendments to the Constitution of the JEA and to submit these for approval to the chairman of the Board of Governors of the Association."[4]

In reporting this development to the Executive Committee, Rooney indicated the changes that would be necessary in article VII in order to implement the provincials' directive.[5] After recalling the several amendments already attached to the constitution since its approval by Father Janssens in 1948, he continued: "It seems to me that now it may be time for a complete overhauling of the Constitution of the JEA."[6] The Executive Committee agreed with his suggestion and moved that an *ad hoc* subcommittee be appointed to prepare a draft. This subcommittee, subsequently approved by the provincials, was appointed on February 16, 1959, and included, in addition to Chairman Edward Rooney, three hard-working province prefects.

Joseph C. Glose, whose genial countenance was known to countless scholastics who had attended his classes in psychology at Woodstock College, was province prefect for colleges and universities in the New York Province. At the public celebration of his golden jubilee in the Society in 1960, he was aptly characterized as "a cheerful companion, a true friend, a happy religious and a gentle servant of God."[7] Father Glose, a member of the Executive Committee for ten years, had concentrated his energy and paternal interest on the academic formation of the young Jesuits entrusted to his care. It was said that he always had time to listen.

The New York Province prefect for high schools was also a ten-year veteran of the Executive Committee. Lorenzo K. Reed, who had been a successful principal at Canisius High School in Buffalo, was the first to be prepared for any meeting. He had a good grasp of detail, was famous for doing his homework, and enjoyed solving problems. Thoroughly familiar with the Society's legislation on education, he was, when the occasion arose, a valuable ally of the JEA president. He would be a key member of the subcommittee.

The third member of the committee was from New England, which facilitated collaboration by reason of geographical propinquity. Joseph D. FitzGerald, who had just completed his assignment as an inspector, was, on the death of Arthur Sheehan, appointed province prefect for high schools. This was a curious assignment since his administrative career had been exclusively with colleges (and he would later serve as president of Fairfield University). Although he could be decisive when the situation demanded it, he was essentially a diplomat who preferred conciliation to confrontation. A conservative by nature, and firmly committed to tradition, he would not easily endorse innovations.

In reporting to the provincials, Rooney anticipated "that several drafts of the Revision will have to be submitted before it is ready for presentation to the Board of Governors."[8] At this point, he was unaware of the difficulties he would encounter, and the provincials were equally unrealistic in requesting a draft "well in advance" of their 1960 meeting.[9]

With the provincials' deadline in mind, the subcommittee lost no time in getting down to work. From beginning to end, the procedure for revision followed a pattern which involved, in addition to the contribution of the subcommittee, the Executive Committee, the presidents and rectors, and of course the Board of Governors. What began in a flurry of activity eventually broke down into a tedious process of point and counterpoint. At the first meeting of the subcommittee, at the JEA Central Office on March 16, 1959, the members reexamined the constitution that had been promulgated in 1948, together with the amendments that had been approved since that time. The chairman then recalled developments within the JEA, such as the growth of conferences and the establishment of the JRCA, which required a more explicit reference in the constitution. The occasion also offered, as the chairman pointed out, "an opportunity for a declaration on the juridical effect of approval by the Board of Governors of the JEA of resolutions, recommendations, and other actions taken by the JEA."[10] The advantage of adopting bylaws was also discussed.[11]

At the next meeting, in June, the subcommittee continued to compose a draft of a new constitution. Under consideration were proposals to revise the method of financing the association, for defining the voting procedures of province prefects, and, as proposed by Robert Harvanek, for giving constitutional recognition to province directors of special studies.[12] The subcommittee had now reached article VI in its revision, and in a desperate effort to meet the provincials' timetable, the first draft was completed in March. A decision was made to omit mention of the director of special studies, since his work was technically independent of the JEA, and inclusion of a treasurer as an officer of the association was also deferred until the question of incorporation could be settled.

The revision of the constitution, which consumed the better part of five years, was unnecessarily complicated by reason of an intricate pattern of review and the multiplication of committees.[13] Approval was also delayed by appeals to several levels of authority. It would be tedious to record every detail in the long process toward consensus, but a brief chronology is important in order to understand the interaction of several groups.[14] The subcommittee completed its "First Draft" in March 1960 and submitted it to the Executive Committee. After annotations by that committee, the draft was again remanded to the subcommittee, which completed a "Second Draft," with bylaws, in November 1960. This draft was circulated by province prefects among the administrators in the individual provinces for their comments. After incorporating these suggestions, the document was submitted by Father Rooney to the Board of Governors at its May 1961 meeting.[15]

The subsequent response of the provincials was clearly influenced by the Conference of Presidents. At their 1961 meeting in Denver, the presidents appointed a four-man committee to receive, tabulate, and clarify those comments which each president had agreed to submit. The Presidents' Committee, at a hastily convened meeting at Seattle University in March, prepared an agenda for a plenary session of the conference, scheduled for April.[16] To avoid the charge of secrecy, Father Lemieux invited Leo Kaufman, province prefect of Oregon, to attend the meeting as Rooney's representative. This subcommittee of four proposed that (1) the Conference of Presidents petition the Board of Governors for a hearing at which the former's chairman, Paul Reinert, would indicate the broad outline of a new constitution, and (2) the presidents ask for a year's delay on any decision, during which time an institute might be held to determine the fundamental purpose of the JEA.[17] In the meantime, the better to prepare for the March meeting of the Executive Committee, Rooney asked Lemieux to send him "at his earliest convenience the comments he received from the presidents."[18] The president of the JEA was not made happier when he was informed that this request would have to be cleared with Father Reinert, "since our instructions were to review the suggestions and then send them on to him, who, in turn, would directly submit them to you."[19] This reply was a harbinger of things to come.

Although Rooney was unsuccessful in obtaining the comments sent by the presidents to their committee, the members of the Executive Committee were eminently successful in eliciting opinions from the presidents in their respective provinces. Two examples, both from the South, illustrate the tenor of their remarks. W. Patrick Donnelly, president of Loyola, New Orleans, in replying to a letter from Edward A. Doyle, province prefect, wrote that he had reviewed "the proposed second draft of the revision and had discussed it with others."[20] It was, he agreed, "an orderly document" and provided for the several functions of the organization "as conceived by the makers of the constitution."[21] He then went to the heart of the matter.

> The key to the whole constitution seems to be in the Executive Committee and in that committee's functions. If I can judge from my past meetings of Jesuit presidents, that particular group will not be happy in being excluded entirely from the executive committee as to representation. As you know, in some provinces the presidents of colleges and universities do not have great confidence in province prefects of studies' knowledge of college and university affairs and do not think that in those instances the prefects of studies adequately represent university and collegiate higher education. . . . Whether this is right or wrong is another question, but I do think it represents the thinking and the wish of the group of Jesuit presidents.[22]

Father Donnelly's colleague in the New Orleans Province was A. William Crandell, president of Spring Hill College in Mobile, Alabama, who became a very important spokesman for the presidents' efforts to influence negotiations on revision of the constitution. Tall, broad shouldered, and darkly handsome, he had the bearing and manners of a Southern gentleman. As a former member of the Board of Governors—he had been provincial from 1950 to 1956—his opinions were taken seriously by that elite group. In a sense, it could be said that Crandell gave respectability and credibility to Father Reinert's campaign to change the constitution. It is interesting to note, however, that since 1960, when he became president, his perspective on the JEA had changed dramatically from the days of his provincialate. He later acknowledged that his concept of the Executive Committee had undergone a transformation upon his arrival at the president's office, which became for him a source of new ideas.

His letter to Father Doyle is a classic statement of the presidents' position. Father Crandell believed, first of all, "that the presentation to the Board of Governors of the revised Constitutions [*sic*] should be delayed for a full year."[23] During that time, an opportunity should be given to various sectional or national groups to prepare their own reports and, if they wished to do so, submit them directly to the board. As Father Donnelly had stressed, careful consideration should be given to those sections of the constitution which refer to the province prefect of studies "so that his position in the governing structure of the Society may be clearly understood."[24] He then became technical.

> He [the Province Prefect] is a most important staff officer of the Provincial and not a line officer in the chain of command. This distinction

should be clearly made in all passages pertaining to his duties. Thus it seems to me that his duties in the educational institutions of the Province should be "to inspect and to report to the Provincial" rather than "to supervise."[25]

Reminding Father Doyle that no legislative power in the Society may come between the provincial and the local superiors, Father Crandell admitted that, with Father General's approval, "the Board of Governors is a quasi-legislative body for all of the institutions in the Assistancy."[26] In its operations, the board depends heavily upon the recommendations of the Executive Committee. For that very reason, he argued, "the Presidents feel that this committee should not be made up exclusively of staff officers but should contain a representation of the line officers who serve the Provincials in positions of authority in the colleges and high schools."[27] In explanation of his change of heart, he added: "I had not thought of this matter before I heard it discussed in the Presidents' Conference but after thinking it over I believe that it is a very valid opinion that should be given full consideration in the preparation of the revised Constitutions of the JEA."[28]

Against this background, the Conference of Presidents met in April at the Chalfonte-Haddon Hotel in Atlantic City. Because of a tight schedule, the report of the Seattle meeting was submitted, without a reading, to the assembled presidents for a brief period of private perusal.[29] The report, submitted by Edmund Morton in place of the absent Father Lemieux, was not accepted. At that point, Paul Reinert announced that he had requested, and received, an invitation to present the proposals of the presidents to the Board of Governors at its May meeting. With this incentive, and under the guidance of Reinert, chairman of the conference, the report was revised and accepted with unanimous approval.[30]

With a hastily written covering letter, Father Reinert sent a copy of the report, which he had personally typed, to Father Rooney, who was in Atlantic City for the annual meeting of the JEA. Promising "a more legible copy at a later date," Reinert explained that he would "discuss this proposal before the Provincials at their St. Louis meeting."[31]

This seven-page "Report of the Conference of Presidents" crystallizes the radically new approach of its authors. Although it disclaimed any intention of criticizing the contributions of the association and the valuable services of its president, the conference sincerely believed "that there is need for an entire re-thinking of the purpose, structure and, especially, the function of the JEA itself."[32] As the presidents saw it, the basic problem was that "neither among the national or provincial officers is there anyone who is identified with any of the *Institutions* that constitute the Jesuit Educational Association."[33] This situation "clearly presents the fundamental weakness" of the association, "whose direction is totally from without."[34] From this major premise, the presidents made specific recommendations for revision.

In their new scheme of organization and representation, the authority and function of the Board of Governors would remain intact. Below that level, four basic units (scholasticates, province prefects, colleges and universities, and secondary schools) would be represented by four permanent commissions, each with its proper chairman.[35] "Commissions, therefore, are the permanent constituents representing the variety of educational endeavors of the Society in the American Assistancy."[36] Moreover (this was the novel contribution of the presidents), "to achieve the unity which is the avowed purpose of the J.E.A. and to coordinate the work of the four distinct units," there should be an *Executive Committee* representative of the four commissions.[37] The presidents urged that this committee be composed of three representatives from the four commissions, and the president of the JEA.

An Executive (or Coordinating) Committee was the heart of the presidents' proposal, whose purpose, of course, was to eliminate the Executive Committee as currently constituted. Borrowing language almost *verbatim* from Father Crandell, the report made the technical distinction between line and staff officers, a combination of which would best serve the interests of all. A committee so constituted "would bring the Board of Governors into vital contact with those administrators who have been designated by higher superiors with the authority and entrusted with the responsibility of answering to the Society and to the Church for the well-being of these institutions."[38] In summary, the service work could still be performed by the province prefects, as staff officers, but "quasi-legislative proposals should be committed to a newly-formed Executive Committee."[39]

The intervention of the Conference of Presidents had thrown the subcommittee, and its chairman, off balance and off schedule. At their March meeting, the members of the committee decided to submit a progress report to the Board of Governors, rather than attempt a third draft of the constitution. Suggestions from the provinces had not been adequately assimilated and they could not, at that point, predict the exact form of the presidents' proposal. The subcommittee then agreed that the progress report, after giving reasons for not completing the draft, should contain a statement of certain facts which would help to dispel misconceptions of the uncompleted draft. Secondly, it would state the basic issues extracted from the comments and criticisms that had been sent to the subcommittee; clarify the position of the Executive Committee on these issues; and, finally, compose a list of suggestions that the Executive Committee felt were particularly valuable and should be considered for incorporation in the revised constitution.[40] In submitting this report to the provincials, Father Rooney reminded them that "no further steps can be taken by the Executive Committee until we know whether or not the Board of Governors approves of the radical changes in the organization of the JEA proposed by the Conference of Presidents."[41]

Although several important questions were before the board at its Saint Louis meeting, revision of the constitution was probably the most delicate.[42] The provincials found themselves in a difficult dilemma, since there were, obviously, two contending philosophies of organization, each with its own rationale. In possession of the progress report and the presidents' proposal, and further enlightened by oral presentations from both Rooney and Reinert, the board thought it prudent to postpone a decision. Since the divergence was too great for an immediate compromise, the board took the following action. First, it delayed, for at least a year, a final decision on revision of the constitution. Second, it directed the president of the JEA to appoint a committee that would consist of three province prefects, one college or university president, one secondary school representative, and one representative from the scholasticates, to study ways and means of improving the structure of the JEA and to offer suggestions for such an improved structure. Third, the provincials indicated, in detail, how the members of this committee were to be selected and chosen by their respective committees and commissions, with the president of the JEA acting as chairman. Finally, this committee was directed to report to the Executive Committee at its Spring 1962 meeting; the Executive Committee would, in turn, report to the Board of Governors in May 1962.[43]

In immediate compliance with the provincials' instructions, the president of the JEA contacted by letter those groups from which a representative would be chosen for the special committee. The selection procedure was carried out according to prescriptions, and on October 17, 1961, six Jesuits were appointed to the committee. Men of experience and sound judgment, they were concerned only with the success of the apostolate of education in the United States and the means to achieve it; they were not beguiled by pet projects. For the most part, they were familiar names: Joseph K. Drane, province prefect, Maryland; Herman J. Hauck, province prefect, California; William P. LeSaint, dean, Faculty of Theology at West Baden College; Julian L. Maline, province prefect, Detroit; Paul C. Reinert, president, Saint Louis University; Gerald R. Sheahan, principal, Saint Louis University High School; and Edward B. Rooney, chairman. Losing no time, Rooney suggested that the first meeting take place at John Carroll University, Cleveland, November 18 and 19.[44]

The provincials now expected a resolution of the differences and the committee prepared for a very important meeting. Father Rooney fully realized that his concept of the Jesuit Educational Association, which he had worked so hard to shape in his own image, would now be tested against another model of shared supervision. In the proposals and counterproposals that had thus far been made, three questions, which affected some basic assumptions within the JEA, continued to surface with unfailing regularity. These questions concerned (1) the legislative, or juridical, force of decisions handed down by the Board of Governors, (2) the authority of province prefects as members of the Executive Committee, and (3) the role of the presidents as line officers in the JEA In the past five years, Rome had furnished some answers and hinted at others.

At an early meeting of the Sub-Committee on Revision, the precise authority of a "response" of the Board of Governors came up for discussion. There was unanimous agreement that "strictly speaking, a Provincial can interpret a response the way he wishes, or could even neglect it."[45] However, in order to salvage some authority, the committee concluded that the force of a response was derived from an agreement—a kind of interprovince compact theory. Consequently, the subcommittee included in its first draft a statement to the effect that "actions agreed upon by the Board of Governors of the Association are binding on all constituent members."[46]

Father Rooney, who wanted support for this statement, pressed for an authentic interpretation. In the summer of 1960, as the debate continued, he submitted three questions to Father General Janssens.

1. When the Board of Governors gives a response and it appears in the Response or in the summary of the Response sent to officials of our educational institutions, is it binding on all concerned?

2. Is a Provincial free to disregard a Response in his own Province? (Presupposing that the Response was made by the unanimous decision of the Provincials.)

3.  Am I correct in thinking that by establishing and approving the JEA
    and its Constitution, an entity has been set up within the Society, viz.,
    the JEA, and by putting the Provincials over this entity as its Board
    of Governors, the Society intends that this group, viz., the Board of
    Governors, as a group has authority over the Association?[47]

In his reply, the General cited two pertinent documents as the
bases of his explanation. In promulgating the *Instruction*, Father Ledochowski had written: "It aims moreover at reorganizing our educational
institutions, *leaving untouched the inviolable principles of our Institute
and its Ratio Studiorum.*"[48] Secondly, the function of the Executive
Committee, under article 3 of the *Instruction*, "is to assist the Provincials in order that those things, ordained and approved by legitimate
authority for each Province, may be committed to execution."[49] Using
these citations as guidelines, the General responded to the three *quaesita*
put to him by the JEA president.

First, "the colleges are not bound to follow the 'Responses' unless
the General, for the entire Assistancy, or the Provincial, for his own
Province, promulgates them as mandatory." Second, "according to our
Institute, a Provincial is not bound by a decision that has been
unanimously agreed upon by the Provincials. In case of later dissent,
however, it would be proper to advise the Chairman of the previous
Provincials' meeting and the President of the J.E.A." Third, "in practice, it is the function of the J.E.A. President and the Executive Committee to decide which items the General or the Provincials are proposing for the Assistancy or for individual Provinces."[50] The Institute is
quite clear on these points, and the General was only confirming what
everyone knew and admitted.

The position of the province prefect and the function of the Executive Committee, however, were more difficult to define. The solution to these closely connected questions had eluded Rooney since his
appointment in 1937, although he had always insisted that his primary
interest was in qualified prefects of studies. In a letter to the General,
which was provoked by a particular situation, he asked: "I wonder if
you would give consideration to the idea of requiring that appointment
to the office of Province Prefect of Studies must have the approval of
Very Reverend Father General."[51] If such were the case, he added, "it
would be necessary to indicate that the man had the necessary qualifications for the position."[52] Janssens probably had no intention of
forcing the provincials to justify their appointments. Although he admitted a certain validity to Rooney's arguments, he decided against any
change in the established practice since the advantages did not out-
weigh the disadvantages.[53]

Father Rooney was grateful for a straightforward answer. Even though it was not to his liking, he was not discouraged, and continuing the campaign, he pressed the General for a statement on the composition of the Executive Committee, its supervisory function and independence. Since the presidents had already asked for two places on the Executive Committee, he urged Janssens to state "that the make-up of the Executive Committee is established by the *Instructio* and cannot be changed except by Father General."[54] While he admitted that the committee is advisory, he wanted another statement to the effect "that as Province Prefects, they are to have all authority necessary for their office."[55]

The following year, in his conference with the General, Rooney returned to this subject with renewed vigor. As he saw it, esteem for the office of province prefect was in decline, assignments were made at the whim of the provincial, who was likely to support a rector in any confrontation, and the presidents resented any supervision.[56] This was the real problem. "They [the presidents] do not feel that anyone who is not *at their level of authority* should be interposed between them and the provincial."[57] Rooney conceded that it was sometimes a question of personalities, but he saw "a more serious issue, viz., the right of *supervision by the General and the Provincial*, both individually and collectively through officials over our educational institutions."[58]

Supervision was the heart of the matter, and Rooney's comment struck a sensitive nerve at the Roman Curia. Shrewdly gauging this reaction, the JEA president reminded the General that "if the JEA is crippled or weakened, the only antidote [to the presidents' independence] will vanish."[59] In confirmation of Rooney's arguments, the General had at hand the minutes of the recent provincials' meeting at which Paul Reinert had presented his proposal for reorganization. In its comment, "the Board of Governors found serious difficulties with the plan as presented by Father Reinert."[60] After consultation with his Assistants, the General supported Father Rooney's position. Addressed to the chairman of the most recent provincials' meeting, the formal response was clear and, it appeared, decisive.

> With regard to the JEA, it seems most important that a committee, independent of the colleges and universities, should continue to function in a supervisory role over these institutions at the behest of and as an aid to the Fathers Provincial. Consequently, the JEA must not become dependent upon a committee of Rectors, Presidents etc. It is the mind of his Paternity that everywhere in the Society there should exist a type of supervision over our schools which depends on the Provincials, not, indeed, on the schools themselves.[61]

This response of the Vicar General, communicated to the president of the JEA by John McGinty, chairman of the Board of Governors, strengthened the hand of Father Rooney and added to his confidence as he opened the meeting of the special committee at John Carroll University in Cleveland. All the members of the committee, who had been supplied with the relevant documents, were present. In his introductory remarks, the chairman reviewed the history of the constitution from the early drafts in 1938 to its approval, in several forms, by Fathers Ledochowski and Janssens.[62] He described in greater detail the more recent events, including the proposals of the Conference of Presidents and the action of the provincials, leading to the appointment of the special committee.[63] In his explanation of the function of the committee, in which he repeated the instructions of the Board of Governors, Rooney made two points which, he hoped, would keep the discussions within bounds. Admitting the criticisms and suggestions that had been made by different groups, he added: "It strikes me that while we should be alert to needed changes we must also be careful to protect what has been advantageous in that structure."[64] Secondly, "it should be clearly remembered that the purpose of the JEA is to furnish a means of cooperation between the individual Jesuit institutions of a province and of the Assistancy, and to strengthen the bond of unity among those institutions."[65] In his opinion, these were the parameters within which the committee should operate.

Inasmuch as the background and the problems were described above, it is not necessary to review in every detail the sessions of this two-day meeting. It was, in fact, a congenial group, which avoided the temptation to rehearse the dialogue of old positions. The committee members agreed that they should answer two questions. First, "what kind of organization of the JEA do we wish consistent with the *Instructio* and other Society legislation?"[66] Second, "what structure will best transact the business of this organization?"[67]

In considering the second question, the committee made a genuine, and original, contribution in defining and describing the "services" of the association. This was an unambiguous response to the presidents, who had correctly insisted that the "service function" of the JEA be clearly distinguished from the "regulatory function" of the provincials. In its final form, the constitution reflected the committee's recommendations on this aspect of the association.[68]

In addition to *pro forma* revisions in membership, objectives, regional units, voting procedures, and the amendment process, the special committee addressed the two substantive questions which were crucial to the presidents' proposal and, therefore, the most delicate. The answer to one necessarily affected the other. At the third session, on Sunday, November 19, the committee discussed the structure of the organization—a structure that would achieve the purposes, services, and aims of the association.[69] Following Father Rooney's lead, and influenced no doubt by Father Swain's letter, the committee voted "to retain the Executive Committee membership as before, but modify functions of the members so as to have them consult Presidents and Rectors before meetings and represent their positions to the Executive Committee."[70] It also recommended, in another critical decision, to reduce the number of commissions to three, namely, one on scholasticates, another on colleges and universities, and a third on secondary schools. Each commission, with due regard to geographical representation, would be composed of three province prefects, three presidents or rectors, and three academic administrators.[71]

Although the record is silent on the point, one can only assume that Paul Reinert was outvoted on both substantive issues. As events turned out, the presidents were keenly disappointed in the recommendation to retain the Executive Committee as originally designed, rather than create a new committee that would be representative of four commissions. In the meantime, the recommendations of the special committee were turned over to the JEA Sub-Committee on Revision, with the suggestion that they be incorporated into a tentative draft. The draft should be submitted to the special committee and then, with whatever comments were necessary, to the Executive Committee.

In a series of meetings between January and April 1962, marked by signs of impatience on the part of some, a tentative third draft of the revised constitution was finally completed. A needlessly complicated process, it involved the reconciliation of positions taken by the Executive Committee and the two *ad hoc* committees. (To most parliamentarians, it would have seemed extraordinary that Edward Rooney was the chairman of all three committees.) To the end, problems persisted on the extent of the authority of the Board of Governors, the concept of supervision, the function of the province prefects, the organization of province units, and the relationship of conferences to commissions.[72] Almost in desperation, and with the conviction that nothing better could be achieved, the Executive Committee voted to submit the third draft of the constitution, which had been approved on April 6, to the Board of Governors.[73]

But that was not the end of the story. Since he had won the battle on the retention of the Executive Committee, which had always been his principal concern, Father Rooney probably did not suspect that he would ultimately lose the war. Informed by Father Reinert, at their January 1962 conference, that Father General wished the province prefects to continue in their customary role, the presidents reacted with ominous silence. Nor does any overt dissension appear in the minutes of their spring meeting at the University of Detroit. However, behind the scenes there was an epistolary exchange at a very high level. A. William Crandell, the new chairman of the Presidents' Conference, had evidently written to the General, in late March, urging his favorite thesis on the reorganization of the JEA. The content of his letter can easily be deduced from the answer, whose wording was very carefully drawn.

Acting as agent for the General and the vicar general, the American Assistant reviewed the reasons for the General's original decision as contained in the vicar's letter of October 9, 1961. Father Small then repeated that "the point to be assured and guaranteed . . . is the existence of a supervisory body of Province Prefects, which depends on the Provincials and not on the schools themselves."[74] He added, rather enigmatically, that "this reply does not indicate that Father General (or Father Vicar) wants the Executive Committee to remain just as it is, without any change in its membership."[75] Consequently, "it does not seem out of order for the Conference of Presidents to present its reorganizational suggestions through the proper channels."[76] In a second letter, with what appeared to be further support from Rome, the Assistant informed Father Crandell that "Father General approves of the Presidents' Conference submitting their proposals, as outlined by your reverence, to the meeting of the Fathers Provincial."[77]

The president of the JEA was surprised, but grateful, to receive from Father Small copies of his letters to Father Crandell. In his letter of acknowledgment, Rooney reminded the Assistant "that the very same request was made to the Provincials last year . . . and it was not accepted."[78] He added, with resignation, "of course this does not preclude the possibility of reconsideration."[79] While dutifully protesting that "whatever the Provincials decide and what Father General approves will be perfectly alright [*sic*] with me," he hoped (with understandable weariness) "that this matter is going to be settled soon. It has been dragging on all too long and I am sure that everyone will be pleased to have it over with."[80]

Actually, matters were slowly but surely coming to a head. Whether the timing was calculated or not, on Monday, May 7, one day before he was to present his report to the provincials, Rooney received from Crandell a copy of a "Memorandum to the Board of Governors from the J.E.A. Conference of Presidents." Crandell was scheduled to present the memorandum to the board that very afternoon. The presidents, who hoped that the ideas in the memorandum would "be incorporated in the new constitution of the Association," came quickly to the point.[81] Candidly admitting that "these proposals . . . are substantially the same as those presented . . . to the Board of Governors last year," the conference repeated its recommendation that the Executive Committee of the association consist of the president of the JEA, his two assistants, and three members from each of the four commissions — a total of fifteen members.[82] The commissions would be "empowered to elect or appoint, in any manner suitable to them, their representatives on the Executive Committee."[83] Appropriate conferences would operate under the commissions. The memorandum clearly reflected the views of Fathers Reinert and Crandell, who, it appeared, were more determined than ever to ensure that the presidents have an active voice in shaping decisions that would affect colleges and universities.

There was, indeed, a problem, but the presidents were equal to the occasion. They had devised a means whereby the presidents would have membership on the Executive Committee and, at the same time, the province prefects would exercise the supervision required by the General. Although, as the presidents admitted, the impression was created that the conference "was trying to dominate the J.E.A.," that was not the case. "The Conference of Presidents does not want to interfere in any way with the duties of the Province Prefects acting as a group" for the supervision of the institutions.[84]

In the proposal as submitted, the right of supervision was ensured in two ways. First, "that the Commission of Province Prefects be empowered to report directly to the Board of Governors, without reference to the Executive Committee, on all matters pertaining to the proper supervision of the institutions of the JEA or any special assignments that may have been given to it directly by the Board of Governors," and second, "that the President of the JEA and the three Province Prefects of the Executive Committee be empowered to discuss with the Commission of Province Prefects any matters on which they feel the Commission would like to submit a report of its own in addition to the report of the Executive Committee."[85] Although there was a parliamentary legerdemain in this intricate constitutional procedure, as events turned out it seemed to satisfy both the General and the presidents. Ultimately, it satisfied everyone but the president of the association.

Appearing before the provincials on May 8, Father Rooney complained that this was the second time that the presidents had "effectively by-passed the Executive Committee by presenting its recommendations after the close of the spring meeting of the Executive Committee."[86] Then, depending upon hastily prepared notes, (later organized in a six-page report) he repeated his standard objections, namely, that the presidents' proposal effectively made two executive committees, multiplied meetings, and placed a commission between the provincials and the province prefects. In summary, he doubted that Province Prefects would be as independent as Father General wished or as free to supervise as the presidents pretended.[87]

The following day, Rooney wrote out a more detailed criticism of the Crandell memorandum and, with the permission of Father Provincial James Coleran, chairman, submitted it to the Board of Govenors.[88] In this critique, he pointed out that a commission of province prefects placed the provincials' representatives, their special collaborators, on the same level as other commissioners. Moreover, he argued, since the commissions would elect their own representatives on the Executive Committee, the provincials would have no control over its composition. His conclusion was that "the proposal should be rejected" and that the third draft, prepared by the subcommittee and the special committee, should be accepted.[89]

Confronted again with two divergent propositions, the provincials took refuge in silence. As Rooney reported to the province prefects, "no response is made of the [revision] item."[90] However, as he later confided to the General, he received a letter from Father Provincial Coleran, dated May 14, 1962, in which he was informed that "it was the conclusion of the Provincials that this revision should be given further consideration and for this reason a commmittee [of Provincials] was named; for the present the Provincials prefer not to disclose the members of the Committee."[91] Then, standing on his rights as national secretary of education of the American Assistancy, Rooney asked that if the provincials approved Father Crandell's memorandum, "I be given an opportunity to send you further comments on the proposal."[92]

Although the provincials' committee had been hard at work on a revision of the constitution for an entire year, not a word of its progress was communicated to the Central Office of the JEA. The three members of this committee, whose identity was temporarily shielded by the Board of Govenors, had administrative and academic backgrounds that may have influenced their sympathies. The chairman, James J. Shanahan, provincial of the Buffalo Province, had been president of St. Peter's College and was known to share the viewpoint of the Conference of Presidents. The second member, John M. Daley, the Maryland provincial, had earned his Ph.D. in American history at Georgetown University, where he had also served for a number of years as graduate dean. John R. Connery, the third member, was provincial of the

Chicago Province. He had taken his doctorate in moral theology at the Gregorian University; taught that subject at West Baden College, where he was a popular professor; and then moved to the Bellarmine School of Theology at North Aurora, Illinois. Although these men had friends among the presidents, all were innocent of any previous connection with the province prefects.

Father Shanahan reported orally for his committee at the 1963 meeting of the Board of Governors. With no surprises, his committee, following the presidents' lead, proposed that the major commissions report directly to the board and that the *coordinating* committee handle common problems. The role of the national secretary of the JEA would be one of service, not supervision.[93]

In the course of Rooney's annual conference with Father General (at Villa Cavalletti, outside Rome) in July 1963, Father Assistant Small evidently hinted at the provincials' objections to the Executive Committee.[94] Rooney's retort, of course, was that the Executive Committee was simply functioning according to the *Instruction*, the constitution, and the letters of the General. In any case, after repeating his request to see any revision that might be approved, the General "said that he would see to it that no change was made in the JEA constitution without my seeing any proposed revision."[95] True to his word, in a letter written shortly after the Roman conference, Harold Small, acting as surrogate for the General, asked Father Rooney to submit his comments on a document entitled, "Constitution of the Jesuit Educational Association," which had been sent to Rome by the American provincials after their May 1963 meeting. It was more than a *pro forma* request, as the Assistant added: "It seems to me that it would be helpful if you not only gave your frank opinion, as I know you will, but also if certain ideas were adopted, which you oppose, how they might be modified to make them less unacceptable."[96]

To his surprise, and disappointment, the document — in its essence — reflected the proposal which Father Crandell had consistently and vigorously urged for the past three years. In his criticism, omitting articles that were noncontroversial and those that were incorporated *verbatim* from the third draft, Father Rooney concentrated his fire on article V, A, paragraph 5: "There shall be a Coordinating Committee . . . composed of three duly elected representatives from each of the [four] Commissions."[97] In opposing this committee, which would replace the Executive Committee, he rehearsed all the arguments which he had advanced for the past three years. He agreed that "the present set-up of the JEA can be improved," but the coordinating committee, as proposed and constructed, was not the answer.

In his final arguments, Rooney, for the first time, introduced a personal element. "I never heard," he wrote to the General, "a serious complaint about the operation of the JEA until the Conference of Presidents came into being."[98] In his judgment, it was the "supervision" of the province directors of education, as exercised through the Executive Committee, that had originally generated the resentment of the presidents. At the end of this thirteen-page memorandum, Father Rooney attached a draft "in which I have incorporated my proposals as well as all the changes proposed by the Provincials which I believe are workable."[99]

Alas, his courageous and vigorous efforts to defeat the presidents' proposal were to no avail. Although he was excluded from the final negotiations, Rooney was at last informed that a decision had been made. In a letter from the New York provincial, who was also chairman of the Board of Governors, he was told that "Very Reverend Father General . . . has approved a revision of the Constitution of the Jesuit Educational Association."[100] Father McGinty then continued with an expansive paragraph which was designed to bring a measure of consolation to the president of the JEA:

> The Fathers Provincial, and the Jesuits who are engaged in educational work in the Assistancy, know well how much of the success of the J.E.A. has been due to your wise and courageous leadership and your unbounded devotion to its well-being. You and the members of the Executive Committee, past and present, deserve our thanks and our acclaim. Let me, in the name of all, acknowledge our admiration and gratitude for what you have accomplished, and our complete cooperation in your implementation of the new Constitution.[101]

In the same communication to Father Rooney, the provincial enclosed a copy of the text of the revised constitution, together with a copy of the General's official letter of approval. Father Janssens, first noting that the educational apostolate in the American Assistancy "had matured academically and expanded significantly" in the past twenty-five years, observed that "a primary agent effecting union and cooperation among those educational institutions . . . has been the Jesuit Educational Association."[102] Gratitude was due, of course, to all who conducted the affairs of the organization, but "especially to Father Edward B. Rooney, without whose energetic and talented efforts the JEA would not have attained its present level of achievement."[103]

But even though the General admired Father Rooney, he obviously did not agree with him. The General supported the Conference of Presidents:

This revision . . . modifies the organization of the JEA, by establishing four Commissions to promote the function and interests of their members: the Commission on Secondary Schools, the Commission on Colleges and Universities, the Commission on Houses of Studies, and the Commission of Province Directors of Education. A *Coordinating Committee* consisting of three duly elected representatives of each of the four Commissions, with the President of the JEA as an *ex officio* member and Chairman of the Committee will take the place of the former Executive Committee, and will serve to coordinate the activities common to the several Commissions and advise the Board of Governors in administering the Association.[104]

There was, therefore, one point on which the General and the president of the JEA were in agreement. The modification, or revision, of the old constitution lay precisely and essentially in the creation of the Coordinating Committee and its satellite commissions.[105]

In any case, everyone breathed a sigh of relief that the suspense had ended. *Roma locuta est. Causa finita est.* The General, after noting that the revision "merited the unanimous recommendation of the Fathers Provincial," added his blessing: "I am pleased at this time, to grant my approval for the promulgation of the revised Constitution of the JEA."[106] With a covering letter, appropriately released on the Feast of Saint Ignatius, the chairman of the Board of Governors sent copies of the new constitution to members of the American Assistancy.[107]

The debate within the American Assistancy triggered by the revision of the constitution symbolized the pain that often accompanies change as the old order gives way to the new. It was natural for one who had exercised a proprietary protectorate over the association for twenty-seven years to look upon a radical reform as a personal rejection, even censure, of his contribution. But that was not the point. The presidents and provincials were reading the signs of the times. The president of the JEA and his Executive Committee, as everyone admitted, had done an extraordinary service, in a relatively short time, in welding together the educational efforts of the American Assistancy. The presidents realized, however, as Father Rooney apparently did not, that Jesuit universities in the United States had to keep pace with other American universities in the race for excellence and influence.

# 11. The New Order, 1964–1968

THE YEAR 1964 WAS a watershed in the history of Jesuit higher education in the United States. Not only had the presidents won the tacit permission of the provincials to expand their colleges and universities with very little reference to "higher superiors"; they had also designed a revised constitution that guaranteed the freedom they coveted. Having slipped their Roman moorings, these Jesuit institutions glided smoothly into the mainstream of American academic life and discovered that their vessels were seaworthy. The presidents, some of whom were hesitant in the beginning, as new commanders often are, used the authority that had been conferred upon them with respect and, in general, used it wisely.

The mid-1960s was not an ideal time to test the presidents' navigational equipment and skills. With the death of President John F. Kennedy in November 1963, Lyndon B. Johnson, his successor, was faced with a bad situation in Southeast Asia that would ultimately destroy his political life. The sparks from the war in Vietnam, which began in earnest in the summer of 1964 with the Tonkin Gulf Resolution, ignited the campuses of American universities, which three years later erupted into riots and anti-war demonstrations. The climax came in 1970, when four students at Kent State University were killed by Ohio National Guardsmen. Jesuit campuses, of course, were not immune from student unrest. From Boston College on the East Coast to Santa Clara on the West, Jesuit students had to leave their ivy halls for the rice paddies of Vietnam.[1] But Vietnam was probably only the catalyst. The students, who were born as World War II ended, seemed hyperactive; they mistook liberty for license and freedom for irresponsibility. Suspended classes and canceled examinations made it an anxious time for college administrators.[2]

Other movements contributed to a changing world. The Catholic Church itself was in the process of removing four centuries of barnacles

188

from Peter's bark. The Second Ecumenical Vatican Council (1962–1965) "opened the windows," as Pope John XXIII put it, to allow fresh air to enter the chancel and enable the Church to look out upon the modern world. Through serious dialogue with the basic elements of society and with a renewed accent on social justice, the Council attempted an *aggiornamento* with all aspects of the human family, and one of the documents approved by the Council was the *Declaration on Christian Education*.[3] It was not one of the more profound statements of the conciliar fathers, but it answered the challenge of those who would deny the Church the right to teach. It also gave conciliar support to the Jesuit apostolate of education.

In an excellent introduction, G. Emmett Carter, cardinal-archbishop of Toronto, claimed that the document's distinction "is the insistence upon the integration of Christian education into the whole pattern of human life in all its aspects."[4] Moreover, in conformity with the spirit of Vatican II, "the contrast is with a form of thinking and acting of another age when it was considered best to keep Christians away from the world lest they be contaminated thereby."[5] The archbishop added:

> The present Declaration spells the official and definitive end of any possible false thinking on this score. The Church here states with utmost clarity that it has no desire to remain away *from* the world in a form of isolation but that Christian education is *in* the world and, in a sense, *for* the world, since man must always work out his salvation in the concrete situation in which God has placed him. . . . [6]

With that brief explanation, the document takes on added meaning. Historically occupied with schools of higher learning "and with individual branches of knowledge studied according to their own proper principles and methods," the Church

> intends thereby to promote an ever deeper understanding of these fields, and as a result of extremely precise evaluation of modern problems and inquiries, to have it seen more profoundly how faith and reason give harmonious witness to the unity of all truth. . . . The hoped-for result is that the Christian mind may achieve, as it were, a public, persistent, and universal presence in the whole enterprise of advancing higher culture, and that the students of these institutions may become men truly outstanding in learning, ready to shoulder society's heavier burdens and to witness the faith to the world.[7]

Emphasizing a spirit of cooperation that would have delighted Father Janssens, the *Declaration* urged the colleges and universities to unite in a mutual sharing of effort; together they can promote international conferences, allot fields of scientific research, share discoveries, exchange teachers temporarily, and foster among themselves whatever else contributes to more helpful service.[8]

If the presidents of Jesuit colleges and universities needed further encouragement, they now had a magisterial sanction for their ambitious plans. At least that is the way the *Declaration* was interpreted by those who took the time to study it. But — as was the tendency with other conciliar documents, often to the amazement of the fathers who had approved them — there was a predisposition to assume a broader meaning — or "flexibility" — than had been intended. Added to the statement of the Council was the generous interpretation of Pedro Arrupe, who, anxious to please, was quick to delegate authority to responsible people. In many ways, though not in *every* way, the advent of a new General abetted the presidents' plans.

After a steady decline in health during the summer and early fall, John Baptist Janssens, who bore his infirmities bravely, died a peaceful death on October 5, 1964.[9] Convoked by Vicar General John Swain, the Thirty-first General Congregation, on Saturday, May 22, 1965, elected the provincial of the Japanese Province the twenty-eighth successor to Saint Ignatius of Loyola.

Pedro Arrupe, the new Superior General of the Society of Jesus, was born on November 14, 1907, at Bilbao, a city in the Basque region of northern Spain. Interrupting his study of medicine at the University of Madrid, he entered the Society at Loyola (a hallowed shrine) on January 15, 1927. To broaden his background, he was, as a scholastic, introduced to the customs, habits, and manners of American Jesuits. After completing his course in theology at Saint Mary's College, Kansas, where he was ordained to the priesthood in 1936, he was guided through the tertianship by Father Francis X. McMenamy, the beloved instructor at Saint Stanislaus in Cleveland.

Father Arrupe arrived in Japan in 1938 and for the next twenty-seven years dedicated his efforts and talents to the remarkable people of that mission. His character, already marked by his Basque origins, was influenced during his long sojourn in Japan by Eastern practices and Oriental modes (and persisted even at the Roman Curia). When the atomic bomb was dropped on Hiroshima, Arrupe, who was instructing the novices at Nagatsuka, a suburb, led the first rescue party into the stricken city. Using his knowledge of medicine, he converted the novitiate into a hospital and treated the victims.[10] With his high forehead, piercing dark eyes, and gaunt, ascetic face, he had the distinctive visage of a Spaniard. His warm smile, however, was a key to the compassion and tender care he exercised toward his subjects throughout his generalate.[11]

His career as a Jesuit had not been closely identified with the apostolate of higher education, but he was fully aware, as a missionary, of the enormous contribution of Sophia, the Jesuit university in Tokyo, to the success of the Japanese mission. He realized, as provincial, that education was the key to conversion and to influence. As General, one of his closest collaborators would be Vincent T. O'Keefe, the former president of Fordham University, who was privy to and sympathetic toward the presidents' program. The Thiry-first General Congregation itself, though it followed the lead of Vatican II in emphasizing the pastoral apostolates, reminded Jesuits that the intellectual apostolate is "one of the primary ministries of the Society."[12] On account of the "ever-growing ·importance of universities and institutions of higher learning, . . . we must see to it that the Society and its priests are present to this work."[13] Moreover, Arrupe was convinced of the logic of Father Janssens oft-repeated admonition, which found—so to speak— an echo in Vatican II: "Jesuits should have a high regard for scholarly activity, especially scientific research properly so-called, and they are to view this as one of the most necessary works of the Society."[14]

Shortly after the completion of the first session of the Thirty-first General Congregation, the General took advantage of two opportunities to clarify his personal thoughts on education. Granted that he was specifically addressing the administrators and teachers in secondary schools, his message to the French Assistancy, nevertheless, concerned the basic question of the educational apostolate.

> They say [he wrote to the delegates at Amiens] that other apostolic ministries are today more efficacious. I cannot believe it, for nothing is more useful to contemporary society than to prepare for it men of solid character and personality whom that same society now so critically needs.[15]

Moving to another country and a larger stage, Father Arrupe accepted an invitation to deliver an address at the 1966 National Meeting of the JEA at Loyola University, Chicago. It was his first visit to the United States after his election as Superior General, although he had several times, while provincial, canvassed the American Assistancy for support in men and money for the Japanese mission. On this occasion, at the microphone before an expectant audience of presidents, deans, and principals, the General seemed genuinely impressed with the achievements of the system.

I am proud that everywhere in your marvelous country you have qualified our schools professionally; you are recognized and accredited. You sit in high level deliberation at planning tables with your fellow educators from state schools and from other private schools. Men of good will everywhere look upon our Jesuits in education as partners who are intent on developing constantly better schools. They consider us as peers and colleagues who furnish a component part of the total American educational program. . . . America will always need a parallel educational system that can speak with positive conviction and teach with authority of absolute values, a system where morality and virtue can be explicitly and formally cultivated.[16]

One sentence in that address seemed innocuous but had a very sharp point. "I encourage you to devote yourselves unquestioningly and unreservedly to the life of scholarship."[17] Then, almost as an afterthought, he added: "There is harmony and high compatibility in the role of priest and teacher."[18] This observation, which many may think self-evident, was a reference to a current crusade by certain, predominantly young, Jesuits to replace the intellectual apostolate with social programs. These young members of the Society professed to see incompatibility between the priest and the researcher—some, indeed, held that the intellectual ministry is an apostolate by "default" and, in their judgment, should be pursued only until priest-teachers could be replaced by laymen.[19] The controversy, which should not be characterized as a "movement," was carried on in the pages of the *JEQ*, and symposia were held to justify the ministry of the priest-scholar.

This development caught the presidents by surprise and they marshaled their most impressive spokesmen to combat it. At a 1964 Woodstock Symposium, which included three presidents, Vincent T. O'Keefe, reenforcing the arguments of his co-panelists Michael P. Walsh and Paul Reinert, came down hard in favor of the intellectual apostolate which had served Jesuit higher education so well in the past.[20] These presidents who had fought hard to persuade the provincials to their position on expansion, were keenly aware—apprehensive—of the probable consequences of a successful challenge to the intellectual apostolate, the very foundation of the Jesuit edifice of higher education. Fortunately, the Thirty-first General Congregation supported the presidents and warned those who might question the efficacy of the educational apostolate "against the illusion that they will serve God better in other occupations which can seem more pastoral, and they are to offer their whole life as a holocaust to God."[21]

In the broad context of these developments in the Society and the Church, the presidents explored the possibilities for accelerating the potential of their institutions. Nominally—although they were now operating under the aegis of the Commission on Colleges and Universities and the revamped Coordinating Committee—they were still accountable to the venerable president of the association. As far as they were concerned, the sooner a change was effected, the better.

Since, in the revision of the constitution, the case had gone against Father Rooney, it would have made more sense to change the top management in 1964. However, due to the death of Father Janssens and the formalities surrounding the election of a new General, the appointment of a successor was postponed and Rooney was charged with the responsibility for the reorganization of the association under the new constitution.[22] In his letter of July 25, the New York provincial had written that, in his opinion, "the first and most important task is the establishment of the Coordinating Committee."[23] Until this was accomplished, since it "will take considerable time," he asked the JEA president to carry on in what amounted to a "caretaker" management. When the province directors of education met at Regis College, Denver, in August 1964—their first meeting as a commission under the new constitution—they elected their own officers and then the three members of the Coordinating Committtee. Then, as instructed by Father McGinty, they made plans to assist in the formation of other commissions and the eventual membership of the Coordinating Committee.[24]

While these constitutional legalities were gradually implemented, the presidents, meeting at Saint Louis University, were unsuccessful in solving some problems of their own. Although they had talked a lot, and written more, about "university centers," there was no common understanding of what was meant by that designation. Their dilemma was whether to follow Michael Walsh's lead or Robert Henle's, since there was a notable divergence in their respective approaches to this question. As Father Swords, secretary of the Commission on Colleges and Universities, explained to the Board of Governors: "Father Henle proposes a really high-powered, predominantly graduate program of research institutes, consultant departments in all professions, more along the lines of post-graduate work."[25] Such an intensive academic program would necessarily require an interprovince exchange of qualified Jesuits. Father Walsh, however, urged "a more complex and expanded university concept with freedom to undertake more programs and to grow larger and more complex."[26] Since the Walsh blueprint did not involve interprovincial cooperation, "the Presidents of the larger universities seemed to favor the idea of Father Walsh but there are still many hazy ideas concerning both proposals."[27]

Once again, the deeper question was manpower, a discussion of which always made every president nervous. Whether large, medium, or small, all institutions were fearful lest they be called upon to make a sacrifice for the sake of the others. At Saint Louis, Father Crandell pointed out that expansion ultimately depended upon the provincial and, therefore, "there should be more thinking between the Presidents and Provincials about the number and location of University Centers."[28] Father Shanahan, who had traveled to St. Louis from Buffalo, then inserted into the record an excerpt from a letter of the vicar general, written only a month before the commission met, urging a resolution of the problem. His comment went to the heart of the matter, and deserves to be quoted at length.

> The report of the JEA Commission on Colleges and Universities on the establishment of University Centers brings into focus a problem for which the Commission should seek a solution. All the Universities think University Centers fall within the scope of American Jesuit higher education, but the "Complex Universities" recommend "a small number" of such centers, while the "Medium Complex Universities," which would be expected to contribute manpower, advocate "no more than one."
>
> If the creation of one or more University Centers means that the other "Complex Universities" would be limited in their academic offerings, the Center or Centers should be determined as soon as possible to prevent fruitless expansion and odious contraction and hasten the advent of such creative academic collaboration. Therefore, the Commission should clearly define the term "University Center" and explicitly state the limitations and obligations of those Universities not so designated; and should seek to determine the number and location of this Center or Centers.[29]

Rome, obviously, was telling the presidents to make up their minds and to submit a concrete plan. But, as the record makes clear, the presidents were either unwilling or unable to forge a consensus on what was, from the beginning, a nebulous idea. Always the realist, with little time for concepts, Walsh lamely admitted that he and Father Henle had written their papers, the basis for the whole discussion, to answer objections which had been raised in reference to the expansion of Jesuit universities. In the papers, "we merely wished to get across the idea that our schools should be permitted to grow at their own pace."[30]

In the end, the whole discussion was "academic." Although the question would surface from time to time, as if it were a ritual reminder of greater things to come, the large, complex universities, such as Georgetown, Fordham, and Boston College in the East and Saint Louis, Marquette, and Loyola (Chicago) in the Midwest, continued to respond to the needs of their constituencies, the managerial skills of their presidents, and the availability of resources. By an infusion of lay personnel in both staff and faculty, these institutions laid the foundation for graduate programs that could, in a true sense, be characterized as "University Centers," though that terminology was never applied. The interprovince cooperation, which had been advocated for best results, was never implemented. Each president had to depend upon his own powers of persuasion to convince the provincial of the needs of his institution.[31]

In a related development, the presidents were beginning to realize, as Rooney had predicted, that additional staff assistance would be needed to manage the empire they had created. They were convinced that an executive director of the Commission on Colleges and Universities would be the answer to their problems — and their prayers. Although the oft presented plan had thus far defied national acceptance, since it involved the consensus of autonomous provincials, the presidents were sanguine that a reasonable and equitable interchange of Jesuit personnel could be arranged. This would be the executive director's first mandate.

However, the job description for that position, as drawn up by a subcommittee chaired by Vincent O'Keefe, would have discouraged any normal person from accepting the challenge. Even Father Shanahan, a model of industry, felt that the job "in its present form . . . includes too many duties for one man."[32] In addition to routine office management, he would supervise interprovince and interinstitutional exchanges, act as a liaison with national and international associations, promote publicity, establish a clearing house for information, and in general represent the presidents in a surrogate capacity.[33] Although his relation to the presidents was clear, his relationship, if any, to the JEA was vague.

In his attempt to unravel the mystery, at his meeting with the provincials in April 1965, Father Swords was unable to shed much light on the subject. "His [the Executive Director's] role was envisaged," Swords explained, "as on an indirect relationship with the Jesuit Educational Association, but having no authority in it, nor being responsible to the Jesuit Educational Association President."[34] An honest man, as those who knew him would testify, he admitted that "this was an area that was not clear."[35] The provincials were in total agreement with that conclusion, and one "suggested later that it would be most important to redefine the functions of both offices . . . so that we don't end up with two independent men."[36]

Actually, neither the provincials nor the new General, who had been warned by Rooney in his first conference with him, accepted the arguments for an executive director.[37] However, in a final effort to influence the provincials, the presidents recommended for the position a trusted lieutenant with impeccable credentials. Surely, A. William Crandell, a former provincial and president of Spring Hill College, who recently had been succeeded in that office by William J. Rimes, would bring distinction, prudence, and experience to the position.[38] But, at this point, the provincials had other plans for Father Crandell, whose future duties, in fact, would closely approximate those that would have been assigned to an executive director of the Presidents' Commission. The long-expected and, for some, eagerly awaited change in JEA leadership was about to take place.

The change in leadership, when it came (in 1966), was a dramatic moment in the history of the JEA. For twenty-nine years, in good times and bad, Edward Rooney, as national secretary of education and president, had presided over the councils of the association. But there is always a temporal limit to human endeavors.[39] In a letter written just five days before the election of Father Arrupe, the American provincials were informed that the new General would consider the appointment of a successor to Father Rooney.[40] The following October, they agreed that a replacement should be sought, and the matter was resolved in a letter from the General to the Oregon provincial, who was acting as chairman at that time. The General agreed that Paul Reinert was a good choice, but, since he would remain in St. Louis, no change should be made until an executive assistant had been chosen for ordinary administration. The General added that "it will be up to the New York Provincial to advise Father Rooney of the appointment of his successor. . . . Father Rooney should be given a new appointment in keeping with his experience."[41]

As was proper, the Jesuits of the American Assistancy were the first to know. In an announcement on March 3, 1966, Father Rooney, who had already been informed, was assigned to Jesuit Missions as educational representative.[42] In a subsequent press release, it was announced that Paul C. Reinert, while remaining chief executive officer at Saint Louis, would be the new president of the JEA, effective March 15. A. William Crandell was designated vice president and Paul V. Siegfried, former director of education in Detroit, was appointed secretary-treasurer of the organization.[43] Typical of more surprises to come, the constituent members were simultaneously informed that the National Office would be relocated in Washington, D.C., where Crandell would preside over the day-to-day operation. The *new order* had been established.[44]

Paul Clare Reinert, a man of enormous energy, superior managerial skills, and proven qualities of leadership, was the most experienced administrator in the American Assistancy. Intimately familiar with and fraternally accepted by the community of higher education in the United States, he was committed, insofar as the Society's Institute would allow, to the Americanization of Jesuit colleges and universities. He had conservative critics, whom he might characterize as timid, but he had strong support where it counted among the presidents and deans. There was a hint of coming attractions in a memorandum to the provincials for the reorganization of the JEA, which he submitted after his appointment but before the public announcement.[45] Shortly thereafter, Reinert was invited to a very important meeting at the provincial's residence in Buffalo, with the American Assistant in attendance, at which final arrangements were agreed upon for the future direction of the JEA.[46]

The new president lost no time in presenting his progressive ideas to the Board of Governors (many of which have since become standard practice). Reporting to the provincials "on university problems facing the Society and the Church today," he first singled out "the large question of the right of the lay faculty to have a voice in establishing policy and the need of some means for the lay faculty to express opinions."[47] Related questions, he believed, "may call for re-organization in the structure of the Catholic or Jesuit university today."[48] Included in these bold initiatives were the appointment of Jesuits to the faculty by vote of the departments; the autonomous status of universities, with the concomitant obligation to resist directives from ecclesiastical authorities; the possibility of separating Jesuit communities, through legal incorporation, from the universities; and the special relationship of the university to the public.[49]

This last consideration, which touched upon the legal creation of all church-related, independent institutions as public trusts, introduced the question of the composition of boards of trustees. Father Reinert was strongly in favor of revising Jesuit boards of trustees with the addition of laymen, a novel idea at that time. At the fall meeting of the provincials, he submitted his reasons for the proposed changes, which, he fully realized, represented a radical movement away from traditional Jesuit control of certain aspects of the educational apostolate. Reorganization of boards of trustees and separate incorporation of Jesuit communities, he argued, would (1) create a sounder academic policy structure, (2) better represent the segments of society that had a vested interest in the enterprise, (3) enhance the participation of laity in Catholic activities, (4) promise more substantial support from a larger pool of involved donors, and (5) — a suggestion that reflected the decrees of the General Congregation — make for a more appropriate arrangement in relation to the Jesuit vow of poverty.[50]

Moving from the general to the particular, he explained to a spellbound audience how the system might work, using Georgetown and Saint Louis as examples. While it was clear that each case would have to be judged on its own merits and the property rights of the Society would have to be secured, Reinert urged the provincials to approve the idea of experimentation by a few institutions that might wish to move in that direction. He left the regional superiors with plenty to think about and much to ponder.[51]

In lending its support to the new order, the Commission on Colleges and Universities had not been idle. At an important meeting in June 1966, the presidents produced a brief document, in the form of a recommendation, which placed the Jesuit university in its modern setting. In order to preempt an objection from Rome, the presidents were at pains to distinguish the major difference between the Society's experience in education in the United States and its history in Europe.

> American Jesuit colleges and universities as institutions of higher learning are chartered not by the Society or by the Congregation of Seminaries and Universities, but by the United States in which they lie. In addition, the continuance of their charters, as well as extensions or changes in the same, depend upon the regulatory authority of State government. For this reason, American Jesuits engaged in higher education are stewards of the public trust and must, as such, acknowledge a clear and direct obligation to the civil authority that gives their institutions civil existence.[52]

It was a question, therefore, of stewardship and of service to the community. But "community" in the broad sense was understood as in Vatican II's *Constitution on the Church in the Modern World* and *Declaration on Religious Liberty*. Although "stewardship" included expert and devoted service to the Church, the presidents maintained that "we falsify our public trust if we do not admit that our obligation is to serve the community in terms of its needs and its moral demands upon us."[53] Not only that, but in America "the academic aims, structure and quality of our institutions rest in large part on criteria established by the accrediting agencies" to which Jesuit colleges and universities must conform.[54] Conscious that they were also addressing officials beyond the Atlantic, the commissioners concluded that, in the ancient tradition, "the Society [must] adapt itself to the norms and the institutions which the American experience has painfully evolved."[55] On this preamble, the presidents then dealt with the training, assignment, and removal of Jesuits in American Jesuit universities and colleges.

In general—since it is not necessary to follow the argument in detail—the authority of the appropriate academic officer would be paramount in all decisions and intrusion by the provincial would be minimal.[56] Although the presidents concentrated their fire on the academic relationship of Jesuits to the university, in time they broadened their sights so as to withdraw almost all academic decisions from the purview of the provincials. The provincials themselves seemed sympathetic to this shift in the source of administrative authority; at least, there was no open opposition. This change of heart reflected, no doubt, the background of the men who now formed the Board of Governors. James Shanahan had been president of St. Peter's College in Jersey City; John F. X. Connolly was the former president of the University of San Francisco; John M. Daley had been dean of the Georgetown University Graduate School; and Robert Harvanek, while he might not always agree with the presidents, was familiar with their problems and their positions.

Father Reinert, and the presidents, received support for their thesis from an unexpected quarter. Invited to address the 1966 JEA National Meeting, Andrew Greeley, widely known sociologist of the National Opinion Center, was under instructions not to single out the good characteristics of Jesuit education (which, many thought, was an unnecessary admonition). Although he was *ex professo* critical of certain aspects of Jesuit education, he was close to the mark when he contended "that the problems of Jesuit higher education in the United States are essentially American problems . . . which are to be expected in a religious order as it adjusts to the American environment."[57] Furthermore, since the "solutions to present problems must be American solutions," Father Greeley suggested that "applying American solutions to American problems is in the finest tradition of the Society."[58]

In response to Greeley's analysis, Reinert agreed that the Catholic Church in America was passing through "a period of traumatic transition" from the Tridentine to the Vatican Church. He also conceded, reverting to a favorite theme, that an outstanding characteristic of the Church in America was "the emergence of the layman as a necessary and vital force in policy-making and administration of every facet of the Church's program."⁵⁹ All of this was grist for the presidents' mill, and, as they had hoped, the point of the exchange was not lost upon the provincials, who commented upon it at their May 1966 meeting.

Even though certain questions on governance had still to be resolved, Father Reinert was ready to make his first move. However, a small, dark cloud on the horizon might cause trouble. On more than one occasion, Father Janssens had tried to interest Father Rooney in the establishment of an International Secretariate of Education. Rooney had always discovered reasons to resist these overtures since, as he suspected, they might lead to his replacement at the National Office. The matter was revived under Father Arrupe and, indeed, written into the legislation of the Thirty-first General Congregation.⁶⁰

At the 1966 fall meeting of the American provincials (held at the Roman Curia due to their presence at the Congregation), Father Reinert, a delegate from Missouri, presented a synopsis of the reaction of the JEA commissions. According to his report, "some few rejected the idea as dangerous and unnecessary, although the majority saw some usefulness in a modern information center where accurate information could be gathered."⁶¹ However, and this was the point at issue, "universally it was emphasized that this information center and its personnel should not be given any authority for decision-making."⁶² In an attempt to soothe the presidents' fears, the General sent a long letter to the Maryland provincial, who, now that the JEA central office was located in Washington, D.C., was chairman of the Board of Governors. Among other things, he wrote:

> The Fathers Provincial need not worry that the Secretariate of Education will be exercising dangerous and unnecessary interference in the decision-making of our educational institutions. . . . The General Congregation did not wish this and my only desire is to supply an organ for improving our apostolate of education.⁶³

Apparently, the JEA vice president was not entirely satisfied. In a letter to the General's Assistant — an old ally from the Presidents' Conference — he wrote:

> As you know, I, and many others, are quite fearful of what the Secretariate might develop into. We would prefer to have you and Harold Small interpreting American Jesuit Education and its needs and respon-

sibilities to Father General rather than to have the intervention of a worldwide secretariate. Please keep this in mind as the secretariate develops and help us to avoid a very undesirable bureaucracy.[64]

Six months later, after further consultation with his Assistants, the General appointed John E. Blewett, an American Jesuit from Wisconsin and former dean of Sophia University in Tokyo, as his advisor in educational affairs and executive secretary of the International Center of Jesuit Education.[65] Father Blewett, who would be the first to avoid controversy and foster conciliation, made an immediate effort to describe his office "so that misunderstandings may be swept away and the good intended through the appointment more effectively furthered."[66] (In retrospect, the anxieties of the JEA officers seem to have been exaggerated, indeed unfounded. The secretariate has been largely concerned with the coordination of international projects, usually in Europe, and the collection of information. There has never been an attempt to interfere with the administration of American institutions.)

With these reassurances, and satisfied that the time was ripe, Saint Louis University was the first Jesuit institution to restructure its board for complete administrative and corporate autonomy. To all intents and purposes, it would be independent of Roman and provincial supervision. (The pioneer is always remembered, as the late Charles Lindbergh could testify, and deserves to be recognized.) On June 23, 1967, in one of the most significant events in the history of Saint Louis University and the American Assistancy — as described by Paul Reinert — "a newly constituted board, consisting of Jesuits and laymen, met for the first time."[67]

Two historical innovations marked this occasion, which would be of subsequent importance to American Jesuit colleges and universities. Of the twenty-eight trustees invited to join that board, ten were Jesuits and a majority (eighteen) were laymen. Though President Reinert was an *ex officio* member, the chairman of that board was Daniel L. Schlafly, a distinguished Catholic layman of St. Louis. Before he accepted the president's invitation, he was assured "that the board would have total control of the properties and policies of St. Louis University."[68] Schlafly confirmed this in a press conference when he said: "While the board will not and should not be involved with the day-to-day administration of the University, it will nevertheless have the final authority over the University's long-range policy."[69]

In a simultaneous action, which also was unique, the thirteen Jesuits who had voted to restructure the board also voted to create a separate corporation embodying the Jesuit community. Legally distinct from the university, with no rights or responsibilities in relation to that corporation, the assets of the Jesuit community included its residence, facilities, and other related material needs. As administrators and faculty members, the Jesuits would contract with the university for their services and receive compensation according to their academic rank or position.[70]

Contrary to what might have been expected, this unusual move involved no change in the original charter of Saint Louis University, although new bylaws were formulated to ensure the Jesuit character of the university. Basically, the new structure was an effort to make the board and its actions better reflect the university's several constituencies; to capitalize on the emergence of laymen (after Vatican II) in highly responsible positions in Catholic enterprises; and to separate the policymaking function from the internal administration of the university, "in keeping with modern university practice."[71] In approving this arrangement, the General pointed out "that the change was in line with a decree on education which was adopted . . . by the 31st General Congregation."[72] Since permission to restructure boards of trustees in colleges and universities in the American Assistancy would find support in this decree, it may be helpful to quote the relevant paragraphs.

> According to the mind of the Second Vatican Council, a close collaboration with the laity is recommended. On the one hand, we can give them help. . . . On the other hand, let Jesuits consider the importance for the Society itself of such collaboration with lay people, who will always be the natural interpreters for us of the modern world, and so will always give us effective help in this apostolate. Therefore, we should consider handing over to them the roles they are prepared to assume in the work of education, whether these be in teaching, in academic and business administration, or even on the board of directors.
>
> It will also be advantageous to consider whether it would not be helpful to establish in some of our institutions of higher education a board of trustees which is composed partly of Jesuits and partly of lay people; the responsibility both of ownership and of direction would pertain to this board.[73]

Saint Louis University had set the pace, and others were eager to march to the same drummer. In the summer of 1967, a questionnaire was circulated among the presidents which requested information on their plans for the restructuring of boards of trustees and the separate incorporation of Jesuit communities. The responses clearly revealed that a majority was projecting changes in the near future.[74]

But the matter was not as simple as Reinert's account had led people to believe. Although the General had the decree of the Congregation as a guide, he seemed perplexed as to his role, if any, in this legal tangle. An opportunity for further inquiry came over the question of a revised list of permissions that must be referred to Rome. Father Sponga, in a letter to Father Reinert, wrote that the General, "before approving a revision of the List of Permissions, which colleges and universities should obtain from Father General . . . would like a clear statement on the authority and responsibility which the Society, and in particular the General, has in the administration of Jesuit colleges and universities."[75] The General had been told "that the Board of Trustees, Jesuit or lay, in a public service corporation established for the purpose of education enjoys ultimate authority and responsibility over such institutions. If this be the case," the General continued, "we must face and resolve this existential situation before we can review and plan realistically our educational commitments."[76]

While the presidents were meeting in Washington, the provincials had gathered at North Aurora in Illinois. The first session of their meeting "was devoted entirely to a discussion of the timely and rather involved question of ownership, authority, and responsibility in our universities, colleges and high schools."[77] The discussion was led by John J. McGrath, a priest of the Steubenville Diocese, who had practiced law before entering the seminary and, as a canonist, was then teaching comparative law at The Catholic University. He was considered an expert, and his publication on American institutions had been well received.[78]

In the meantime, accelerating the flow of information, Edward Sponga, chairman of the Board of Governors, with Joseph Drane as an assistant, was commissioned to draw up a statement on ownership, separate incorporation, and freedom. Although it was further revised, after consultation and additional suggestions, it is one of the clearest expositions of the legal position of Jesuit institutions as public trusts. The statement seeks "to establish that our colleges-universities and our high schools (those at least which are civilly incorporated) are not ecclesiastical property by virtue of Canon Law or, if they were initially, were alienated upon becoming civilly incorporated."[79] For this reason, "Jesuit rights and responsibilities in institutions run under their auspices [were] defined juridically by the State in the charter and by-laws of the corporation enforced by civil law."[80]

This would be true, moreover, even if all members of the board remained Jesuits, since American law does not oblige church-related institutions to place laymen on the board. Granted the premise — though the statement has here been abbreviated—one must logically conclude "that permission from Rome is not needed (or really possible) to alienate property, although the wish of superiors' should play its proper role in the formation of the conscience of the individual Jesuit trustee."[81]

The formation of the conscience of the Jesuit trustee, with the co-relatives of responsibility and freedom, was to some extent a theological problem. The Sponga statement had several questions on this point but no definite answers. In the new system, "which put religious authority on the outside of the institutions, . . . what about the possible conflict between an institution trustee and his religious superior, v.g., the Provincial?" More particularly, "what is to be done in a situation where, e.g., a bishop or even the Holy See might demand that a President or Board of Trustees be obliged by the religious superior to adopt a certain policy about matters taught in a given institution?"

As chance would have it, there was just such a question before the presidents at this time. Augustin Cardinal Bea, S.J., former rector of the Biblical Institute and a scripture scholar of international reputation, in a private document had questioned the propriety of engaging non-Catholic teachers of the Old Testament for undergraduate students.[82] When the cardinal's comment was brought to the attention of the General, Father Arrupe demanded an explanation and a justification of the presidents' position. The presidents, having decided to take a stand, were determined to protect the rights they had claimed in the discussion over institutional autonomy. Rejecting the suggestion that they adopt a set of procedures for this type of case, since each institution was theoretically free to devise its own approach, they submitted, instead, a policy statement. In essence, the statement said: "In employing teachers for Sacred Scripture, the same procedure should be used as is used for the employment of any other faculty member in the various departments of the university."[83]

Perhaps it was this type of response—a logical conclusion from the presidents' premise—that gave the General temporary reservations on the full implications of the "new order." In any case, in a letter to the Maryland provincial he asked ten searching questions which went to the heart of the matter in the event that civil prerogatives were fully implemented.[84] The presidents' responses left little doubt that though the Jesuit character would or could be preserved, the institutions would be totally emancipated from the General's authority.

The questions reflected areas of concern. "Should a Board of Trustees . . . govern a college or university independently of any outside Jesuit authority?" The answer was affirmative. "If the Board of Trustees is independent of outside Jesuit authority, should the [Jesuit]

President be subject to the Board?" Yes, they answered; "American educational practice requires that the President of the college be a creature of the Board of Trustees." Again, "Why should the Society of Jesus permit its name to be identified with an institution in which the responsible superiors of the Society can exercise no authority?" The firm commitment, they explained, is more important than the name or structure.

There was another question, the answer to which had intrigued several Jesuits who had commented on the impending divorce between Rome and institutions in the United States. "How would one define or describe a Jesuit college or university in which the Provincial of the area and the General of the Society of Jesus have no authority to determine its academic, religious or financial practices and policies?" The answer to this query was probably the least satisfactory. In brief, "it would be, in American terminology, a private, independent, church-related institution sponsored by the Society of Jesus on behalf of that segment of the American public that wishes to perpetuate . . . a style of education that emphasizes traditionally Jesuit values."[85]

At this point, it would appear, all official and unofficial constituencies had contributed their expertise to this classic and historic discussion. The Coordinating Committee, the Commission on Colleges and Universities, the other three commissions, and experts whose advice had been solicited had all submitted their opinions and, implicitly, had cast their votes.[86] Meeting in 1968 at Puerto Rico, in the presence of the General and with this mountain of information before them, the provincials' subcommittee of the JEA proposed that the fathers provincial of the American Assistancy submit the following requests to Father General:

> That he permit, where desired and feasible, the establishment as separate and distinct [but cooperating] corporations, those Jesuit communities whose primary apostolate is an educational institution; [that] permission be given to revise the corporate structure of the existing educational corporations . . . so that laymen could be added to the Board of Trustees in any proportion; [that] in the event [after separate community incorporation] of a decision of withdrawal of the Society from an educational institution [permission be granted] to revise the corporation so as to replace Jesuits on the Board with persons who are non-Jesuits.[87]

In practice, the General accepted these proposals.

It would be unnecessarily tedious to trace the transition of individual colleges and universities. The collected literature is extensive and, we presume, institutional archives provide documentation for the rewriting of bylaws and the restructuring of boards.[88] One example, in an abbreviated account, will illustrate the caution with which these transitions were accomplished, the concern for preserving the traditions of the Society, and the care with which presidents and boards thought out the legal implications. Michael P. Walsh, who had been a leader in this "modern movement," was succeeded as president of Boston College, on July 1, 1968, by W. Seavey Joyce, a Harvard Ph.D. in economics and former dean of the School of Management. At the meeting of the Board of Trustees on January 25, 1968, at which he submitted his resignation, Father Walsh introduced two pieces of business with important implications for the future. He asked the members of the board to study the documents, which he had distributed, on the separate incorporation of the Jesuit community of Saint Louis University. With his customary prescience, he predicted that this topic might come up for consideration in, as he was fond of saying, the not-too-distant future. He also called for a final review of the new bylaws of Boston College.[89]

Article III, section 11, of these bylaws provided for a board of directors (twenty-five members or more) which "shall have all necessary and convenient powers to direct and manage the business and affairs of the corporation, hereinafter referred to as the University." The directors would be elected by a majority vote of the entire board of trustees, which, it must be remembered, was still comprised of ten Jesuits.[90] With high hopes and serious intent, the board of directors of Boston College met for the first time on October 8, 1968.

While there were obvious advantages in having, at Boston College and elsewhere, the assistance of a high-powered board of lay experts to manage the affairs of the university, two governing boards was not the ideal solution. At Boston College, legal ownership of the university, and all its assets, was still vested in the Jesuit board of trustees; supervision of those assets, however, resided in the board of directors. It was generally understood from the beginning that this was a transitional arrangement. At a meeting of the Jesuit board of trustees in September 1971, there was a discussion of combining the two boards, and on September 24 it was voted unanimously to remove the two-board system with a simultaneous revision of the bylaws.[91] The new bylaws, which purposefully did not set a number or percentage for Jesuit membership on the board, also referred to Boston College "as a University in the Jesuit tradition." The new board of trustees, which now included Jesuits and laymen and -women, met for the first time on December 8, 1972.[92] After one hundred and nineteen years, the destiny of Boston College was entrusted to a board that was dominated, at least numerically, by laymen and -women, who would hereafter determine the policy of that institution. This legal conversion, in which the university trustees contracted for Jesuit services with the separately incorporated community, was gradually duplicated at Jesuit colleges across the country with incidental differences.

Obviously, as many pointed out, this radical restructuring of the educational mission of the Society in America was not without risks. In a long letter to the executive secretary of the Conference of Major Superiors of Jesuits, Michael P. Walsh, who had moved on to the presidency of Fordham University, identified some of the problems that could develop, on trustee boards and separately incorporated Jesuit communities, unless the most experienced legal counsel was employed to draft bylaws and indentures.[93]

Apart from legal guarantees, the greatest protection, as events would prove, came from the integrity of the board members — Catholic, Protestant, and Jew — who, faithful to a rich inheritance, were determined to perpetuate the Jesuit commitment to higher education in America. These members often suggested, and always supported, the statements that underscored the reasons for the existence of the institutions they supervised.[94]

The mission and identity of church-related colleges and universities have always been a concern of the Church. In an excellent statement on higher education, the United States Catholic Conference, which represents the bishops, insisted that "the Catholic identity of these institutions should be evident to faculty, students and the general public."[95] Cognizant of the changes that were taking place, the Conference recommended that "policies, practices, programs, and general spirit should communicate to everyone that the institution is a community of scholars dedicated to the ideals and values of Catholic higher education."[96] As guardians of this tradition, "trustees and administrators have an extremely important role to discharge in maintaining fidelity to the nature of this institution and the kind of education the students experience."[97] This was a fundamental position which merited continued emphasis.

The former academic vice president at Boston College, a Jesuit of long experience in the supervision of academic programs at a complex university, in addressing a workshop for trustees made the same point: "One of the first and primary responsibilities of trustees of academic institutions is to see to it that the institution is so conducted as to fulfill its professed mission and goals."[98] In his opinion, the trustee has two paramount obligations: to ensure that the institution fulfills its "stated purpose" and "that it is managed in ways that are fiscally viable."[99] Internal administration is best left to the administrators.

Although reservations have been raised, the results of the restructuring of Jesuit boards of trustees have been generally beneficial. Prominent merchants, academic leaders, members of the judiciary, public figures, distinguished physicians and lawyers, freely contributing their services, have interpreted Jesuit institutions to the world and have explained the realities of the world to these same institutions.[100] With broad experience and diverse backgrounds, these trustees have proved reliable guides in piloting the colleges and universities through the tricky currents of modern society. Their financial advice in managing portfolios, their prudent insistence on matching revenues with expenses, and their supervision of a president himself, have given a professionalism that, in some instances, had been lacking.

In summary, the new boards, opening doors hitherto closed, have assisted in creating new and better relationships with almost all segments of the American public. In the eyes of those who can most help or hinder the apostolate of education, the Jesuit colleges and universities had come of age and were treated as partners in the American academic enterprise.[101]

# 12. The Presidents Assume Full Responsibility, 1968-1970

THE GOVERNANCE OF JESUIT colleges and universities in the late 1960s and early '70s was not made easier by unrest on campus and complications beyond the campus. The increase in student enrollments, the pressure for construction, the accent on research, the introduction of student aid on a large scale — all of these factors combined to forge a closer partnership between colleges and the federal government. Experts in the prediction and interpretation of federal legislation had a high priority on campus. At the same time, many Jesuit and non-Jesuit presidents were fearful that colleges might become the junior partner in this financial alliance, subject to the normal hazards of inequality. It is a rule of thumb that those who supply the funds ordinarily specify how the money should be managed and spent.

In this uneven equation, strangely enough, academic freedom — in one form or another — became the index of eligibility. Although it meant different things to different people, it was an issue for faculty and students alike, who sometimes collaborated to the advantage of both groups. The administration, forced into the role of adversary, formed the third group.

Since Jesuit colleges had now, by choice and design, taken on the native features of American colleges, they shared in the benefits as they inherited the problems. In a certain sense, the problems were compounded in a church-related institution. For example, the presidents and boards in Jesuit institutions probably devoted more time to the question of academic freedom than their counterparts in other universities. The American Association of University Professors, due to the proliferation of cases at this time, was extremely active in revising its statements on this sensitive subject.

Anxious to avoid a confrontation with the AAUP, the Commission on Colleges and Universities asked Patrick H. Ratterman, S.J., vice president for student affairs at Xavier University, Ohio, to keep the commission informed on developments and to refine his ideas on the position the JEA should take.[1] (Ratterman later accepted an invitation to act as chairman of a special committee which commented in depth on the most recent AAUP statements.) His own position, which was expanded in two informative articles, was that a consensus of all interested parties was the only solution to the escalation of campus unrest.[2] In fact, he would be prepared to defend the thesis "that campus consensus is just about the most interesting and important thing that can be discussed in relation to any particular university or college."[3] The Jesuits could probably find reasons to debate that conclusion. Admittedly, arriving at a consensus of administration, faculty, and students had not been the traditional view or method of asserting authority on a Jesuit campus.[4]

Academic freedom as it applied to faculty was more important and, indeed, more complicated, but it had to be addressed since it was tied to the constitutionality of government support of church-related colleges and universities. In an address to Jesuit presidents, Wilbur G. Katz, professor at the University of Wisconsin Law School, readily agreed that "the Documents of Vatican II, and their implementation, have done much to improve the image of the Catholic church and the Catholic college and university in the public mind."[5] These new perceptions, "gradually dispelling the fears that many have of the Catholic church as an authoritarian body with a closed mind," have had a favorable effect "on academic freedom on the Catholic campus [and are] undoubtedly improving the climate of public opinion regarding governmental aid to church-related colleges."[6] In his closing remarks, Dr. Katz referred to the recently issued AAUP "Statement on Academic Freedom in Church-related Colleges and Universities," which he had co-authored and which he recommended to the close study of the presidents.[7] Katz considered academic freedom very important for the viability of Jesuit institutions. "Without proper academic freedom on the campus," he said, "the mission of the Church and of the Church-related educational institution can very easily become confused, to the detriment of the educational institution seeking government funds for support."[8]

The solution, however, was not as clear or simple as Dr. Katz assumed. In a Church-related institution, academic freedom impinges on basic relationships to authority in general and, in particular, to the teaching authority of the Church, namely, the magisterium.[9] These were realities that would not disappear, nor could they be wished away by appealing to the necessity of federal aid for the support of the apostolate of education. The presidents, who were conscious of this problem, were reasonably successful in reconciling their obligations to the magisterium with the requirements of federal and state governments. Indeed, they hesitated to move as far or as fast as their Jesuit expert advisors were ready to concede. It was well known that Jesuit presidents, if not openly critical, were privately unhappy with the statement by the administration of Webster College, St. Louis, — formerly Catholic — which chose "to become a private secular college in no way legally related to a religious congregation or to a diocese."[10]

There was an extraordinary accumulation of experience (and, one might add, wisdom) among the twenty-eight presidents of Jesuit colleges and universities. They were quick to see the implications in the two suits under litigation in Maryland and Connecticut.[11] It was, more than ever, a time for cooperation and mutual assistance. In these instances, and others, there was substantial agreement with the advice given by Charles M. Whelan, S.J., professor at the Fordham University Law School, an asociate editor of *America*, and an acknowledged authority on the First Amendment. Father Whelan stressed the importance of emphasizing the secular excellence of Jesuit education, since only the secular aspects would justify federal assistance to institutions wherein theology and philosophy are treated as all other academic disciplines. However, since the law allows the incorporation of Church-related institutions, "we should not spontaneously do through fear what our opponents are trying to force us to do through the courts."[12]

Paul Reinert, shortly after assuming the presidency of the JEA, had made a similar point. In suggesting the necessity of a "rationale of education," he proposed that Jesuits attempt to formulate a statement of position "to determine the degree of agreement we can reach, and thereby to avoid inconsistent and even dishonest statements as well as the danger of becoming more secular than we want to be."[13] Warming to his subject, Reinert eloquently recommended that "we [Jesuits] state our basic curricular characteristics, formulate our minimum philosophic commitments, describe our environmental factors, explain selection of faculty members who genuinely agree with this position — and then defend *this* education as both eligible and worthy of financial support."[14]

The tension created by court cases, the delicate diplomacy required in negotiating federal grants and loans, the constant necessity of legal counsel to avoid hidden pitfalls, made the presidents understandably cautious. On the other hand, each case was a learning experience.

The Maryland case in particular, which was brought to the courts in 1967, accelerated the movement toward the restructuring of boards of trustees. At the same time, it was clear that more laymen must be appointed to high administrative positions, such as vice president, dean, and department chairman, in order to refute the accusation of religious domination. Moreover, it was recommended, within the council of presidents, that lay faculty, whose tenure, promotion, and sabbaticals should be warmly endorsed on merit, should also be encouraged to become active in the committee work of the university.[15] In view of past misunderstanding, it was strongly advised that the distinction between the president and the religious superior be clearly drawn to avoid a confusion of roles in dealing with civil authorities.[16]

With so much at stake, the presidents of Catholic universities — not only in the United States but around the world — agreed that it was a propitious time to compose a statement on the nature of the contemporary Catholic university that would satisfy both Church and State. The spadework was initiated under the auspices of the North American region of the International Federation of Catholic Universities. A panel of educators, drawn from an international pool, met from July 20 to 23, 1967, at a comfortable lodge at Land O'Lakes, Wisconsin, which was placed at the disposition of the group by the University of Notre Dame. With Theodore M. Hesburgh, C.S.C., the distinguished president of that institution (and also of IFCU) presiding, the panel attempted to formulate a definition of a Catholic university through a delineation of its distinctive characterstics.

A basic conviction of the committee members was "that the Catholic university not only can and must be a university in the authentic sense of the word, both traditional and modern, but that, in fact, a Catholic university properly developed can even more fully achieve the ideal of a true university."[17] Throughout the statement the accent was on autonomy, modernity, and excellence, and there was no ambiguity on the importance of independence.

> To perform its teaching and research functions effectively the Catholic university must have a true autonomy and academic freedom in the face of authority of whatever kind, lay or clerical, external to the academic community itself. To say this is simply to assert that institutional autonomy and academic freedom are essential conditions of life and growth and indeed of survival for Catholic universities as for all universities.[18]

Based on that premise, "the Catholic university participates in the total university life of our time, has the same functions as all other true universities and, in general, offers the same services to society."[19] But there *is* an important difference. Such a university has "distinctive characteristics," so that "the Catholic university must be an institution, a community of learners or a community of scholars, in which Catholicism is *perceptibly present* and *effectively operative.*"[20] The statement developed these ideas as they refer to interdisciplinary dialogue, research, public service, and administration.

The Land O'Lakes Statement, as it came to be called, was in reality a position paper that had been commissioned and composed in preparation for the Eighth Triennial Congress of the International Federation of Catholic Universities, which was held at Lovanium University, Kinshasa, the Congo, September 10–17, 1968. The federation, although an independent organization, was responsible (at least obliquely) to the Roman Congregation for Catholic Education, which at that time was presided over by Gabriel Cardinal Garrone.[21] Through the leadership of Father Hesburgh, the popular and effective president of IFCU, the American influence was stronger than the numbers suggest.[22] The Kinshasa Statement, entitled "The Catholic University in the Modern World," reflecting perhaps a closer relationship to the Roman Congregation (underscored by the presence of Cardinal Garonne), was more forthright in admitting a religious affiliation than the Land O'Lakes Statement. After describing the teaching, research, and public service common to all universities, the statement acknowledged that "the Catholic university brings to its task the inspiration and illumination of the Christian message."[23]

There was an attempt to strike a balance, or compromise, on the question of freedom and independence. Although they would probably deny that there was a loss of autonomy, the educators gathered in the Congo, numerically dominated by Latin American, European, Asian, and African delegates, added that the Catholic institutional commitment "includes a respect for and a voluntary acceptance of the Church's teaching authority."[24] For his part, reporting to the Coordinating Committee of the JEA on the Kinshasa meeting, Paul Reinert said that "the meeting resulted in a clarification of the role of the Catholic university with the understanding that a juridical tie with Rome is not an essential note of a Catholic institution."[25] Cardinal Garrone, he added, was an interested spectator at the daily debates.

Taking everything together, the delegates were convinced that Catholic universities, in their role of service to local communities and the larger world of international society, "merit wide support not only from the general public but also from governmental sources and philanthropic institutions."[26]

The Kinshasa Statement had its influence on American educators. A month later, in a second Land O'Lakes Statement (October 10, 1968), there was much more emphasis upon the integration of the Christian message (never explicitly called Catholic) into the standard teaching and research activities of the Catholic university. There was also renewed insistence that "Christian faith is no obstacle to the objectivity of academic scholarship."[27] Moreover, Christian colleges must be secure enough in their commitment to untiring, honest scholarship that they can offer incentives to professors who can teach; to scholars, energetic in their discipline, who can witness to the priorities of Christ; and to friends who would not be afraid to confront students with a model of what it means to be truly educated.[28] But the statement was careful to reaffirm the position of the American presidents: that, for the freedom it needs, "in the face of all authority outside the academic community, the Christian college must assert its autonomy and academic freedom."[29] This was the only possible position, "because the Christian community itself has come to recognize that it has neither the responsibility nor the right to impose moral or religious values on its members, either by institutional authority, courses of indoctrination, or disciplinary structure. Indeed, by its very nature commitment cannot be imposed at all."[30] This was a thesis which John Courtney Murray, a Jesuit hero of Vatican II, could wholeheartedly support.

As collaborating architects of these blueprints of a Catholic university, the Jesuit presidents seemed satisfied with the design that had been drawn at Land O'Lakes and Kinshasa. They also agreed that any attempt to distinguish between a Catholic and a Jesuit university would involve a distinction with very little meaning. As a matter of fact, the spectacular growth in quality, service, and influence of several Jesuit universities closely paralleled the reality envisioned by the two statements. By the ordinary measurements of success—faculty, students, student programs, academic awards, and distinguished alumni—several Jesuit universities in the United States were ranked as good as other well-known private institutions, and better than many.

But candor compels the conscientious recorder to note that the picture had its gray areas when viewed from another perspective. In his presidential address to the delegates at Kinshasa, Father Hesburgh confessed that he saw "many valid reasons for optimism and for pessimism as I look at Catholic universities on a world wide scale." He also saw ample reason "both for great hope and some fear, too."[31] In his paper, to illuminate his reasons for optimism and pessimism, Hesburgh referred extensively to a book that had appeared that very year. The

authors, two shrewd and acute observers of the academic scene in
America, wrote:

Sweeping reforms that concentrated on a relatively small number of institutions might well enable leading Catholic colleges and universities to
improve their competitive position vis-à-vis non-Catholic institutions.
The more important question is not whether a few Catholic universities
prove capable of competing with Harvard and Berkeley on the latter's
terms, but whether Catholicism can provide an ideology or personnel for
developing alternatives to the Harvard-Berkeley model of excellence. Our
guess is that the ablest Catholic educators will feel obliged to put most
of their energies into proving that Catholics can beat non-Catholics at the
latter's game. But having proved this, a few may be able to do something
more. There is as yet no American Catholic university that manages to
fuse academic professionalism with concerns for questions of ultimate
social and moral importance. . . . If Catholicism is to make a distinctive
contribution to the over-all academic system, it will have to achieve such
a synthesis on the graduate level.[32]

In a further effort to prove that "Catholics can beat non-Catholics
at the latter's game," the presidents of Jesuit universities, who were
restructuring their boards, decided that it would be useful to reorganize
their own association. The signs of the times all indicated that, at this
point in history, it was anachronistic for the presidents of American institutions of higher learning, albeit Jesuit, to report beyond their boards
of trustees to another, and higher, board within the Jesuit hierarchy of
authority. The provincials themselves had begun to question the function of the Board of Governors as a court of last resort for appeals from
heads of institutions. Much less did they relish the role of supervisors in
an operation that had become more complex every year.

Consequently, in his report to the Coordinating Committee on his
return from Kinshasa, Father Reinert urged each of the four commissions to make a self-evaluation of its operation under the revised constitution. He suggested, also, that the Coordinating Committee reassess
the effectiveness of its functions during that same three-year period.[33]

The following March, a discussion of changes in the structure of
Jesuit institutions quickly turned into a debate on the merits of the JEA
itself. A key question was asked by one of the members: "When our institutions *become* independent of the Provincials, what function does
the Board of Governors have in the JEA?"[34] One proposal saw advantages in a voluntary association of autonomous and independent institutions which could provide for itself a board of trustees or directors; "but

these trustees need not necessarily be a Board of Provincials."[35] In what the committee members now perceived to be an archaic structure, the *semblance* of power was part of the problem. At the same time, they realized that "the horizontal influence of the Province upon the institution, by way of Provincial control over his men, is still very real."[36]

The stark heading on the page of the minutes, "Whither the JEA?" indicated the *status questionis*. The Commission on Colleges and Universities, meeting at the University of Detroit on April 7, 1969, moved the discussion closer to a solution, and two alternatives were presented by the JEA president. First, the JEA could be more precisely defined and restructured "as the administrative arm of the American Provincials in regard to the educational apostolate of the Society in this country."[37] In that sense, the organizational pattern, and the authority of the provincials, would remain much the same as in the revised version of the constitution. If that were the preferred option, it was seen, even by the provincials, to violate the normal autonomy and institutional self-determination of an American college or university.[38]

In the second alternative, which came closer to the mark, "the JEA could be defined and restructured as a voluntary educational association of Jesuit high schools, colleges and universities operating, like such organizations as the Association of American Colleges, to promote the best interests of these institutions with their unique educational ideals and objectives."[39] In that plan, there would be a jurisdictional and pastoral relationship between the Society and the individual Jesuit; the relationship with the institution would be more familial than jurisdictional.[40] A suggestion was made which eventually led to a formal division within the association: there would be only two commissions—one for colleges and universities and one for high schools.

When the presidents met at the Shoreham Hotel in the nation's capital in October, it was suggested that "the present JEA Commission on Colleges and Universities establish a new and independent organization entitled 'Association of Jesuit Colleges and Universities' [AJCU] which would resemble in its structure and services the Association of American Colleges."[41] Since, as Father Reinert pointed out, a constitution and bylaws would be required for the AJCU, he suggested that the presidents submit their basic ideas at this meeting as elements that should be included in the new documents. For additional information, Reinert called attention to two documents (which had been distributed before the meeting) that could be helpful in stimulating and guiding their thoughts.[42] At the close of the meeting, a committee on restructuring was appointed and was asked to submit a report containing the constituent parts of a new constitution.[43]

The discussion at the Washington meeting, as reported in the *Proceedings*, makes interesting reading. Although the interventions are not identified, it is clear that the presidents were divided in their enthusiasm for a new organization and constitution. Some questioned the note of urgency that had been quietly implied; others doubted the wisdom of a new organization at the precise time when, at the provincial and Roman levels, the Society was implementing changes of its own. Let the ecclesiastical dust settle, they said. Moreover, there was concern that the demise of the JEA would mean a loss of union, strength, and leadership at a time when those qualities were most needed, in the face of new federal relationships. Furthermore, it was the provincials' office to certify the "Jesuitness" of an institution; for the AJCU to assume that responsibility would expose it to the accusation of an intramural agreement based on mutual self-interest.

But the positive arguments prevailed. As the lines were drawn on this in-house debate, the critical discussion turned on the role of a board and who should control it. If a new organization were created, it was generally agreed that the presidents, in some form or other, should replace the Board of Governors. This move seemed not only appropriate but even necessary, since, as was reported, "the Provincials do not wish to remain as the Board of Governors."[44] It was equally clear that a majority of the presidents would exclude lay membership on the board. (Among other duties, it might be called upon to consider the "Jesuitness" of an institution, which, it was reasonably argued, should be determined by Jesuits.) Since, as conveyed to the presidents, "the Provincials have already instructed us to proceed with plans," a timetable was worked out which set January as the date for installing an interim Board of Presidents.[45]

In retrospect, the decisive meeting took place, according to schedule, at the Shamrock Hotel in Houston. The commission was called to order by its chairman, Paul L. O'Connor, of Xavier University, who, after disposing of routine business, turned the meeting over to Father Toland, chairman of the JEA restructuring committee. In his opening remarks, Toland asked the presidents to act as a Committee of the Whole in the discussions to follow. Furthermore, in order to confine remarks within manageable bounds, comments were restricted to the present and future status of the Commission on Colleges and Universities. "We have nothing to say about the other Commissions of the JEA."[46]

Presenting the report of his committee, Father Toland pointed out that, in his opinion, there were three key issues: (1) the Board of Directors and its composition, (2) the structure of the AJCU, which should be simpler than that of the JEA, and (3) membership and representation within the AJCU.

During this critical meeting, as the Committee of the Whole discussed one point after another, consensus was obtained on the substantive issues. All agreed that there should be a national organization of Jesuit colleges and universities to improve their educational effectiveness. The Board of Directors, which should be composed of the presidents of the member institutions, should have the requisite authority to govern the association, with the power to determine policies. The board would elect from its membership a chairman, vice chairman, and secretary who, with two other elected members from the board, would constitute an Executive Committee. Commissions, with membership drawn from member institutions, would be established and, when appropriate, dissolved by the Board of Directors. Commissions might also appoint conferences. As would be stated in the bylaws, the president of the association would be a Jesuit, appointed by the Board of Directors and serving under such conditions as would be set by the board.[47]

It was appropriate that, as this story comes to a close, the presidents met in the Mandarin Room of the Haddon Hall Hotel in Atlantic City. Though not Chinese, they were distinguished Jesuit officials. Whether this omen was good or bad, poor weather conditions, combined with an air traffic controllers' "sick out," interrupted the arrival of delegates for the crucial Easter Monday meeting. Since only fourteen presidents, one-half of their total number, were in attendance as the meeting opened, there was the delicate question of the necessary quorum to conduct "affairs of state," but as the session progressed, more presidents arrived, establishing a majority for the business at hand.[48]

The chairman, Terrence Toland, presented for discussion the proposed constitution of the AJCU, the text of which had been prepared by his committee after receiving the blessing of the presidents at their previous meeting. In February the draft had been submitted to the Coordinating Committee for its comments and to the provincials' Committee on Education. The Coordinating Committee had serious reservations on two points. Is it not a mistake, nine members asked, to limit membership on the Board of Directors of the AJCU to the Jesuit presidents? "The replacement of Provincials by Presidents is no solution to our problems within the JEA."[49] Again, did the constitution and bylaws sufficiently delineate the "Jesuitness" of these institutions and clearly indicate the characteristics that must be found in them? These were proper questions since, as all knew, the jurisdiction and supervision of the provincials would be withdrawn.

In the end, the presidents, with minor modifications, voted to approve the draft of the constitution, which was based on the consensus that had been obtained in January. They were more convinced than ever that the Board of Directors should be composed of, and limited to, Jesuit presidents, who, they argued, through firm control of the association could best guarantee the continuation of the Jesuit apostolate of education in its pristine spirit.[50] In approval of the bylaws, the debate concentrated on number 5, "Liaison with Other Organizations," which included the provincials' Committee on Education. A few presidents wished to omit that particular bylaw entirely; a majority felt it should be retained as it formed the only link with the provincials — indeed, with the body of the Society.[51] As finally accepted, the bylaw reads (and deserves to be quoted):

> Liaison with the Jesuit Provincials shall be accomplished through contact and communication between the Presidents of the AJCU and the Executive Secretary of the Conference of Major Jesuit Superiors (CMSJ) and by the establishment, from time to time, of "ad hoc" committees. The Executive Committee of the Association shall meet annually with the Jesuit Provincials' Committee on Education.
>
> Liaison shall also be established between the AJCU and the Jesuit High School Association, the Jesuit Houses of Study, Province Prefects of Studies and other national and international organizations with common interests.[52]

Two immediate casualties of the new association, one scientific, one literary, were further proof of the passing of an era. In discussing various items at the January meeting, the commission agreed that the Jesuit Research Council of America, whose entire history had been controversial, should be dissolved as a separate corporation. Provision was made for its continuance as a conference (or commission) under the supervision of a staff officer of the Central Office, who would act as its secretary. The discontinuance of the *Jesuit Educational Quarterly*, the serial badge of the JEA for thirty-two years, was more difficult to understand and explain. It is true that a questionnaire had confirmed that it was not read by a large percentage of the membership — a charge that could be made against many journals — and it was moderately expensive to publish. However, in the judgment of a number of Jesuit *literati* it served a useful purpose, and many lamented the decision to cease publication of *JEQ* in favor of an AJCU newsletter which would be issued in its place.[53]

The final act in this organizational drama, which had opened with the promulgation of the *Instruction* thirty-six years earlier, came to an end quickly and, all things considered, quietly. In a letter to the American Assistant in Rome, the chairman of the provincials' Committee on Education petitioned the Roman authorities to approve, for a period of two years, the constitution and bylaws of the proposed Association of Jesuit Colleges and Universities.[54]

Apparently, the curial advisors saw no insuperable complications. Andrew Varga, a special assistant to the General, responded for Father Arrupe, who, as president, was occupied in presiding at meetings of the Union of Superiors General. By commission of Father General, Varga approved the new organization "under the condition made by the Fathers Provincial that in the meantime they [the Presidents] would give further thought to a more representative Board of Directors which would not be composed merely of Presidents."[55]

Influenced, no doubt, by the same legitimate concerns that had agitated the Coordinating Committee, Varga suggested that "a Board composed only of Presidents seems to be contrary to the wider participation in government in the Society and especially in the colleges and universities where trustees, lay faculty and students are participating."[56] In other words, in Father Varga's opinion, without broader representation at the base and at the top, the AJCU was in danger of becoming a fraternity of college presidents.[57] With a brief covering letter of his own, Father Sheahan forwarded Father Varga's letter of conditioned approval to Paul Reinert and other officials of the American Assistancy.[58]

To all intents and purposes, the presidents of Jesuit colleges and universities had assumed complete control and direction of the apostolate of higher education in the United States. It was the beginning of a new era in the long history of Jesuit education.

# Epilogue

ALTHOUGH EMANCIPATED FROM the immediate supervision of the provincials, the Association of Jesuit Colleges and Universities, since its foundation in the summer of 1970, has not lost its Jesuit identity, motivation, or purpose. The Board of Directors, in fact, has worked strenuously (and successfully) to enhance the academic influence of Jesuit institutions and to promote institutional cooperation among its constituent members. In this latter endeavor, the AJCU has been more successful than the organization it replaced. Moreover, there has been greater stability among the presidents, who, responsible to the directives of their boards of trustees, have been continued in office to the advantage of the several colleges and universities.

While the number of Jesuits, for reasons beyond the control of the institutions, has declined, the provincials' commitment to the apostolate has never waned. Working through the Jesuit Conference, which was designed and approved in the summer of 1972, the provincials selected as their first study the Jesuit apostolate of education in the United States. Project I, as it came to be called, was specifically intended to examine the Jesuit mission in higher education.[1] As a result of this four-year study, the provincials reaffirmed their "corporate commitment to this apostolate in the Jesuit colleges and universities in the United States."[2] Furthermore, lest there be any misunderstanding, they pledged themselves "to continue to prepare and assign young Jesuits to this apostolate."[3]

The American provincials were strengthened in their resolve by previous statements of Father General Arrupe. In an address to the rectors and presidents of Jesuit universities gathered in Rome, on August 5, 1975, the General gave a ringing endorsement of this apostolate and based his remarks in part on the history of the Society and the Gospel mission "to teach."[4] A year later, taking a more academic approach and repeating the arguments of his predecessor and the mandate of the recent Congregation, he emphasized the necessity of continuing the intellectual apostolate. Among other things, he wrote:

> But apart altogether from these references, it is clear that the Society as a "body" could not do justice to the intellectual dimension attaching to our key apostolic options unless a sufficient number of its members are committed with a special priority to research, to science and, more broadly, to an apostolate that is explicitly intellectual. And further, what better means do we have, in many cases, for carrying out these tasks than well-organized centers, universities, colleges, research institutes, periodicals.[5]

The dream of the Inter-Province Committee of 1921 has become a reality. From Ledochowski, Janssens, and Arrupe, the charge to excel has gone out to the Jesuit colleges and universities in the United States and to those who direct them. This network of twenty-eight institutions, with undergraduate, graduate, and professional schools, and in 1981 an enrollment of 172,081 students, is irrefutable proof of the determination of contemporary Jesuits to honor the traditions of the past.[6]

# Appendix A

Questionnaire submitted by Father General
W. Ledochowski to American Provincials
March 12, 1927

1. Give exact total numbers of Catholics, Protestants and Jews in the student-body, in each of the different departments, indicating also the number, if any, of those who claim no religious affiliation.

2. Give same of professors, indicating first, number of Ours, then of laymen, Catholics, Protestants, Jews, no belief.

3. What departments, if any, have non-Catholic Deans? Is he Protestant or Jew?

4. Why are non-Catholic professors and Deans employed? Is anything being done to substitute Catholics for them?

5. What authority does the Rector exercise in the matter of selecting or discharging professors and Deans?

6. What care is taken to make sure that professors propound nothing that is contrary to faith or morals?

7. To what extent are text books by Catholic authors insisted on?

8. What is done for the religious instruction of the Catholic students?

9. a) What is done directly to promote a better knowledge of the Catholic religion among non-Catholic students?
   b) Is anything done positively to promote conversions among them?

10. In places where non-Catholic students are numerous, what provisions are made to prevent non-Catholic influences?

11. In general is any direct influence exercised over the moral conduct of the students?

12. a) In what department are women students admitted?
    b) How many are actually in attendance, divided, as in question 1, according to department and religion?
    c) Is special care taken here to forestall moral dangers?

13. Is there a crucifix in each of the class-rooms or lecture rooms?

14. Is it expressly stated in any catalogue, prospectus or bulletin of the University that it is an "un-denominational" institution?

15. a) In general, of what practical utility is the University to the cause of religion?
    b) Can the Catholic students be said to be better Catholics after their University course and because of it?
    c) Do they as a rule take a more active and efficient part in Catholic movements as zealous lay leaders?
    d) Are the non-Catholic students at least better disposed towards the church as a result of their attendance at the University?

# Appendix B

Summary of Recommendations by
Commission on Higher Studies, 1931

PART I. UNITED PURPOSE AND CONCERTED ACTION

1. That there be organized at once a really functioning interprovince organization.

2. That this organization be known as the *Association of Jesuit Universities, Colleges and Secondary Schools of the United States.*

3. That there be in each province two Standing Committees on Studies: *The Province Committee on Secondary Schools* and *The Province Committee on Colleges and Universities,* and that each consist of three well-chosen men.

4. That there be in each province two General Prefects of Studies; one for the secondary schools, the other for the colleges and universities; and that these two be members and chairman *ex officio* of the respective standing committees on studies in each province. That the chairman of the standing committee on college and university studies be particularly chosen for the position on account of the qualifications stated by Reverend Father General in his letter of December 8, 1930, in establishing the present Commission.

5. That the Association operate through a National Executive Committee to be composed of the chairmen of the respective standing committees on college and university studies in the seven provinces.

6. That this National Executive Committee meet once a year or oftener if necessary and report directly to Very Reverend Father General and to the Fathers Provincial at the close of each meeting.

7. That this Association have a full-time Permanent or Executive Secretary who will be nominated by the National Executive Committee, approved by the Fathers Provincial and appointed by His Paternity.

8. That the Executive Secretary be *ex officio* chairman of the National Executive Committee of the Association, and be provided with a suitable office

and the necessary assistants and equipment to enable him to fulfill the duties outlined in Part I, Section 6 of this report.

9. That, as an emergency measure, His Paternity himself immediately select and appoint from the American Assistancy the first Executive Secretary and give him the power and authority of an Educational Commissioner (*Commissarius*) for the Assistancy.


## PART II. COMPARATIVE STANDING OF OUR INSTITUTIONS

1. That very definite measures be taken to secure adequate endowment not only by the colleges but particularly by the graduate and professional schools.

2. That each college and university be required to have an institutional and departmental budget system.

3. That the books of each university and college be set up according to modern methods with a competently trained bookkeeper in charge who will operate under the supervision of the Procurator.

4. That all our institutions introduce a cost accounting system and that the books be audited at regular intervals by a certified public accountant.

5. That all financial statements given to the public be frank and adequate and issued only over the signature of a certified public accountant.

6. That educational statements be issued only by competent officials of the college or university and that duplicate copies of these statements be kept on file at the institution.

7. That effective means be used to establish and maintain contacts with those who can help our institutions financially or educationally.

8. That our institutions publish Statutes and By-Laws directing their whole administration.

9. That definite norms for appointment, tenure and promotion be formulated in the Statutes.

10. That the choice of lay professors for our faculties in any rank above that of instructor fall hereafter only on Doctors recognized for their scholarship.

11. That those of Ours who show special talent in a particular line be encouraged to foster and develop it; that a general attitude of sympathetic encouragement of scholarship and scholarly activities be manifested in our communities; and that Superiors effectively discourage any contrary attitude.

12. That the standards described in Part II, Sections 7–14 be carefully adhered to in all our colleges.

13. That our graduate schools be located only at strategic points throughout the country; that those now existing be further strengthened; and that others be organized only as we are able to supply the faculty and equipment that will make them equal the best.

14. That the following norms be recommended for the Master's degree:

(1) *Advanced Standing.* — To accept for credit towards the Master's degree, one-third, and, in the case of the major, one-fourth of the graduate

work done in other recognized graduate schools, is admitted to be reputable practice and as such is recommended as a maximum for advanced standing.

(2) *Requirement of Minor (or Minors).* — It is recommended that, in general, the determination of the candidate's schedule of work be left in the hands of the department in which he specializes. It then rests with the department to allow or to prescribe courses in related departments.

(3) *Length of the Master's Course.* — For full-time students, one academic year should be required. Six summer sessions of six weeks each will ordinarily meet this requirement. Wherever possible, summer session work, in order to be counted toward the degree, should be immediately preceded or followed by a regular semester's work.

(4) *Master's Thesis.* — A thesis should be required of all candidates in order to give the student some appreciation of investigational work and to provide him with some training in the technique of research.

(5) *Foreign Language Requirement.* — A reading knowledge of French *or* German should be required of all candidates for the Master's degree.

(6) *Final Comprehensive Examination.* — A final comprehensive examination, oral or written, or both, before a committee of the graduate faculty, should be required.

15. That there be strict conformity to the requirements set forth in Part II, Sections 22 and 23, for the conferring of the degree of Doctor of Philosophy.

16. That our professors and officials maintain close contacts with the outside educational world.

17. That the standards of our professional schools excel those required by the accrediting organizations.

18. That the National Executive Committee under the direction of the American Commissioner initiate steps towards the formulation of a distinctively Jesuit educational plan for our American colleges and universities.

## PART III. ACCREDITING AGENCIES

1. That every Jesuit institution of higher education obtain membership in all of the respective accrediting associations, regional and national, for each of its schools and colleges.

## PART IV. ACADEMIC DEGREES AND EDUCATIONAL TRAINING

1. That the doctorate in some particular field be regarded as the academic goal of all in the same sense as the profession is the ecclesiastical goal.

2. That the successful completion of two years of college work be the normal academic entrance requirement of the Society.

3. In order to prepare Ours for their normal goal, the doctorate, it is urgently recommended:

(1) That the curriculum of each Scholastic be arranged individually in accordance with his previous college record, his talent, and the specialty to which he is to be devoted;

(2) That this specialty be determined by a comprehensive examination at the end of the lower division college studies;

(3) That lower division Juniorates be maintained for those who have not yet satisfied the requirements of the Church, the Society, or the American educational system for entrance upon upper division work;

(4) That, in accordance with the result of the comprehensive examination and previous records, each Scholastic be devoted to a given branch of learning, and that he be sent to an upper division Juniorate which is equipped for advanced study of that branch;

(5) That the provinces cooperate in the establishment, proper equipment, and maintenance of standard upper division Juniorates at our recognized Jesuit universities;

(6) That those who are chosen to specialize in philosophy be sent directly to a Philosophate after the comprehensive examination and receive there the special spiritual care proper to the upper division Juniorates.

4. That in accordance with the requirements of the Church, the Society and the American system, the first two years of philosophy be organized as an upper division undergraduate curriculum for all, during which the less difficult questions in each subject are to be covered.

5. That a third year of philosophy of strictly graduate standard be required of all, who, in the undergraduate course, will have shown themselves qualified in the comprehensive examination for two years' advanced standing.

6. That those, who have outstanding talents in philosophy, be selected for a further two years of graduate study, during which they will qualify for both the canonical and the American degree of Doctor of Philosophy.

7. That those either not entering on graduate work in any field or failing to qualify for the mastership be not permitted to teach in our schools, since they are ineligible according to the best American educational practice.

8. That the full three years of regency be given to those Scholastics who have received the master's degree, but about whose qualifications for the doctorate there may be doubt.

9. That those Scholastics who are to go on to the doctorate in any subject be assigned during their regency either as assistants to high school or college teachers in their own field or as teaching fellows in the universities; and that they be supplied during that time with the necessary books, journals, supervision and encouragement to continue their studies for the doctorate.

10. That all Scholasticates, including Juniorates, Philosophates and Theologates, be located within easy reach of our recognized universities and in intimate association with them as integral parts, thus sharing their library and other facilities, which must be available to every advanced student, in order that all the degrees granted to our Scholastics may be accorded that unqualified esteem and recognition which the educators of the country give to the degrees of the foremost institutions.

11. That Ours hold active membership in learned societies in their field, and that such membership be permitted to continue during theology.

12. That every state of scholastic progress in the Society in so far as is possible, be recognized by a corresponding degree either academic or canonical.

13. That all our universities granting the Doctor's degree and not yet recognized, so organize and develop their faculties and facilities that they may obtain recognition by the Association of American Universities as universities of complex organization with graduate schools.

14. That every university granting the Doctor's degree strive so to develop as to deserve an invitation to become a *member* of the Association of American Universities.

15. That our Jesuit teachers be trained not only for a special *subject*, but for a specific *position* in a particular *institution*.

16. That this assignment be made at the beginning of graduate study for the doctorate, so that the institution for which the man is destined may supervise his training.

17. That this assignment once made be not changed except for grave reasons.

18. That the institution which may thus normally hope to have the services of the man bear the financial responsibilities for his training.

19. That the faculty needs of all our institutions be so budgeted and stabilized that an annual status will become unnecessary and may be abolished.

20. That our Scholastics be given at least fifteen semester hours of education, exclusive of practice teaching before beginning their Regency.

21. That these minimum courses in education include history, principles, administration, psychology and methods.

22. That in addition to the above courses in education each Scholastic be given at least three semester hours of practice teaching under standard conditions.

23. That each newly appointed instructor, particularly each Jesuit teacher beginning his teaching, be taken in hand by the head of the department, who will require a monthly written report of the results the instructor has achieved, the problems he has met, and the proposals for solving these problems; that the head of the department discuss with the instructor actual situations included in the report and the methods employed or to be employed in handling them; and with a view to cooperation rather than criticism, that he arrange frequent visits to the instructor's classroom as a means of carrying out the plans previously agreed upon.

24. That men be chosen as heads of departments who are conspicuous not only for their knowledge of their subject, but for their proven executive ability.

25. That deans of colleges or of university schools be normally chosen from among heads of departments and that the tenure of office, both of heads of departments and of deans, be conditioned only on their success.

26. That the size and complexity of our universities seem to indicate the need of putting into practice the dual organization mentioned in Part IV, Chapter 17, of the Constitutions of the Society.

27. That each college and university president at the beginning of his administration be required by the Father Provincial to submit a program for the development of the institution under his guidance covering a period of at least five years, which, when and as approved, is to be continued and developed by his successors; each successor in turn submitting a similar plan.

# Appendix C

## Policies and Procedures Regarding Expansion of Jesuit Institutions

### POLICIES ON EXPANSION

1. We should be ready to accept as many students as "furnish solid grounds for the hope that they will go through with their studies to the end with real success"* and for whom we can provide the teaching and physical facilities necessary to give the kind of an education we wish to give.

2. We will be ready to expand present physical facilities and teaching staffs to the extent compatible with our financial resources, actual or readily available.

### PROCEDURES

While these are the general policies that should guide our decisions in regard to expansion, there are many other considerations as well as practical procedures that administrators should bear in mind while making particular application of these policies to specific questions of expansion. Among them, the following might be listed:

1. All plans for expansion of existing facilities will be subject to the approval of higher superiors. Wherefore, provincials and province consultors, with the advice of province prefects of studies, should endeavor to develop province policies on expansion so as to make certain that expansion will aim at the greater good both of the province and of the individual institution.

* Cf. letter of Very Reverend John Baptist Janssens, General of the Society of Jesus on the occasion of the canonization of Saint John De Britto and Saint Bernardino Realino, June 22, 1947, II, 6.

2. In our endeavor to meet the long-term needs of Catholic education, we must bear in mind the need for vocations to the priesthood and religious life and, consequently, areas from which such vocations are likely to come should be given a preference in our decisions on expansion. Moreover, provinces will do well to develop a long-term practical program for fostering religious vocations.

3. Plans for expansion should be made to coordinate with, rather than to be in competition with plans of the hierarchy for expansion.

4. Definite measures should be developed by each school to determine who can profit by the education we wish to give in our schools. For this purpose, a scientific study should be made of student records over a suitable number of years so as to develop criteria for identifying the capable student. Such criteria will include, for example, the required I.Q., character of previous preparation, prerequisite subjects, general prospect of success, etc. Such criteria are necessary since it would be unfair to admit students who are certain to fail because they lack the ability to meet the requirements of the course or school they enter.

5. Different criteria should be developed for the different courses or curricula offered by the institution.

6. Plans for expansion should include a rigorous policy concerning entrance requirements and the preservation of high scholastic standards. If such policies are adhered to strictly, many inferior students can be eliminated, and this, in itself, will create considerable expansion of facilities for capable students.

7. Given such criteria for identifying the students capable of profiting by a Jesuit education, and policies on admissions, expansion should be considered only to the extent that sufficient facilities are or can be made available. By this is meant:

a. That we have or can recruit a sufficient number of Jesuits and competent lay-teachers to care for the students we accept, keeping in mind that among the means proper to attain the aims of Jesuit education are: a program of religious instruction and practice adapted to the stage of development of the student; an adequate course in scholastic philosophy which, together with religion, will constitute a norm to be applied to all the facets of modern life; the well-tried Jesuit method of teaching which not only aims at solid intellectual training but also aims at the formation and development of the abilities and qualities of the individual student; personal interest in individual students which will reflect itself not only in teaching and example but also by wise counsel and advice.

b. That we have or can procure the financial resources to provide adequate salaries for the laymen on our staffs.

c. That we have or can procure the adequate classrooms, laboratories, libraries, dormitories, and recreational facilities without incurring unreasonable debts.

8. It is obvious that the number of laymen in strictly professional schools will outnumber Jesuits. This may be true also, but to a lesser degree, in colleges,

whereas in secondary schools every effort should be made to have preponderance of Jesuit members on the teaching staff. But wherever laymen are employed they should be those whose character and educational background are such as to make them apt members of a team striving for the aims of Jesuit education. To assure this unity of spirit, a program of indoctrination in the history, aims, and methods of Jesuit education should be provided for lay members of our faculties.

9. Plans for expansion should include a program of recruitment and training of competent lay-teachers.

10. Plans for expansion should be long-range in scope, taking into account future as well as present manpower and financial conditions. Nor should such plans be on a province basis only. Rather they should include a conscious effort to coordinate our growth not only within provinces but throughout the Assistancy, so that our total American Jesuit personnel, facilities, and resources will be used most advantageously. Such Assistancy-wide planning would find particular application in the development of inter-province scholasticates, in emphasis on specialized graduate fields, and in the program of special studies for Ours.

11. Other things being equal, preference for expansion should be given to those areas and levels of education where the distinctive aims of Jesuit education can best be achieved and the distinctive procedures of Jesuit education can best be observed.

12. Plans for expansion should also include a careful plan for the most efficient utilization of administrative and teaching personnel, as well as the efficient and economical use of physical facilities.


Source: JEA-Response of Board of Governors to Report of President, May 1958
(IV K, pp. 8-10)

# Abbreviations

| | |
|---|---|
| AAU | Association of American Universities |
| AAUP | Association of American University Professors |
| ACE | American Council on Education |
| AJCU | Association of Jesuit Colleges and Universities |
| AR | *Acta Romana* |
| ARSI | Roman Archives of the Society of Jesus |
| BCA | Boston College Archives |
| BG | Board of Governors |
| EBR | Edward B. Rooney, S.J. |
| EC | Executive Committee (JEA) |
| FUA | Fordham University Archives |
| JBJ | John B. Janssens, S.J. |
| JEA | Jesuit Educational Association |
| JEQ | *Jesuit Educational Quarterly* |
| JRC(A) | Jesuit Research Council (of America) |
| MUA | Marquette University Archives |
| NCA | North Central Association |
| NCEA | National Catholic Educational Association |
| NEPA | New England Province Archives |
| S.J. | Society of Jesus (Jesuit) |

# Notes

PREFACE

1. Walter J. Ong, S.J., *American Catholic Crossroads* (New York, 1959), p. 93.


1. THE INTER-PROVINCE COMMITTEE, 1921-1931

1. The Society of Jesus was suppressed, as a religious order, by Pope Clement XIV in 1773. In 1805, through a special petition of two ex-Jesuit bishops, John Carroll of Baltimore and his coadjutor Leonard Neale, Gabriel Gruber, General of the Society in the Russian Empire, where the papal bull of suppression had never been recognized, allowed former Jesuits in America to be aggregated privately to the Russian body. The Society was restored throughout the world by Pope Pius VII.

2. William V. Bangert, S.J., *A History of the Society of Jesus* (St. Louis: Institute of Jesuit Sources, 1972), p. 494.

3. Quotation appears in *ibid.*

4. *Woodstock Letters*, vol. 29 (1900), appendix.

5. *Ibid.*, 51, no. 3 (1922): 469.

6. *Ibid.*, 67, no. 1 (March 1938): 58–62.

7. In references to colleges or universities, the terms "president" and "rector," unless otherwise noted, are used to designate the same office.

8. "Report," meeting of Inter-Province Committee on Studies, 1921, p. 1. The minutes of the annual reports of the Inter-Province Committee (1921–1931) fill a volume of 125 pages. Two copies of this volume are located, as part of the Jesuit Educational Association collection, in the University Archives, Boston College. Hereafter, these documents will be referred to as "Inter-Province Reports." For a fuller description of these reports, see Matthew J. Fitzsimons, S.J., "*The Instructio*, 1934–1949," *Jesuit Educational Quarterly*, 12, no. 2 (October 1949): 69–78.

9. They were Joseph H. Rockwell, Maryland–New York; Francis X. McMenamy, Missouri; Francis X. Dillon, California; Emile Mattern, New Orleans; John M. Filion, Canada.

10. Also present were Fathers C. A. Buckley, dean, University of Santa Clara; C. F. Carroll, dean, Gonzaga University; E. P. Tivnan, president, Fordham University; W. C. Nevils, dean, Georgetown University; M. J. O'Mailia, dean, Canisius College; J. B. Furray, rector, Saint Ignatius College (now Loyola University), Chicago; J. F. McCormick, rector, Creighton University; J. M. Walsh, dean, Spring Hill College; M. J. Walsh, dean, Loyola University, New Orleans; W. H. Hingston, rector, Loyola College, Montreal.

11. "Inter-Province Report," 1921, p. 2.

12. *Ibid.*

13. In an official notice to the superiors of the Maryland–New York Province, Father Provincial Rockwell announced the appointment of Father Francis M. Connell as the first prefect general of studies of that province. Joseph H. Rockwell to Father Superior, New York, June 1, 1922, JEA File, Boston College Archives (hereafter BCA).

14. "Inter-Province Report," 1921, p. 9.

15. *Ibid.*

16. *Ibid.*

17. By ordination of Father General Francis Xavier Wernz, December 8, 1909, the fathers provincial of the United States and Canada were enjoined to meet annually to consider the editorial policy, financial statement, and general "status" of the weekly periodical *America*. The procedure at the annual meeting was therefore to review, first of all, the report of the editor of *America* and then proceed to other business, which from 1921 to 1931 included the report of the Inter-Province Committee. Since *America* was located in the Maryland–New York Province, the provincial of the province was, again by direction of Father Wernz, *ex officio* chairman of the provincials' meeting. See "Ordinatio ARP Francisci Xav. Wernz de Novo Periodico Libello in America Septentrionali Publicando," Woodstock Letters, 39, no. 2 (1910): 212–221; also *Acta Romana*, 1 (1906–10): 163–175.

18. "Minutes," provincials' meeting, April 20, 1921, p. 4. These documents, located in the New York Province Archives, can be found in the New England Province Archives from 1922 on. In that year, New England, formerly a *regio*, was established as a vice province, and Father Patrick F. O'Gorman, vice provincial, began to attend the provincials' meetings.

19. A brief summary of these recommendations will indicate the basic topics under discussion. The committee recommended the physical and administrative separation of colleges and high schools situated on the same campus; restriction of the name "college" to those institutions commonly referred to as such in America; conformity to regional education association requirements; the "units" for admission to and graduation from college; and the departmental divisions in a liberal arts college.

20. For a biographical sketch and summary of his accomplishments, see Joseph A. Slattery, S.J., "Very Reverend Father Vladimir Ledochowski, Oc-

tober 7, 1866–December 13, 1942," *Woodstock Letters*, 72, no. 1 (March 1943): 1–20. See also *Acta Romana*, 10 (1941–1945): 479–486.

21. This document, issued January 12, 1899, criticized the alleged American position that the Church should modify her doctrines to suit modern situations and adapt her teachings to popular theories. For the most detailed account of this controversy, see Thomas T. McAvoy, C.S.C., *The Americanist Heresy in Roman Catholicism, 1895–1900* (University of Notre Dame Press, 1963).

22. W. Ledochowski to R. P. Joseph Rockwell, provincial, October 20, 1921, Roman Archives of the Society of Jesus (ARSI), *Registr. Maryland*, VI: 141. The content of the letter is summarized in its title: "Permanens Ac Provinciis Americae Commune Consilium De Externorum Collegiis Et Scholis Altis." (This title is usually rendered in English as "The Permanent National Council for the Colleges and High Schools of the American Provinces.") It may be helpful to recall, as explained briefly in note 17, that the provincial of the Maryland–New York Province was, for administrative purposes, *primus inter pares*. Ordinary business with the provinces of the American Assistancy, which was established by the 26th General Congregation in 1915, was conducted between the Roman Curia and the provincial of Maryland–New York. That provincial submitted the report of the provincials' meeting to Father General, who, in turn, would acknowledge to that provincial. He would then communicate the General's comments to the other provincials. Father Thomas Gannon, Maryland–New York, was elected first American Assistant in 1915.

23. *Ibid.*

24. *Ibid.*

25. *Ibid.*

26. "Inter-Province Report," 1922, p. 17. Albert C. Fox was reelected chairman. While the membership of the committee remained relatively stable over the years, there were yearly replacements. In 1922, three new members appeared: R. H. Rankin, dean, Fordham University, replacing Father Tivnan; F. M. Connell, Xavier High School, New York; and F. D. Sullivan, regent, Loyola University, New Orleans, replacing M. J. Walsh.

27. See James L. Burke, S.J., *Jesuit Province of New England: The Formative Years* (Boston: privately printed, 1976).

28. "Inter-Province Report," 1922, pp. 21–22.

29. *Ibid.*, p. 22.

30. *Ibid.*

31. *Ibid.*

32. *Ibid.* "During all the years of Jesuit educational pioneering, from the founding of Georgetown down to 1921, no attempt seems to have been made to organize the several provinces and the many Jesuit high schools and colleges on a national scale. The diversity of social, cultural, and economic conditions in different sections of the country . . . was probably the chief obstacle. Another was the fact that the national groups of Jesuits, who were the founders of American Jesuit education, reflected and to an extent clung to the diverse traits and traditions of their origin—English, French, Belgian, Italian, Ger-

man." Allan P. Farrell, S.J., and Matthew J. Fitzsimons, S.J., *A Study of Jesuit Education* (New York: privately printed, 1958).

33. For a fuller treatment, see John S. Brubacher and Willis Rudy, *Higher Education in Transition* (New York, 1958); Frederick Rudolph, *The American College and University: A History* (New York, 1962).

34. William K. Selden, *Accreditation: A Struggle over Standards in Higher Education* (New York, 1960), p. 37.

35. "The failure of one college in this matter would reflect discreditably on all other Jesuit institutions." "Inter-Province Report," 1922, p. 19.

36. "Inter-Province Report," 1923, p. 24. In addition to six fathers who had already worked with the committee, there were two new members: F. X. Twellmeyer, prefect of studies of the New Orleans Province, and Francis Cavey, dean, Spring Hill College.

37. *Woodstock Letters*, 64, no. 2 (1935): 280–281. Saint Xavier College changed its name to Xavier University on August 4, 1930.

38. "Inter-Province Report," 1923, p. 26. Jesuit presidents of an earlier day had had a running controversy with the Board of Regents of the University of the State of New York on that very question. For a further discussion of this issue, see Allan P. Farrell, S.J., and Matthew J. Fitzsimons, S.J., *op. cit.*, pp. 66–70.

39. "Inter-Province Report," 1923, p. 26.

40. *Ibid.*

41. At a later date, omitting any reference to an "in-house" proposal, the provincials "were of the opinion that where possible, means should be taken to acquire the recognition of standardizing agencies necessary to maintain a proper rating." "Minutes," Provincials' Meeting, 1929, p. 8.

42. "Minutes," Provincials' Meeting, Saint Louis University, May 22–23, 1923, p. 3.

43. "Minutes," Provincials' Meeting, College of Saint Francis Xavier, New York, January 11, 1924, p. 3.

44. *Ibid.* It is interesting to note that one province seems to have anticipated a decision of the fathers provincial. In the Missouri Province *Newsletter* (September 1923, no. 1), the editor refers to "the third annual convention of the Jesuit Educational Association, Middle-West Division, [which] was held at Campion College, August 16–18." It was the first use of that name.

45. The provincials' meetings in 1923 and 1924 were, to some extent, subordinated to the business of the 27th General Congregation, which was held in 1923. At that congregation, Father Emile Mattern, former provincial of New Orleans, was elected American Assistant to succeed Father Anthony Maas.

46. "Inter-Province Report," 1923, p. 24.

47. In 1922, the committee had called the attention of the provincials to a report of the American Council on Education which contained the following advice: "A college should have a live, well-distributed, professionally administered library of at least 8000 volumes, exclusive of public documents, bearing specifically upon the subjects taught and with a definite annual appropriation for the purchase of new books." See "Report of the Committee on Col-

lege Standards," *Educational Record*, 3, no. 3 (July 1922): 210-214. Albert C. Fox, S.J., president of Marquette University, representing the Catholic Educational Association, was a member of this prestigious committee, appointed by the American Council on Education.

48. *Ibid.*, p. 212.

49. "Inter-Province Report," 1923, p. 30.

50. *Ibid.*

51. *Ibid.*

52. *Ibid.*

53. *Ibid.*, p. 31.

54. Normal prudence came to the rescue of the committee. It was stipulated that "before [the material] is presented to the standardizing agencies," a copy must be sent to each provincial, to the prefect of studies of the four provinces, and to each member of the committee.

55. "Inter-Province Report," 1924, p. 41.

56. *Ibid.*

57. "Inter-Province Report," 1926, p. 3. (The pages of the 1926 Report are not numbered consecutively.)

58. Accrediting agencies in general confined their evaluation to undergraduate departments. The Association of American Universities, however, more frequently examined graduate programs.

59. The state of Montana had recently deprived Jesuits of the right to teach in high schools because they had not fulfilled specific requirements in education courses. See "Inter-Province Report." 1923, p. 31.

60. "Inter-Province Report," 1924, p. 40.

61. W. Colman Nevils, S.J., to Very Rev. Joseph M. Piet, S.J., Washington, D.C., June 27, 1924 (BCA).

62. It is interesting to note that in departments of education in Jesuit colleges, qualified laymen "could be confined to those courses which deal largely with the mechanics of education, reserving courses in the history, principles and psychology of education to our own Jesuit teachers." "Inter-Province Report," 1923, p. 33.

63. June 27, 1924.

64. See *Woodstock Letters*, 66, no. 1 (1937): 277-291.

65. "Minutes," Special Meeting of Provincials of the American Assistancy, April 19-20, 1924 (Provincial Archives, New York).

66. *Ibid.*

67. *Ibid.*

68. "Inter-Province Report," Buffalo, 1925, p. 44.

69. *Ibid.*, p. 45. It should be remembered that the provincials, each in his own province, continued to appoint the members of the committee.

70. *Ibid.*, p. 46.

71. This sixth annual meeting of the Inter-Province Committee was held at Santa Clara, May 16-19, 1926. Father Connell acted as chairman and Father Charles F. Carroll was secretary.

72. The three titles were: "Standard Requirements for Our Schools,"

"Special Recommendations Concerning Our Schools," "Miscellaneous Recommendations Bearing on Our Schools Only Indirectly." In general, the eight-page digest, under numerous headings, briefly described the standard requirements for a good college and, even more briefly, for a good high school. See *Quinquennial Digest* (of Inter-Province Committee annual reports, 1921–1925), Provincial Archives, N.Y.C. Also, "Inter-Province Report," 1926.

73. "Inter-Province Report," 1926, p. 2.

74. "Minutes," Provincials' Meeting, Santa Clara, May 31–June 1, 1926 (NEPA).

75. *Ibid.*

76. "Minutes," Provincials' Meeting, Saint Louis University, April 21–22, 1927. The provincials conceded that the unexpected transfer of their meeting from New Orleans to St. Louis was an extenuating circumstance in the absence of the committee representative.

77. "Inter-Province Report," 1927, p. 51.

78. *Ibid.*

79. *Ibid.*

80. See above, pp. 9–10.

81. "Minutes," Provincials' Meeting, May 31–June 1, 1926.

82. The provincials' reply is contained in the 1926 Report, p. 1. Strictly speaking, the provincials of the American Assistancy had no authority to establish a national association. They could only confirm the Inter-Province Committee, already approved by Father General, as a surrogate.

83. "Inter-Province Report," December 31, 1927–January 3, 1928.

84. J. L. Burke, *op. cit.*, pp. 12–13.

85. New faces were in attendance: William I. Lonergan, associate editor of *America* (California Province); Charles J. Deane, dean of Fordham College; William T. Tallon, rector, Saint Joseph's College, Philadelphia; Cornelius L. Bulman, assistant dean, Holy Cross College; Joseph C. Kearns, dean, Loyola University, New Orleans. Edward P. Tivnan, rector of Weston, as a courtesy was invited to take part in the proceedings of the meeting.

86. See *Woodstock Letters*, 63, no. 3 (October 1934): 459–461.

87. "Inter-Province Report," 1928, *passim*. The committee members at Weston College agreed that this problem was not confined to Jesuit schools. The democracy of the American system of higher education, they noted, favors the average student, not the gifted.

88. "Inter-Province Report," 1928, p. 5.

89. *Ibid.*, p. 6.

90. *Ibid.*

91. "Minutes," Provincials' Meeting, New Orleans, April 11–12, 1928.

92. *Ibid.*

93. The provincials were not entirely unresponsive. The honors courses, recommended for talented students, were approved. The province prefects of studies were also advised to encourage the publication of Jesuit textbooks and to exchange lists of titles in order to avoid "useless" duplication.

94. The minutes of the provincials' meeting (Boston College, April 3–4, 1929) allude to a communication from Father General to the American provincials. "Referring to the Interprovince Committee on Studies, Very Rev. Fr. General says its purpose should be to draw up schemes to help the Fathers Provincial in the matter of studies; that it probably is too large and does not seem to have produced results commensurate with the labor and money expended."

95. This was in response to comments by Father General Ledochowski in a letter dated 7 June 1928. This letter will be referred to in detail in chapter 2.

96. The ninth meeting was held December 31, 1928–January 3, 1929 (see "Inter-Province Report," 1929, pp. 73–81, *passim*). Anticipating by a decade the appearance of the *Jesuit Educational Quarterly*, the committee called for a "Jesuit Journal of Education to be the joint work of the Several Provinces." It would be a vehicle for articles of young Jesuits and a source of unity and cooperation in the American Assistancy.

97. *Ibid.*, p. 75.

98. *Ibid.*, p. 76.

99. *Ibid.*, p. 78. With worldly wisdom, the committee recommended that "editors and their staffs should be generously supplied with tickets, invitations, etc. for all college activities, especially for pay affairs." This was all the more necessary since "nearly all of our Jesuit institutions are suffering from the delusion that we are better now than we actually are."

100. See Louis J. Gallagher, S.J., *Edmund A. Walsh, S.J.: A Biography* (New York, 1962). Father Gallagher was the author of five additional books (two were novels).

101. See L. J. Gallagher, "Bobola, Andrew, St.," *New Catholic Encyclopedia*, 2: 624–625.

102. See L. J. Gallagher, S.J., "Notes from a Russian Diary," *Woodstock Letters*, 54, no. 1 (1925): 54–69; no. 3, pp. 206–238. The relics of Saint Andrew are now interred in Warsaw.

103. New England was advanced from a vice province to a province on July 31, 1926, and was represented by Father Gallagher for the first time on the Inter-Province Committee in 1927.

104. "Minutes," Provincials' Meeting, Boston College, April 1929, p. 3.

105. *Ibid.* During these years a debate was taking place within the Catholic Church in America and the Society of Jesus concerning the position of the Newman Movement in higher education. There were many who felt that the rapid growth of Catholic colleges in the United States was made at the expense of the Newman Movement. See John Whitney Evans, "John LaFarge, *America*, and the Newman Movement," *Catholic Historical Review*, 64, no. 4 (October 1978): 614–643. While the American provincials did not sanction the direction of Newman Clubs by Jesuit chaplains, "which would probably be misunderstood and might embarrass us at this time," they were not opposed to Jesuits' "giving the spiritual exercises to these clubs whenever asked to do so." "Minutes," Provincials' Meeting, Saint Louis University, April 1927.

106. *Ibid.*, Boston College, 1929, p 7.

107. *Ibid.*

108. The ninth annual meeting of the Inter-Province Committee was at Georgetown University, December 31, 1929–January 3, 1930. Six American provinces and the Canadian province were represented. See "Inter-Province Report," 1930, pp. 82–91.

109. *Ibid.*, p. 89.

110. "Minutes," Provincials' Meeting, University of Detroit, April 23–24, 1930, p. 10.

111. The restrictions placed on regents and advisors severely limited their efficiency. They served as advisors to the rector only; there was to be no conflict with house consultors; there was no obligation on the part of the rector to share the financial balance with advisory boards. If shown, it must be done with the advice of the consultors. *Ibid.*, p. 11.

112. *Ibid.*, Boston College, 1929, p. 3.

113. Eleventh (and last) Annual Meeting of the Inter-Province Committee, Loyola University, Los Angeles, December 31, 1930–January 2, 1931. See "Inter-Province Report," 1931, pp. 92–114.

114. *Ibid., passim.* A *Quinquennial Digest* was published under a separate cover. The *Digest*, so far as the evidence indicates, was neither approved nor circulated.

115. In this instance, the committee's labors did not go entirely in vain. While the Maryland–New York and New England provinces decided that they could meet "the imperative exactions of external agencies . . . without notable departure from the existing schedule of studies," the other provinces felt that it would be necessary "to modify the existing schedules substantially in accordance with the suggestions submitted by the Inter-Province Committee." "Minutes," Meeting of Provincials of the United States and Canada, Toronto, Canada, May 5–6, 1931, p. 9.

116. Father Samuel H. Horine, prefect general in the Missouri Province, later provincial and active in the Inter-Province Committee, was delegated to interpret the 1931 report to the provincials.

117. It may be helpful to quote the exact words: "Labores 'Interprovince Committee on Studies' non minori laude digni sunt. . . . Volo omnino ut huius 'Committee' experientia et praeteriti labores novae Commissioni de Studiis Altioribus subsidio sint et auxilio, ac proinde arcta cooperatio inter utrumque coetum vigere debet. Interea tamen, ut patet 'Interprovince Committee' labores suos suspendere debebit." Letter of W. Ledochowski, S.J., to American Provincials, Rome, March 10, 1931.

## 2. THE COMMISSION ON HIGHER STUDIES, 1931–1934

1. W. Ledochowski to Fathers Provincial of the American Provinces, Rome, March 12, 1927. See file entitled "Epistolae etc. de Coll's & Univ's Americanis," ARSI, Rome.

2. *Ibid.*

3. *Ibid.*

4. *Ibid.*

5. At the end of his covering letter, the General casually asked the provincials about "the state of affairs at Notre Dame University along the lines of the Questionnaires." He was leaving nothing to chance in preparing for his next encounter with the cardinal-prefect.

6. The questionnaire appears as appendix A.

7. See file "Epistolae etc. de Coll's & Univ's Americanis," ARSI, Rome.

8. W. Ledochowski to the Fathers and Brothers of the American Assistancy, Rome, January 7, 1928. (ARSI). This letter is also available in the archives of American provinces.

9. *Ibid.*

10. A further insight to Father Ledochowski's philosophy of education may be found in his letter to the Spanish provincials (Rome, December 17, 1928), "The Apostolate of Education," and the letter to the provincials of the Italian assistancy (Rome, March 28, 1930) on "The Promotion of Christian Education." See *Selected Writings of Father Ledochowski* (Chicago, 1945), pp. 643–657.

11. Letter of January 7, 1928.

12. *Ibid.*

13. *Ibid.* The encyclical of Pope Pius XI *On the Christian Education of Youth* (December 31, 1929) incorporates some of the ideas of Ledochowski. *The Papal Encyclicals, 1903–1939*, ed. Claudia Carlen, IHM (McGrath, 1981), pp. 353–369.

14. Letter of January 7, 1928. In the first official break with Jesuit tradition, nuns and laywomen were admitted to an eight-week summer session at Marquette University. On the advice of the provincial, the president of Marquette, James McCabe, presented the case to the General for his approval. Since no specific regulation had been imposed to the contrary, women were again registered in the summers of 1910 and 1911. The response from Rome arrived in the spring of 1912, when Father General Francis Wernz gave permission for "ladies and even nuns" to attend Marquette. See Raphael N. Hamilton, *The Story of Marquette University* (Milwaukee, 1953), pp. 124–127.

15. Letter of January 7, 1928.

16. *Ibid.*

17. As a result of the letter, the provincials now insisted upon the appointment of a full-time spiritual director in professional schools; moreover, they began to provide for the appointment of a qualified head of departments of religion. "Minutes," Provincials' Meeting, Boston College, April 1929.

18. *Ibid.*, Detroit, April 1930, p. 4.

19. The Congregation of Procurators, in accordance with the Institute of the Society, is convened to advise the General on the advantages or disadvantages of calling a General Congregation.

20. Ledochowski to American Provincials, Rome, December 8, 1930 (ARSI).

21. *Ibid.*

22. *Ibid.*

23. In his letter of December 8, 1930, the General was singularly silent on the work of the Inter-Province Committee, which had strongly recommended many, if not all, of the points he made.

24. The Society, as all clerical congregations, had to satisfy the requirements of the apostolic constitution *Deus Scientiarum Dominus* in preparing candidates for the priesthood.

25. *Ibid.*

26. *Ibid.*

27. Ledochowski to the Provincials of the American Assistancy, Rome, March 9, 1931 (NEPA). The appointees represented the six provinces of the American Assistancy: California, Maryland–New York, Chicago, New Orleans, New England, Missouri.

28. Ledochowski to R. P. James Kilroy, Rome, March 9, 1931 (NEPA).

29. See Victor J. Blum, S.J., "James Bernard Macelwane, S.J., *American Geophysical Union*, 37, no. 2 (April 1956), 135–136.

30. See Thomas Clancy, S.J., *Our Friends* (Loyola University, 1978).

31. For brief biographies of Fathers Charles F. Carroll, Albert C. Fox, and Edward P. Tivnan, see chapter 1.

32. These meetings were held in St. Louis, New Orleans, San Francisco and Santa Clara, Boston, and, finally, Chicago.

33. This report, hereafter referred to as *Report of Commission on Higher Studies*, is available for reference at Boston College Archives.

34. *Ibid.*, p. 7.

35. *Ibid.*

36. See JEA File, box 15, BCA.

37. *Report of Commission on Higher Studies*, p. 6.

38. The *Report of the Commission on Higher Studies* was divided into four parts: "I, United Purpose and Concerted Action," "II, Comparative Standing of Our Institutions of Higher Learning," "III, National and Regional Accrediting Agencies," "IV, Academic Degrees and Educational Training of Ours." The report also contains three appendixes.

39. To this proposal, Father General had commented: "Valde quoque mihi placet quod RVa animadvertit de nova aliqua associatione Collegiorum nostrorum instituenda qua proprias nostras normas ac methodos stabilire ac liberius sequi possitis. Libentissimo igitur approbo ut RVa hac de re cum ceteris Provincialibus in proximo vestro conventu agat." See "Minutes," Provincials' Meeting, April 3–4, 1929.

40. *Ibid.*

41. See chapter 1, p. 15.

42. "Minutes," Provincials' Meeting, May 1931, p. 11.

43. *Ibid.* The following year, however, when Father Macelwane asked that the members of the commission be released from their regular assignments during May, June, and July, "several of the Provincials did not see how they could prudently grant the request." All agreed that it would be "very imprudent" to take a dean away from his college in May and early June. "Minutes," Provincials' Meeting, Fordham University, May 3–4, 1932.

44. Part IV of the Constitutions recognizes the educational apostolate as a means to the end for which the Society was founded, and provides for the acceptance of colleges and universities. See *Constitutiones Societatis Jesu et Epitome Instituti* (Rome, 1943). For a translation of part IV of the Constitutions of the Society of Jesus, see George E. Ganss, S.J., *Saint Ignatius' Idea of a Jesuit University* Milwaukee, 1954).

45. *Report of the Commission on Higher Studies*, p. 16.

46. *Ibid.*

47. *Ibid.*, p. 19.

48. *Ibid.*, p. 20. With or without official sanction, and obviously anticipating approval, the letterhead of the commission's stationery carried the same title.

49. *Ibid.*

50. *Ibid.*, pp. 20–21.

51. *Ibid.*

52. See JEA File, box 15, BCA.

53. *Report of the Commission on Higher Studies*, p. 26.

54. *Ibid.* A "commissarius" in the Society (there have been very few in Jesuit history) has temporary but ultimate authority from the General in the area to which he is appointed. The commissioners, who debated the merits of "visitor" versus "commissarius," preferred a commissarius because his duties would be different from those usually assigned to a visitor. If he had to deal with external agencies, a commissioner would be more acceptable. Finally, "commissarius" would be less likely to connote disciplinary reform. See JEA File, box 15, BCA.

55. *Report of the Commission on Higher Studies*, pp. 26–28, *passim*.

56. Although Tivnan, at this point, was entirely in favor of a commissarius, he himself would not be a candidate for that office. In a letter to the chairman, he wrote: "I agree with the ideas expressed in your letter to the General, with the exception of the suggestion that I be designated to play the part of our educational Mussolini. . . . But I do hope that someone will jog the [General's] elbow if he tries to shoot in my direction." Tivnan to Macelwane, Boston College, August 22, 1932, box 15, BCA.

57. As proof of the commission's thoroughness, the minutes of the final meeting, which was held at Loyola University, Chicago (July 3–23), comprise a volume of more than 200 pages. The extended session was due to Father Tivnan, who was convinced "that if we are to achieve any results which might be incorporated in a report to Father General, we must decide to sit together for a succession of meetings covering at least a month" (Tivnan to Macelwane, Boston College, March 24, 1932; box 15, BCA). It would be helpful for the reader to consult the "Summary of Recommendations" (pp. 181–192), which became an integral part of the *Report* and reflected the commission's conclusions on the four issues raised by the General. This "Summary" is included as appendix B.

58. Those teaching in juniorates, philosophates, and theologates were particularly interested in, and generally critical of, that section of the *Report*

which designed a course of studies for Jesuits that would, while protecting ecclesiastical requirements, also prepare scholastics for higher degrees.

59. This letter is dated December 8, 1932, but the name of the writer has been deleted. See "Minutes," Provincials' Meeting, 1930–1940 (NEPA).

60. This communication, unsigned, undated, is in the files of the minutes of the provincials' meetings. In point of fact, one of the commissioners had second thoughts on the wisdom of this recommendation. "The Commissarius idea is a red flag. I think it unfortunate that we used the term." Tivnan to Macelwane, Boston College, June 26, 1933; box 15, BCA.

61. Ledochowski to Provincials of the American Assistancy, Rome, April 5, 1932 (NEPA). The title "scriptor" was common in the catalogs of European provinces and, since the Jesuits did not administer universities in Europe, this title designated those who were engaged in the intellectual apostolate at a high level.

62. *Ibid.* In a related subject, the General requested the American provincials to prepare men in Sacred Scripture and theology in order to take their places beside European Jesuits on the faculties of the Biblical Institute and the Gregorian University. Ledochowski to Edward Phillips, Rome, April 4, 1933 (NEPA).

63. Ledochowski to Provincials, Rome, April 2, 1932 (NEPA).

64. Edward Tivnan to James Macelwane, Boston College, May 18, 1932; box 15, BCA.

65. *Ibid.*

66. Tivnan to Macelwane, Boston College, June 26, 1933 (box 15, BCA). In the same letter Tivnan wrote: "I have not the least hope that anything will come of all our work even if the General does take the modified action I expect."

67. *Ibid.*

68. *Ibid.*

69. A biography appears in "Office of Public Information," Saint Louis University, October 9, 1959.

70. A two-page summary of this conversation (n.d.) is in the file of the provincials' meetings, 1930–1940 (NEPA).

71. 47, no. 7 (May 21, 1932): 163–164, and no. 11 (June 18, 1932): 257–258.

72. See *Report of Commission on Higher Studies*, appendix 2, pp. 198–208.

73. "A National Plan for Catholic Higher Education." Indicative of this position was a form letter sent to the diocesan priests of the Diocese of St. Augustine by Rev. M. J. Brown, chairman of the Diocesan Committee of the Society of Friends of the Catholic University of America, Winter Haven, Florida, November 4, 1935. In that letter Father Brown wrote: "The Catholic University of America is the Catholic center of scholarship and teacher-training for our country . . . and, because of its membership in the Association of American Universities, conferring upon its students degrees recognized by all accredited agencies."

74. See abstract of *Proceedings* of National Catholic Educational Association, June 26-29, St. Paul, Minnesota: "Meeting of Jesuit Representatives;" JEA File, BCA.

75. In 1931-32, 797 master's degrees were awarded by Catholic graduate schools; of that number, 447 were from Jesuit institutions. In 1932-33, the total was 833, of which 543 were from Jesuit schools. In those two years combined, 131 doctorates were awarded by Catholic graduate schools, and 66 were from Jesuit institutions. Box 15, Commission on Higher Studies, BCA.

76. Wlodimirus Ledochowski, *Ad Omnes Provinciarum Praepositos Aliosque Societatis Superiores, "De Ministeriorum atque Operum Delectu Nostrorumque ad Ea Institutione,"* Rome, June 29, 1933; *Acta Romana*, 7 (1932-1934): 454-493.

## 3. THE GENERAL APPOINTS A "COMMISSARIUS," 1934-1937

1. For a brief history of the foundation, purpose, and function of this organization, see *The American Council on Education: Its History and Activities, 1934-1935* (an ACE Publication, 744 Jackson Place, Washington, D.C.).

2. Raymond M. Hughes, "Report of the Committee on Graduate Instruction," *Educational Record*, 15, no. 2 (April 1934): 192-234.

3. *Ibid., passim.*

4. *Ibid.*, p. 194. The procedure, as explained by the committee, was fair and thorough. After all the institutions and departments (the study, as concluded, covered thirty-five fields) that offered the doctorate were identified, the national learned society in each field was asked to provide (as far as possible) a list of the distribution of 100 well-known scholars among the special branches of the field. Each scholar, in turn, was requested to check those institutions which, in his judgment, had an adequate staff to prepare candidates for the doctorate. He was also asked to "star" departments of the highest rank. Those institutions and departments checked by a majority (though failing of a majority of stars) were placed in the group of those adequately staffed and equipped. *Ibid.*, pp. 193-194.

5. April 2, 1934.

6. For the source of this statement, see Matthew J. Fitzsimons, S.J., "The *Instructio*, 1934-1949," *Jesuit Educational Quarterly*, 12, no. 2 (October 1949): 69-78.

7. Ledochowski to the Fathers and Scholastics of the American Assistancy, Rome, August 15, 1934; *Acta Romana*, 7 (1932-1934): 920-923.

8. *Ibid.*

9. *Ibid.*

10. *Ibid.*

11. *Ibid.*

12. *Ibid.*

13. Ledochowski to the Provincials of the American Assistancy, Rome, August 15, 1934; *Acta Romana*, 7: 923–927.

14. *Ibid.*

15. *Ibid.*

16. *Ibid.* This appointment, as the General explained, was made in accordance with the eleventh decree of the Second General Congregation of the Society. The title "commissarius" is not easily rendered by the English word "commissary," which has a double meaning, and even less so by the Russian derivative "commissar."

17. *Ibid.* Due to a series of unanticipated circumstances, the *Instruction* was not made permanent until 1948. These included the promulgation of a new version of the *Ratio Studiorum Superiorium* in 1941, which was related, in some of its aspects, to the *Instructio*; the Second World War, which interrupted communications between Rome and the American provincials; and the illness and death of Father Ledochowski in 1942.

18. The full title was *Instructio Pro Assistentia Americae De Ordinandis Universitatibus, Collegiis, Ac Scholis Altis Et De Praeparandis Eorundem Magistris.* This is usually rendered in English as "Instruction for the American Assistancy on the Administration of Universities, Colleges and High Schools and the Preparation of Their Teachers. *Acta Romana*, 7 (1932–34): 927–935.

19. The author hopes that the present historical endeavor will serve, in some measure, to rehabilitate the memory of Father O'Connell, although he recognizes that there are Jesuits who will not agree entirely with this interpretation.

20. *Jesuit Educational Quarterly*, 21, no. 4 (March 1959): 263–264. See also his obituary (Fr. Daniel M. O'Connell), *The Chronicle* (Chicago Province), October 1959.

21. Father O'Connell, for reasons of his own, did not preserve the records of his three-year tenure. Superiors have speculated that, due to the delicate nature of his correspondence as commissarius, he decided to destroy his files. After Father O'Connell's death, Father Edward B. Rooney, who succeeded Father O'Connell as national secretary of education, in a letter dated September 19, 1958, wrote to Father William J. Schmidt, provincial of the Chicago Province, asking "if anyone had gone through [Father O'Connell's] files and if so, if they found materials which belong to the JEA." In his reply to Father Rooney, dated September 23, 1958, Father Schmidt wrote: "With reference to any JEA file material, we had alerted and checked with Father McGrail, then Rector of West Baden College, to check for JEA materials among Father O'Connell's notes. He assured us that he himself went through everything and found nothing. Father McGrail had asked Father O'Connell about this some time previously and received the answer that absolutely nothing was there." Fortunately, copies of Father O'Connell's official correspondence and reports are preserved in the Roman Archives in a file identified as *JEA: 1935: Dan M. O'Connell, Commissarius.* Through the courteous cooperation of Father Georges Bottereau, assistant archivist at the Roman Curia, the author was able to obtain copies of 160 pages from the O'Connell

File. These materials are now in the JEA File, University Archives, Boston College. Subsequent references will be to the O'Connell File, BCA.

22. Obviously, Jesuit high schools comprised an important segment of the apostolate of education in the United States. However, since they are only marginally connected with the thrust of this study, there will be no attempt to document Father O'Connell's directions with regard to them.

23. Daniel O'Connell to James T. McCormick, Loyola University, Chicago, January 1, 1935; O'Connell File, BCA.

24. Notes on Boston College; O'Connell File, BCA. Doctoral programs were reinstated at Boston College in 1952.

25. The commissarius also visited the Boston College Law School, founded in 1929, and applauded its recognition by the American Bar Association. He made suggestions that would improve the chance of recognition by the Association of American Law Schools, which was already accorded to seven Jesuit law schools. O'Connell File, BCA.

26. Notes on Holy Cross; O'Connell File, BCA.

27. *Ibid.*

28. O'Connell File, BCA.

29. The committee included William J. Murphy, province prefect of studies, chairman; James H. Dolan, socius to the provincial; Louis J. Gallagher, president, Boston College; Francis J. Dolan, president, Holy Cross; John E. Lyons, rector, novitiate. In a three-page memorandum (found in the O'Connell File), Father Francis P. Donnelly, who had spent eleven years teaching in New England, disagreed with the proposed changes in curriculum. Implicitly, he was criticizing Father O'Connell and the work of the committee.

30. *AAU, Journal of Proceedings and Addresses of the First Annual Conference* (Chicago, February 27-28, 1900), p. 7.

31. See above, chapter 1, p. 8.

32. See *Proceedings and Addresses*, AAU, Conf. 34-36, 1932-1934. The Catholic University of America is a charter member of the AAU. No Jesuit institution has been elected to membership in this association.

33. Fernandus Payne to Aloysius J. Hogan, S.J., Indiana University, November 26, 1935; O'Connell File, BCA.

34. *Ibid.*

35. *Ibid.*

36. O'Connell to Zacheus J. Maher, Loyola University, Chicago, December 15, 1935; O'Connell File, BCA.

37. O'Connell to Maher, Loyola University, Chicago, December 17, 1935; O'Connell File, BCA. Emile Mattern, American Assistant to the General, died in Rome, July 31, 1935. Zacheus Maher, former provincial of the California Province, was appointed to succeed Mattern on September 3, 1935.

38. *Ibid.*

39. "Notes on Fordham University"; O'Connell File, BCA.

40. It may be of interest to note that, in the course of his visitations, the commissarius recommended that certain talented Jesuits, with established reputations, be granted the doctorate in philosophy or theology by Father

General. At Fordham, for example, he recommended George Bull, Moorhouse I. X. Millar, and Walter Somers. The authority to award the doctorate to Jesuits who, prior to the papal document *Deus Scientiarum Dominus* of 1932, had passed an *examen rigorosum* in philosophy and/or theology, had been granted to the Jesuit General by Pope Julius III, and confirmed by Pius IV and subsequent popes. Technically granted by the General himself, the Gregorian University acted as witness and registrar of the degree. See *Acta Romana*, 7 (1932–34): 785–86.

41. *Ibid.*

42. O'Connell File (n.d.), BCA.

43. *Ibid.*

44. *Ibid.*

45. For a good account of the controversy, see Joseph T. Durkin, S.J., *Georgetown University: The Middle Years* (Washington, D.C., 1963).

46. "Notes on Georgetown," submitted to the provincial of the Maryland–New York Province; O'Connell File, BCA.

47. *Ibid.*

48. *Ibid.*

49. *Ibid.*

50. *Ibid.*

51. *Ibid.*

52. *Ibid.*

53. *Ibid.* The commissarius agreed that "Georgetown can be proud of its Law School." However, "the Medical School should carry out the directions of the American Medical Association inspectors." Referring to article 17 of the *Instruction*, Father O'Connell directed that, in the future, deans and heads of departments (especially psychiatry) should be appointed from among qualified Catholics (*ibid.*). Since it would unduly interrupt the narrative, the author has not made a practice of citing the *Instruction*. The commissarius, however, in his instructions to the provincials, was very careful to base his directives on the appropriate article of the *Instruction* of Father Ledochowski.

54. This narrative does not do justice to the meticulous attention to details which characterized O'Connell's visitations. He also visited Loyola College, Baltimore, which he urged to seek undergraduate recognition from the AAU; Canisius College, Buffalo, where he raised a question of master's degrees; Saint Peter's College, Jersey City, which had just received accreditation from the Middle States Association; Saint Joseph's College, Philadelphia, which had been continued on the association's list but with a warning to improve the undergraduate program.

55. For an interesting account of these early years, see William Barnaby Faherty, S.J., *Jesuit Roots in Mid-America* (Florissant, 1980), and George E. Ganss, S.J., *The Jesuit Educational Tradition and Saint Louis University: Some Bearings for the University's Sesquicentennial, 1818*–1968 (a publication of the Sesquicentennial Committee of Saint Louis University, 1969).

56. "Notes on the Missouri Province"; O'Connell File, BCA.

57. *Ibid.*

58. *Ibid.*

59. *Ibid.*

60. In his "notes" to Father Maher the commissarius wrote: "Even Father R. Kelley, the Rector, admitted to close Denver would be for the greater good of the Province, but immediately his personal feelings enter in (he contracted the debts) and he fights to keep it open, ECCE, V. Rev. Fr. Assistant, the difficulties of an economic plan for gaining high recognition for Jesuit institutions of higher learning. We are in large numbers still riding in the covered wagon." *Ibid.*

61. *Ibid.*

62. See "Some Notes on the Association of American Universities"; O'Connell File, BCA.

63. For example, he was not entirely pleased with the report submitted by A. Schwitalla, dean, on "Religious Care and Guidance for Students" in the Medical School (see O'Connell File, BCA). In "Directions on Saint Louis University," O'Connell explained article 7 of the *Instruction*, which "makes clear the Catholic note for our institutions" and the *personalis alumnorum cura.* Articles 11–17 contain the stipulation for Catholic professors and deans.

64. In a detailed, five-page memorandum on the Saint Louis University Graduate School, O'Connell evaluated each department which gave the master's degree or Ph.D., or both, on the basis of its periodicals, collections, professors. He then added his directives and indicated the degrees to be given in the future. O'Connell File, BCA.

65. "Directions on Saint Louis University"; O'Connell File, BCA. Unfortunately, Father O'Connell did not live to see the completion of the imposing Pius XII Memorial Library at Saint Louis University.

66. "Comments to Zacheus Maher" (n.d.); O'Connell File, BCA.

67. Joseph Walsh to W. Ledochowski, New Orleans, June 14, 1935. See also an exchange of correspondence between Walsh and O'Connell, February through March 1935. O'Connell File, BCA.

68. See the letter of J. W. Hynes, S.J., to James Macelwane, S.J., Loyola University, New Orleans, November 13, 1936; JEA File, BCA. On October 17, 1936, President Hynes delivered an excellent paper, which was well received, at the regional meeting of the Association of American Colleges: "Developments in the Relation of Catholic Institutions to the Standardizing Associations." This paper is preserved in the JEA File, BCA.

69. Walter Fitzgerald to Daniel O'Connell, Holy Family Mission, May 15, 1935; O'Connell File, BCA.

70. O'Connell to Fitzgerald, Omaha, May 25, 1935; O'Connell File, BCA.

71. Fitzgerald to O'Connell, Portland, June 7, 1935; O'Connell File, BCA.

72. In 1935–1936 there were twenty-six colleges and universities in the continental United States administered by the Society of Jesus. However, Saint John's University, Toledo, founded in 1898, closed its doors in 1936. Father O'Connell and the provincial of the Chicago Province, John J. Clifford, were

in agreement on this action. Saint Mary's College, Kansas, founded as an Indian school in 1848, closed in 1931 due to exigencies of the Depression.

73. The complete record is preserved in the O'Connell File in the Archives at Boston College.

74. *JEQ*, 21 (March 1959): 263.

75. See "Wernersville–Juniorate"; O'Connell File, BCA. The alternative was St. Joseph's College, Philadelphia, but that institution "is in trouble with the Middle States [accrediting agency]; Wernersville would be liable to rigid inspection and Pennsylvania authorities are more bothersome" (*ibid.*). The plan to integrate Woodstock and Georgetown was not successful due to the academic independence of Woodstock.

76. *Ibid.* Father Connell, who had done so much to advance the apostolate of education in Maryland–New York, died on June 15, 1935.

77. An extended explanation of the function and early history of the Jesuit Educational Association (JEA) will be given in chapter 4.

78. JEA File, BCA.

79. Undated memo to Zacheus Maher; O'Connell File, BCA. Father O'Connell did not get his wish.

80. Samuel K. Wilson, S.J., to James B. Macelwane, S.J., Chicago, May 21, 1937; JEA File, BCA.

81. *Ibid.*

82. *Ibid.* In fact, this was the plan that was finally adopted. See below, chapter 5.

83. Edward J. Power, *A History of Catholic Higher Education in the United States* (Milwaukee, 1958), p. 237, n. 55.

84. *Catholic Higher Education in America* (New York, 1972), pp. 372–377.

85. See *Norms*, etc., JEA File, BCA.

86. "Minutes," meeting of Executive Committee, April 2, 1937, Louisville; JEA File, BCA.

87. These figures are available in province catalogs of the American Assistancy.

88. In the interest of privacy, it would not be appropriate to cite names and the academic disciplines to which, it was suggested, they be assigned.


## 4. THE EXECUTIVE COMMITTEE, 1937–1946

1. The Visitor's authority is defined by the General in the terms of his commission. His function, described by his title, is to observe and to submit his observations to Rome. In 1957, Father Bolland met an untimely death in a public transportation accident in Rome.

2. At the 28th General Congregation, held in Rome (March 12–May 9, 1938), Maurice Schurmans, provincial of the Province of Northern Belgium, was elected vicar general to assist the ailing Ledochowski.

3. For these and subsequent references, see the *Instruction*, which is easily available in libraries and archives of Jesuit institutions.

4. "Minutes," Provincials' Meeting, May 1936 (NEPA).

5. Ledochowski to Provincials of the American Assistancy, Rome November 16, 1936 (NEPA). Other points in this letter responded to the provincials' questions concerning the juniorate curriculum, the sequence of courses in philosophy, and the difficulties in assigning scholastics to special studies while insisting, at the same time, on a regency experiment. Important as these questions are, this study will concentrate on the formation and administration of the Jesuit educational organization.

6. "Minutes," May 1936 (NEPA).

7. Ledochowski to Provincials, November 16, 1936 (NEPA).

8. See chapter 3, pp. 50–51.

9. "Minutes," Convention of Jesuit Representatives, April 15, 1936; JEA File, box 6, BCA.

10. *Ibid.*

11. The Graduate Committee was composed of tried and true veterans: James Macelwane, chairman; Samuel Knox Wilson, president, Loyola University; Charles Deane, Fordham University; William Murphy, province prefect of studies, New England; John W. Hynes, province prefect of studies, New Orleans; and Leo F. Robinson, prefect of studies, Oregon.

12. Sensitive to slights, the committee was annoyed at the omission of Jesuit institutions from a publication entitled *Les Universités-Catholiques* by René Algrain (Paris, 1935). This was another example, according to committee members, of a "contemptuous ignoring of our American educational effort, Jesuit and other, that was begun by the *Annuaire Général des Universités Catholiques*." This omission was another incentive for devising additional means for getting public recognition. "Minutes," Executive and Graduate Committee Meeting, April 2, 1937. See *Executive Committee Meetings*, vol. 1, April 1935–October 1944; JEA File, BCA.

13. The same evening, at another location, Julian L. Maline, province prefect of studies for secondary education, Chicago, was presiding over a meeting of high school delegates. The province prefects for higher education, who helped to shape the future course of the Executive Committee, were Allan P. Farrell, Chicago; W. G. Gianera, California; William J. Murphy, New England; Francis J. McGarrigle, Oregon; William J. McGucken, Missouri; Edward B. Rooney, Maryland–New York; and Andrew C. Smith, New Orleans.

14. "Minutes," April 2, 1937 (BCA).

15. *Ibid.*

16. Ledochowski to Edward B. Rooney, Rome, October 19, 1937; Private Papers of EBR, box 2 (Personal Documents), BCA. There was no question of reviving the office of commissarius. The matter was settled in precise Latin: *"quin tamen Commissarius constituatur hoc enim officium nunc esse terminandum statutum est."*

17. See "Biographical Data," Edward B. Rooney, S.J., Private Papers, box 2, file 9, BCA.

18. "Minutes," Executive Committee Meeting, Loyola University, Chicago, December 12–13, 1937 (BCA).

19. A summary of the situation is contained in "Minutes," EC, December 1937 (BCA).

20. For background, see chapter 2, pp. 34–35.

21. Rita Watrin, *The Founding and Development of the Program of Affiliation of the Catholic University of America, 1912 to 1939* (Washington, D.C., 1966), p. 157.

22. *Ibid.*

23. Apart from his quarrel with the Jesuits, Deferrari was not notably successful in selling his program to other Catholic colleges. According to Anselm Keefe, O. Praem., dean of Saint Norbert's College, Wisconsin, it would not help his college, nor, in his opinion, would it help Catholic University, to enter into a program of affiliation with a group of institutions, 52 percent of which had no educational standing. He conceded, however, that "it is undoubtedly a labor of love actuated by the highest spirit of Christian charity for the Catholic University of America to gather under its wings a mixed brood (some of which are educational ugly ducklings)" (Watrin, *ibid.*, p. 172). Moreover, the College and University Department of the NCEA considered the "affiliation program" a duplication of the benefits already granted by that organization.

24. The Catholic University of America, it should be remembered, was a charter member of the Association of Graduate Schools in the Association of American Universities. Membership carried academic distinction since the original group was limited in number. No Jesuit graduate school has ever been admitted to that privileged circle; nor has any other Catholic university been inducted. This in itself is not an indictment, since membership has not been increased for many years. It was in good part because membership was frozen that the AGS initiated a movement for a new organization that would be truly representative of American graduate schools. The Council of Graduate Schools in the United States, as the new organization was called, held its first annual meeting in 1961. Several Jesuit graduate schools are charter members of that association. (See *Council of Graduate Schools in the United States, Proceedings of Annual Meetings, 1961–1962.*) For a good description of the intricacies of classification within the AAU, see Thurber M. Smith, S.J., "Recognition by the Association of American Universities," *JEQ*, 12, no. 1 (June 1937): 40–43.

25. Ledochowski to R. P. Dolan, Rome, June 23, 1938 (NEPA).

26. *Ibid.*

27. *Ibid.* In this letter, Father General suggested that, for public relations purposes, the provincials refer to Father Maher's excursion as a "good will tour."

28. George O'Donnell, S.J., dean of the Boston College Graduate School, reported a conversation he had with Dean William Pierson of the University of North Carolina. Asked if AAU members would accept degrees from nonmember institutions, Dean Pierson replied: "From those on the approved list,

there would be no problem; from those not on the approved list, he could not be sure." Dean Charles Lipman, of the University of California, informed Father Rooney that the competence of the teacher applicant would be the deciding factor ("Minutes," Executive Committee Meeting, Santa Clara, November 2–5, 1938). There were six Jesuit institutions on the AAU's approved list, as distinct from membership.

29. *Ibid.*

30. *Ibid.* Members of the subcommittee were E. Rooney, A. Farrell, J. Keep, W. McGucken, and W. Murphy.

31. "Report of the National Secretary to Reverend Provincials of American Assistancy, May 2, 1939" (see "President's Report to Board of Governors with Responses," vol. 1, 1939–1944; JEA File, BCA). Father Rooney actually made such a proposal to the provincials in May 1939. Voicing an ominous prediction that, if the present situation continued, "our schools" could be placed in a position of isolation, "were all or a large majority of other schools to ask for affiliation." With regard to membership in the AAU, "Saint Louis University and Fordham are thought best prepared to take steps to secure membership." The Executive Committee carefully avoided indicating its preference. The provincials asked for more information and that was the end of it. ("Minutes," Provincials' Meeting, New Orleans, May 1939; NEPA). In the meantime, Father Rooney was invited to join the Advisory Committee of the NCEA. In that organization, he found a sympathetic ally in George Johnson, an influential member of the Catholic University faculty. See "Memorandum of Meeting of the Advisory Committee of the NCEA" (JEA File, BCA).

32. Edward B. Rooney, S.J., to Joseph Corrigan, D.D., New York, April 20, 1940 (Archives of Catholic University of America).

33. *Ibid.*

34. Joseph Corrigan, D.D., to Edward B. Rooney, S.J., April 29, 1940 (Catholic University Archives).

35. *Ibid.*

36. In a letter to the province prefect of studies in California, Rooney wrote that he was attaching a memorandum of the interview of himself and McGucken with Deferrari. The memorandum, however, is not in the file. EBR to Hugh M. Duce, New York, May 17, 1940 (box 2, JEA File, BCA).

37. "Minutes," Executive Committee Meeting, Loyola University, Chicago, September 16–18, 1940.

38. Only a small percentage of men's Catholic colleges and a slightly higher percentage of women's colleges took advantage of Catholic University's proffered protection.

39. "Minutes," JEA Executive Committee, Chicago, December 13, 1937. Hereafter, reference will be to "Minutes," EC (with date). The minutes of Executive Committee meetings form part of the JEA Collection, BCA.

40. Edward B. Rooney, S.J., to William M. Magee, S.J., New York, August 22, 1938; box 1, Doc. 301, BCA. Father Magee was provincial in Chicago; the same letter was sent to each provincial.

41. The members were Rooney, McGucken, Hynes, and Farrell.

42. *Ibid.* Rooney to Magee, August 22, 1938.

43. *Ibid.*

44. "Minutes," EC, November 1938, pp. 9-10.

45. *Ibid.*

46. *Ibid.* The same provincial preferred the title "Executive Secretary" to "Executive Director." The latter title prevailed.

47. *Ibid.*

48. Ledochowski to American Provincials, Rome, July 31, 1939 (*JEQ*, 3, no. 2 [September 1940]: 69).

49. *Ibid.*

50. Zacheus J. Maher to James H. Dolan, Camarillo, California, June 21, 1940 (NEPA).

51. *Ibid.*

52. 3, no. 2 (September 1940): 71-78.

53. Article VI, paragraph 1.

54. *Ibid.*, paragraph 3.

55. "Minutes," EC, April 19, 1938.

56. *Ibid.*, November 1938. Originally, a nine-member board of associate editors was selected. This format changed with the years, and members of the Executive Committee automatically formed the Advisory Board.

57. *JEQ* contains 32 volumes: vol. 1, no. 1 (June 1938) to vol. 32, no. 4 (March 1970).

58. "Report of the National Secretary to the Jesuit Educational Association," Kansas City, Missouri, March 26, 1940 (*JEQ*, 3, no. 1 [June 1940]: 7). In September 1980, the librarian of a distinguished non-Jesuit university contacted the author to investigate the possibility of acquiring a complete set of the *JEQ*.

59. "Minutes," EC, November 1938.

60. Outline of report presented by the national secretary to provincials of American Assistancy, New Orleans, May 2, 1939 (BCA).

61. "Minutes," EC, October 23-25, 1939.

62. *Ibid.*

63. *Ibid.*

64. The revised edition of the *Instruction* was published in *JEQ*, 11, no. 2 (October 1948): 69-95. The original text, as noted above, was printed in *Acta Romana*, 7 (1932-1934): 927-935.

65. Another house organ was the *J.E.A. Special Bulletin*, inaugurated on February 1, 1939. An important vehicle by which the central office communicated with the membership concerning current events affecting Jesuit institutions, it included other items of interest to provincials, presidents, and deans. It was the main source of information during the war years, 1942-1945. The JEA *Directory*, which became official for the academic year 1946-47, was the third publication. As early as 1944, Edward B. Rooney (EBR) had asked province prefects to prepare lists of rectors, deans, assistant deans, and principals for inclusion in a directory. Gradually, the *Directory* expanded to in-

clude enrollment statistics, commissions, conferences, and other items of interest.

66. "Report" of Executive Director to Board of Governors, St. Louis, May 4, 1943, p. 5. Hereafter this reference will read: "Report," EBR to BG, (date).

67. For example, the provincials predicted that article 31, which stipulated that scholastics be sent for a master's degree after philosophy, "will be the cause of serious difficulties to the Provincials." They argued that (1) it would be impossible to send all scholastics to special studies; (2) all scholastics were not apt for special studies; (3) an article should not be incorporated that cannot be observed. See "Report," EBR to BG, May 1945.

68. See *Acta Romana*, 10 (1941–1945): 472.

69. *Ibid.*, pp. 628–631.

70. *Ibid.*, 9 (1938–1940): 16.

71. "Report," EBR to BG, May 1945.

72. *Ibid.*

73. See *ibid.*, New Orleans, May 1946.

74. Norbert de Boynes to EBR, Rome, February 27, 1946 (printed in *JEQ*, 9, no. 2 [October 1946]: 5).

75. "Response," BG, May 1946.

76. See "Minutes," Executive Committee Meetings, 1937, 1938, 1939, *passim*.

77. Each Jesuit college and university has preserved (in its archives) the record of its wartime involvement: the flight of students by way of enlistment in the armed forces; the army, navy, and marine programs sponsored by the government; the adaptation of curricula and "retooling" of faculty. With a serious effort at cooperation, Jesuit institutions made a substantial contribution to ultimate victory. The JEA *Special Bulletins* (1941–1946) are the best source of information on the involvement of the JEA in the war effort. See JEA Collection, BCA.

78. "Minutes," EC, Loyola College, Baltimore, January 1942.

79. *Ibid.*, Santa Clara, October 1942.

80. *Ibid.*

81. *Ibid.*

82. Those decisions, however, will be documented in the history of each institution. Such details go beyond the limits of this account.

83. "Report" of Executive Director to Provincials, 1943, p. 11.

84. From 1937 to 1941, the four Catholics on the council were Rooney; George Johnson, Catholic University; Alphonse Schwitalla; and Ross Hoffman, professor of history, Fordham University. *Ibid.*, p. 10.

85. See "Reports" of EBR to Provincials, May 1942 and May 1943. EBR was appointed to the National Japanese American Student Relocation Council, which became a semiofficial committee, the War Relocation Authority. The council was organized to assist American citizens of Japanese origin, upon release from relocation centers, in the continuation of their studies. "Minutes," EC, April 27–29, 1943, p. 4.

86. "Minutes," Executive Committee Meeting, December 1943, p. 6.

87. *Ibid.*

88. The members of that committee were A. Farrell, chairman; M. J. Fitzsimons, New York; John J. McEleney, Fairfield College Preparatory School (and later archbishop of Kingston, Jamaica); Miles O'Mailia, Saint Joseph's College, Philadelphia; and Albert F. Poetker, University of Detroit. *Ibid.*

89. *Ibid.*

90. "Obituary: William J. McGucken, S.J., 1889-1943," *Woodstock Letters*, 73, no. 1 (March 1944): 63-67. See also *J.E.A. Special Bulletin*, no. 29 (November 15, 1943), for a tribute by members of the Executive Committee.

91. *Ibid.*

92. "Response," Board of Governors, Santa Clara, May 1944, pp. 1-2.

93. There was an additional bonus. The excellent performance of "Jesuit students," in competition with students from other arts and sciences colleges in wartime programs of various kinds, helped to overcome the "inferiority complex" that had characterized some Jesuit institutions. At the same time, it was revealed that the science requirement was a weak link in the Jesuit curriculum. After the war, the science requirements were emphasized, and mathematics became the key to success in those programs.

5. POSTWAR EXPANSION, 1946-1950 (Commissions and Institutes)

1. The congregation met at the Jesuit headquarters in Borgo Santo Spirito, Rome, from September 6 to October 23, 1946.

2. See *Acta Romana*, 14 (1961-1966): 493-503; also "John Baptist Janssens, S.J.," *JEQ*, 14, no. 2 (October 1946).

3. *Acta Romana*, 14 (1961-1966): 308-309.

4. Rome, June 5, 1947; *ibid.*, 11: 283-287.

5. Rome, June 27, 1947; *ibid.*, pp. 299-336.

6. Two additional ministries are described and urged as works proper to the Society: the foreign missions and that spiritual apostolate toward those whom the General referred to as *"neo-pagani."*

7. See *Catholic Mind*, "The Catholic Priesthood," 34 (1936): 41-79.

8. *Acta Romana*, 11: 316.

9. *Ibid.*, pp. 54-59.

10. *Ibid.*, p. 319.

11. *Ibid.*

12. *Ibid.*, p. 320.

13. *Ibid.*, p. 321.

14. *Ibid.*

15. John B. Janssens to EBR, Rome (113), March 29, 1947 (*JEQ*, 10, no. 1 [June 1947]: p. 4). In this letter, Father Janssens refers to a letter of Norbert de Boynes, who while vicar general encouraged American Jesuits to follow the

*Ratio*, revive classical studies, and update the philosophical courses. *Ibid.*, 9, no. 1 (June 1946): 5-6.

16. "Report of Executive Director," *ibid.*, 11, no. 1 (June 1948): 5-14. For an interpretation of the "Letter on Ministries" by a university president in an effort to motivate his Jesuit faculty, see Paul C. Reinert, S.J., "The Intellectual Apostolate," *JEQ*, 13, no. 2 (October 1950): 71-78.

17. *Acta Romana*, 11: 569-571. For the *Instruction*, see *ibid.*, pp. 571-579. Hereafter, *Acta Romana* will be referred to as *AR*.

18. *Ibid.*, p. 569; emphasis added.

19. *Ibid.*

20. *Ibid.*

21. *Instructio and Constitution of the Jesuit Educational Association* (privately printed by the JEA, New York, September 1948). The General's letter and the two documents were also published in *JEQ* (11, no. 2 [October 1948]: 69-94).

22. John Baptist Janssens to EBR, Rome, March 25, 1949; *JEQ*, 12, no. 1 (June 1949): 4.

23. *Ibid.*

24. For a good description of the magnitude of the problems, and proposed solutions, see "Higher Education for American Democracy," *Report of the President's Commission on Higher Education*, vols. I-VI (New York, 1946). Despite its value, one section of the *Report* was sharply criticized by the NCEA and the JEA. The commissioners, in a majority vote, recommended federal aid for public colleges and universities but voted against such aid for independent institutions. Two Catholics on the commission, Monsignor Frederick Hochwalt of NCEA and Dr. Martin R. P. McGuire of Catholic University, strongly objected to this discrimination. On the other hand, the commission recommended federal scholarships for capable and needy students at all institutions. See "Report" of EBR to BG, May 1948. See also Albert I. Lemieux, S.J., "Report of the President's Commission on Higher Education," *JEQ*, 11, no. 1 (June 1948): 25-34.

25. "Enrollments," *JEQ*, vol. 7, no. 3 (January 1945); *ibid.*, vol. 11, no. 3 (January 1949). In these four years, two new Jesuit colleges had been founded: Fairfield University and LeMoyne College.

26. Those who are interested in an account of the war and postwar years at individual colleges and universities may wish to consult several monographs that were written after 1946. One of the more complicated questions, which demanded a policy decision, concerned the granting of degrees to former students who, while members of the armed forces, had completed course work at other institutions. The Association of American Colleges had discussed this problem at length. In brief, Jesuit colleges, in an effort to be helpful, accepted credits from accredited colleges. However, most Jesuit institutions required the students to complete a certain number of courses in philosophy and theology as a prerequisite for graduation. See letter of EBR to Deans of Colleges and Universities, July 28, 1944; JEA box 31, file 104-10, BCA.

27. For a description of all these items, see JEA *Special Bulletins*, nos. 61 through 74, 1946 and 1947 (BCA).

28. "Minutes," EC, Boston College, October 1944. The members of the subcommittee were Hugh Duce, Matthew Fitzsimons, Edward Bunn, Julian Maline, and Wilfred Mallon, chairman.

29. "Minutes," EC, New Orleans, April 1945.

30. "Report," EBR to BG, Inisfada, New York, May 1945.

31. The following names were suggested: John C. Murray, theology professor, Woodstock; Robert Henle, dean, Faculty of Philosophy, Saint Louis; William G. Griffith, dean, School of Business, Fordham.

32. "Report," EBR to BG, Loyola University, New Orleans, May 4, 1946.

33. In writing a historical account, the author must be selective. Many topics were on the agendas of Executive Committee meetings in the postwar years, such as college and university statutes, lay boards of advisors, recruitment of lay faculty, retirement plans, athletics, accreditation, and curricular recommendations. However, in the author's opinion, the work of the commissions and the organization of the institutes and workshops most directly affected the academic development of Jesuit institutions in these years.

34. The five commissions were: Secondary Schools, Liberal Arts Colleges, Professional Schools, Seminaries, Graduate Schools.

35. *Constitution*, art. VII, 4.

36. "Minutes," EC, Loyola College, Baltimore, September 1945. The other members of the commission were M. G. Pierce, Boston College; J. F. Quinn, University of Detroit; L. A. Walsh, Fordham; M. G. Barnett, Marquette.

37. Father Maxwell, who had completed his term as president of Holy Cross College, was appointed rector of Cranwell Preparatory School. Father Percy had been active and influential in the Association of American Colleges during his presidency of Loyola University, New Orleans, and was scheduled to serve as president of the Association of American Colleges in 1946. However, his retirement from Loyola forced the association to nominate another candidate. See "Report," EBR to BG, New Orleans, May 1946.

38. "Minutes," EC, September 1945. This study became all the more necessary when, in its preliminary findings, the commission reported the striking variations in required units, texts, and systems. Although the Executive Committee discussed the preparation of Jesuit textbooks, "the controversy now current among teachers of philosophy on the subject of the Thomistic synthesis" made it difficult to agree on common texts. "Minutes," EC, April 1947.

39. "Response," BG, May 1946.

40. In 1946–47 the members of this commission were G. Dumas, Fordham; C. E. Schrader, University of Detroit; W. J. Schlaerth, Fordham; J. H. Guthrie, Georgetown; and E. J. Drummond, Saint Louis, chairman.

41. See "Report of the Special Committee Accrediting Graduate Study," AAU *Journal of Proceedings and Addresses*, 46th Annual Conference, October 11–13, 1945.

42. In 1946 there were 34 member institutions of the AAU, and Catholic University was the only Catholic member. Of the 266 colleges and universities

on the approved list, 24 were Catholic institutions. Of these, 15 were women's colleges and 9 were men's, and of that number 7 were Jesuit. See "Report," EBR to BG, May 1946.

43. *Ibid.*, New Orleans, May 1946.

44. *Ibid.* The Jesuit institutions on the approved list were Boston College, Creighton, Fordham, Georgetown, Holy Cross, Marquette, and Saint Louis.

45. "Response," BG, May 1946.

46. Julian A. Maline to Edward B. Rooney, Chicago, April 16, 1946; JEA File, box 2, BCA.

47. Floyd Wesley Reeves (*et al.*), *The Liberal Arts College* (Chicago, 1932), p. 254. This book is based on surveys of thirty-five colleges related to the Methodist Episcopal Church. See also George Zook and M. E. Haggerty, *Principals of Accrediting Higher Institutions* (Chicago, 1936). This work comprises a series of monographs on the subject.

48. With a public notice (October 1948), the AAU terminated its activities "in the field of accrediting undergraduate institutions." On this occasion, the final list of approved institutions was published as an appendix of *Proceedings and Addresses of the 49th Annual Conference*, Philadelphia, October 28–30, 1948. Jesuit institutions remained as before.

49. "Problems Associated with Increased Graduate Enrollment," AAU *Journal of Addresses and Proceedings*, October 23–25, 1947.

50. "Minutes," EC, April 1946.

51. The function of a Jesuit regent was to provide liaison between the president of the institution and the lay dean of the professional school.

52. "Report," EBR to BG, May 1948.

53. *Ibid.*

54. *Ibid.*

55. *Ibid.*

56. The same was true of the other professional schools. For a good example of a detailed report in a professional area, see "Report on Nursing Education," EBR to BG, May 1949, appendix D.

57. "Report," EBR to BG, Chicago, 1948.

58. It was decided that the Commission on Seminaries would consist of the deans of the philosophates, with the office of chairman rotating annually. This commission had its own importance since the philosophates were academically affiliated with particular colleges in order that scholastics might receive collegiate credit toward the bachelor's or master's degrees. "Minutes," EC, April 1947; also "Report," EBR to BG, May 1946.

59. For the origins of the Institute, see "Minutes," EC, April 1946.

60. *Proceedings of the Denver Principals' Institute*, Regis College (privately printed by the JEA) (JEA Collection, BCA).

61. For a good summary, see Joseph R. N. Maxwell, S.J., "The Denver Principals' Institute," *JEQ*, 9, no. 2 (October 1946): 69–76. See also "Denver Institute Proceedings: Course of Studies," *ibid.*, no. 3 (January 1947): 145–156.

62. "Minutes," EC, April 1947.

63. *Ibid.*

64. *Ibid.*, October 1947.

65. *Ibid.*

66. This paper is reprinted in *JEQ*, 9, no. 2 (October 1948): 113-122.

67. In the absence of Professor Wrenn, his paper was read by William F. Kelley, S.J., then a graduate student at the University of Minnesota, and some years later president of Marquette University.

68. These facts and figures, correlated and organized, comprise a bound volume: *Academic Policies and Practices in American Jesuit Colleges of Arts and Sciences and Schools of Business Administration* (private circulation, St. Louis, Missouri, 1948) (BCA). This item does not provide a study nor does it constitute a manual or interpret the data; it merely records the facts as reported on the completed questionnaire.

69. *Ibid.*, see appendixes IV and V, pp. 122-134.

70. "Minutes," EC, April 1947, p. 3; "Response," BG, May 1947, p. 5.

71. See JEA *Directory*, 1948-1949 (BCA).

72. With the exception of philosophy, lay professors taught 65 percent of the classes in arts as against 35 percent for Jesuits. If the natural sciences were also counted, the Jesuit average would be much lower. See *Academic Policies and Practices, etc.*, pp. 63-68.

73. As a matter of fact, to see things in proper perspective, Matthew J. Fitzsimons, S.J., delivered the first paper, "Objectives of a Jesuit College." All of the papers and edited versions of discussions are contained in a large volume: *Proceedings of the Institute for Jesuit Deans*, edited by Wilfred M. Mallon, S.J. (private circulation, Regis College, Denver, August 3-13, 1948). (BCA).

74. *Ibid.*, Foreword, p. 1.

75. *Ibid.* For a more comprehensive account of this topic, see Paul A. Fitz-Gerald, S.J., "The Historical Development of the Office of the Jesuit College Dean," *JEQ*, 24, no. 4 (March 1962): 212-222; also Charles F. Donovan, S.J., "The Dean's Responsibility for Academic Excellence," *ibid.*, pp. 223-230.

76. Edward B. Bunn, S.J., W. Edmund FitzGerald, S.J., and Matthew J. Fitzsimons, S.J., "Jesuit Deans' Institute-Denver, 1948," *JEQ*, 11, no. 2 (October 1948): 95-112, 110.

77. *Ibid.*

78. *Ibid.*, p. 111.

79. These resolutions are attached as appendix III (pp. 303-309) to *Proceedings of the Institute for Jesuit Deans*.

80. "Response" of BG to "Report" of EBR, May 3, 1949. To continue the momentum initiated by the institute, the Executive Committee suggested the inauguration of a Training Center for Jesuit Administrators. Saint Louis University seemed a logical place, in view of Father Paul C. Reinert's academic training and practical experience. See "Report" of EBR to BG, May 1949.

81. "Response," BG, May 1949. A Jesuit Guidance Institute was held in the summer of 1949 at Fordham University. A National Jesuit Institute on College Religion took place at Holy Cross College, August 2-14, 1951. The second Institute for College Deans was held at Santa Clara, August 3-13, 1955.

82. "Response," BG, May 1949.

83. "Both departments" referred to the secondary and postsecondary divisions of the JEA.

84. Depending upon the location, which was determined by the NCEA, the annual meeting was frequently hosted by a Jesuit college or university.

85. The author was a delegate to the annual meeting from 1954 to 1966.

86. The principal papers delivered at the annual meeting were published in subsequent issues of *JEQ*.

87. See chapter 6 for an extended account of the policies and procedures developed by the Office for the orderly expansion of Jesuit institutions. Athletics would be a good example of an activity that was outside the purview of the committee. When the Executive Committee expressed concern at basketball schedules that interfered with class lectures and examinations, it was reported "that some school authorities consider the matter of athletics beyond the scope of the supervision of the Province Prefects." "Minutes," EC, April 1949, p. 18.

88. *Ibid.*, October 1947.

89. *Ibid.*, March 1948.

90. *Ibid.*, April 1949.

91. The Executive Committee made a positive contribution to the recruitment of lay faculty. A code was submitted, approved, and accepted by the colleges which governed negotiations wherein one Jesuit college negotiated with a lay faculty member in another Jesuit college. See "Minutes," EC, April 1946, which contains the code, and *ibid.*, October 1948. See also "Recruiting of Lay Faculty," *JEQ*, 9, no. 3 (January 1947): 144.

92. The JEA worked most closely with the NCEA, the National Council of Independent Schools, the American Council on Education, the Association of American Colleges, and of course the regional accrediting associations.

93. Members of the Executive Committee were also active: Julian Maline was vice president and member of the executive committee of the North Central Association; Andrew Smith was vice president of the Southern Association; Hugh Duce was a member of the Executive Committee of the Western Association; Samuel Knox Wilson was chairman of the Commission on Colleges of the North Central Association.


6. ACCENT ON QUALITY, 1950-1955

1. Memorandum of Conference with Very Reverend Father John Janssens, Rome, September 16, 1947. See *Personal and Confidential Memoranda of Conferences of JEA President with Fr. General and/or Fr. Vicar;* JEA Collection, book I, BCA.

2. *Ibid.*, p. 2.

3. *Ibid.*

4. Originally appointed Visitor to the Maryland-New York Province (December 1919-February 1921), Father de Boynes was subsequently appointed Visitor to all American provinces. See *Memoriale Visitationis Provin-*

*ciae Marylandiae – Neo Eboracensis Relictum a R. P. Norberto de Boynes Visitatore,* August 31, 1921–September 13, 1921 (IV, 1.3, pp. 12–13); Provincial Archives, Maryland Province.

5. *Ibid.*

6. The Latin makes it clear that the Visitor was creating a new office: *"Creetur Praefectus Generalis studiorum liber ad omni alio officio, cujus munus determinabitur a Patre Provinciali cum ejus consultoribus et aliquibus viris in educatione peritis."* See *Directiones Relictae Reverendo Patri Provinciali Provinciae Marylandiae-Neo Eboracensis a Reverendo Patre Norberto de Boynes, ejusdem Provinciae Visitatore,* January 25, 1922 (IV 4' pp. 9–10); Provincial Archives, Maryland Province.

7. Memorandum on the Office of Province Prefects of Studies in the United States, August 10, 1954; book II, E and F, BCA.

8. *Ibid.*

9. From 1922 to 1954, according to a study done by Rooney, 56 fathers held the position of province prefect; 15 were full time throughout their tenure; 7 were full time during part of their tenure; 34 were part time throughout their tenure. For this reason, Rooney wrote in his memorandum to the General: "My own experience, over the past seventeen years, makes it abundantly clear to me that part-time province prefects of studies just do not work out. Their interests are split; and so is their time. . . . Not the least of all, the part-time province prefect suffers in prestige." *Ibid.*

10. "Response" of BG, May 3, 1949, p. 7.

11. *Ibid.* The provincials did not wish to confuse the technical roles of socius and province prefect; the socius is *ex officio* a provincial consultor. It had once been proposed to Father Ledochowski that general prefects be named provincial consultors. He answered: "This proposal I cannot entertain, as I do not wish to attach the office of Consultor to any particular class of persons, with the exception of the Socius." *Acta Romana,* 7: 926.

12. "Response," BG, May 3, 1949.

13. The other members of the committee were Hugh Duce, California; Wilfred Mallon, Missouri; and John Nash, New York ("Minutes," EC, October 1949).

14. *Ibid.,* April 1950.

15. *Ibid.,* appendix I, p. 1.

16. *Ibid.*

17. "Response," BG, April 1951.

18. The following Eastern provincials were members of the subcommittees: David Nugent, Maryland; John J. McMahon, New York; William E. FitzGerald, New England.

19. The statement was attached to the "Response," BG, April 1953.

20. New York, May 15, 1954. The letter and statement are in *JEQ,* 17, no. 1 (June 1954): 5–14.

21. Article I, "Educational Assistant to the Provincial." *Ibid.,* p. 8.

22. Confidential Memorandum, September 11, 1954, p. 7; book I, BCA.

23. Memorandum on Statement on "The Duties and Functions of the Province Prefect of Studies," Memorandum and Reports on Special Subjects by the JEA President, December 31, 1947 to September 30, 1964, book II, E, BCA.

24. *Ibid.*

25. *Ibid.*

26. Article III, Director of Special Studies, "Duties and Functions, etc." *JEQ*, 17, no. 1: 12-13.

27. Article III, 4; *ibid.*, p. 13.

28. Confidential Memorandum, September 16, 1947; book I, p. 3, BCA.

29. It was at this conference that Rooney asked the General to rule on the authority of the presciptions made by Daniel O'Connell. The General answered that, *per se*, "such prescriptions still held." However, given the long period of time that had elapsed, "Provincials would certainly have the power to change prescriptions made by Father O'Connell." *Ibid.*

30. *Acta Romana*, 12: 403-412, p. 410. On that occasion, making the interpretation official, he added: *"Hoc est primum quod de ministeriis nostris temporum necessitabus aptandis intendebam. Catholici simus, magisque Catholici in dies efficiamur."*

31. The author's experience was probably typical. From start to finish, the Jesuit graduate student dealt exclusively with the director of special studies, who, needless to say, made his own report to the provincial.

32. "Response," BG, May 1952, p. 3.

33. *Ibid.* The "Annual Report on Special Studies" appeared regularly, beginning in 1942, in the March issue of *JEQ*.

34. Mehok was succeeded in 1955 by Richard D. Costello of the New England Province.

35. "Minutes," EC, April 1953.

36. "Status of Special Studies, 1952-1953," *JEQ*, 15, no. 4 (March 1953): 241-246, p. 241.

37. According to figures published in Rome, the increment in the total number of priests in the American provinces dropped steadily from 144, reported in 1947, to 60 in 1951. Figures for those years also showed a decrease in the number of scholastics; 1946 was the leanest year of all, with a minus 92. See *Prospectus Societatis Jesu Universae*. This item is distributed throughout the Assistancy with the province catalogs.

38. In that year there was a total of 181 Jesuits in graduate studies, an increment of 8 over the previous year. In 1942, the first year that a report was filed, there were 80 Jesuits in full-time graduate study. In 1966, the last year that Rooney reported, there were 412.

39. The 173 graduate students in 1952-53 were distributed among 47 universities. Of this number, 27 were in secular universities. A large group, 30, was in attendance at Saint Louis University.

40. "Minutes," EC, April 1952, p. 7.

41. *Ibid.*, August 1952, p. 13.

42. "Response," BG, May 1952.

43. "Minutes," EC, October 1953, p. 6.

44. "Scholarly Publications: American Assistancy, 1953–54," *JEQ*, 17, no. 4 (March 1955): 239–247.

45. "Response," BG, May 1953, p. 10.

46. "Minutes," EC, October 1953, p. 6.

47. *Ibid.*

48. The CCICA, organized in 1946, was established to encourage and recognize Catholic scholarship. From the beginning, it was supported by the JEA, both financially and intellectually, and in the early years several Jesuits were installed as officers of the commission. "Minutes," EC, April 1947 and January 1952.

49. An extended report of the subcommittee is attached as appendix A to the minutes (EC, October 1953).

50. Moreover, Jesuits who earned their doctorate at Catholic universities were as productive, if not more productive, as Jesuits who trained at public or secular institutions.

51. As a point of interest, the original GI Bill of Rights expired July 25, 1956. The $14.5 billion program enabled 7,800,000 veterans to receive an education.

52. "Report," EBR to BG, May 1949. For example, when Boston College decided to reinstate Ph.D. programs in 1952, Rooney reviewed the reasons and the General approved the decision.

53. For an excellent resumé of the discussion, within the JEA, of the Latin requirement for the A.B. degree, see the unpublished paper of Charles F. Donovan, S.J., "Boston College's Classical Curriculum" (BCA).

54. Confidential Memorandum, September 11, 1954, book I, pp. 3–5 (BCA).

55. *Ibid.* The obvious reference is to three newly founded schools: Le Moyne College in 1946 and Wheeling College and McQuaid Jesuit High School in 1955.

56. *Ibid.*

57. *Ibid.*

58. *Ibid.*

59. *Ibid.*

60. *Ibid.*

61. Memorandum for JBJ from EBR re Expansion of Jesuit Education in the U.S., New York, February 5, 1955; book II, G, BCA.

62. *Ibid.*

63. *Ibid.*

64. *Ibid.* See "Policies and Procedures Regarding Expansion of Jesuit Institutions" appendix A.

65. "Policies and Procedures on Expansion," no. 10.

66. Confidential Memorandum, October 12, 1955; book I, p. 1. The advantages and disadvantages of expansion were, of course, debated by other colleges and associations. For an example of the dilemma facing small colleges, see "President's Report" (James Stacy Coles), *Bowdoin College Bulletin* (1953-54), p. 24; also an address by Robert I. Gannon, S.J., speaking to the proposition; "Establishment of a New University in New York," Long Island University, February 18, 1954; also "Minutes," "The Ohio Committee on Expanding Student Population," June 4, 1954. Frederick E. Welfle, S.J., president of John Carroll University, was the secretary of that committee. All of these items are found in the JEA Collection, box 34, file 109, BCA.

67. "Report," EBR, May 1956. It was at this meeting (May 1956) that the Board of Governors approved the change of title for the executive director. Henceforth, in line with other associations, Rooney's title would be "President" of the Jesuit Educational Association.

68. Personal Memorandum (conference of EBR with JBJ), Frascati, August 26, 1958; book I, BCA.

69. *Ibid.*

70. See *Proceedings*, Conference of Presidents of Jesuit Colleges and Universities, Georgetown University, Washington, D.C., January 3-4, 1958; JEA Collection, BCA.

71. *Ibid.* p. 42.

72. *Ibid.*

73. January 15, 1958. This was typical of a number of journals. The daily press, with some exceptions, was more sympathetic. The *New York Times* (February 9, 1958) gave the facts and figures on expansion. Referring to Jesuit colleges, the *Times* wrote: "Plans at 28 institutions in U.S. pass $127,000,000 as Enrollments Rise." Programs in excess of $5,000,000 included those at Boston College, Creighton University, Georgetown, John Carroll, Loyola–Chicago, Loyola–New Orleans, and Seattle, the *Times* said. In the 28 colleges there was a total enrollment of 110,934 students. At this news conference, the presidents also announced the establishment of a National Jesuit Commission on Research, which will be explained in detail in a later chapter.

74. "Response" of BG, May 1958.

75. This memorandum is dated December 26, 1956.

76. Personal Memorandum of Conference of EBR with JBJ, August 16, 1957, book I, BCA.

77. *Ibid.*

78. *Ibid.* Someone, in a letter to the General, had evidently tried to place the blame on the accrediting agencies for forcing the Jesuit institutions into a curriculum straitjacket. Rooney defended the agencies and said that they "will go along with us if we can defend the program." *Ibid.*

79. *Ibid.*

80. "Policies and Procedures," no. 3.

81. In a case involving Youth Progress program grants, Laurence M. O'Neil, president of Jesuit High School in New Orleans, in a letter to Most

Reverend Joseph F. Rummel, archbishop of New Orleans (November 7, 1949), made a courteous, clear, and scholarly defense of Jesuit exemptions. JEA Collection, box 34, BCA.

82. Leo J. Robinson, S.J., to Edward B. Rooney, S.J., Portland, May 13, 1947.

83. *Ibid.*

84. The Law of Exemption is stated in canon 615: *"Regulares, noviciis non exclusis, sive vires sive mulieres, cum eorum domibus et ecclesiis, ab Ordinario Loci jurisdictione exempti sunt, praeter quam in casibus jure exceptis."* Canons 1336, 1338, 1382 give the Ordinary jurisdiction over all in his territory in prescriptions that pertain to religion and morality. The problem arose in reconciling these two areas of activity.

85. The members of the Committee of Five were: John J. Crowley, W. Edmund FitzGerald (who resigned in 1950 when appointed provincial in New England), Thomas E. Henneberry (rector, Bellarmine College, New York), James J. Maguire (president, Loyola University, Chicago), and Arthur J. Sheehan. This committee submitted its report on April 25, 1952. See JEA box 32, file 135-01, BCA.

86. There were a few cases at the university level. Paul L. O'Connor, president of Xavier University, in what he considered a conciliatory gesture, supplied information on the Theology Department to the archbishop of Cincinnati at his request. Informed of this, the General immediately reminded the provincial in Chicago of the exemption from canon 1382. His language was very clear: "This privilege is not to be renounced, even implicitly. Even though the privilege may seem doubtful in certain instances, it must be protected." *Proceedings*, Conference of Presidents, Rockhurst College (January 4–6, 1959), appendix H, p. 38.

87. The Executive Committee cited as outstanding examples of cooperation and financial generosity the archbishops of New York, Baltimore, Cincinnati, Boston, Los Angeles, and Brooklyn.

88. "Report" of the Committee of Five, p. 13.

89. For a copy of the draft, see JEA box 32, file 135.08, BCA.

90. The authors acknowledged, in their covering letter, that "it would be better to incorporate most of the report in our Memorandum."

91. As the colleges and universities expanded, with the recruitment of lay faculty in philosophy and theology and the addition of controversial courses in those departments, there was heightened concern on the part of the bishops. This situation initiated a more serious confrontation, as is clear from Roman documents issued in more recent times.

92. A National Institute on College Religion was held at Holy Cross College in August 1951; the second Institute for Jesuit College Deans was held at Santa Clara in August 1955. The *Proceedings* of these institutes are available in the JEA Collection, BCA.

93. *JEA Special Bulletin*, no. 163, May 6, 1953; also no. 162, February 25, 1953 (BCA).

94. *Ibid.*, no. 163, May 1953.

95. *Ibid.*, nos. 162–165, *passim.*


7. THE EMERGING ROLE OF JESUIT PRESIDENTS,
   1940–1960

1. *Report of the Commission on Higher Studies*, p. 175.

2. *Ibid.*, p. 177.

3. "*Cura universalis, vel superintendentia et gubernatio Universitatis penes Rectorem erit; qui idem esse poterit qui in Collegio praecipuo Societatis praeest . . .* ," part IV, chapter 17, 1.

4. This document is simply entitled: *Normae Quae Determinant Relationes Rectorem Inter et Praesidem Universitatis Fordhamensis* (box 34, BCA).

5. It is vitally important to note the difference between rector of the *university* and rector of the *Jesuit community*, which was a later development.

6. See JEA Collection, box 34, BCA.

7. Joseph P. Sweeney, S.J., to Edward B. Rooney, S.J., New York, March 29, 1943; JEA File, box 34, file 131.10, BCA.

8. *Ibid.*

9. Gannon on *Normae*, exhibit C, March 31, 1943; JEA Collection, box 34, file 131.10, BCA.

10. *Ibid.*

11. *Ibid.*

12. *Ibid.*

13. J. H. Fisher, "Notes on the Normae," exhibit A, 1943; JEA Collection, box 34, file 131.10, BCA.

14. *Ibid.*

15. *Ibid.*

16. Joseph A. Murphy, S.J., "Criticism of the *Normae* of the Rector-President Arrangement at Fordham University," exhibit B, March 31, 1943; box 34, file 131.10, BCA.

17. *Ibid.* By a strange turn, Father Murphy was appointed rector of Fordham in 1947.

18. *Ibid.*

19. N. de Boynes, S.J., to Zacheus J. Maher, S.J., Rome, January 17, 1945; box 34, file 158.03, BCA. The *Revised Norms* went into effect July 1, 1944. If anything, these *Norms* clarified and emphasized the office of rector of the university. The *Norms* repeated that the president, juridically, "is an official of the Rector and in the exercise of his office is, in fact, an assistant of the Rector." Obviously, Father Gannon had not won his case.

20. Vincent A. McCormick, S.J., to Zacheus Maher, S.J., Rome, January 17, 1945; JEA File, box 34, file 158.03, BCA.

21. *Ibid.*

22. *Ibid.*

23. Zacheus J. Maher, S.J., to Vincent A. McCormick, S.J., Pough-keepsie, N.Y., February 4, 1945; JEA File, box 34, BCA.

24. Edward B. Rooney, S.J., to Vincent A. McCormick, S.J., New York, March 27, 1945; JEA File, box 34, BCA. There is also an important letter in the file from F. X. McMenamy, tertian instructor at Saint Stanislaus, Cleveland, to Father Rooney (March 4, 1945). McMenamy, an acknowledged authority on the Constitutions, was in favor of the dual arrangement and saw no constitutional problems.

25. EBR to Vincent McCormick, New York, March 27, 1945; box 34, file 158.03, BCA.

26. At their 1946 meeting in New Orleans, the provincials devoted an entire afternoon to a discussion of the plan then in operation at the three universities. At the request of the vicar general, the chairman, Henry L. Crane, appointed a committee to draw up a *postulatum* (petition) for the next General Congregation, "asking that this form of local government be given the Society's approval." This committee consisted of Fathers Provincial Joseph J. King (California), Leo D. Sullivan (Chicago), and Francis A. McQuade (New York). These provincials were also requested to report on the dual-control experiments in their respective provinces. "Minutes," Provincials' Meeting, 1946 (NEPA).

27. "Report," EBR to BG, May 1946.

28. "Response," BG to EBR, May 1946.

29. See JEA Collection, box 34, file 158.07, BCA. The members of the subcommittee were Arthur J. Sheehan (N.E.), Andrew C. Smith (N.O.), Matthew J. Fitzsimons (N.Y.), chairman.

30. *Report on Dual Administrative Control*, p. 12. At the University of Detroit there was an unusual arrangement. A. H. Poetker had the title "Executive Dean" but, to all intents and purposes, acted as president in all academic matters. This was done with the approval of C. H. Cloud, rector-president, who in a statement to the Academic Council clarified the responsibilities of Poetker. Poetker to EBR, Detroit, March 30, 1945; box 34, file 158.03, BCA.

31. *Report on Dual Administrative Control*, pp. 12–13.

32. Vincent A. McCormick, S.J., to EBR, Rome, May 20, 1945; box 34, file 158.03, BCA.

33. "Report" of subcommittee, p. 15.

34. "Memorandum" of Conference, EBR and JBJ, Rome, September 16, 1947; book II, BCA.

35. The five members were Edward B. Rooney, chairman, and Edward B. Bunn, Julian L. Maline, Wilfred M. Mallon, and Arthur J. Sheehan.

36. EBR to W. M. Mallon, S.J., New York, November 24, 1948; box 34, file 158.03, BCA.

37. The document is entitled "Minutes of Meeting of Special Sub-Committee of the Executive Committee on Possible Division of Executive Functions in Jesuit Colleges and Universities" (St. Louis, Missouri, December 16–21, 1948); box 34, file 158.07, BCA.

38. Memo of telephone conversation, EBR and John McMahon, December 14 or 15, 1948; box 34, file 158.03, BCA.

39. According to John Hynes, this was the original proposal of the Commission on Higher Education. See "Memorandum" re Rector-President (Ad Third Proposal), August 4, 1946 (box 34, file 158.03, BCA). See above, p. 111.

40. The intricacies of canon law and the Jesuit constitutions are explained in a letter from John J. Crowley to Arthur J. Sheehan, Weston College, December 31, 1948; box 34, file 158.03, BCA.

41. "Minutes," Special Sub-Committee, 1948, p. 10.

42. *Ibid.* p. 11.

43. *Ibid.*, pp. 11–12. The subcommittee noted two disadvantages: According to common practice, the rector could be removed after six years; secondly, since the superior did not have final authority, there could be a tendency to appeal to the rector, thus defeating the primary purpose of the division of labor. It might be useful to point out that, prior to the separate incorporation of Jesuit community and university, the juridical entity (sole ownership of the entire complex) was vested in the *domus religiosa*. For that reason, as Father Crowley noted in his letter to Father Sheehan, the religious superior, even though dependent, should not approach the rector hat in hand, as it were, for a gratuitous hand-out in preparing his budget for the community.

44. The fourth option provided for a rector-president and vice presidents for the "immediate administration and coordination of large areas of complex institutions, such as academic and financial" (*ibid.*, p. 12). There was nothing innovative about this arrangement, which had become the normal administrative structure in Jesuit universities. Although this design of governance relieved the rector of the personal management of educational details, it left in the hands of one man the ultimate responsibility for the educational enterprise and for the paternal government of the Jesuit community.

45. Edward B. Rooney to Members of the Sub-Committee, St. Louis, December 21, 1948; box 34, file 158.03, BCA.

46. "Memorandum" of Conference of EBR with JBJ, Rome; book II, BCA.

47. Seattle University was a special case. A. A. Lemieux was the president and religious superior of the Jesuit community. The rector of Seattle University (Christopher A. McDonnell at this time) was also the rector of Seattle Preparatory School. The reason for this unusual arrangement was that, even though the two schools were geographically separated, the local Ordinary would allow only one canonically erected religious foundation.

48. "Minutes," EC, April 1954. Members of the subcommittee were James L. Burke (N.E.), chairman; Joseph K. Drane (Md.); and Joseph C. Glose (N.Y.).

49. Edward B. Bunn, who was knowledgeable on the fine points of governance, insisted that the regents at Georgetown University played a useful role. For a fuller explanation, see "Report of Sub-Committee on Role of Regents in Jesuit Institutions, EC "Minutes," October 1955, appendix E, p. 31.

50. "Response" of BG, May 1954.

51. *Ibid.*, May 1956.

52. "Report" of EBR to BG, May 1957.

53. *Ibid.*

54. Paul Blanshard, an extreme Jeffersonian liberal who was particularly aggressive in challenging Catholic positions (*American Freedom and Catholic Power*, 1949) claimed that American Jesuits did not have full legal ownership of their institutions. He argued that ultimate control was in the hands of the Jesuit General, an alien. It is true that the Society of Jesus was never a legal corporation in the United States and, therefore, did not own these institutions. However, all Jesuit institutions were legally incorporated, and members of the Society formed the legal corporations as trustees and officers. See *Proceedings*, Conference of Presidents, 1958, p. 3.

55. See JEA *Special Bulletin*, no. 226 (BCA), for a good account of the origins of the Research Council.

56. "Report" of EBR to BG, May 1957.

57. "Response" of BG, May 1957.

58. *Proceedings*, Conference of Presidents, 1958, p. 35.

59. "Report" of EBR to BG, May 1958, appendix B, pp. 53A-B-C. See also "Response" of BG, 1958, p. 4. Although it never operated within the constitutional ambit of the Jesuit Educational Association, it would be an oversight not to acknowledge the existence and valuable contribution of the American Association of Jesuit Scientists, which was founded in 1922 and discontinued in 1966. This association, with a national constituency, was especially effective in encouraging the participation of its younger members. It also published a journal which (in 14 bound volumes) may be consulted at the Boston College Archives.

60. "Report" of EBR to the BG, May 1958, appendix B. For additional correspondence on the JRCA, see JEA box 28, file 59.1, BCA.

61. Since membership in the JRCA was optional, only 22 institutions (out of 28) formed the original group of cooperating members. The six that joined at a later date were Boston College, Fairfield, Georgetown, Loyola (Baltimore), Santa Clara, and Wheeling.

62. These reports are in box 7, BCA.

63. Joseph P. Kane, who now serves as vice president of the Association of Jesuit Colleges and Universities, succeeded Robillard as executive director in 1967.

64. The success of this venture subsequently convinced the presidents that the national office of the JEA should be located in the nation's capital.

65. The members of the board were drawn nationally—for example, C. G. Duncombe, Detroit; L. W. Friedrich, Marquette; W. F. Kelley, Creighton; C. M. Gorman, University of San Francisco; F. L. Canavan, Fordham.

66. See *Proceedings*, Conference of Presidents, Rockhurst College, June 4-6, 1959.

67. The recruitment and retention of lay faculty will be discussed in a

later chapter. The presidents also discussed at length a proposal submitted to Father Rooney by Raymond Reiss, president of Reiss Manufacturing Corp. of New York. Reiss, with a businessman's orientation, strongly urged creation of a National Board of Advisors in order to overcome what he perceived to be a public relations problem within the JEA. The idea, for several reasons, was never enthusiastically supported by the presidents, nor by the president of JEA.

68. *Proceedings*, 1959, p. 52.

69. *Ibid.*, p. 53.

70. *Ibid.*

71. "Report" of EBR to BG, May 1959, p. 8.

72. *Ibid.* p. 9.

73. *Ibid.*

74. Conferences, unlike commissions, were not explicitly mentioned in the JEA Constitution. They were, however, provided for in article VIII, A, 4, b, which sanctioned "the meetings of the associations of Jesuit philosophers, scientists, historians, and representative groups in other fields." Again, unlike commissions, whose officers were appointed by the JEA president, conferences, by virtue of the same article, were permitted to elect their own chairman and secretary. In short, in the government of the association, conferences were at the lowest level of influence.

75. "Report" of EBR to BG, May 1959, p. 9. See also Presidents' File, March 1959, JEA Collection, 131.034, BCA.

76. "Report" of EBR to BG, May 1959, p. 9.

77. *Ibid.*

78. *Ibid.*, p. 10.

79. *Ibid.*

80. *Ibid.*

81. *Ibid.*

82. "Minutes," EC, March 1959, pp. 4–5 and 27–28.

83. "Response" of BG to "Report" of EBR, May 1959, p. 3.

84. *Ibid.*

85. *Ibid.* The revision of the JEA Constitution will be examined in chapter 10.

86. *Ibid.*

87. "Minutes," EC, September 1959, p. 32.

88. *Ibid.* For appointment of an assistant for higher education, see chapter 10.

89. *Proceedings*, Conference of Presidents, 1960, p. 23.

90. *Ibid.*, pp. 24–25.

91. *Ibid.*, pp. 25–26.

92. Edward B. Rooney to Presidents of Jesuit Colleges and Universities, New York, May 25, 1960; Presidents' File, JEA Collection, BCA.

93. *Ibid.*

94. "Response" of BG to "Report" of EBR, May 1960, p. 17.

95. *Ibid.* In a related response, the provincials agreed with the JEA presi-

dent that, in view of limited manpower and current priorities, the need for appointing specialized academic assistants to the National Office superseded the need for a "Public Relations Specialist." For the resolution of this question, see chapter 10.


## 8. COORDINATION AND COOPERATION, 1955-1965

1. *Proceedings*, Conference of Presidents, 1959, appendix D, p. 27.

2. *Ibid.*

3. As one example, Casassa cited a group of institutions in Southern California: Occidental College, Claremont Graduate School, Redlands University, and Whittier College shared faculties, courses, and library resources.

4. "Minutes," EC, March 1948, p. 4.

5. *Ibid.*, p. 5.

6. "Report" of EBR to BG, May 1948, p. 7.

7. *Ibid.*, pp. 7-8.

8. "Minutes," EC, September 1950, p. 7.

9. *Ibid.*, August 1951, p. 2.

10. *Ibid.*, April 1952, p. 8.

11. John B. Janssens to Leo D. Sullivan, Rome, April 20, 1948 (NEPA). Father Sullivan was provincial of the Chicago Province and chairman of the provincials' meeting in 1948.

12. John B. Janssens to Joseph D. O'Brien, Rome, April 1, 1951.

13. John B. Janssens to John J. McMahon, Rome, April 25, 1952 (NEPA). In that same letter the General, while complimenting the provincials on sending 191 Jesuits to graduate studies, lamented the fact that no one was being prepared for preaching, "unless it be the three listed under speech." University studies, he wrote, should not bring about "the loss of our pulpits."

14. *Ibid.*

15. *Ibid.* The General was not always consistent. In that very year, 1952, he approved, as previously noted, three new doctoral programs at Boston College Graduate School.

16. Agenda items attached to Janssens letter of April 25, 1952.

17. *Ibid.*

18. A copy of this report is in box 28, file 54.01, BCA.

19. Preface to report.

20. Part III was completed in a later document, which will be described below.

21. Father Rooney had reported to the Board of Governors: "At Father General's explicit request, I sent him a copy of this report on March 13, 1953, as he wished to see it in connection with a special problem that had been submitted to him." "Report" of EBR to BG, May 1953, p. 30.

22. "Response" of BG to "Report" of EBR, May 1954, p. 12.

23. "Report on Graduate Study," *Bulletin*, NCEA, 51, no. 1 (August 1954) ("Proceedings and Addresses," 51st Annual Meeting): 212.

24. *Ibid.*, 52, no. 1 (August 1955): 129.

25. Under that title, the address was published in *Thought*, 30 (1955): 351-388.

26. "Catholics and the Intellectual and Social Apostolate," *Bulletin*, NCEA, 52, no. 1 (August 1955) ("Proceedings and Addresses," 52nd Annual Meeting): 156.

27. *Ibid.*

28. *Thought*, 30 (1955): 353.

29. *Ibid.*, p. 374.

30. *Ibid.*, p. 375.

31. *Ibid.*

32. "Why Is the American Catholic Graduate School Failing to Develop Catholic Intellectualism?" *Bulletin*, NCEA, 53, no. 1 (August 1966): 179-189.

33. *Ibid.*, *passim.*

34. *American Catholic Dilemma* (New York, 1958).

35. *Ibid.*, p. 25.

36. Studies completed in the '50s clearly show that Catholic students, while shunning the rewards of academic applause in the pursuit of pure science in the graduate schools, were overrepresented in law and medicine. They preferred the community prestige and the financial remuneration associated with those professions. For additional studies on these and related questions, see James Hennesey, S.J., *American Catholics: A History of the Roman Catholic Community in the United States* (New York: Oxford University Press, 1981), chapter 20, "Cross and Flag"; also Denis W. Brogan, *USA: An Outline of the Country, Its People and Institutions* (London, 1941). For an in-depth analysis by an astute observer, see Richard Hofstadter, *Anti-Intellectualism in American Life* (New York, 1963); also Merle Curti, *American Paradox: The Conflict of Thought and Action* (New Brunswick, N.J., 1956), and Walter J. Ong, S.J., *Frontiers in American Catholicism* (New York, 1957).

37. In view of its importance, it seems odd that the debate on American Catholic intellectualism was never explicitly discussed by the Executive Committee; nor did Father Rooney assess its implications for Jesuit education in his reports to the Board of Governors. However, at the annual meeting of the JEA in 1956, Graduate School delegates (and their commission) discussed Institutional Plans for Preeminent Doctoral Programs and Evolving Plans for New Doctoral Programs." See *JEQ*, 19, no. 1 (June 1956): 5-6.

38. Raymond V. Schoder to Edward B. Rooney, Nigmegen, Netherlands, May 30, 1956; box 28, file 54.01 BCA.

39. EBR to RVS, New York, July 5, 1956; box 28, file 54.01, BCA.

40. "Minutes," EC, April 1958, p. 22.

41. "Report" of EBR to BG, May 1958, p. 36. Arthur North was the only graduate dean to speak in favor of the Institute.

42. "Minutes," Meeting of Graduate Commission, January 31, 1958. The minutes of Graduate Commission meetings are preserved in chronological order in box 28, file 54.01, BCA.

43. Entitled "Report of the Committee on a Preeminent Department of

Classical Languages at Fordham University," it is attached as appendix D to EBR's "Report" to BG, May 1958.

44. "Report," p. 5.

45. "Response" of BG to "Report" of EBR, May 1958, p. 14.

46. "Minutes," Meeting of Graduate Commission, December 7, 1958.

47. February 5, 1958; Fordham University Archives (FUA).

48. *Ibid.*

49. Arthur A. North to Edward F. Clark, Office of the Graduate Dean, March 22, 1958; FUA.

50. Edward F. Clark to Laurence J. McGinley, Office of the Academic Vice President, May 13, 1958; FUA.

51. Laurence J. McGinley to Arthur A. North, Office of the President, May 19, 1958; FUA.

52. *Ibid.*

53. *Ibid.*

54. The revision was edited by Paul A. FitzGerald, S.J., dean of the Boston College Graduate School and chairman of the Graduate Commission. With a preface by Edward B. Rooney dated July 24, 1958, *Principles and Policies* was printed and circulated by order of the Board of Governors. Although over 600 copies were printed, this item is not easily available. Three copies are filed with the JEA Collection (BCA). See "Report" of EBR to BG, May 1958, p. 51.

55. *Principles and Policies*, p. 7.

56. *Ibid.*, p. 11.

57. *Ibid.*, p. 12.

58. *Ibid.*, p. 11. Edward A. Doisy received the Nobel Prize in 1943 for his original work in physiology and biochemistry. For this reason, in a report designated "confidential," Father Henle suggested a pilot study of the Biochemistry Department at Saint Louis University in order to evaluate its potential for preeminence.

59. *Principles and Policies*, p. 11.

60. The selected fields were basic medical sciences, classical languages, economics, education, history, law, literature, philosophy, physics, political science, psychiatry, psychology, social work, sociology, and zoology-anthropology. *Ibid.*

61. *Ibid.*, p. 14.

62. This document, dated October 15, 1955, is in the Marquette University Archives (MUA). As ultimately agreed upon, the departments included philosophy, biology, anatomy, physiology, microbiology, and pathology.

63. Father Drummond later served as vice president of the Medical Center at Saint Louis University, and still later (1979) was acting president of that institution.

64. The members of the committee were Eugene F. Gallagher, prefect of studies in Missouri, later in Wisconsin; Edwin Quain, academic vice president, Fordham University; Robert J. Henle, dean of the Graduate School, Saint

Louis University. For selection of committee members, see letter of E. J. Drummond to E. F. Gallagher, Office of Academic Vice President, September 19, 1955; MUA.

65. Eugene Gallagher to Leo J. Burns, Milwaukee, March 9, 1957; MUA.

66. *Ibid.*

67. Donald M. Mackensie to Edward J. O'Donnell, Chicago, June 25, 1957; MUA. Mackensie added that "the Board felt Marquette University should be commended for having voluntarily withdrawn from this level of work in 1944." *Ibid.*

68. *Ibid.*

69. E. J. O'Donnell to Lawrence W. Friedrich, Office of the President, September 19, 1957; MUA.

70. Leo J. Burns to Edward J. Drummond, Milwaukee, September 19, 1955; MUA.

71. Memorandum of Conference of EBR with JBJ, October 12, 1955; book I, BCA.

72. *Ibid.* Rooney also spoke to the Assistant, Vincent McCormick, who "had some very nice things to say about Marquette." *Ibid.*

73. Edward B. Rooney to John B. Janssens, New York (n.d., but probably March 1957); BCA, box 36, file 22.

74. *Ibid.*

75. *Ibid.*

76. Vincent A. McCormick to Edward B. Rooney, Rome, March 19, 1957; box 36, file 22, BCA.

77. *Ibid.*

78. "Memorandum," E. J. Drummond to the President (E. O'Donnell), September 3, 1957; MUA.

79. Edward B. Rooney to Vincent A. McCormick, New York, May 13, 1957; box 36, file 22, BCA. The Marquette Medical School had a special administrative and financial relationship to the university.

80. *Ibid.*

81. In 1961 Marquette applied for, and received, permission to establish an important doctoral program in Religious Studies. Designed as a "Training Course for College Theology Teachers," it fulfilled a critical need in that academic area. The inauguration of the program is fully documented in the files of the MUA.

82. "Memorandum," Conference of EBR with JBJ, July 1956, p. 6; book I, BCA.

83. *Ibid.*

84. For an interesting, though not entirely accurate, appraisal of the impact of programs at Santa Clara on its students, see Julian Foster, "Some Effects of Jesuit Education: A Case Study," in Robert Hassenger, ed., *The Shape of Catholic Higher Education* (Chicago, 1967), pp. 163–190. See also Gerald McKevitt, S.J., *The University of Santa Clara: A History, 1851–1977* (Stanford, 1979), pp. 278 sqq.

85. "Memorandum," Conference of EBR with JBJ, August 1958, p. 6; book I, BCA.

86. *Ibid.*

87. *Ibid.*

88. "Report" of EBR to BG, May 1959; see appendix D, pp. 67–70.

89. "Response," BG to EBR, May 1959, p. 9.

90. Provincials' Meeting, May 1959, San Francisco, May 10–12, 1960. See also "Response" of BG to "Report" of EBR, May 1960, pp. 6–7.

91. Arthur S. Adams, "To Whom It May Concern," Washington, D.C., November 17, 1960; box 36, file 17.01, BCA. These testimonials were submitted to the JEA to facilitate proposals for federal funds and to support appeals to private foundations for special programs.

92. William K. Selden, "To Whom It May Concern," Washington, D.C., November 22, 1960; box 36, file 17.01, BCA.

93. Theodore A. Distler, "To Whom It May Concern," Washington, D.C., November 15, 1960; box 36, file 17.01, BCA.


## 9. THREE AREAS OF CONCERN, 1960–1965

1. "Minutes," EC, March 1959, pp. 9–10. See also *Epitome Instituti* (S.J.), no. 814.

2. Leo D. Sullivan visited Marquette, Saint Louis, Creighton; Francis J. Corkery visited Detroit, Loyola (Chicago), Loyola (New Orleans); Joseph D. FitzGerald visited Loyola (Los Angeles), University of San Francisco, Seattle, Gonzaga; A William Crandell visited Georgetown, Fordham, Boston College.

3. "Minutes," EC, March 1959. See also Edward B. Rooney to Vincent A. McCormick, New York, July 8, 1959; box 36, file 22, BCA.

4. "Memorandum of Conversation," EBR with Vincent McCormick, Rome, December 3–13, 1959; box 36, file 22, BCA.

5. *Ibid.*

6. John B. Janssens to John J. McGinty, Rome, November 26, 1960 (NEPA). In sending a copy of this letter to the other American provincials, Father McGinty informed them that he had asked Father Rooney to undertake this study. Rooney was unduly optimistic in assuring McGinty that he would have the report ready for the next meeting of the Board of Governors, which was scheduled for May 1961. John J. McGinty to James E. Coleran, New York, December 17, 1960 (NEPA).

7. Janssens to McGinty, November 26, 1960.

8. *Ibid.* The General also suggested the usefulness of a program "to indoctrinate" Catholic and non-Catholic teachers, who were not educated in Jesuit institutions, "in the principles and purpose of Catholic and Jesuit education." *Ibid.*

9. "Memorandum," Conference, EBR with JBJ, September 11, 1954; book II.

10. *Ibid.* Later in his 1956 conference with the General, Rooney pleaded for higher salaries for lay teachers since "failure to meet the salary problem was resulting in our losing some of our very best lay teachers" (p. 5, book II).

11. Edward B. Rooney to John B. Janssens, New York, November 18, 1960; box 36, file 22, BCA.

12. This memorandum is attached to the covering letter of November 18, 1960.

13. *Ibid.* In the academic year 1957–1958 there was a total of 1,476 teachers in Jesuit high schools in the United States; of that number, 1,060 were Jesuits and 416 were laymen. However, in that same year in Jesuit colleges and universities there was a grand total of 5,007 faculty members; of that number, 1,425 were Jesuits and 3,582 were lay faculty members. The professional schools accounted for a large percentage of lay faculty.

14. *Ibid.*

15. See JEA *Directory, 1958–1962.* The 14 JEA Conferences were dominated by lay men and women.

16. "Response" of BG to "Report" of EBR, May 1959, p. 7.

17. Edward B. Rooney to Harold O. Small, New York, November 2, 1960; box 36, file 22, BCA.

18. *Ibid.*

19. John B. Janssens to all Major Superiors, Rome, May 21, 1960; *Acta Romana*, 13: 775–776. Father Small was duly appointed American Assistant by the 30th General Congregation. See Pedro Arrupe to all Major Superiors, Rome, July 8, 1965; AR, 14: 619–620.

20. See *AR*, 13: 772–774; also JBJ to All Major Superiors, Rome, March 9, 1961 (*ibid.*, 14: 38).

21. John R. Swain to All Major Superiors, Rome, October 7, 1964; *ibid.* 484–885; also *ibid.*, pp. 618, 842.

22. The memorandum is dated May 17, 1963; book III, BCA.

23. *Ibid.*

24. *Ibid.*

25. "Recruiting of Lay Faculty: A Proposed Statement." Prepared by E. J. Drummond and W. F. Kelley, March 22, 1961; box 36, file 22, BCA.

26. For the official version, see "Revised Statement on Recruitment of Lay Faculty," *JEQ*, 25, no. 2 (October 1962): 129–130.

27. Strange to say, Father Rooney was not entirely happy with the provincials' decision since the *JEQ* contained letters of the General. See "Report" of EBR to BG, May 1960, p. 40.

28. John B. Janssens to Carroll O'Sullivan, Rome, March 3, 1960 (NEPA). O'Sullivan was provincial of the California Province.

29. Carroll O'Sullivan to James E. Coleran, San Francisco, March 14, 1960 (NEPA). Coleran was provincial in New England.

30. *Proceedings*, Conference of Presidents, 1960, pp. 7–11.

31. *JEA Special Bulletin*, no. 274, May 31, 1961.

32. *Ibid.*

33. "Response" of BG to "Report" of EBR, May 1960, p. 13. Members of the subcommittee were: Joseph K. Drane (Maryland), chairman; Edward A. Doyle (New Orleans), Jerome J. Marchetti (Missouri).

34. See "Minutes," EC (March 1961), appendix E, for text of the report.

35. Philosophy was the topic of the hour. In a conversation with Vincent McCormick in New York in 1960, Rooney learned that a Congress of Philosophers had been called by the General. It consisted of a small group of selected Jesuits from different provinces. Joseph Wulftange of West Baden College, attended as the American delegate. The Congress was held in Rome, and Paolo Dezza was in general charge. "Minutes," EC, April 1960, p. 3.

36. *Ibid.*, p. 19.

37. "Response," BG, to "Report" of EBR, May 1960, pp. 4–6.

38. *Ibid.*

39. These members were Charles S. Casassa, Edward A. Doyle, Bernard Cooke, Matthew Rooney, Victor A. Yanitelli, Robert F. Harvanek.

40. There were two institutes, one preceding and one following, which augmented the impact of the Workshop on Philosophy and Theology. The Third National Institute for Deans was held at Gonzaga University, Spokane, August 4–14, 1961, under the direction of William F. Kelley, the academic vice president at Creighton University. Its purpose was to explore the dean's role in achieving academic excellence in the college under his charge. This provided an ideal background for discussing philosophy and theology as academic disciplines. A Guidance Institute was held at Boston College, August 7–15, 1963, under the direction of James F. Moynihan, chairman of the Department of Psychology at that institution. The results of this institute were of assistance in exploring and understanding the religious, moral, and spiritual formation of Jesuit students.

41. Personal Memorandum, Conference of EBR with JBJ, Rome, July 22, 1960; book II, BCA.

42. These five volumes are preserved in the JEA Collection, BCA.

43. Robert J. Henle, S.J., "The 1962 Loyola Workshop: A Comment," *JEQ*, 25, no. 4 (March 1963): 237–242. This item is followed by a "Statement of Positions" (pp. 243–264), which is reprinted from volume V, chapter IV, "Final Report of the Workshop."

One of the first fruits of the workshop was an excellent volume, by three of the participants, which brought to a wider audience a selection of papers, discussions, and conclusions of the workshop. See J. Barry McGannon, S.J., Bernard J. Cooke, S.J., George P. Klubertanz, S.J., eds., *Christian Wisdom and Christian Formation: Philosophy and the Catholic College Student* (New York: Sheed and Ward, 1964). This book has a foreword by Edward B. Rooney, S.J.

44. *Ibid.* (*JEQ*), p. 236.

45. *Ibid.*

46. *Ibid.*, p. 237.

47. *Ibid.*, p. 239.

48. *Ibid.*, pp. 244–255.

49. *Proceedings*, Conference of Presidents, Atlantic City (January 12–13, 1963), p. 1.

50. *Ibid.*, pp. 4–5.

51. "Response," BG, May 1963, p. 3.

52. These reports are not available to the researcher.

53. "Report" of EBR to BG, May 1960, p. 42 (emphasis added). It was later implied that Rooney may have exaggerated the meaning of the Assistant's alleged remarks. See below, p. 167.

54. "Minutes," EC, April 1960, p. 12.

55. "Report" of EBR to BG, May 1960, p. 42.

56. In further recognition of his talents, Father Harvanek served as provincial of the Chicago Province (1967–1973).

57. Rooney noted in his charge to the Executive Committee that "one of the first steps toward such a study would be to gather a bibliography concerning the objectives of Jesuit institutions." Francois de Dainville, S.J., an editor of *Etudes*, assisted Rooney in listing titles in French, Spanish, Italian, Latin; there was nothing in English. "Minutes," EC, April 1960, p. 12, and *ibid.*, appendix B, p. 37.

58. See John W. Donohue, S.J., *Jesuit Education: An Essay on the Foundations of Its Idea* (New York, 1963). The *Ratio Studiorum*, it should be remembered, is a plan of studies; it does not consider (primarily) the objectives.

59. See *Proceedings of the Santa Clara Institute for Jesuit College Deans* (August 1955). Privately circulated by the JEA.

60. "Objectives of the Catholic Liberal Arts College," *ibid.*, pp. 9–21, p. 10.

61. *Ibid.*, p. 11.

62. *Ibid.*, p. 12.

63. *Ibid.*, pp. 22–33. Jocosely or otherwise, there were a few at the institute who, in rebuttal, quoted from Cardinal Newman's *Idea of a University:* "Liberal education makes not the Christian, not the Catholic, but the gentleman."

64. *Proceedings*, p. 22.

65. *Ibid.*, p. 25.

66. *Ibid.*, p. 31. For an exhaustive explanation, see George E. Ganss, *St. Ignatius' Idea of a Jesuit University* (Milwaukee, 1956).

67. "What Is a Good Statement of the Objectives of a Liberal Arts College?" *Proceedings*, p. 36.

68. *Ibid.* For a summary of the entire program, see Neil G. McCluskey, S.J., "Deans' Institute, Santa Clara, 1955," *JEQ*, 18, no. 2 (October 1955): 69–80.

69. "Minutes," EC, September 1960, p. 31. The complete report is attached to these minutes as appendix B, pp. 44–46.

70. *Ibid.*

71. *Ibid.* Father Harvanek's thesis appears to be confirmed by more recent scholarship. In an interesting publication, John W. O'Malley, S.J., professor at the Weston School of Theology, examines the connection between Renaissance humanism and traditionally Christian moral and religious virtues. He writes: "Humanistic texts were studied not only for their stylistic qualities. There was also a spirituality implicit in them. . . . This religious direction of the humanistic movement has not yet received the attention it deserves in the history of the early Society. It throws the educational program of the Jesuit *Ratio* into a new light." "The Jesuits, St. Ignatius, and the Counter Reformation: Some Recent Studies and Their Implications for Today," *Studies in the Spirituality of Jesuits*, 14, no. 1 (January 1982): 18–19.

72. "Minutes," EC, March 1961, appendix C, pp. 44–47.

73. *Ibid.*

74. "Response" of BG to "Report" of EBR, May 1961, pp. 12–13. Emphasis added.

75. *Ibid.* At this time, under orders from the Board of Governors, Rooney added Paul A. FitzGerald, National Office of the JEA, and Adrian J. Kochanski, province prefect from Wisconsin, to the subcommittee, thereafter known as the Committee of Five.

76. "The Objectives of the American Jesuit University—A Dilemma," *JEQ*, 24, no. 2 (October 1961): 69–87. At this very time, Father Harvanek had relinquished his place on the Executive Committee and had returned to West Baden College as professor of philosophy and director of special studies for the Chicago Province.

77. *Ibid.*, p. 74.

78. *Ibid.*

79. *Ibid.*, pp. 185–186.

80. "The Role of the Jesuit University," *JEQ*, 25, no. 4 (March 1963): 210–222.

81. *Ibid.*, p. 212.

82. *Ibid.*, p. 216.

83. *Ibid.*, p. 219.

84. *Ibid.*, p. 222.

85. Comment on "The Role of the Jesuit University," *ibid.*, pp. 223–226, p. 226.

86. *Ibid.*, p. 226.

87. *Ibid.*

88. The consolidated report is found in the *addendum* to EBR's "Report" to BG, May 1963.

89. *Ibid.*

90. "Responses," of BG to "Report" of EBR, May 1963, p. 4.

91. See *JEQ*, 26, no. 4 (March 1964): 197–204. Technically, Father Walsh was responding to the report of the Committee of Five on "Objectives." In reality, he was formulating a rebuttal to Father Harvanek's article.

92. *Ibid.*, p. 197.

93. *Ibid.*

94. *Ibid.*, p. 198.

95. *Ibid.*, p. 199.

96. *Ibid.*, p. 201. Some thought it would be difficult to reconcile this blueprint with the position papers of the Loyola Workshop.

97. *Ibid.*, p. 204.

98. See *Proceedings*, pp. 43-49. Under the revised constitution (which will be explained in chapter 10), the Conference of Presidents was replaced by the Commission on Colleges and Universities.

99. *Ibid.*

100. The statement was forwarded to the Board of Governors with a covering letter from A. A. Lemieux to John V. O'Connor (Seattle, September 17, 1964); NEPA.

101. See *Proceedings*, Commission on Colleges and Universities, pp. 1-3.

102. *Ibid.*, p. 2.

103. As president of a well-known college, Father Swords was invited to submit his comments, in article form, "on the manpower, the expansion and the future prospects of the four year, single purpose, liberal arts college" (Paul A. FitzGerald to Raymond J. Swords, New York, February 4, 1964). Father Swords declined, on the score that it might appear to be a dispute between Holy Cross and Boston College. In the same letter, Swords remarked that Vincent Beatty, president of Loyola College, Baltimore, had heard objections to the Santa Clara Statement from members of his faculty (Swords to FitzGerald, Worcester, February 6, 1964). Box 28, file 51.01, BCA.

104. See "Statement of the Presidents of Jesuit Colleges and Universities Regarding the Development of Jesuit Higher Education" (n.d.). In file of "Minutes," Provincials' Meeting, 1964 (NEPA).

105. "Memorandum" to Father Provincial re Statement of Presidents of Jesuit Universitites and Colleges, September 28, 1964. Provincials' Meeting, 1964 (NEPA).

106. See *Proceedings*, Commission on Colleges and Universities, Saint Louis University, January 9-10, 1965, pp. 4-5.

107. *Ibid.*

108. EBR to John L. Swain, New York, January 25, 1965; box 36, file 21, BCA.

109. John L. Swain to EBR, Rome, February 19, 1965; box 36, file 21, BCA.

110. *Ibid.*

111. EBR to John L. Swain, New York, March 12, 1965; box 36, file 21, BCA.

112. John L. Swain to EBR, Rome, March 22, 1965 (box 36, file 21, BCA). The vicar general took this occasion to thank Father Rooney for his explanation of the origin of the JEA subcommittee on "objectives."

113. "Minutes," EC, August 1963.

114. "Report" of EBR to BG, April 1964.

115. These responses from the province prefects were carefully tabulated by Eugene F. Mangold, administrative assistant to Father Rooney. Four provincials favored continuation of the committee; four preferred to discontinue its action; three voted to remand the matter to the Board of Governors. These reponses are attached to an interoffice communication, EFM to Edwardo [Rooney], February 14, 1964. Box 35, file 4.04, BCA.

## 10. THE REVISED CONSTITUTION, 1959–1964

1. See *Proceedings* of Conference of Presidents, p. 24.
2. "Report" of EBR to BG, May 1958; *addendum*, p. 35a.
3. *Ibid.*
4. "Response" of BG to EBR, May 1958; *addendum*, p. 13.
5. "Minutes," EC, September 1958, p. 7.
6. *Ibid.*, p. 9.
7. "Minutes," EC, September 1960, p. 4.
8. May 1959, p. 30.
9. "Response" of BG to "Report" of EBR, May 1959, p. 7.
10. "Minutes," meeting of Sub-Committee on Revision of Constitution, March 16, 1959; box 35, file 4.04.2, BCA.
11. *Ibid.*
12. "Minutes," meeting of Sub-Committee, June 12, 1959.
13. A Jesuit, involved in the process, was heard to remark—with amusement—that the Constitutional Convention (Philadelphia, 1787) had completed its work in three months.
14. In general, the lines were drawn between the Executive Committee and the Presidents' Conference. There are seven voluminous files in box 35, BCA.
15. See "Report," EBR to BG, May 2–4, 1961, pp. 24–27.
16. Members of the subcommittee, all from the West Coast, were A. A. Lemieux, chairman, University of Seattle; John F. X. Connolly, University of San Francisco; Patrick A. Donohue, Santa Clara; Edmund W. Morton, Gonzaga.
17. "Minutes," EC, March 1961, pp. 20–23; see *ibid.*, appendix, pp. 35–43.
18. "Minutes," Sub-Committee Meeting on Revision, March 13–14, 1961, p. 3.
19. *Ibid.*
20. W. Patrick Donnelly to E. A. Doyle, Loyola University, New Orleans, February 16, 1961; box 35, file 4.05, BCA.
21. *Ibid.*
22. *Ibid.*
23. A. William Crandell to E. A. Doyle, Spring Hill College, Mobile, February 21, 1961; box 35, file 4.05, BCA.

24. *Ibid.*

25. *Ibid.*

26. *Ibid.*

27. *Ibid.*

28. *Ibid.*

29. "Minutes," Conference of Presidents, April 3, 1961; box 28, file 74.041, BCA.

30. *Ibid.*

31. Paul Reinert, S.J. to Ed[ward] B. Rooney, S.J., Chalfonte-Haddon Hotel, Atlantic City, April 6, 1961; box 28, file 74.041, BCA.

32. This document is entitled: "Revision of the Constitution of the Jesuit Educational Association: Report of the Conference of Presidents of Jesuit Colleges and Universities to the Board of Governors"; box 28, file 74.041, BCA.

33. *Ibid.*

34. *Ibid.*

35. *Ibid.*

36. *Ibid.*

37. *Ibid.* As finally approved, it was called the Coordinating Committee.

38. *Ibid.*

39. *Ibid.*

40. "Minutes," Sub-Committee meeting, March 1961, pp. 4–5; box 28, file 4.04.2, BCA.

41. "Report" of EBR to BG, Saint Louis, May 2–4, 1961, p. 27. The progress report is attached as appendix B, pp. 59–66.

42. It was at the 1961 Saint Louis meeting that the Board of Governors moved a vote of thanks to Father James E. Coleran for contributing a member of the New England Province to the National Office of the JEA. At the May 1960 provincials' meeting, Paul A. FitzGerald, dean of the Boston College Graduate School, was appointed assistant for higher education to the president of the JEA. This was a disappointment to the presidents, who, as indicated above, had urged the appointment of a "specialist in public relations." For the record, however, let it be said that, in his many dealings with the presidents over a six-year period, the author received unfailing cooperation and was the recipient of many kindnesses. See "Minutes," Meeting of Sub-Committee of Functions of Specialists in Higher Education and Secondary Education, March 25, 1960; box 28, file 49.045, BCA. Also "Report" of EBR to BG, 1960, pp. 34–35.

43. "Response" of BG to "Report" of EBR, May 1961, pp. 6–7.

44. Edward B. Rooney to members of the Special Committee on Revision of the JEA Constitution, New York, October 17, 1961; box 35, file 4.05.1, BCA.

45. "Minutes," Meeting of Sub-Committee, March 24–25, 1960; box 35, file 4.04.2, BCA.

46. *Ibid.*

47. Excerpt from memorandum to Very Reverend Father General, John

B. Janssens from Reverend Edward B. Rooney, August 16, 1960; box 35, file 21, BCA.

48. Ledochowski to the Fathers and Brothers of the American Assistancy, August 15, 1934 (emphasis added).

49. *Instruction*, titulus I, art. 3, #2,b (trans. from the Latin).

50. John B. Janssens to Edward B. Rooney, Rome, 23 September 1960; box 35, file 21, BCA.

51. EBR to JBJ, New York, March 24, 1961; box 35, file 21, BCA.

52. *Ibid.*

53. JBJ to EBR, Rome, April 15, 1960; box 35, file 21, BCA. In the General's exact words: "Incommoda enim, quae ex eiusmodi nova dispositione sequi possint, praesertim quod ad regimen Provinciae et relationes cum Praeposito Provinciae attinet, compensari non videntur emolumentis quae sperantur."

54. Personal Memorandum, Conference of EBR with JBJ, July 22, 1960, p. 6; book II, BCA.

55. *Ibid.* This question was examined in chapter 4.

56. Personal Memorandum, Conference of EBR with JBJ, August 31, 1961, pp. 2-3; book II, BCA.

57. *Ibid.*

58. *Ibid.*

59. *Ibid.*

60. "Minutes," Provincials' Meeting, St. Louis, May 1-7, 1961; NEPA.

61. Joannes L. Swain to Linus Thro, Rome, October 9, 1961 (NEPA). As provincial in Missouri, Father Thro was chairman of the provincials' meeting. (Trans. from Latin.)

62. "Minutes" of Meeting of Special Committee on Revision of the Jesuit Educational Association Constitution, John Carroll University, Cleveland, Ohio, November 18-19, 1961 (box 35, file 4.05.2, BCA).

63. "Minutes" of the Special Committee (pp. 7-8) contain an annotated list of documents which served as background to the committee's discussions.

64. *Ibid.*, p. 8.

65. *Ibid.*

66. *Ibid.*, p. 11.

67. *Ibid.*

68. *Ibid.*, pp. 11-12.

69. "Minutes," Special Committee; Work Copy for Third Session, November 19, 1961.

70. *Ibid.*, p. 3.

71. *Ibid.*

72. See "Minutes," EC, University of Detroit, April 1962, pp. 24-31. Conferences had a more important role in the revised constitutions.

73. For a complete copy of the third draft, see *ibid.*, appendix B, pp. 1-18.

74. Harold O. Small to A. William Crandell, Rome, April 9, 1962 (box 36, file 22, BCA).

75. *Ibid.*

76. *Ibid.*

77. Harold O. Small to A. William Crandell, Rome, April 20, 1962; box 36, file 22, BCA.

78. EBR to Harold O. Small, New York, May 2, 1962; box 36, file 22, BCA.

79. *Ibid.*

80. *Ibid.*

81. This memorandum, received in the JEA office Monday, May 7, 1962, is dated May 1, 1962 and signed by A. William Crandell, S.J. (box 35, file 4.05.1, BCA).

82. *Ibid.*

83. *Ibid.*

84. *Ibid.*

85. *Ibid.*

86. See *Excerpt from Oral Report of the J.E.A. President,* May 7, 1962; box 35, file 4.05.1, BCA.

87. *Ibid.*

88. See *Comments on Proposal Presented by Father A. William Crandell, S.J.,* Boston, May 9, 1962 (box 35, file 4.05.1, BCA).

89. *Ibid.* Father Rooney was unaware, of course, that the provincials, quite apart from the proposals for revision, were not entirely satisfied with his administration. After Father Crandell had left the room on May 7, following his presentation, the board went into an executive session. The provincials noted that "among other reasons for reorganization are the lack of communication; too much and too detailed supervision by the J.E.A.; the supervision has become mediocre; the presidents wish more voice in the decisions formulated by the J.E.A." See "Minutes," Provincials' Meeting, Loyola House, Boston, May 7–12, 1962, p. 19 (NEPA).

90. "Minutes," EC, San Francisco, August 17–20, 1962.

91. EBR to John B. Janssens, New York, May 17, 1962; box 36, file 21, BCA.

92. *Ibid.*

93. "Minutes," Meeting of Provincials of the American Assistancy, Detroit, May 5–12, 1963, p. 10; NEPA.

94. Personal Memorandum of Conference of EBR with JBJ, July 6, 1963; book II, BCA.

95. *Ibid.*

96. Harold O. Small to EBR, Rome, July 30, 1963 (box 36, file 22, BCA).

97. "Memorandum," EBR to JBJ, August 23, 1963 (box 35, file 4.05.3, BCA).

98. *Ibid.*

99. *Ibid.*

100. John J. McGinty to Edward B. Rooney, New York, July 25, 1964; box 35, file 4.05.4, BCA.

101. *Ibid.*

102. John B. Janssens to John J. McGinty, Rome, June 22, 1964; box 35, file 4.05.4, BCA.

103. *Ibid.*

104. *Ibid.* Emphasis added.

105. In the revised constitution, see article V, no. 6. The constitution is filed in box 35, file 4.05.4, BCA.

106. Janssens to McGinty, June 22, 1964. It is interesting to note that, in his letter, the General again emphasized the importance of cooperation "especially on the level of graduate studies, and a sharpening of the profile of the Jesuit alumnus, as sketched by the Loyola Workshop."

107. John J. McGinty to Fathers and Brothers of the American Assistancy, New York, July 31, 1964 (box 35, file 4.05.4, BCA). The revised *Constitution of the Jesuit Educational Association* was published in *JEQ*, 27, no. 2 (October 1964): 87–98.


11. THE NEW ORDER, 1964–1968

1. Although much of the literature on Vietnam has been self-serving, the following items are instructive: Frances FitzGerald, *Fire in the Lake* (Boston: Little Brown, 1972); David Halberstram, *The Best and the Brightest* (New York: Random House, 1972); Theodore Roszak, *The Making of a Counter-Culture* (Garden City, N.Y.: Doubleday, 1969).

2. For further enlightenment, see Seymour Martin Lipset and Philip G. Altback, eds., *Students in Revolt* (Boston: Houghton Mifflin, 1969); Edward J. Bander, ed., *Turmoil on the Campus* (New York: H. W. Wilson Co., 1970); Donald L. Light Jr. and John Spiegel, *The Dynamics of University Protest* (Chicago: Wilson-Hall, 1977).

3. *The Documents of Vatican II*, Walter M. Abbott, S.J., general editor (New York: Guild Press, 1966), pp. 631–655.

4. *Ibid.*, p. 635.

5. *Ibid.*

6. *Ibid.*

7. *Declaration on Christian Education*, sec. 10 (in *ibid.*, 648). For harmony between culture and Christian formation, see *Pastoral Constitution on the Church in the Modern World* (*Gaudium et Spes*), sec. 62 (in *ibid.*, p. 268). See also John W. Donohue, S.J., *Catholicism and Education* (New York: Harper and Row, 1973).

8. *Declaration on Christian Education*, sec. 12 (in *Documents* of Vatican II, p. 650.)

9. Harold O. Small, the American Assistant, penned an affectionate remembrance of His Paternity: "John Baptist Janssens: Some Reflections," *Woodstock Letters*, 94 (Winter 1965): 27–31.

10. The General has written an eyewitness account: *Yo Viví la Bomba Atomica* (Madrid, 1952).

11. See *Current Biography Yearbook, 1970,* Charles Moritz, ed. (New York, 1971), pp. 19–21; also, for journalistic details, *New York Times,* May 24, 1965.

12. *Documents of the 31st and 32nd General Congregations of the Society of Jesus* (St. Louis: The Institute of Jesuit Sources, 1977), decree 28, 535, p. 236.

13. *Ibid.,* 535, p. 236.

14. *Ibid.,* decree 29, 547, p. 240.

15. "Reverend Father General to the Fathers of the French Schools," Rome, August 25, 1965, in *JEQ,* 28, no. 2 (October 1965): 69–74, p. 70.

16. Peter Arrupe, "The Jesuit Apostolate of Education," *JEQ,* 29, no. 1 (June 1966): 5–11, p. 7.

17. *Ibid.,* p. 9.

18. *Ibid.*

19. See Peter M. Quay, S.J., "Jesuit, Priest, and Scholar: A Theory of Our Learned Apostolates," *JEQ,* 28, no. 2 (October 1965): 98–121. For a response to this article, see Charles Frankenhoff, S.J., "Some Comments on: 'Jesuit, Priest and Scholar,'" *ibid.,* no. 4 (March 1966): 245–248. Six years earlier, John B. Janssens had detected the faint order of this malaise. In a letter, which reviewed the history of the apostolate of education, he admonished young Jesuits to engage in this apostolate if assigned to it by superiors (Rome, September 15, 1960; *Acta Romana,* 13: 816–824).

20. See Robert Fitzgerald, S.J., ed., "Jesuits and Catholic Students in American Catholic Higher Education: A Symposium," *Woodstock Letters,* 93, no. 3 (July 1964): 253–281; also, Robert Fitzgerald, S.J., ed., "Jesuits and Higher Education: A Symposium," *ibid.,* 94, no. 1 (Summer 1965): 245–274.

21. *Documents,* etc., decree 29, 549, p. 241.

22. Father Rooney's tenure had come up for discussion on previous occasions. As far back as 1951, the Board of Governors was unhappy at Rooney's excessive involvement in international associations and had even appointed a committee (Frs. J. McMahon, W. E. FitzGerald, and D. Nugent) to suggest a substitute during his extended absences from the country. (See "Minutes," Provincials' Meeting, Santa Clara, April 1951; NEPA). More recently, the provincial in Detroit, writing to the provincial in Boston, "[had] wondered over the past year or two whether the Fathers Provincial should not consider a new director of the JEA. Father Rooney has been in charge now for many years and perhaps someone else might give a different direction and impetus to the organization." John A. McGrail to James E. Coleran, Detroit, April 6, 1962; NEPA.

23. McGinty to Rooney.

24. There is an interesting preamble to that meeting, which took cognizance of the fact that it was the end of one era and the beginning of another. "Minutes," EC, August 1964.

25. "Minutes," Provincials' Meeting, Spring 1965; NEPA.

26. *Ibid.*

27. *Ibid.*

28. *Proceedings*, Commission on Colleges and Universities, January 9–10, 1965, p. 1.

29. John L. Swain to James J. Shanahan, Rome, December 10, 1964; NEPA.

30. *Proceedings*, 1965, p. 2.

31. In one of his last observations on a favorite theme, Father General Janssens had written to Father Provincial McGinty: "Through the years the JEA has worthily developed cooperation and strengthened unity among the educational institutions of the Assistancy, but it seems that the colleges and universities in their current exposition of goals and future requirements hesitate to assign cooperation a stronger supporting role in their plans. Let not Provincials delay unduly on assessing the manpower within a Province, since much of this was accomplished in drawing blueprints for expansion, but press on to explore intra-Provincial and regional collaboration. Rome, March 4, 1964; NEPA.

32. *Proceedings*, 1965, p. 2.

33. In short, the presidents concluded: "He should be the type of person the provincials would not hesitate to recommend as the President of one of our major universities." *Ibid.*, appendix C, p. 31.

34. "Minutes," Provincials' Meeting, 1965.

35. *Ibid.*

36. *Ibid.*

37. See Personal Memorandum of Conference with Very Reverend Father General Pedro Arrupe, Monday, September 20, 1965 (at the Curia, Rome) (book I, BCA).

38. *Proceedings*, Commission on Colleges and Universities, 1966, p. 25.

39. There were unfounded rumors of retirement in 1962 on the occasion of the 25th anniversary of Rooney's appointment as Executive Director of the Jesuit Educational Association. For the Testimonial Program, see JEA box 9, 25th Anniversary, BCA; also "A Tribute, 1937–1962," *JEQ*, 25, no. 2 (October 1962): 73–75.

40. John L. Swain to Thomas D. McMahon (vice provincial, Buffalo), Rome, May 17, 1965; NEPA.

41. Pedro Arrupe to John L. Kelley, Rome, December 16, 1965 (Curia Files; Portland, Oregon).

42. After the announcement, there was an outpouring of cordial and sincere testimonials, from provincials and classroom teachers alike, to Father Rooney and the *old order*. These are preserved in the Private Papers of EBR, box 5, file 31–7, BCA.

43. For a description of the news release, see *ibid.*

44. In order to present the image of a complete reorganization (or "new deal," as Father Reinert put it), Fathers FitzGerald and Mangold, after assisting in the transition, were reassigned to works in their respective provinces.

45. Father Reinert, it might be noted, did not always get all that he requested. For example, his first choice was to identify Crandell as executive director of two commissions; Siegfried, similarly, of the other two. This proved

unsatisfactory. He then suggested vice president for each. In the end, as already indicated, the provincials preferred vice president and secretary-treasurer. See "Minutes," Provincials' Meeting, 1966; NEPA.

46. Although it did not touch the substance of the reorganization, in order to meet some of the criticisms leveled at the previous administration, Reinert circulated among Jesuits and lay personnel, administrators, and faculty a detailed *Questionnaire on the Functions and Services of the J.E.A.* Not surprisingly, many Jesuits and most lay colleagues were unfamiliar with the inner workings of the organization. It was generally perceived as an association for the support of administrators. The questionnaire, with responses, is preserved in the JEA Collection, BCA.

47. "Minutes," Provincials' Meeting, Spokane, May 6-8, 1966, p. 8.

48. *Ibid.*

49. *Ibid.*

50. "Minutes," Provincials' Meeting, Rome, September-October, 1966, p. 17.

51. The implementation of these recommendations would involve the revision of bylaws, an interpretation of canon law, a division of structure whereby the title to property might be separated from academic authority.

52. *Proceedings*, Commission on Colleges and Universities, Gonzaga University, June 1966, appendix L, p. 112.

53. *Ibid.*

54. *Ibid.*

55. *Ibid.*

56. "It goes without saying that any Jesuit may petition for his removal from any assignment and that the Provincial must have entire liberty to accede to such a request" (*ibid.*). The procedure for the selection, training, and assignment of Jesuits is still a relevant question. With a covering letter dated June 21, 1982, John J. O'Callaghan, S.J., president of the Jesuit Conference, published *Guidelines for the Assignment of Jesuit Personnel in Higher Education.* As Father O'Callaghan notes, such a document "is one practical application of our previously stated commitment to engage in a national corporate apostolate."

57. See Andrew M. Greeley, "The Problems of Jesuit Education in the United States," *JEQ*, 28, no. 2 (October 1966): 102-120, p. 102.

58. *Ibid.*

59. Paul C. Reinert, "In Response to Father Greeley," *ibid.*, pp. 121-129, p. 121.

60. "To help Father General in fostering the whole work of education, a secretariate of education should be established. Its task will be to collect and distribute information about the apostolate of education carried on by Jesuits and also to promote alumni associations and periodic conventions." Decree 28, no. 31.

61. "Minutes," Provincials' Meeting, p. 20.

62. *Ibid.*

63. Pedro Arrupe to Edward J. Sponga, Rome, December 13, 1966; NEPA.

64. A. William Crandell to Vincent T. O'Keefe, Washington, D.C., January 6, 1967; box 35, file 22, BCA.

65. Pedro Arrupe to All Major Superiors, Rome, June 29, 1967; *AR*, 15: 48–49.

66. John E. Blewett, "International Center of Education," *JEQ*, 30, no. 3 (January 1968): 131–138, p. 132.

67. See Paul C. Reinert, "First Meeting of a Board," *JEQ*, 30, no. 2 (October 1967): 112–117, p. 112; also "An Innovation in Higher Education: The Board of Trustees of Saint Louis University," BCA.

68. *Ibid.*, p. 115.

69. *Ibid.*

70. *Ibid.*, p. 114. Later (1973), the Jesuit community purchased a residence hall from the university.

71. *Ibid.*, p. 113.

72. *Ibid.*, p. 114.

73. *Documents* of 31st General Congregation, decree 28, no. 27.

74. At this time, 26 boards were exclusively Jesuit; 2 had a mixture of Jesuit and laymen. Eighteen institutions planned to include laymen on the board in the near future; 8 intended to continue a Jesuit board. Twenty-one were giving serious thought to the separate incorporation of the Jesuit community.

75. October 10, 1967. Quoted in *Proceedings*, Commission on Colleges and Universities, Washington, D.C., October 13–14, 1967, p. 12.

76. *Ibid.*

77. Excerpts from the Minutes, Provincials' Meeting, October 5–9, 1967; NEPA.

78. *Catholic Institutions in the United States: Canonical and Civil Law Status* (Washington, D.C.: Catholic University of America Press, 1968).

79. "Action Proposed on Ownership — Separate Incorporation — Responsibility and Freedom," October 9, 1967; box 9, Board of Governors, BCA. For an in-depth explanation, see also Joseph K. Drane, S.J., "Juridical Substructures of American Jesuit Educational Institutions," *JEQ*, 31. no. 2 (October 1968): 67–90.

80. "Action Proposed on Ownership."

81. *Ibid.*

82. See *Proceedings*, Commission on Colleges and Universities, October 1967, pp. 12–14. See also Edward J. Sponga to Paul C. Reinert, Baltimore, October 21, 1967; box 9, Board of Governors, BCA.

83. *Proceedings*, October 1967, appendix A, p. 18.

84. Pedro Arrupe to Edward J. Sponga, Rome, November 27, 1967; Maryland Province Archives.

85. *Proceedings*, Commission on Colleges and Universities, San Francisco, April 15, 1968, appendix B, pp. 12–17.

86. The minutes of the Coordinating Committee, 1966–1971, and the *Proceedings*, Commission on Colleges and Universities, 1967–1970, document the

position of the presidents in their march toward autonomy. These items are preserved in the JEA Collection at BCA.

87. See *Report of the Provincials' Committee of the J.E.A.*, prepared for the meeting of the North American and Canadian Provincials at Puerto Rico, May 13–18, 1968; box 9, Board of Governors, BCA.

88. Although not yet open to researchers, the JEA Collection includes two boxes entitled "Separate Incorporation of Institution and Jesuit Community."

89. A complete file of the minutes of the Board of Trustees of Boston College, 1863–1982, is kept in the University Archives.

90. Many of the directors were former members of the Board of Regents. Established in 1960, this board was comprised mainly of prominent businessmen who acted as advisors to the president.

91. On November 9, 1971, by act of the Massachusetts Legislature, the original limitation of ten members of the Board of Trustees was removed.

92. In the meantime, W. Seavey Joyce had resigned and, effective September 1, 1972, J. Donald Monan, S.J., was 24th president of Boston College.

93. Michael P. Walsh to John V. O'Connor, Bronx, February 28, 1969; box 9, BG, BCA. In a surprise comment, Walsh wrote: "There is need for some group to restudy Father McGrath's thesis on ownership. It is possible that expert counsel would indicate that for historic reasons, or arrangements of the past, that the Jesuits actually owned the college or university. I would say that this is one of the most urgent and critical problems that should be resolved before others go into the problem of separate incorporation and Boards of Trustees." *Ibid*.

94. There are a number of excellent statements. Examples: "The Jesuits at Boston College," "The Jesuits at Georgetown," "On Being Jesuit," at Wheeling College; "Goals and Guidelines," at Santa Clara.

95. *Catholic Higher Education and the Pastoral Mission of the Church* (Washington, D.C., November 13, 1980), p. 3.

96. *Ibid*.

97. *Ibid*.

98. Charles F. Donovan, S.J., "The Role of Trustees in Promoting the Jesuit Character of Our Institutions" (Boston College, June 4–5, 1980). BCA.

99. *Ibid*.

100. The Association of Governing Boards of Universities and Colleges, a new organization with an office in Washington, D.C., came into existence at this time. The executive vice president, J. L. Swingle, was very anxious that the chairmen of Catholic boards join the association.

101. Harvard University, in conferring an honorary Doctor of Laws degree on J. Donald Monan, S.J., president of Boston College, at the commencement exercises on June 10, 1982, acknowledged a new relationship in this concise citation: "With the philosopher's dedication to truth and goodness, he has given fresh strength to the mission of an admirable neighbor." The *Boston Globe*, in an editorial the next day, caught the meaning of the occasion. "This

symbolic event officially ends generations of rivalry — some good-natured and some not — between two groups of alumni and socio-political strains. It confirms an era of mutual respect between two major universities that began long ago."

## 12. THE PRESIDENTS ASSUME FULL RESPONSIBILITY, 1968-1970

1. *Proceedings*, Commission on Colleges and Universities, Los Angeles, January 13-16, p. 2.

2. "Student Rights and Freedom: A Comment on the Joint Statement," *JEQ*, 31, no. 1 (June 1968): 35-52, and "University Governance and Campus Consensus," *ibid.*, 32, no. 3 (January 1970): 149-177.

3. "University Governance," p. 164.

4. A variety of images of Jesuits and Jesuit institutions are reproduced in *Findings and Implications of a National Survey of Knowledge and Opinion of Key Groups Regarding Jesuit Higher Education in the U.S.*, 3 vols. (Conducted for JEA by Nowland and Company, Greenwich, 1964). BCA.

5. *Proceedings*, Colleges and Universities, Minneapolis, January 14, 1968, p. 1.

6. *Ibid.*

7. For the complete statement, see *ibid.*, appendix A, pp. 12-13.

8. *Ibid.*, p. 2.

9. For a further examination of these questions, see George McCauley, S.J., "Christian Authority," *ibid.*, appendix B, pp. 14-29; also Ladislas M. Orsy, S.J., "Academic Freedom in Theological Research and the Teaching Authority of the Church," *ibid.*, appendix C, pp. 30-39.

10. For "Webster Statement," see *Proceedings*, Commission on Colleges and Universities, January 1967, appendix B.

11. The Maryland case — the Horace Mann League vs. Board of Public Works — involved four church-related colleges: two Catholic (St. Joseph's of Emmitsburg and Notre Dame of Maryland) and two Protestant (Western Maryland College and Hood College). These four colleges were given matching grants by the state of Maryland which were challenged in the courts. The decision by the Maryland Court of Appeals went against three of the institutions. Hood College (United Church of Christ) was declared to be sufficiently nonsectarian so as to be eligible to receive state grants. An appeal to the Supreme Court of the United States was denied. 242 Md 645, 220 A.2d 51 (1966).

In the Connecticut case — Tilton vs. Richardson — a suit was brought against certain federal officials and four Catholic colleges (Sacred Heart University, Fairfield University, Annhurst College, Albertus Magnus College). The plaintiffs charged that these officials had approved grants (not loans) of federal funds to these institutions for five construction projects. They claimed that the grants were unconstitutional under the First Amendment since they supported sectarian institutions propagating the Roman Catholic faith. Ably represented by Attorney Edward Bennet Williams, the institutions won their case in the state court and in the Supreme Court. 403 U.S. 672 (1971).

12. "Minutes," JEA Coordinating Committee, Saint Louis University, March 8–9, 1969, pp. 10–11.

13. *Ibid.*, North Aurora, June 14–16, 1966, p. 9.

14. *Ibid.*

15. See "Jesuit-Lay Relationships," in *Proceedings: J.E.A. Denver Workshop on Jesuit Universities and Colleges: Their Commitment in a World of Change* (Regis College, August 6–14, 1969). In these years the percentage of Jesuits to lay faculty had changed dramatically. In the late '60s, Jesuits comprised about 20 percent of faculty and administration. BCA.

16. *Proceedings,* Commission on Colleges and Universities, January 1967, p. 7.

17. See preamble to "Statement of the Nature of the Contemporary Catholic University," Land O'Lakes, Wisconsin, July 23, 1967.

18. "Statement of the Nature of the Contemporary Catholic University."

19. *Ibid.*

20. *Ibid.*

21. On June 28, 1948, the *Foederatio Universitatum Catholicarum* was established, by the Holy See, according to a decree of the Sacred Congregation of Seminaries and Universities (later changed to Catholic Education). Its first statutes were approved by the Roman Congregation on January 11, 1951. New amendments to the statutes, which were adopted at Boston College in 1970 by the 9th General Assembly, took notice of the developments of the federation and better defined its mission. Concerning its specific goals, "the Federation intends more explicitly to promote a closer collaboration among Catholic institutions of higher education themselves as well as with all universities and international organisms interested in the diffusion of knowledge and in research."

22. It might be of interest to note that, on this occasion and in this setting, Robert Drinan, S.J., dean of the Boston College Law School, delivered a major address on "Human Rights."

23. Kinshasa Statement.

24. *Ibid.*

25. "Minutes," September 21–22, 1968, p. 4.

26. Kinshasa Statement.

27. Second Land O'Lakes Statement.

28. *Ibid.*

29. *Ibid.*

30. *Ibid.*

31. "Opening Address," 8th General Conference of the International Federation of Catholic Universities.

32. Christopher Jencks and David Riesman, *The Academic Revolution* (New York: Doubleday, 1968), p. 405.

33. "Minutes," Dupont Plaza Hotel, Washington, D.C., September

21-22, 1968, p. 3. Reinert also reminded the committee members that the terms of office of the present staff (Reinert, Crandell, Siegfried) would terminate in the spring of 1969. Recommendations for replacements were in order.

34. "Minutes," Coordinating Committee, Saint Louis University, March 8-9, 1969, p. 11. Emphasis added.

35. *Ibid.*

36. *Ibid.*, p. 12.

37. *Proceedings*, p. 4.

38. *Ibid.*, p. 5.

39. *Ibid.*, p. 4.

40. Anticipating eventual independence of institutions, the chairman of the provincials' JEA Committee looked upon the proposed Association of Jesuit Colleges and Universities (first use of that name) as analogous to the Association of Higher Education; but also "as somewhat analogous to a voluntary accreditation association, with the accreditation being the right to use the name Jesuit." Provincials would offer Jesuit manpower to a "Jesuit" institution as long as it maintained its "accreditation"; similarly, Jesuit communities would continue to serve an institution as long as its "Jesuitness" or "Jesuit accreditation" was acknowledged. Gerald Sheahan to Paul Reinert, St. Louis, August 29, 1969; Provincial Archives, St. Louis, Missouri.

41. *Proceedings*, Commission on Colleges and Universities, October 10-11, 1969, p. 1.

42. One was: *Guidelines for Jesuit Higher Education: The Consensus Statements, Recommendations and Committee Reports of the J.E.A. Denver Workshop on Jesuit Universities and Colleges: Their Commitments in a World of Change* (Regis College, Denver, August 6-14, 1969); BCA. The second was a document prepared by A. William Crandell entitled: "Elements and Notes for Consideration in Formulating a Constitution for the AJCU."

43. The members of the committee were Malcolm Carron (Detroit), A. William Crandell (JEA), Robert Henle (Georgetown), Albert Jonson (San Francisco), James Maguire (Loyola, Chicago), and Terrence Toland (Saint Joseph's), chairman.

44. *Proceedings*, October 1969, p. 4.

45. *Ibid.*, p. 5.

46. The Commission on High Schools restructured its own organization, and in August 1970 submitted a constitution and bylaws for approval. With Roman and provincial approval, this organization is now known as the Jesuit Secondary Education Association (JSEA), whose central office is in Washington, D.C.

47. *Proceedings*, Commission on Colleges and Universities, January 10-11, 1970. For the text of the committee report on restructuring, see *ibid.*, appendix A, pp. 13-17.

48. *Proceedings*, Commission on Colleges and Universities, March 30, 1970.

49. "Minutes," Coordinating Committee, Rowntowner Motor Inn, New Orleans, February 21-22, 1970. The three members on the committee, who

represented the commission, spoke in favor of the presidents' position and in support of the constitution as drafted.

50. As stated in article III, membership in the association is voluntary. However, the charter members were the twenty-eight (28) Jesuit colleges and universities in the United States as of September 1970.

51. There is no reference to the provincials in the AJCU constitution.

52. The constitution and bylaws are attached to *Proceedings*, March 30, 1970, as appendix A, pp. 10–15.

53. A notice of termination appeared in volume 32, no. 4 (March 1970). "Publication of the *Jesuit Educational Quarterly* will cease with this issue. During the coming academic year, 1970–71, while plans for the restructuring of the JEA are being implemented, a study will be made of the advisability of resuming publication at a later date." To date, there has been no resumption of publication.

54. Gerald Sheahan to Harold O. Small, St. Louis, May 23, 1970; Provincial Archives, St. Louis, Missouri.

55. Andrew C. Varga to Gerald R. Sheahan, Rome, June 6, 1970; AJCU File, Washington, D.C.

56. *Ibid.*

57. Since the AJCU has functioned since 1970, the response of the presidents obviously fulfilled the condition to the satisfaction of the General.

58. Gerald R. Sheahan to Paul C. Reinert, St. Louis, June 10, 1970; AJCU File, Washington, D.C.


### EPILOGUE

1. Published by the staff of the Jesuit Conference, *Project I* comprises six progress reports. Each report documents the results of a particular study.

2. "The Jesuit Mission in Higher Education," a letter from the American provincials (Easter, 1978).

3. *Ibid.*

4. *Project I*, "The Jesuit Apostolate of Education in the United States," no. 6 (October 1975), pp. 43–57.

5. Pedro Arrupe, "A Letter to the Whole Society on the Intellectual Apostolate," Rome, December 24, 1976; *Acta Romana*, 16: 996–1009 (English version).

6. For enrollment statistics, 1980–81, see *AJCU Higher Education Report*, September 1982, p. 6.

# Bibliography

PRIMARY SOURCES

*1. Unpublished*

Annual Responses of Board of Governors of JEA to President of JEA, 1939–1964
Annual Reports of President of JEA to Board of Governors of JEA, 1939–1964
Confidential Memoranda of Conferences of Edward B. Rooney with Roman
    Officials of the Society of Jesus
Correspondence, Members of Commission on Higher Studies of American
    Assistancy of the Society of Jesus
Daniel M. O'Connell Correspondence, 1934–1937
Letters of Pedro Arrupe
Letters of John B. Janssens
Letters of Wlodimir Ledochowski
Minutes of JEA Committees and Commissions
Minutes, JEA Executive Committee
Minutes of Provincials' Meetings, 1921–1969
Official Correspondence between Officials of the JEA
Official Correspondence between Roman Officials and Officers of the JEA
Private Papers of Edward B. Rooney
Proceedings, Presidents' Commission on Colleges and Universities, 1958–1970
Reports of Inter-Province Committee, 1921–1931

*2. Published*

Letters of Pedro Arrupe
Letters of John B. Janssens
Letters of Wlodimir Ledochowski

OFFICIAL PUBLICATIONS

*Acta Romana*
*AJCU Higher Education Report*

*Constitution, AJCU* (1970)
*Constitution of the Jesuit Educational Association* (1948)
*Constitutiones Societatis Jesu et Epitome Instituti* (Rome, 1943)
*Documents of the 31st and 32nd General Congregations of the Society of Jesus*
*Documents of Vatican II*
*Findings and Implications of a National Survey of Knowledge and Opinion of*
    *Key Groups Regarding Jesuit Higher Education in the U.S.* (3 vols., 1964)
*Instructio* (1934)
*J.E.A. Directory* (1947–1970)
*J.E.A. Special Bulletin* (1939–1963)
*The Jesuit Mission in Higher Education* (1978)
*The Jesuit Order and Higher Education in the United States, 1789–1966* (1966)
*Kinshasa Statement*
*Land O'Lakes Statement*
*Principles and Policies Governing Graduate Programs in Jesuit Institutions*
    (1958)
*Proceedings,* JEA Institutes and Workshops, 1948–1969
*Project I: The Jesuit Apostolate of Education in the United States*
*Revised Constitution* (1964)
*Report of the Commission on Higher Studies of the American Assistancy of the*
    *Society of Jesus, 1931–1932*
*Selected Writings of Father Ledochowski* (Chicago, 1945)
*Studies in the Spirituality of Jesuits*

JOURNALS, MAGAZINES, NEWSPAPERS

*America*
*American Geophysical Union*
*Boston Globe*
*Bulletin* (Association of American Jesuit Scientists)
*Catholic Historical Review*
*Catholic Mind*
*Educational Record*
*Jesuit Educational Quarterly*
*Journal of Proceedings and Addresses* (Association of American Universities)
*New York Times*
*Proceedings and Addresses (NCEA Bulletin)*
*Proccedings of Annual Meetings* (Council of Graduate Schools in the U.S.)
*Thought*
*Woodstock Letters*


SECONDARY SOURCES

Algrain, René. *Les Universités-Catholiques.* Paris, 1935.
*American Council on Education: Its History and Activities, 1934–1935.* ACE
    Publication, 744 Jackson Place, Washington, D.C.

Arrupe, Pedro. *Yo Viví La Bomba Atomica*. Madrid, 1952.

Bander, Edward J., ed. *Turmoil on the Campus*. New York: H. W. Wilson, 1970.

Bangert, William V., S.J. *A History of the Society of Jesus*. St. Louis: Institute of Jesuit Sources, 1972.

Brogan, Denis W. *USA: An Outline of the Country, Its People and Institutions*. London, 1941.

Brubacher, John S., and Willis Rudy. *Higher Education in Transition*. New York, 1958.

Burke, James L., S.J. *Jesuit Province of New England: The Formative Years*. Boston: privately printed, 1976.

Carlen, Claudia, I.H.M., ed. *The Papal Encyclicals, 1903-1939*. McGrath Publishing Co., 1981.

Curti, Merle. *American Paradox: The Conflict of Thought and Action*. New Brunswick, N.J., 1956.

Daley, John M., S.J. *Georgetown University: Origin and Early Years*. Washington, D.C., 1957.

Donohue, John W., S.J. *Jesuit Education: An Essay on the Foundations of Its Idea*. New York: Harper and Row, 1963.

_____. *Catholicism and Education*. New York, 1973.

Durkin, Joseph T., S.J. *Georgetown University: The Middle Years*. Washington, D.C., 1963.

Faherty, William Barnaby, S.J. *Jesuit Roots in Mid-America*. Florissant, Mo.: St. Stanislaus Historical Museum, 1980.

Farrell, Allan P., S.J. *The Jesuit Code of Liberal Education*. Milwaukee: Bruce, 1938.

Farrell, Allan P., S.J., and Matthew J. Fitzsimons, S.J. *A Study of Jesuit Education*. New York, 1958.

FitzGerald, Frances. *Fire in the Lake*. Boston: Little Brown, 1972.

Gallagher, Louis J., S.J. *Edmund A. Walsh, S.J.: A Biography*. New York, 1962.

Ganss, George E., S.J. *The Jesuit Educational Tradition and Saint Louis University: Some Bearings for the University's Sesquicentennial, 1818-1968*. Saint Louis University, 1969.

_____. *St. Ignatius' Idea of a Jesuit University*. Milwaukee: Marquette University Press, 1954.

Halberstram, David. *The Best and the Brightest*. New York: Random House, 1972.

Hamilton, Raphael N., S.J. *The Story of Marquette University*. Milwaukee: Marquette University Press, 1953.

Hassenger, Robert, ed. *The Shape of Catholic Higher Education*. Chicago, 1967.

Hennesey, James, S.J. *American Catholics: A History of the Roman Catholic Community in the United States*. New York: Oxford University Press, 1981.

"Higher Education for American Democracy." In *A Report of the President's Commission on Higher Education*, vols. 1–4. New York, 1946.

Hofstadter, Richard, *Anti–Intellectualism in American Life*. New York, 1963.

Jencks, Christopher, and David Riesman. *The Academic Revolution*. Garden City, N.Y.: Doubleday, 1968.

Light, Donald L., Jr., and John Spiegel. *The Dynamics of University Protest*. Chicago: Wilson-Hall, 1977.

Lipset, Seymour Martin, and Philip G. Altback, eds. *Students in Revolt*. Boston: Houghton Mifflin, 1969.

McAvoy, Thomas T., C.S.C. *The Americanist Heresy in Roman Catholicism*. Notre Dame, Ind.: University of Notre Dame Press, 1963.

McGannon, J. Barry, S.J.; Bernard J. Cooke, S.J.; and George P. Klubertanz, S.J., eds. *Christian Wisdom and Christian Formation: Theology and the Catholic College Student*. New York, 1964.

McGrath, John J. *Catholic Institutions in the United States: Canonical and Civil Law Status*. Washington, D.C.: Catholic University of America Press, 1968.

McGucken, William J., S.J. *The Jesuits and Education*. Milwaukee, 1932.

McKevitt, Gerald, S.J. *The University of Santa Clara: A History, 1851–1977*. Stanford, 1979.

Melville, Annabelle. *John Carroll of Baltimore*. New York, 1955.

Ong, Walter J., S.J. *Frontiers in American Catholicism*. New York, 1957.

————. *American Catholic Crossroads*. New York, 1959.

Power, Edward J. *A History of Catholic Higher Education in the United States*. Milwaukee: Bruce Publishing Co., 1958.

————. *Catholic Higher Education in America*. New York, 1972.

Reeves, Floyd Wesley, *et al*. *The Liberal Arts Colleges*. Chicago, 1932.

Roszak, Theodore, *The Making of a Counter-Culture*. Garden City, N.Y.: Doubleday, 1969.

Rudolph, Frederick. *The American College and University: A History*. New York, 1962.

Selden, William K. *Accreditation: A Struggle over Standards in Higher Education*. New York, 1960.

Watrin, Rita. *The Founding and the Development of the Program of Affiliation of the Catholic University of America, 1912–1939*. Washington, D.C., 1966.

Zook, George, and M. E. Haggerty. *Principles of Accrediting Higher Institutions*. Chicago, 1936.

# Index

AAC. *See* Association of American
  Colleges
AAU. *See* Association of American
  Universities
Accreditation
  movement toward, 8–9
  professional schools and, 83–84
Accrediting agencies, 7–8, 9, 147–148,
  199. *See also* Council on Educa-
  tion; North Central Association;
  Standardizing agencies
ACE. *See* American Council on
  Education
Adams, Arthur S., 147
Affiliated program, Catholic University
  and, 59–60, 61–62
AJCU. *See* Association of Jesuit Colleges
  and Universities
Alumni associations, formation of Jesuit,
  18, 19, 20
American Association of University Pro-
  fessors (AAUP), and academic
  freedom, 209–210
American Council on Education (ACE),
  108, 147
  and doctoral degrees, 36–37, 38
  JEA as member of, 56
  president of, 70
American Medical Association, and
  accreditation of medical schools,
  83–84
Aquirre, Cardinal Gregorio Maria, 16
Arbesmann, Rudolph, O.E.S.A, 139,
  140, 141
Arrupe, Pedro, S.J., 153, 221–222

biography of, 190–191
Association of American Colleges, 70,
  108, 216
Association of American Law Schools
  (AALS), 83
Association of American Universities
  (AAU), 8, 10, 36, 38, 41, 108–109
  Catholic University and, 60–61
  Georgetown University and, 44, 45,
  50
  graduate programs and, 81–82
  Loyola and, 51
  purpose of, 42
  qualifying for, 34, 35
  recognition by, 46, 52
  Saint Louis University and, 47
Association of Jesuit Colleges and Uni-
  versities (AJCU), formation of,
  216–220, 221

Bea, Cardinal Augustin, S.J., 204
Berger, Charles A., S.J., 101
Bier, William C., S.J., 101
Blewett, John E., S.J., 201
Blum, Victor J., S.J., 122
Board of Governors, 174, 199
  authority and role of, 175, 177–178,
  181, 183
Board of Trustees
  governing role of, 204–205
  laity on, 202, 205, 206
  reorganization of, 198–208
Bolland, John, S.J., 54
Boston College, 49
  board of directors of, 206

graduate degrees at, 40, 41
meeting of Inter-Province Committee
     at, 18
rector–president and, 119
Bouscaren, Timothy, S.J., 107
Bowles, Frank H., 82
Bunn, Edward B., S.J., 71, 117, 119
Burghardt, Walter J., S.J., 101
Burke, James L., S.J., 158
Burns, Leo, S.J., 104, 144, 155
Burrus, Ernest J., S.J., 101
Butler, Nicholas Murray, 8


Campion College, 4–5
Carroll, Charles F., S.J., 14, 26
     biographical sketch of, 16
Carroll, John, S.J., 44
Carter, Cardinal G. Emmett, 189
Casassa, Charles S., S.J., 125–126, 131,
     156
Catholic Commission on Intellectual and
     Cultural Affairs, 100, 136
Catholic University, definition of a, 212,
     213. *See also* Land O'Lakes
     statements
Catholic University of America, The, 19,
     21, 34, 44
     affiliation program of, 59–62
Clark, Edward F., S.J., 140, 141
Clark, William F., S.J., 92–93
Clarke, Norris, S.J., 101
Codd, William J., S.J., 90
Co-education. *See* Women at Jesuit
     institutions
Coleran, James, S.J., 184
College of the Holy Cross, 40, 41
Commissarius, 36–53
     appointment of, 38
     provincial visits of, 40–42, 44–49
     recommendation on universities of,
          42, 43, 44
     suggested appointment of, 31
     suspension of the office of, 54, 55
Commission on Colleges and Univer-
     sities, 167, 193, 194, 195–196,
     210, 216
Commission on Graduate Schools,
     81–82, 131–133, 134, 135
     preeminent departments and,
          141–143

Commission on Higher Studies, 20,
     21–35
     criticisms of, 32–33
     first appointments to, 26–28
     first report of, 28, 32
     organizational structure proposed by,
          29–31
     questionnaire sent by, 28–29
Commission on Liberal Arts Colleges, 81
Commission on Professional Schools,
     83–84, 121
Commissions, reactivation of JEA, 80–83
Committee on Graduate Studies, JEA,
     50, 56, 57
Committee on Objectives of American
     Jesuit Universities, 158–162
Committee on Postwar Jesuit Education,
     79–80
Conference of Presidents, 121–130, 162
     and revision of JEA constitution,
          172–176
Connell, Francis M., S.J., 22, 23, 50
     biography of, 12–13
Connery, John R., S.J., 184, 185
Connolly, John F. X., S.J., 199
Constitution of the Jesuit Educational
     Association, 62–66
     rector-president plan and, 113–114
     revision of, 172–176, 182–183,
          186–187
Cooper, Russell, 87
Corrigan, Joseph, D.D., 61–62
Crandell, A. William, S.J., 146, 173,
     174, 175, 182, 183, 185, 194, 196
Crowley, Francis M., 34
Crowley, John, S.J., 107, 115
Cummings, Edward, S.J., 14


Daley, John M., S.J., 184, 185, 199
Deane, Charles J., S.J., 26
     biography of, 27–28
De Boynes, Norbert, S.J., 68, 74, 93,
     113
*Declaration on Christian Education*,
     189–190
Deferrari, Roy J., 59–60, 62
Degrees
     doctoral (*see* Doctoral degress)
     encouragement of advanced, 32
     necessity for advanced, 49, 50, 52

selection of scholastics for advanced, 34

Didusch, Joseph, S.J., 50

Distler, Theodore A., 148

Doctoral degrees, 25
colleges qualified to grant, 36–38
necessity for, 10–11, 49, 50, 52
studies for, 96–97
*See also* Graduate programs; Special studies program

Dollard, Stewart E., S.J., 135

Donnelly, Francis, S.J., 43

Donnelly, W. Patrick, S.J., 126, 172

Doyle, Edward A., S.J., 172

Drane, Joseph K., S.J., 177, 203

Drummond, Edward J., S.J., 144

Dubourg, Louis W.B., 46

Duce, Hugh, S.J., 71, 81, 116

Duncombe, C.G., 122

Dunne, Peter Master, S.J., 101

Dunne, William J., S.J., 114, 116

Education, national secretary of, 54, 55, 57. *See also* Commissarius; Pedagogy

Egan, Joseph, S.J., 116

Eisenhower, Milton, 87

Ellis, John Tracy, 136

Eurich, Alvin, 165

Executive Committee, JEA, 54–73, 173, 174, 175
co-education and, 69
commissions and institutes of, 80–89
Edward B. Rooney and, 58–62
formation of, 54–58
function of, 178–179
governing constitution of, 62–66
postwar education and, 71–73
publication of *Instruction* by, 78
retention of, 181
revised membership of, 183
revision of *Instruction* by, 66–69
war efforts and, 69–71

Expansion of Jesuit schools, 101–106

Expansion of Jesuit universities, 188, 193–194

Faculty, lay. *See* Lay faculty

Farrell, Allan P., S.J., 57

biography of, 65–66

Feeney, Leonard, S.J., 13

Female religious, in Jesuit institutions, 22, 23. *See also* Women at Jesuit institutions

Fisher, John Harding, S.J., biography of, 111–112, 113

FitzGerald, Joseph D., S.J., 170

Fitzgerald, Walter F., S.J., 48–49

Fitzgerald, William J., S.J., 120

Fitzsimons, Matthew, S.J., 63

Fleege, Urban, 135

Ford, John C., S.J., 101

Fordham University, 62, 116
classics department of, 139, 140
dual administration of, 110–111, 114
first rector-president of, 118–119
graduate school of, 42, 43, 44

Fox, Albert C., S.J., 4, 8–9, 26

Gallagher, Eugene F., S.J., 144

Gallagher, Louis J., S.J., 43
biography of, 18–19

Gallen, Joseph, S.J., 107

Gannon, Robert Ignatius, S.J., biography of, 110–111, 112

Ganss, George E., S.J., 160, 161

Garrone, Cardinal Gabriel, 213

Georgetown University, 19
graduate programs at, 44–45
integration of juniorate courses at, 50

Gianara, William G., S.J., 81

Gilpatric, C. Edward, S.J., 163–164

Glose, Joseph C., S.J., 170

Graduate Commission. *See* Commission on Graduate Schools

Graduate programs, 99, 131–148
intellectual caliber of, 136–137
revival of Marquette's, 143–146
*See also* Doctoral degrees; Special studies program

Graduate Schools, 34–35, 38
accreditation of, 42
commission on, 81–82, 131–133, 134, 135, 141–143
lay professors and, 11–12
norms for, 50–52, 56, 57
students in, 98

Grattan, John, S.J., 50

Greeley, Andrew, 199
Grimaldi, William M.A., S.J., 101
Guthrie, J. Hunter, S.J., 119

Hamilton, Raphael N., S.J., 71
Hanselman, Joseph, S.J., 7
Harvanek, Robert F., S.J., 101, 158,
    161, 162–163, 164, 168, 199
Hauck, Herman J., S.J., 146, 158, 177
Henle, Robert J., S.J., 101, 123–124,
    156, 157, 159–160, 193
Henneberry, Thomas, S.J., 103
Hesburgh, Theodore M., C.S.C., 212,
    213, 214
Heyden, Francis J., S.J., 101
Hogan, Aloysius, S.J., 42, 43, 44
Honors Course System, 17
Horine, Samuel H., S.J., 46, 47
Hudson, N. Paul, 83
Hughes, Raymond M., 36
Hussey, James, S.J., 114, 116
Hutchins, Robert, 25
Hynes, John W., S.J., 26, 33, 48, 58
    biography of, 27

IFCU. *See* International Federation of
    Catholic Universities
*Inspectores*, 149, 152, 154, 158
Institutes, JEA, 85–89
*Instruction on Studies and Teaching*,
    37–39, 49, 52, 219
    publication of, 78
    revision of, 66–67
Intellectual apostolate, 221–222
    questioning of, 192
Intellectualism, dearth of Catholic,
    136–138
International Association of Universities,
    109
International Federation of Catholic
    Universities (IFCU), 212
International Secretariate of Education,
    200–201
Inter-Province Committee, 1–20, 222
    graduate schools and, 11–12
    initial meeting of, 2, 4–5
    purpose of, 13–14
    quinquennial digest of, 14–15, 17

waning support for, 17, 19, 20
Inter-Province Executive Committee,
    55–73

Janssens, John Baptist, S.J., 58
    biography of, 74–75
    death of, 190
    expansion of Jesuit schools and, 103,
        104, 105
    graduate school coordination and,
        133–134
    letter on ministries by, 75–77, 150
    review of JEA constitution and,
        186–187
JEA. *See* Jesuit Educational Association
JEQ. *See Jesuit Education Quarterly*
Jesuit communities, separate incorpora-
    tion of, 198, 202, 206
Jesuit education, objectives of, 158–168
Jesuit Educational Association (JEA)
    accommodation with hierarchy by,
        106–108
    annual meetings of, 89–90
    Commission on Graduate Schools of,
        131–133, 134, 138
    commissions of, 80–85, 154
    Committee on Graduate Studies of,
        50, 56, 57
    and Committee on Objectives of
        Jesuit institutions, 158–162
    conference of Presidents and,
        124–130
    constitution of, 62–66, 78, 169–187
    Executive Committee of (*see* Execu-
        tive Committee, JEA)
    first national meeting of, 56
    formation of a, 39
    and graduate studies, 50
    institutes sponsored by, 85–89
    *Instruction* and, 57
    philosophy at Jesuit schools and,
        156–158
    and prefect of studies, 93–96
    publications of (*see Jesuit Educa-
        tional Quarterly*)
    restructuring of, 215–219
    and World War II, 69–73
*Jesuit Educational Quarterly* (JEQ), 64,
    65

editor of, 97
lay faculty and, 154
listing scholarly publications in,
99–100
objectives of Jesuit schools and, 162,
163, 164
Jesuit Institute of the Humanities, proposal for, 138
Jesuit institutions
and federal government, 209
investigating Catholicity of, 149–150
philosophy in, 154–158
postwar expansion and, 74–91,
101–106
praise for, 147–148
as public trusts, 203–204, 205
quality of, 98–101
relation to diocesan authorities of,
106–108
women and non-Catholic students at,
22, 23
*See also* Jesuit universities
Jesuit Research Council of America
(JRCA), establishment of, 121–122
Jesuit universities
committee on objectives of American,
158–162
dual administration of, 110–120
expansion of, 188, 193–194
Jews, in Jesuit institutions, 21, 22
Johnston, Robert, S.J., 34, 47
Joyce, W. Seavey, S.J., 206
JRCA. *See* Jesuit Research Council of
America
Juniorates, integration with universities
of, 49–50

Kane, John J., 136
Kaufman, Leo, S.J., 172
Katz, William G., 210
Keelan, Vincent L., S.J., 119
Kehoe, John J., S.J., 119
Kilroy, James, S.J., biography of, 15–16
Kinshasa Statement, 213, 214
Klubertanz, George, S.J., 101

Land O'Lakes Statement, 213
Lauer, Quentin, S.J., 101
Law schools. *See* Professional schools

Lay faculty, 11–12, 212
as administrators, 120
and expansion of Jesuit schools, 103
graduate schools and, 11–12
and JEA institutes, 87–88
in Jesuit schools, 150–154
non-Catholic, 153, 204
and policy decisions, 197, 200
Ledochowski, Wlodimir, S.J., 19, 20,
21, 178
appointment of commissarius by,
36–53
biographical sketch of, 5, 6
death of, 67
and Inter-Province Executive Committee, 55–56
letter to American Assistance by,
22–24
and letter on ministries, 35, 75–77,
96, 101, 150
questionaire to provincials by, 22–23
reform of graduate education and,
37–39, 40
and role of Jesuits in education,
24–25
and university presidents, 110–111
Lemieux, Albert A., S.J., 126, 146, 172
LeSaint, William P., S.J., 177
*Letter on Jesuit Ministries*, 35, 75–77,
96, 101, 150
Liberal Arts Commission, 81
Linehan, Daniel, S.J., 101
Lonergan, William I., S.J., 240
Lord, Daniel, S.J., 107
Loyola University (Chicago), 116
Loyola University (New Orleans), 8, 9,
27, 48
Lucey, Francis E., S.J., 45
Lucey, William L., S.J., 101

McCarron, Hugo, 50
McCormick, James T., 41
McCormick, Vincent A., S.J., 95, 105,
112, 114, 145, 149, 152, 158, 167
biography of, 75
Macelwane, James Bernard, S.J., 28, 32,
46, 56, 57
biography of, 26–27
Committee on Graduate Studies and,
50

defense of Commission on Higher
  Studies, 33
MacFarlane, Joseph, S.J., 107
McGinley, Laurence, S.J., 125, 129, 141
  biography of, 118–119
McGinty, John J., S.J., 150, 152, 180
McGrath, Brian, S.J., 161
McGrath, Earl, 87, 165
McGrath, John J., 203
McGucken, William J., S.J., 46, 57
  biography of, 72
McMahon, John, S.J., 95, 116, 117, 134,
  135
McMenamy, Francis X., S.J., 61, 190
McNutt, Paul V., 71
Magni, Alexis, S.J., 68
Maher, Zacheus, S.J., 46, 47, 64, 69,
  114
  and support of Catholic University,
  60–61
Maline, Julian L., S.J., 71, 80, 82, 85,
  98, 100, 116, 118, 177
  biography of, 86
  and Committee on Professional
  Schools, 83
Mallon, Wilfred, S.J., 79, 85, 87, 98,
  100, 117
  biography of, 86
  and Committee on Professional
  Schools, 83
Manning, Urban W., S.J., 119
Manresa Retreat League, 27
Marquette University, 11, 43, 46
  revival of doctoral program at,
  143–146
Maxwell, Joseph R.N., S.J., 81, 119, 125
Medical schools, 83–84
Mehok, William J., S.J., 97–98
Merry del Val, Cardinal Rafael, 21, 24
Monan, J. Donald, S.J., 293–294n
Moriarity, Frederick L., S.J., 169
Morton, Edmund W., S.J., 174
Moynihan, James F., S.J., 101
Murphy, Joseph A., S.J., 43, 112, 113,
  116
Murray, John C., S.J., 101, 214
Musurillo, Herbert, S.J., 101

National Catholic Educational Association (NCEA), 2, 7, 10, 15, 56

annual meeting of, 89
college section of, 16, 17
Committee on Graduate Studies of,
  34–35
graduate program coordination and,
  135–136
National Commission on Accrediting,
  148
National Jesuit organization, proposed,
  7, 9–10
National Secretary of Education, 58–62.
  *See also* O'Connell, Daniel M.,
  S.J.; Rooney, Edward Bernard,
  S.J.
NCEA. *See* National Catholic Educa-
  tional Association
Nevils, W. Colman, S.J., 12, 44
Newman Centers, 59
Non-Catholic teachers, 153, 204
Norms
  for graduate schools, 50–52, 56, 57
  for rector-president relationship,
  111–112, 114
North, Arthur A., S.J., 137, 139
North Central Association, 46, 82, 143,
  144
North Central Association of Colleges
  and Secondary Schools, 9

Objectives of Jesuit institutions, 158–168
O'Connell, Daniel M., S.J., 38
  biography of, 39–40
  institutional visits by, 40–49
  and Inter-Province Executive Com-
  mittee, 54–57
  *See also* Commissarius
O'Connor, Paul L., S.J., 217
O'Dea, Thomas F., S.J., 137–138
O'Donnell, Edward J., S.J., 104, 120
O'Keefe, Vincent T., S.J., 191, 192, 195
O'Leary, Arthur, S.J., 44
Ong, Walter J., S.J., 100–101
O'Sullivan, Carroll, S.J., 114, 155

Parsons, Joseph Wilfred, S.J., 34, 61, 62
Pedagogy, courses in, 12
Phillips, Edward C., S.J., 24, 29, 57
Philosophy, in Jesuit institutions,
  154–158
Piet, Joseph M., S.J., 12

# Index

Pope Leo XIII, 6, 59
Pope Pius XI, 32
Pope Saint Pius X, 21
President-Rector relationship, 110–120
Presidents, of Jesuit institutions
    first meeting of, 104–105
    and full responsibility, 209–220
    right of supervision and, 179
    threat to autonomy of, 164, 168
    university administration and,
        110–120
Presidents' Conference, and reorganiza-
        tion of JEA, 182–183, 186–187
Professional schools
    commission on, 83–84, 121
    control and governance of, 120
    emphasis on practical in, 105–106
    standards of, 83–85
Province Prefect of Studies, 92–96
    origin of the office of, 4
    role of, 178–179
Publications, Jesuit scholarly, 88–101.
    *See also Jesuit Educational
    Quarterly*
Pusey, Nathan, 108

Quain, Edwin A., S.J., 139, 140, 141
Quinquennial digest, 11–15, 17

Ratterman, Patrick H., S.J., 210
*Ratio Studiorum* 2, 3, 16, 30, 43, 65
    Commission for the Revision of, 66
    revised, 6, 68
Rectors, and administration of univer-
        sities, 110–120
Reed, Lorenzo K., S.J., 170
Reeves, Floyd, 87
Regents, role in professional schools of,
        120–121
Regional Director of Education, 62
Regis College, Denver, 46, 85
Reid, James H., S.J., 139, 140, 141
Reinert, Paul C., S.J., 120, 125, 172,
        173, 177, 179, 192
    as president of JEA, 196–197, 200,
        201
Richards, J. Havens, S.J., 2, 15
Riedl, John O., 143
Rimes, William J., S.J., 196
Risk, James, S.J., 107
Robillard, James L., 123

Robinson, Leo J., S.J., 106–107
Rockwell, Joseph H., S.J., 7
Rooney, Edward Bernard, S.J.
    biography of, 58–59, 60–61
    challenge to JEA presidency of,
        167–168
    and Committee on Professional
        Schools, 83
    and conference of Presidents, 109,
        127–130
    and coordination of graduate pro-
        grams, 131–132, 134–135
    and diocesan relationships, 107–108
    dual control of universities and,
        112–120
    lay faculty and, 150–154
    and Marquette University, 144–145
    and postwar expansion of Jesuit
        education, 101–106
    review of graduate programs by,
        146–147
    and revision of JEA constitution,
        169–187 *passim*
    as Secretary of Education, 61–62
    special studies program and, 92–96
    successor to, 196
    and war efforts of JEA, 70–73
Roosevelt, Franklin D., 69
Roothaan, Jan, S.J., 2, 6
Rosati, Joseph, 46
Roy, Percy A., S.J., 81

Saint Andrew-on-Hudson, 49, 58
Saint Francis Xavier College, 7
Saint Isaac Jogues Novitiate,
        Wernersville, 50, 112
Saint Joseph's College, Philadelphia, 7,
        58
Saint Louis University, 33, 43
    corporate autonomy of, 201–203
    program recommendations for, 46–47
Saint Xavier College, 8, 9
Salter, John M., S.J., 29
Santa Clara University, graduate pro-
        gram at, 146
Schlafly, Daniel L., 201
Schmidt, William, S.J., 16
Schoder, Raymond V., S.J., 138, 139
Scholarly publications of Jesuits, 99–101.
    *See also Jesuit Educational
    Quarterly*

Scholasticate, integration with universities of, 49–50
Schurmans, Maurice, S.J., 67
Schwitalla, Alphonse M., S.J., 46
  biography of, 33–34
Seattle College, 16, 48
Seattle University, graduate program at, 146
Selden, William K., 148
Shadowbrook, 111
Shanahan, James, S.J., 166, 184, 185, 194, 195, 199
Sheahan, Gerald R., S.J., 220
Sheehan, Arthur, S.J., 71, 94
Sheehy, Maurice, 34, 35
Shields, Thomas E., S.J., 59
Siegfried, Paul V., S.J., 196–197
Small, Harold O., S.J., 152–153, 182, 185
Smith, Andrew, S.J., 48, 58
Smith, Thurber M., S.J., 46
Snavely, Guy, 70
Society of Jesus
  constitution of (see Ratio Studiorum)
  rift with American hierarchy, 58–62
  Superior General of (see Ledochowski, Wlodimir, S.J.; Janssens, John Baptist, S.J.)
Socius, office of, 95
Special studies
  directors of, 94, 96–97
  program evaluation of, 98–101
Sponga, Edward, S.J., 203
Spring Hill College, 48, 146
Standardizing agencies, 29, 30. See also Accrediting agencies
Steiner, Celistine, S.J., 120
Students in Jesuit schools
  non-Catholic, 22, 23
  number of, 2–3
Sullivan, Leo, S.J., 116
Sullivan, Michael X., S.J., 45
Superior, dependent, 118, 119, 120
Swain, John L., S.J., 153, 190
Sweeney, Joseph P., S.J., 112
Swords, Raymond J., S.J., 166, 195

Teachers
  instructions for preparation of, 37–38, 49, 52

non-Catholic, 153, 204
  See also Lay faculty
Theological studies, doctoral degrees and, 11
Tivnan, Edward P., S.J., 11, 26
  biography of, 3
  Commission on Higher Studies and, 33
Toland, Terrence, S.J., 217, 218
Trese, Ralph, 122–123
Trustees. See Board of Trustees

United States Catholic Conference, 207
Universities. See Jesuit universities; Specific universities
University centers, 193–194, 195
University of Berlin, 8
University of Notre Dame, 21, 62
University of San Francisco, 116
University of St. Louis, 62

VanQuickenborne, Charles, S.J., 46
Varga, Andrew C., S.J., 220
Vatican Council, Second Ecumenical, 189, 198, 202, 210
Verhaegan, Peter J., S.J., 46
Vermeersch, Arthur, S.J., 74

Walsh, Edmund A., S.J., 18, 45
Walsh, Joseph M., S.J., 48
Walsh, Michael P., S.J., 124, 125, 164, 165–166, 192, 193–194, 206, 207
Webster College, St. Louis, 211
Wernersville, juniorate at, 50
Wernz, Francis Xavier, S.J., 2
Weston College, 15, 49, 169
Whelan, Charles M., S.J., 24
Willmes, Robert J., S.J., 116
Wilson, Samuel Knox, S.J., 57
  biography of, 50–51
Women at Jesuit institutions, 22, 23, 69
World War II, and JEA, 69–73
Wrenn, Gilbert, 87

Xavier University, Cincinnati, 39, 82

Zema, Demetrius, S.J., 43
Zook, George, 70, 71
Zuercher, Albert C., S.J., 120